George Frideric Handel

A Music Lover's Guide

to

His Life, His Faith

& the Development of *Messiah*

and His Other Oratorios

Marian Van Til

WordPower Publishing
Youngstown, NY

WordPower Publishing
Youngstown, NY 14174
www.wordpowerpublishing.com

Printed on acid-free paper.

ISBN: 978-0-9794785-0-5

Library of Congress Control Number: 2007927893

To the memory of
my father
William R. Van Til (1908-1972)
enjoyer of God, delighter in music, discerner of spirits;
and
my mother
Josie Breuker Van Til (1914-1969)
knitter of wounds, suffering servant, steadfast follower of Jesus.
And to
my husband
Edward Michael Cassidy
daily encourager, faithful confidant, gentle practitioner of all Christian virtues.

Handel lovers all.

As from the pow'r of sacred lays
The spheres began to move,
And sung the great Creator's praise
To all the bless'd above;
So when the last and dreadful hour
This crumbling pageant shall devour,
The trumpet shall be heard on high,
The dead shall live, the living die,
And music shall untune the sky.

From *Song for St. Cecilia's Day*, in honor of Cecilia, patron saint of music
John Dryden, 1687; set by Handel, 1739

Contents

Prologue
Why Write This Kind of Biography of Handel?

George Frideric Handel, more than three centuries after his birth, is enjoying a remarkable rebirth. His *Messiah* is the best-known classical work of all time. Since he wrote it in 1741 it has been heard in numerous countries, and is still heard year after year. Today, not only *Messiah*, but all of Handel's eighteen biblical oratorios and hundreds of his other works are being played, staged, sung, published, recorded and written about as never before. And unlike many composers, he enjoyed great fame in his lifetime, too.

Perhaps you picked up this book because you've noticed this resurgence of interest in Handel and want to know whether the hoopla is justified. Or maybe you know Handel's music well, and his story too, and you'd simply like another take on it. Or perhaps you're one of those listeners who encounter *Messiah* every year and are, each time, profoundly moved by that glorious work, musically and spiritually. And now you want to know the man behind the music.

I have found that when a composer's music deeply moves me I want to get to know that composer, not just as a writer of music but as a person too. I want to know where that music came from, out of what kind of circumstances and out of what kind of heart. Whether you know a lot of Handel's music or only *Messiah* (or none at all), I imagine you're no different than I am in wanting to know Handel the man. That's one reason I've written this book.

What became clear to me about Handel during my years of preparation for this book is that his circumstances and heart were deeply grounded in biblical faith. Though that was assumed in his own day, and continued to be the prevailing view of Handel in the nineteenth century, that view of Handel is no longer assumed, and, in fact, is very often assumed to be wrong. As his music (and especially his opera) is now gaining the broadest hearing it has had since Handel's lifetime, the picture of the composer that increasingly accompanies it is that he was a slightly profane theater animal, a worldly arrogant genius, a pragmatist whose biblical works were written because they put bread (and wine) on the table. That view contorts, even distorts, the outlines of the man that history provides, if one looks, and it tends to skew modern interpretations of his biblical oratorios as well. There is evidence that contradicts this modern view and it needs to be brought forward. That is another reason I've written this book.

Handel's story is of a life lived, a faith nourished, and a calling completed against the background of the late seventeenth century and first half of the eighteenth century in Lutheran Germany and Anglican Britain, and to a lesser extent in Roman Catholic Italy. He was nurtured in a devout Lutheran home and in a time when the spirit of the Reformation was still evident, before the twin spirits of Rationalism and Deism took firm hold where he lived. The picture of Handel here will, I hope, be drawn as true as is possible to the likeness of the flesh-and-blood man of that time who was George Frideric Handel. In the heart of the man we will see a person of deeply ingrained Christian faith, whose life-long generosity and prudent morality reflected that faith.

There are an armful of biographies of Handel, most of them written by scholars, for scholars. This one is simply aimed at music lovers. It is also different because it examines Handel's faith: how it was formed and how it showed itself. Ignoring the permeating role that Christianity played in Handel's life and times, or misunderstanding it because of modern ignorance of what that faith is and how it operated in individuals and society in Handel's day, results in not only an incomplete portrait of Handel, but an inaccurate one. Such a picture would be one that he, his friends and other contemporaries would not readily recognize.

There's one other reason for this book. Though Handel gained fame and fortune in his day, there were many difficult periods in his life. How he reacted to those difficulties is encouraging. Handel's story will resonate with any reader who is struggling or has struggled. From his reaction as a twelve-year-old to the death of his father, to his calm approach to his own death at age seventy-four, and the decades in between, his is an inspiring story. This book tells that story.

~~~

As we set out, a short explanation of the various forms of the composer's name will be helpful. He was baptized Georg Friederich Händel, but even in boyhood spelled his middle name without the second "e." After permanently moving to England in 1712 the composer used the English form of his first name, adopted a hybrid German-English spelling for his middle name, and anglicized his surname by dropping the umlaut on the "a.": *George Frideric Handel.* Many of his English contemporaries wrote his name using the English form of "Frederick." In Italy, where he lived for three-and-a-half years before going to England, and where he visited periodically after living in England, he was referred to as "Hendel" – the pronunciation of Händel in its German form. I will use the English form of his name which Handel himself used, and its German form (Händel) to refer to his parents, siblings and other German relatives.

~

You will note that throughout the book I frequently (and sometimes lengthily) quote from sources in Handel's eighteenth century: from his own surviving letters, from letters his friends wrote and from newspapers and other publications. I've done that because I think it brings immediacy to the story: it is the best way to "get a feel for" his times, for how people then expressed themselves and for what they were thinking.

Please also note the following:

Original spellings, capitalization and punctuation have been maintained in eighteenth century quotations.

Terms in **bold** appear in the glossary.

This book uses a dual-note system. Footnotes are indicated by * and appear on the same pages as the sentences noted by asterisks; footnotes contain additional information that amplifies the main text. Endnotes are indicated by numbers and contain only bibliographical references for each chapter. At the back of the book, they are grouped by subject within each chapter ; thus, many quotations within the text of the book do not have their own endnote number.

Chapter 1
A Thriving Shoot from a German Lutheran Root

The composer Georg Friedrich Händel was born into the heart of Lutheranism in the central German city of Halle on February 23, 1685. Late-seventeenth-century Halle was 168 years and just forty-three miles from the church at Wittenberg where Martin Luther unwittingly unleashed the Protestant Reformation when he nailed his ninety-five theses to the church door in October 1517. During those 168 years, Luther's work had reverberated throughout Germany and beyond, and into the Händel family.

Today, metropolitan Halle, population 300,000, has subsumed the village of Wittenberg. Halle is the largest city in the state of Saxony-Anhalte in what was formerly East Germany. The city of Handel's birth lies along the Saale River, and in his day it was known for producing salt.

A bleak city nearly from its founding, during the Thirty Years War it took some hard knocks, including two sieges. That interminable war had its roots in the Reformation-era struggle between Protestants and Catholics. That struggle also became bound up in the dynastic and imperial ambitions of the Catholic house of Hapsburg. At the end of the war (1648) the Peace of Westphalia turned over control of Halle (and all of the Archbishopric of Magdeburg of which it was a part) to "Great Elector" Friedrich Wilhelm of Brandenburg-Prussia. The change of government would not occur, however, until the death of its then current administrator, Duke August of Saxony. In the meantime, the Elector continued to live in Halle. As it turned out, "the meantime" lasted 32 years.

Herr Georg Händel, the composer's father, was a surgeon, and beginning in 1660 he was employed by Duke August. When the Duke finally died in 1680, Elector Friedrich Wilhelm moved his government to a new palace about twenty miles away at Weissenfels. And, given the opportunity for a better job, Georg Händel went with him. He did not, however, move his family to Weissenfels. He commuted, coming home by coach whenever possible.

Elector Friedrich Wilhelm was Reformed, not Lutheran, and so allowed (demanded, actually) tolerance for Calvinists within his Duchy of Brandenburg. Five years after assuming control of Halle (the year Handel was born), he passed an edict that allowed French Huguenots to settle there. A few years later, Reformed refugees from the Palatinate and a number of Jews also arrived. This tolerance was motivated by the Elector Friedrich's faith, but it was also a smart move: it provided

1

an immediate replenishment to the devastated population of Halle with people who were likely to contribute substantially to the rebuilding of Halle's economy.

Friedrich was tolerant of Pietists as well. The Pietists were Lutherans who wanted to stir their church out of the routine, dogma-heavy and too-intellectual faith they believed it had settled into since Luther's time. They reacted against what they saw as a lethargic church by stressing the need for every individual's conversion and response to God, which would (or should) culminate in a life of devotion and of care for others, especially the poor.

Philipp Jakob Spener, the first impetus behind Pietism, began to hold devotional meetings in 1670. He wanted to bring Christians into closer fellowship and emphasized the need for diligent Bible study. He also stressed the Reformation concept of the "priesthood of all believers" with its implications for Christians' total involvement in both the church and the world. Spener did not intend to leave the existing Lutheran church, but ironically, his repudiation of the importance of doctrine and his desire to limit church membership only to the converted tended to undermine orthodoxy. It brought reactions against Pietism, some of them severe.

From the late 1680s – Handel's childhood – Halle became the center of Pietism, led by Spener's successor August Hermann Francke, a multi-lingual scholar and pastor of a church at nearby Glaucha. The institute Francke founded for destitute children (there were hundreds, casualties of the Thirty Years War and a subsequent plague and fire) grew into a major educational institution. By the time of Francke's death in 1727, more than 2,200 children were being educated and cared for, and the institution influenced the development of Prussian education.[1]

Handel's parents, Georg and Dorothea Händel, were not Pietists, but there are indications that they were strongly influenced by the Pietists around them: the Händels took the "evangelical truth" seriously, as the Pietists did; and they were generous with their wealth and careful to offer help to those in need, like the Pietists.

As a surgeon, Handel's father was part of a medical vocation that was separate from (and not as prestigious as) physician. Since the Middle Ages there had been three categories of medical practitioner: physician, surgeon and barber. There was generally a large social and educational gap between physicians and the other two practitioners, particularly the lowly barber. The medical part of a barber's practice consisted of bleeding his patients. (Any number of ailments were thought to be caused by too much blood in the body.) On the other hand, physicians were men of science and had a high level of education – at least, that was supposed.

Good surgeons were also well-trained but did not practice general medicine as physicians did. A surgeon's primary task was to saw off limbs. And the almost constant war wracking the European continent kept many a surgeon busy at that task, including Georg Händel early in his career. Herr Händel, however, practiced medicine well beyond the surgeon's traditional role. His skill and consequent reputation were high, and he was apparently accorded the deference and prestige of a physician.[2]

In 1636, when Georg Händel was only fourteen, he was brusquely thrust into adulthood. His father died of plague. He was forced to leave school, and then home, to learn a trade. By the time he returned to Halle to settle down at age twenty, he had traveled far as an army surgeon and a ship's surgeon and had apprenticed with two respected and well-known practitioners. Early the next year, 1643, he married for the first time (George Frideric's mother was his second wife).

From the outside the marriage looked like a purely practical union (not unusual at the time), but it was apparently an amiable one. Unusually, Anna Katte Ettinger was ten years older than Georg Händel. She was the widow of a barber, and on their marriage Händel took over her dead husband's practice (also not unusual). He acquired a house in Neumarkt, adjacent to Halle but outside the city wall. In an age of stalking pestilence when many died young, it was an unusually long marriage, just under forty years; and it produced six children.

Within a couple of years of marrying Anna, Georg Händel became the official surgeon for the Giebichenstein region. He had successfully set the badly broken arm of Duke August, which helped to successfully set his career. Even as an elderly man, just a year before his death, he showed no diminution of skill. He removed a swallowed knife from the stomach and throat of a sixteen-year-old, possibly with magnetic poultices. If this sounds like a fable, the story is authenticated by the bill for 50 Reichsthalers which Herr Händel submitted to the court for treating the young man. Elector Friederich paid the bill.

By 1666, the prosperous Herr Händel bought a large house in the best part of Halle, a stone's throw from the ducal palace where he spent part of his working time. There was an interesting side story to that house, and to Georg Händel's career: when the Händels bought their house, wine was being sold from the premises and the place was known as *Zum gelben Hirsch* ("The Yellow Hart"). Händel was granted a renewal of the license to sell both foreign and domestic wines. He leased the wine selling business, apparently quite profitably, to one of Halle's citizens.

Anna Händel and one of the Händel sons died of the plague in 1682. Five of Georg Händel's six children with Anna lived into adulthood, yet only two outlived their father. Despite that, the Händel tombstone indicated that Georg Händel had twenty-eight grandchildren and two great--grandchildren. The memorial stone also summarized his career. He was "former Valet, Physician-in-ordinary, and for 40 years Official Surgeon to the Dukes of Saxe-Merseburg and to the Electors of Brandenberg" (translated from German).[3]

Georg Händel spent very little time alone after his wife's death. Within a year he had Dorothea Taust. He was sixty-one, she was thirty-two. But that vast age difference was no barrier to their enjoying a satisfying fourteen-year marriage based "upon compatibility of soul and true virtue." Handel's mother lived with her elderly husband "until the day of his death, all the time calmly, contentedly and peacefully in Christ," her own funeral preacher years later assured the mourners.[4]

When Georg Friedrich was born a few years into the marriage, the new baby had a half-brother (Karl) and a half-sister (Sophie Rosine) from his father's first marriage. Both Karl and Sophie Rosine were more than thirty years older than baby George, and he was uncle to numerous nieces and nephews who were adults when he was a young child. Despite that, it is likely that the future composer got to know his two half-siblings and their offspring reasonably well. Maintaining ties within extended families was common, and young George's half-siblings lived no great distance away. In fact, Karl Händel (1649-1713), who followed his father both into the medical profession and into service at the Saxon court at Weissenfels, would play an unexpected role in an early but crucial musical incident regarding Handel. But Sophie Rosine is mentioned only in birth and in death. At the time of George's birth, his father was both Honorary Surgeon and Duly Appointed Chamber Servant at the Brandenburg court. The latter position was "granted in recognition of his work during the epidemics" and paid an annual pension of 100 thalers.[5]

Early in the Thirty Years War, Handel's grandfather Valentin Händel, a coppersmith, had moved his family west from Breslau in search of a freer climate in which to exercise their faith (Handel's father was born in 1622). Handel's great-grandfather on his mother's side, Johann Taust, did the same, moving from Bohemia in about 1625

> because of the religious troubles of that time, and the severe persecution
> of those who sympathized with the Confession of Augsburg, and for the

love of the pure evangelical truth..., freely renouncing all his estate, according to the Scripture, Matthew 19: 29, and chose rather to live as a private person here in Halle, than in good esteem and with great fortune, in his Fatherland: for which staunch loyalty Almighty God richly repaid him. [6]

According to Johann Christian Olearius, who preached the funeral sermon when Handel's father died, Georg Händel's parents (the composer's grandarents) "brought him up carefully [in] the fear of God and ensured that he held to all the Christian virtues"; and they educated him at Halle's Stadtgymnasium. A generation later, young George was also sent to the Gymnasium (not to be confused with its current meaning). Education there, for both Handel's father and himself, was part of being brought up in the fear of the Lord.

Unusually, Handel's mother also received an education, and a Christian one. Her family, the stalwart Taust clan, raised generations of Lutheran pastors. Dorothea's father was one of those (and solemnized his daughter's marriage to Georg Händel). He recognized her keen intelligence and schooled her at home; the schools were for boys.

Lutherans, taking their cue from Luther himself, had stressed the need for excellent faith-based education, and the Stadgymnasium offered such learning. In fact, it was the only school in town until 1695 when young George was ten years old. When a second school opened that year it was Francke's Pietist-oriented Institute. This new school may have been no less rigorous than the Gymnasium, but its purpose was to allow paupers' sons to get an education, and Georg and Dorothea Händel and family were comfortably middle class. So George continued at the Gymnasium.

The curriculum there was arduous: the highest classes looked more like university studies do today than like a curriculum aimed at boys of junior and senior high school age. The beginning students were systematically introduced to Bible stories, Luther's Shorter Catechism, reading and writing German and Latin, and counting. The next classes studied, in addition, grammar, syntax, Latin composition, geography and letter-writing. After that, German and Latin poetry were added, and students also began the study of Greek (including the Greek New Testament) and the Latin of Tacitus and Ovid. Finally, the two highest classes took more classical Greek and Latin literature (Cicero, Horace, Socrates, Plutarch), Hebrew writing, logic, "elegant style," oratory, disputation, ethics and physics. Except for the study of literature, notably absent were studies in what we would call the fine arts. Practical music lessons (singing and playing) took place daily at noon, but music was apparently not part of the academic curriculum.[7]

The faith of Handel's father was literally set in stone on the family tomb. The tomb testified that Georg Händel "caused this stone to be set here for remembrance," so he himself no doubt devised some of its words. It declared that his first wife Anna Händel "rests here in her tomb, in God, until the joyful resurrection." And of Georg Händel himself the tomb would proclaim: "[He] in true faith in God and in the precious merits of his Redeemer Jesus Christ, fell asleep on 11th Feb. 1697, and his body rests here till the joyful resurrection of all believers." When he died at age 75, he left Dorothea a forty-six-year-old widow with three children: Dorothea Sophie and Johanne Christianne, aged seven and ten; and Georg Friedrich, who was a few days short of twelve years old. And so George, like his father before him, was thrust at a tender age into an adult world of cares and worries, becoming the male head of the household.

Death's sting was intense and constant in the late seventeenth century. Death swallowed up spouses, parents, babies, older children, siblings, extended family and friends. Rates of infant mortality and women's death in childbirth were high. Just a few years before Handel's birth an epidemic had wiped out more than half the population, and a devastating fire came licking on the heels of disease.

Personal examples of death were everywhere. The elderly father for whom young George grieved had not only been an adolescent when he lost his own father but was only eighteen when his mother died. (And as we've seen, Georg Händel had also buried his first wife and four of his six children from that marriage.) He and Dorothea lost their infant firstborn son the year before George was born, and Dorothea was further acquainted with grief. She experienced her mother's death in 1682, the year before she married Georg Händel; and her father died in 1685, the year George was born. Besides the loss of her husband twelve years later, she would see both of her daughters die, the younger in 1709 at age nineteen, and her namesake in 1718 at age thirty-one. When people were not grieving the loss of family members, there was someone in the town church community with whom, or for whom, to grieve.

The intense education the boy Handel received makes quite plausible his authorship of a floridly stylized but touching poem for his father's funeral: "Ah! bitter grief! my dearest father's heart/is torn from me through death," he wrote five

6

days before his twelfth birthday.* The poem, dated February 18, 1697, appeared in the funeral booklet for Georg Händel. It expresses a young son's loss and his straightforward child's faith. It also demonstrates that Handel's facility for language came early; he would adeptly use at least five languages in his adult life. And it hints at the boy's early love for music (and art), and at his yearning to devote his life to it: he signed the poem "Georg Friedrich Händel, der freien Künste ergebener," that is: "...dedicated to the liberal arts."

The poem's outlook reveals that young George assimilated and assented to his parents' faith. He wrote (paraphrased): "Despite God having taken from me my father's care, yet God lives. I know that from now on He will care and provide for me. He will help me through my anguish and despair."[8] There is no anger at God for depriving him of his father. Such a thought would not have occurred to the boy, or even to most adults of the time. On the contrary, there is the implicit acknowledgment that life is God's to bestow and withdraw. This involves "letting God be God," a concept at the heart of Luther's theology and the Lutheran worldview. Luther described this as acknowledging that God is "all in all" (1 Corinthians 15:28).Luther summed it up: "All things must be God's since nothing can be or become if he would not bring it into existence; and when he stops, nothing can continue to exist." [9]

It is clear that the Händels did not fear death. Even though, Luther said, death was "laid upon man and executed on him through God's wrath" against the sin of the "first Adam," we are freed from that terrifying wrath by the second Adam, Christ. So how can death have any ultimate sting? A looking forward to their own bodily resurrection someday, possible because of Christ's resurrection, was profoundly ingrained in Handel and his family (recall the family tombstone). Raging against death, or a mere stoical acceptance of it in the face of presumed nothingness or perhaps annihilation, would have been incomprehensible – and pagan. Luther asserted that believing-Christians are the only ones who truly understand how utterly terrible death is "under the law," apart from Christ. Conversely, no one need fear the terrors of "sin and the law" if they flee to the mercy God offers in the gospel through Christ.

Hand in hand with anticipation of the Resurrection was the equally deep-

---

*See the entire poem at the end of this chapter.

seated confidence that God governs all things. In the fragile existence of the seventeenth century, knowing God as controller of death as well as life was immense comfort – which the boy Handel confesses in his poem. Underlying young George's confession is the belief that God sees far beyond our limited sight lines and is wholly able to be our help and guide. What point would there be to rail against his will? God takes away, yet he gives far more in return. Job's confession in the midst of calamity, "The Lord gave, the Lord has taken away, blessed be the name of the Lord" (Job 1:21) was frequently repeated and adopted as their own.

Many years later, for many thousands of listeners, Handel would become irrevocably associated with a related confession of Job's, which he so beautifully set in *Messiah*: "I know that my Redeemer liveth and that he shall stand at the latter day upon the earth. And though worms destroy this body, yet in my flesh shall I see God" (Job 19:25). The opening sentence of this confession, in fact, appears on Handel's own grave memorial which still stands in Westminster Abbey. But this comforting verse would be used, first, just eleven years after the death of Handel's father as the text at the funeral of his beloved sister Dorothea Sophie.[**]

Young George's poem doesn't merely parrot adult beliefs, as some music historians have assumed. Later events in Handel's life show that he had learned well his lessons in God's providential care. His early confession of reliance on a living, caring God who preserves his people in his mercy resonates down the years to, and in, the Handel of the biblical **oratorios**. Though Handel himself did not write the texts of his dozen-and-a-half oratorios, he approved them and, of course, worked intimately with them as he set them to music. The oratorio texts reflect the same robust understanding of God's providence that Handel embraced in his childhood home, church and school. It is a scriptural understanding that was basic not only to Lutheran Christianity but to the still Calvinist-infused Anglicanism of Handel's decades in London.

In the short years Georg Händel had with his extraordinary son, he not only trained him "in the fear of the Lord" but showed the boy faith in action: in his profession and in his extra-professional activities. The elder Händel exhibited a

---

[**]Calvin R. Stapert says in *My Only Comfort: Death, Deliverance, and Discipleship in the Music of Bach* (Grand Rapids, Mich.: Wm. B. Eerdmans, 2000, p. 51), "I suspect that one of the reasons for the continuing popularity of Handel's *Messiah* is that its theme, set out so compellingly in the opening tenor solo, is comfort." I concur. Though Charles Jennens, not Handel himself, compiled the Scripture texts used as *Messiah's* libretto, we'll see that Handel's setting reflected his own faith and life-long experience of that comfort.

deep, biblical spirit of charity which his son imbibed. Georg Händel and his famous son after him were generous men who clearly took to heart Jesus's teaching that "to whom much is given, much will be required" (Luke 12: 48).

Helping those whom Christ called "the least of these my brethren" was a concrete way to "seek first his Kingdom," focusing on the next world (which one might enter at any time) even while being wholly involved in this one. C.S. Lewis observed two-and-a-half centuries later in *Mere Christianity* that "if you read history you will find that the Christians who did most for the present world were just those who thought most of the next." "Good works" should be a direct result of gratitude to God for saving us, said Luther and the other Reformers. Good works born of faith are acts by which a person can know that his or her faith is genuine. Love of God must show itself in love for our fellow human beings. "Cursed be the life which someone lives for himself and not for his neighbor," said Luther. "And again, blessed be that life which a man does not live for himself but for his neighbor, serving him with teaching, with admonition, with help, or whatever it may be."

Given that outlook, it is no surprise that Georg Händel provided free medical care to those who couldn't pay for it. And that he and a close associate, Johann Praetorius, rector of the Gymnasium and also a composer, were "members of a small committee formed in 1682 to provide relief for victims of the plague."[10] Based on a review of the extant sources, the early-twentieth century French musicologist and critic Romain Rolland summed up Handel's father as "a man of huge size – serious, strict, energetic, dedicated to his job, also charitable and ready to help."[11] In all of that, his son was not unlike him. The funeral sermon for Handel's father said, "In his whole life he was friendly, zealous, modest, proved to be calm and well meaning towards the poor and suffering, helped many through thick and thin by his skill and profession, even without payment."[11]

Besides generosity, Georg Händel had a well-honed business sense. That capacity, too, he passed on to his son. Despite several financially shaky periods in the composer's life when his operas became a hard sell, Handel would develop a reputation for paying his performers, no matter what. He would live modestly (except, perhaps, in his penchant for good food and fine art), give generously, and regularly invest part of his often considerable income. At the end of his long life he would leave a substantial estate of £20,000, which his will and its codicils liberally distributed. Handel would be essentially the first composer-entrepreneur – a composer who did not make his living by being attached to royal or noble courts, but who independently set and pursued his own course, acting as his own impresario and writing for kings and noblemen only by commission (with one brief exception).

If Handel's father put his faith into practice, so did his mother. Dorothea Händel was a woman whom "the Lord had provided ... with a bright mind and good head above all others of her sex. She made great efforts to have a sound knowledge of Christianity and of the Holy Bible."[12] A woman with such priorities, whose family, like her husband's, had displaced themselves on account of their faith, would work diligently to make sure that her son and two daughters acquired that sound knowledge. That Dorothea Händel carefully kept alive in herself, shared with her husband, and nurtured in her children the biblically Christian faith so important to generations of both their families was attested to at length by Johann Georg Francke's sermon at her funeral at the end of 1730.*

Handel lived in London at the time of his mother's death, and the sermon was printed on his account and sent to him by his brother-in-law. Pastor Francke told of Dorothea's unstinting care of her widowed father after her mother's death in 1681, and of her refusal to "leave him unvisited when the Parsonage at Giebichesnstein was already greatly infected [with 'the contagion raging in those days'], nor considered that death, which had already torn away her young sister, her eldest brother ... and his wife, through this epidemic, might also lay in wait for her in that place. She remained, rather, in the execution of her filial duties, dauntless and confident, realizing that God would uphold her in those dismal times, and could deliver her also from death; indeed [she] often used to relate, to the Glory of God, how his Almighty protection came to be known to her in those days."

After the death of Handel's father, the relationship between Handel and his mother continued to be warm and devoted. They drew strength from the faith they shared, and from each other. In another six years her teenaged son would begin to travel: he would live in Hamburg, in the main cities of Italy, and finally in London, but never again in Halle; and so their mother-son ties would be sustained mainly through letters. Handel would write her frequently and visit her in Germany when possible. (Correspondence between Handel and his brother-in law Michael Dietrich Michaëlsen refers to Handel regularly writing to his mother, but not one of those letters has survived. Dorothea Händel easily lived long enough to see her son's fame

---

*Such sermons were not first of all eulogies, but served as comfort and then warning to the living to get their spiritual houses in order. They can be considered to fairly accurately portray the deceased.

spread far and wide, but it is not necessarily peculiar that it did not occur to her to save for posterity her son's personal letters to her – as a modern mother with a famous son no doubt would.)

Dorothea Händel would live as a widow for thirty-three years. She had extended family around her for support, but she also seems to have been a strong and independent woman. Those qualities apparently developed early and naturally, not merely after her husband died. She had turned down marriage proposals prior to her marrying the elderly Georg Händel, a man of whom Pastor Taust "approved with greatest pleasure." Dorothea was seemingly unconcerned that she herself was creeping beyond a maiden's best marrying age for bearing children. (She had a sister, in fact, who remained unmarried). Yet despite being thirty-two when she eventually married, she bore four children to Georg Händel.

Dorothea's strong, independent intelligence may help explain why her only surviving son seemed to appreciate women with an independent bent and to have had an empathy for women that seems almost modern, even though he himself never married. That understanding of women is evident in the unusual depth, poignancy and illumination of character in the music for so many of the female roles in Handel's operas, oratorios and even some of the Italian **cantatas**. His awareness of his mother's exceptional qualities, character and intelligence, and of his parents' marriage of "compatibility of soul," may also give some psychological insight into the difficulty he may have faced in finding a similarly extraordinary spouse if he ever seriously contemplated marrying. (Handel's younger contemporary William Coxe writes that Handel did consider marriage, once seriously and once not so seriously. More of that later.) Besides the influence of his mother and two beloved sisters, for all of his composing life Handel would work with women as singers and would get to know women's ways – sometimes a mixed blessing, he seems to have thought, but an opportunity and professional relationship most men did not have in that time.

That is the sturdy stock from which Handel sprang. That he accepted as his own his parents' faith and worldview becomes increasingly obvious in his later life. Many years later, the surgeon's famous son would provide the equivalent of "free medical care," feeding and caring for Dublin's and London's orphans through benefit performances of many of his musical works, most notably *Messiah*: in Dublin – for Mercer's Hospital, for prisoners in various jails, and for the Charitable Infirmary on the Inn's Quay; in London – for the Foundling Hospital, of which he became a board member. Handel's younger contemporary, music historian Charles

Burney, writing in 1785 at the one-hundreth anniversary of Handel's birth, noted of *Messiah*: "This great work ... has fed the hungry, clothed the naked, fostered the orphan, and enriched succeeding managers of the Oratorios, more than any single production in this or any country."[12]

Ah, Bitter Grief!

Verses of mourning for his father, written by Handel on February 18, 1697, five days before his twelfth birthday. Translation from the German by Marian Van Til.

Ah, bitter grief! My dearest father's heart is torn from me through death.
Ah, sorrow! Ah, the bitter pain which seizes me, having become an orphan.

My all lies low, my hope vanishes.
He, my counselor and protector, no longer stands beside me!
Ah! My loss! Ah! O heart-piercing wound!
Tell me if a grief like this is to be found [anywhere].

When the sun's golden candle, the light of the world, is veiled, startling, frightening field and hill, so is a child sobered by mourning when his beloved father escapes [this life] so early.

We love the tree which gives shade, which refreshes with its green night.
Much more a child loves him who bestows life and then guides his helpless feet to walk in the right.

A forest trembles when high cedars fall, the fir trees howl, the slender birches blanch. And shall no anguished cry ring out from me while Death's sickle grabs my father's very life?

But if, on the other hand, I were to entirely corrupt the light of my own eyes through a constant stream of tears, still I could never gain him back.
Ah! the loss I must feel [from now on].

God – who has at present taken from me my dear father's care through his death – still lives. He will, henceforth, care and provide for me and help me through all anxiety and distress.

Thus the truly blessed is tearfully mourned, though for the mourner the departure of his dearly beloved father is much too premature.

Georg Friedrich Händel, dedicated to the liberal arts.

Chapter 2
First Immersion in Music

Handel's father has been much abused by historians. For two hundred years it was presumed that he didn't care about music because he wanted his son to become a lawyer instead of a composer (or any kind of musician). The study of law in early eighteenth century Germany focused primarily on philosophical and moral questions about the nature of justice and human agency. That may partly explain why, after his father's death, the teenaged Handel still complied with his father's wishes and enrolled at the University of Halle to study law. (It is assumed he did – there are no specific records of what he studied.) Such an education would have been the kind of mind-expanding study, within a Pietist Lutheran framework, that Handel would not regret, whatever his life's work would be.

Georg Händel's wish that his son go into civil law probably stemmed from wanting him to have an honorable, regular-paying, socially well-regarded profession. Herr Händel must also have been thinking of the time, drawing nearer and nearer, when his wife and daughters would need young George as a solid breadwinner. Händel had no way of knowing the real extent of his son's talent, and how far it would take him.

Handel's father wasn't the only parent in his day to want his musical son to study law. Georg Philip Telemann, four years older than Handel and now known as one of the most prolific composers in history, was in the same predicament. When the two first met, Telemann was on his way "with greatest reluctance" to the University of Leipzig to study law at the behest of his deceased father who had wished him to forego music. Telemann's mother, then very much alive, also adamantly opposed his pursuit of music and had made him diligently promise to give it up. But Telemann's acquaintance with the energetic and no doubt already strong-willed sixteen-year-old Handel proved fatal to Frau Telemann's wishes for her son.

Charles Burney quotes Telemann as saying (perhaps with a chuckle), "From my acquaintance with Handel, who was *already famous* [Burney's emphasis], I again sucked in so much of the poison of music as nearly overset all my resolutions."[1] The friendship between the two then aspiring young composers lasted a lifetime. Of note is that Telemann and Bach also became close friends. Telemann, in fact, was godfather to Bach's son Carl Philipp Emmanuel (and even held him at his baptism), and in 1768 that talented godson succeeded Telemann as director of music in the five churches of Hamburg. When after Telemann's stint at university he took a job in Leipzig as both a church composer and director of the opera, he said of himself and Handel, "In fashioning subjects of melody, Handel and I were continually exercising our fancy, and reciprocally communicating our thoughts, both by letter and conversation, in the frequent visits we made to each other."*

Georg Händel is said not only to have wanted his young son to study law, but to have forbidden him from pursuing music in any form. We first learn that the elder Händel was opposed to his son's pursuit of a career in music from John Mainwaring's 1760 Handel biography, *Memoirs of the Life of the Late George Frederic Handel.* (Mainwaring's biography, still available, was the first about Handel, and the first about any composer as the sole subject of a book).

William Coxe, a much younger contemporary of Handel's, says the same thing about Handel's father in his *Anecdotes of George Frederick Handel and John Christopher Smith.* Coxe surely heard most of his anecdotes from Smith, who was his father-in-law. Smith and his own father, J.C. Smith the elder, knew Handel very well and worked for him for many years; they, like Handel, were natives of Germany who moved to London. Both the Mainwaring and Coxe accounts include many recollections from Handel himself – which doesn't necessarily mean that the chronological details are entirely error-free, as no one's memory is.

Mainwaring says that Herr Händel "strictly forbade [his son] to meddle with any musical instrument; nothing of that kind was suffer'd to remain in the house, nor was he ever permitted to go to any other, where such kind of furniture was in use."[2] That statement has cemented Georg Händel's curmudgeonly reputation, a reputation which persisted almost to the end of the twentieth century. In fact, a 1966 biographer describes Handel's father as having a "morose, misanthropic disposition." Another mid-twentieth century Handel biographer refers to Georg Händel as a man of "severe principles." Fortunately, two more recent studies have corrected that picture. One presents Georg Händel's opposition as "the reasonable fears of an elderly father"; the other chides Mainwaring for giving "a rather exaggerated portrait of the insensitivity of Handel's father."[3]

---

*Burney quoting Telemann, and noting that Hamburg was "a place too distant from Leipsic [sic] for frequent visits between these young Musicians to have been practicable." According to Telemann this took place between 1701-03. Part of that time Handel was still at home and at the university in Halle, part of the time in Hamburg. Burney noted that Leipzig is twenty-four "English miles" from Halle, but 200 from "Hamburgh" (Burney, *Sketch of the Life of Handel,* p. 6).

In any case, the boy Handel is said to have discovered a way to get around his father's prohibition against instruments in the Handel household. Coxe relates the now often-told details this way:

> Handel, though he never possessed a fine voice, could sing as soon as he could speak, and evinced such a predilection for music, that the father carefully kept out of his reach all instruments, with the hopes of weaning his mind from what he deemed a degrading attachment. But the child contrived to obtain possession of a clavicord, which he secreted in the garret, and at night, when he was supposed to be asleep, the young enthusiast was awake; and the imagination may fondly view him striking the strings of his lyre, – that lyre which was to charm all Europe with its energy.[4]

Though the clavichord is essentially a tabletop keyboard instrument and has a contained, gentle sound, it seems far-fetched that a lone child (or even one with a "partner in crime") could have carried this instrument up narrow stairs to a presumably unused garret, that he could have spent many night-time hours playing there without at least his mother and sisters knowing (would not the boy's eventual symptoms of lack of sleep have been questioned?), and that, if his mother knew, she would have conspired with her young son to keep the knowledge from her husband.

If Handel, as an old man looking back at his childhood, related this story to Smith or Mainwaring, he was likely seeing his father through the eyes of a keen and highly talented young boy — eager to get his hands on any and every musical instrument – being reined in by an elderly parent whose energy was fading and whose concern for his son's future was probably not understood by the child. Because Georg Händel had plenty of opportunity for first-hand observation of the role and careers of musicians in both court and church, he may have concluded that it was not the stable kind of profession he wanted for his son (though it was not necessarily a bad-paying one for the exceptionally talented).

It is almost inconceivable that Handel's father did not appreciate music, even deeply appreciate it. Apart from loving the son of his old age who must have showed exceptional musical proclivities nearly from birth, Georg Händel had close friends and associates who were musicians by profession. The wife of the surgeon Händel worked for when an apprentice was the daughter of the important English violinist William Brade. Organist Christian Ritter and royal *Kapellmeister* David Pohle were friends of his (Pohle was also one of the founders of the Halle opera –

there were no faith-related sanctions among Lutherans against opera). Johann Krieger, the esteemed and well-traveled *Kapellmeister* at the Weissenfels court, was a distant relative. Musicologist John Butt suggests that, "given Georg's bimonthly visit to the court from 1688, the two were doubtless well acquainted. Indeed, the Weissenfels opera was the direct successor of the Halle court opera, so it was probably closely and enthusiastically followed by the aging surgeon."[5] This might go some ways toward also explaining young George's delight in opera and his gravitation to it, flames of which delight would be fanned by early visits to Berlin.

Whether Herr Händel was vehemently or only mildly against George's going into music, he unexpectedly changed his mind about it; or at least he relented to the extent that he allowed his precocious son to begin the study of music. A seminal incident involving young Handel's half-brother Karl and the Duke at Weisenfels was the catalyst. Karl Händel was *valet de chambre* at the court in Weisenfels, where their father also worked. George wanted to go along to see his brother on one of their father's regularly scheduled trips to the court. Having been told he could not go, he tenaciously ran after the coach anyway, and was eventually hauled aboard and taken along. It was a day when being feistily disobedient paid-off for a seven- or eight-year-old boy. In William Coxe's version of the story,

> At the Duke's court, Handel was not so closely watched by his father, as at home. He enjoyed many opportunities of indulging his natural propensity; and he contrived, occasionally, to play upon the organ in the Duke's chapel at the conclusion of divine service.
>
> One morning the Duke hearing the organ touched in an unusual manner, inquired of his valet who was the performer. The valet replied that it was his brother; and mentioning at the same time his wonderful talents and predilection for music, and his father's repugnance, the Duke sent for them both. After other inquiries, the Duke was so much pleased with the spirit and talents of the boy, that he pleaded the cause of nature: he represented it as a crime against the public and posterity, to rob the world of such a genius; and, finally, persuaded the father to sacrifice his own scruples, and to permit his son to be instructed in the profession for which he had evinced so strong an inclination. A more interesting scene can hardly be conceived, than Handel listening to the arguments of his powerful advocate, and marking his final triumph over the reluctant prejudices of his parent. The Duke became so much

interested in his success, that, at his departure, he made him a present, and promised his protection as he zealously applied to his studies.[*6]

Whether or not the details are entirely true, Georg Händel did come to the conclusion that he should allow his son training in music after all. He then sent George to the best music teacher teacher in Halle, Friedrich Wilhelm Zachau (sometimes spelled Zackow). Whether Georg Händel acknowledged it or not, this initially set young George on the path toward being a church musician. It allowed him to study, listen to and play much music by Germany's best organist-composers of the previous generations and by his teacher's own generation, as well as by Zachau himself.

From the year before Handel's birth, Zachau had been organist and what might now be called "music director" at Halle's Liebfraukirche (also called the Marktkirche). As a composer Zachau was familiar with the Italian style, the standard of the time, and some of that style is evident in his compositions. Under Zachau, young George received a fine musical education, both theoretical and practical. George analyzed the musical forms of the previous and present generations – especially the **fugue** – and he learned how to construct such forms himself. He was given a thorough grounding in organ and harpsichord (the piano had not yet been invented); he learned how to read and construct **figured bass**, which is fundamental to the structure of **Baroque** music. George also learned to play the violin, and likely the oboe, the latter which became one of his favorite instruments. (One of the recognizable traits of Handel's choral music is the distinctive way he combines oboes, usually in pairs, with the strings and upper voices.)

Eventually young Handel also began to act as substitute organist for Zachau. Zachau made his pupils keep a notebook into which they copied the music of composers they studied. In fact, Handel would retain that notebook all his life, and would dip into it to borrow musical ideas for his own compositions. The notebook contained compositions not only by Zachau himself and some other German Lutherans, but by several Italians as well. (Sadly, it disappeared during the

---

[*]Sources differ as to how old Handel was when this incident took place; perhaps as old as 11. Modern Handel biographer Christopher Hogwood perceptively adds that the account "suggests that in telling the story Handel emphasized the balance of both arguments, and was anxious to show sympathy with his father's dilemma. Although he never experienced them directly, the crises of parenthood appear frequently in the texts of Handel's dramatic music and found a ready response in him" (*Handel*, The Pitman Press, p. 15).

nineteenth century.) Zachau thoroughly grounded his young, eager student in harmonic principles, exposed him to the different national musical styles, made him analyze the good and bad points of compositions of specific composers, and gave him musical subjects to "copy, play and compose." "Thus," Mainwaring concludes, "he had more exercise and more experiences than usually falls to the share of any learner at his years. Zachau was highly pleased with his student, and Handel held Zachau in high regard all his life."[7]

Coxe adds these important details: "At this early period of his life he is said to have composed, every week, during three successive years, a spiritual cantata, or church service for voices, with instrumental accompaniments." Late in life, Handel told J.C. Smith the younger (who once again told Coxe) about the early composing required of him; unfortunately, all of the student- Handel's music is lost.[8]

Handel visited Berlin in 1698 at age thirteen, according to Mainwaring. Berlin was a major musical center, so it's not surprising that while there Handel, young as he was, met the well-regarded Italian composers Bononcini and Attilio. In fact, they were impressed with his skill. This Bononcini was "the same who afterwards came to England while Handel was here, and of whom the former was at the head of a formidable opposition against him [Handel]."[9]

There are chronological problems with this story, which says that Georg Händel and "friends" accompanied young Handel. If George visited Berlin in 1698, it was without his father, as the elder Händel had already been dead for a year. Mainwaring recounts that these friends, acting on the boy's behalf because of his youth, turned down a court appointment for him. They knew that once he was in the Elector's service, if he did excellent work he'd have a hard time extricating himself if he wanted to leave. And if he didn't measure up or caused offense, "his ruin would be the certain consequence." The reasoning of the boy's protectors was sound. This independence was entirely in line, too, with Handel's later attitudes:

> *In the sequel of his life he refused the highest offers from persons of the greatest distinction; nay, the highest favours from the fairest of the sex, only because he would not be cramped or confined by particular attachments.... This noble spirit of independency, which possessed him almost from his childhood, was never known to forsake him, not even in the most distressful seasons of his life.*[10]

In his first twelve years, Handel had seen social independence exemplified by his father. Both father and son seem to have seen themselves not as servants, as both surgeons and composers were regarded to be, but as "professionals." Years later in London, Handel's self-assurance as his own man, his understanding of his own worth as a composer, and his dislike of being beholden to aristocratic employers extended to an impatience even with members of the Royal Family. As humble servants of the monarch, citizens of the realm were not to question the schedules of the monarch or his family. But Handel did. He did not like the musicians – "servants" or not – to be kept waiting. Nor did he take kindly to anyone in the royal retinue, high or low, conversing during the music (a habit of audiences at the time). George II's daughters Princesses Caroline and Anne, at least, would come to be sympathetic to his concerns. As Burney describes it:

> He was heard to say, 'Indeed, it is cruel to have kept these poor people, meaning the performers, so long from their scholars [their music students], and other concerns.' But if the maids of honour, or any other female attendants, talked, during the performance, I fear that our modern Timoetheus, not only swore, but called names; yet, at such times, the princess of Wales [Caroline], with her accustomed mildness and benignity, used to say, "Hush! Hush! HANDEL's in a passion."

~

Handel enrolled in the University of Halle on Feb. 10, 1702, two weeks before his seventeenth birthday. Though it was then five years since his father's death (almost to the day), he still seems to have wanted to honor his father's wishes for him. What his mother's views were we don't know. Given the apparent nature of her character it is easy to conclude that, while not deliberately ignoring the wishes of the deceased husband she had loved, she would have wanted the living son she cherished to develop the immense talent God had given him.

A month after Handel entered the university, when he was still likely living at home with his mother and sisters, he won the first job of his career: organist at Halle's Domkirche, the "cathedral church." Because this church was traditionally the chapel for the administrator of the Arch-bishopric of Magdeburg, when Elector Friedrich took over he asserted his right to control the building. He gave it to a Calvinist congregation. The teenaged Handel had previously filled in for the regular organist who neglected his duties and apparently led a dissolute lifestyle. Given the problems with that organist, the Domkirche consistory was open-minded about Handel being a Lutheran.

Teenaged Handel did not get the chance to display his abilities to the extent he would have in a Lutheran church, but he didn't seem to mind. The Reformed churches restricted their use of music to Psalms and other direct Scripture texts. So Handel's task "on Sundays, on Thanksgiving Days and on other Feast Days" (and on additional days, as necessary) was to "play the organ fittingly at Divine Service, and for this purpose to pre-intone the prescribed Psalms and Spiritual Songs, and to have due care to whatever might be needful to the support of beautiful harmony."[11]

The organ was a fine two-manual instrument with an exceptional bellows that could sustain 180 bars at a measured tempo without refilling, according to a contemporary report. The bellows, of course, in the absence of electricity, had to be pumped by hand (or foot) by someone other than the organist, and boys were usually hired to provide that service. Besides also taking charge of the care of the organ, seventeen-year-old Handel had to make sure that he was "always in Church in good time and before the pealing of the bells ceases." (A sleepy young organist scrambling up the loft stairs before the bell tolled its last and breathlessly sliding onto the organ bench in no physical or spiritual condition to lead the congregation in their musical worship was a scenario the consistory was keen to avoid.)

Further to Handel's conduct and attitude, he was to "render to the Pastors and Elders set over him due honour and obedience" and "to live peaceably with the other Church Officers." (Disagreements between organists and church consistories and councils were frequent; Bach's career was replete with such arguments.) In summary, he was "to lead a Christian and edifying life." That was not only naturally expected, but would in principle help him carry out all other tasks.*

Handel was paid fifty thalers from the "Royal Purse of this province" and given free lodging in the Moritzburg, as organists were. His contract did not stipulate any additional duties, but a document relating to his successor reveals that the organist was also expected to direct singers and instrumentalists in music-making at his lodgings. In a departure from practice in most Reformed churches, he could also make use of an oboe band to help accompany the Psalms and "spiritual songs" of the liturgy, an unusual provision of the job blessed by Elector Friedrich's assent.

---

*Surviving church records indicate that Handel took communion at the church at least twice during the year he was there. Either this Calvinist church did not practice "close" communion (requiring communicants to be members of the church and/or adhere to the Reformed confessions) or they made an exception for their Lutheran organist. Most Reformed churches celebrated communion not more than four times a year. This practice, in fact, was carried over to the Calvinist-influenced Church of England and maintained there during Handel's five decades in London, and well beyond.

There is no record of either the church's dissatisfaction with Handel or of Handel's dissatisfaction with the job, but at the end of his probationary year he left. During that year he undoubtedly mulled over his future. He considered whether he should continue to forge a career as a church musician, keeping in mind that, whatever musical direction he chose, he was responsible for the support of his mother and sisters.

At some point during that year he decided to take another road, and thus to end his association with the Domkirche. That road would take him out of the city of his birth, never to live there again. Handel's successor, one Johann Kohlhardt, it is noted in the consistory minutes, was hired "as much for his pious conduct as for his skill." Presumably, this redeeming quality was noted because it partly made up for his not being the exceptional organist Handel was, not as an implication that Handel's skill outweighed his pious conduct.

Sometime during his year at the university and the Domkirche, Handel may have made another trip to Berlin. It was a likely place for him to dip his toes into the waters of Italian music, especially opera, since as the seat of Elector Friedrich's government the city had a flourishing court opera. (Because Georg Händel had been known to the court, although at Weissenfels, his son may have had an "in.") If the opera bug wasn't already imbedded in Handel, he may have caught it while in Berlin. Mainwaring says that this Berlin trip began to make the young Handel "conscious of his own [musical] superiority"; it whet in him a "passion for fame, which urged him strongly to go out into the world, and try what success he should have in it."[12] After that, Halle had few charms. Apart from anything else, it was hardly a beautiful city. Visitors of that era frequently commented on its dingy, sooty look. So Handel, at age seventeen, resolved to go to Hamburg; and perhaps he was already dreaming, too, of going to Italy, the arts center of the civilized world. In Hamburg he could begin his education in opera, earn a living, and save money so that he could eventually leave, if he wished.

A small paragraph in Mainwaring's account of the young musician's activities at this point gives an interesting glimpse into his relationship with his mother as well as into his own character:

> [*His father's death*] *produced a considerable change for the worse in the income of his mother. That he might not add to her expences, the first thing which he did on his arrival at Hamburgh, as to procure scholars* [*music students*]*, and obtain some employment in the*

*orchestra. Such was his industry and success in setting out, that the
first remittance which his mother sent him he generously returned her,
accompanied with a small present of his own.*

Handel rightly was expected to support his widowed mother, but this
incident also hints at his life-long generosity. Mainwaring notes that, "but a very few
years before his death, being informed that the widow of Zachaw (sic) was left ill
provided for, he sent her money more than once." He wanted to do the same by her
son, "for whose welfare he appeared to be equally anxious," but the son was
apparently a drunk and Handel was advised that "all such services would only
furnish him with opportunities of increasing those sottish habits he had contracted."

When Handel arrived in Hamburg in the spring or early summer of 1703,
he quickly put to work his compelling drive to become a master of his art. He
procured music students, and a position as violinist in the opera orchestra. He soon
took over the much more prominent position of harpsichordist – much more
prominent because the harpsichordist directed the orchestra.* That quickly led to the
debut of his own first opera, *Almira*, composed in 1704 and first produced on
January 8, 1705.

At that point two people came to dominate Handel's life musically and
socially: Reinhard Keiser, manager of the Hamburg Opera and a reputable
composer of both church music and opera; and Johann Mattheson, organist, singer,
composer and aide to the English Resident (Consul), and known to future generations as one of the prominent German music theorists of the eighteenth century.

Opera in Hamburg was not quite the smooth art form it was in Italy. It was
a conglomeration of disparate elements, but it gave Handel an opportunity to learn
much from Keiser, both musically and about how to run an opera company. Handel
would make use of fragments of Keiser's music frequently later in his career. He
obviously watched Keiser with keen interest:

*Keiser's task was to produce a good night out at the theater from a
diverse collection of elements – a musical mixture of "high style" Italian
arias (of which he was no mean composer) with German recitative and*

---

*Sometimes two harpsichords were employed, the first having the prominent position. In Baroque
(non-church) music the harpsichord is the primary keyboard instrument, and, with the cello (and bass, when
needed) makes up the **continuo**: the bass line on which the music is built, "filled in" with chords by the
harpsichord. In some types of music of the period, an organ replaces the harpsichord.

aria, on the basis of librettos whose main plots had to be stretched to accommodate humorous or homely sub-plots and spectacular scenes.[13]

Mattheson was four years older than Handel. The two became friends, though it was a friendship not without controversy, and later may have cooled. They worked together at the opera and went out on musical and social excursions together. One such foray was a trip to Lübeck, where the organist-composer position of the famous Dietrich Buxtehude was to become vacant at his eminent retirement. However, there was an important stipulation accompanying the job: the new organist was required to marry Buxtehude's daughter. No details of this intriguing job requirement are known. Whether Fräulein Buxtehude was undesirable in some way and (or) past the normal marrying age, whether there were no potential husbands locally, or whether her father specifically wanted a fellow musician-composer for a son-in-law can only be speculated. Whatever the case, neither young Handel nor Mattheson was interested in such a commitment in order to procure the job. (Bach also bypassed the position for that reason.) The only detail we have of the excursion to Lübeck is a sentence from Coxe's *Anecdotes*. While presenting a fascinating, if fleeting, glimpse of Handel as a young man (and an allusion to his later vaunted wit) the comment says nothing about Buxtehude or his daughter:

> *They performed this journey in the public caravan, with all the thoughtless hilarity of youth, singing extempore duets, and amusing themselves with all imaginable frolics on the road; to which the affected simplicity and archness of Handel gave an exquisite zest.*[14]

Much later, Mattheson wrote a biographical dictionary of composers and, of course, included Handel. Among many other things, Mattheson remarked on Handel's keen and dry sense of humor. Handel was an excellent straight man, even to the point of playing the simpleton. While a violinist in the opera orchestra,

> *though he ... pretended to know nothing, yet he used to be very arch, for he had always a dry way of making the gravest people laugh, without laughing himself. But his superior abilities were soon discovered, when, upon occasion of the harpsichord-player at the opera being absent, he was first persuaded to take his place; for he then shewed himself to be a great master, to the astonishment of every one, except myself, who had frequently heard him before, upon keyed-instruments.*

Sometimes, however, there was a distinct dearth of humor between the two friends, as in the situation which spurred their notorious duel. Mattheson composed an opera, *Cleopatra*, in which he himself acted and sang the part of Antony while Handel played the harpsichord. After Antony's death early in the work, Mattheson came off-stage and expected to take over as harpsichordist (and conductor). When Handel "refused to indulge his vanity by relinquishing to him this post," as Burney puts it, Mattheson became angry. This caused a literally violent quarrel:

> Mattheson gave him a slap on the face; upon which, both immediately drew their swords, and a duel ensued in the Market-place, before the door of the Opera-house: luckily, the sword of Mattheson was broke against a metal button upon Handel's coat, which put an end to the combat.

The duel occurred December 5, 1704. Later, Handel never mentioned it and Mattheson downplayed it, insisting that "a dry slap on the face was no assassination, but rather a friendly hint, to put him on his guard." Despite the potential seriousness of the incident, the friends were quite soon reconciled and went together on the 30th of December to the rehearsal of Handel's *Almira*. Mattheson sang the principal part, as Handel had planned. Shortly after, Handel wrote his second opera, *Nero* (which is lost to us), and Mattheson also sang its title role.[*] But Mattheson soon quit the stage to become secretary to the British Consul, a position he would keep for sixty years.

We hear nothing again of Handel's "scholars." Later, he would be the music teacher to women in the Royal family, and would particularly value Princess Anne as an excellent musician, connoisseur and friend. But prodding young students to reveal whatever level of excellence they might have been hiding was not high on Handel's lists of priorities – probably because, with few exceptions, the students were quite ordinary, or even mediocre. In 1734 in London he would tell organist, composer and theorist Jacob Wilhelm Lustig, "Since I left your native Hamburg ... nothing on earth could induce me to teach music, with one exception – Anne, the flower of princesses."[15]

---

[*]*Nero's* alternate title was "Die durch Blut und Mord erlangte Liebe," i.e., "Love Obtained by Blood and Murder." American musicologist Ellen T. Harris has introduced a homoerotic interpretation of *Nero* to Handel studies (*Handel as Orpheus: Voice and Desire in the Chamber Cantatas*. Cambridge, Mass.: Harvard University Pres, 2001).

Chapter 3
A Brave New World in Italy

When Handel had saved enough money he set out for Italy. Then twenty-one years old, he arrived in this sun-drenched Catholic land in the latter half of 1706. In the end, he would stay three-and-a-half years, until February 1710. He spent periods in Florence, Rome, Naples and Venice, and probably moved back and forth between Rome and Florence several times. The trail of his movements in and between these famous cities is far harder to track than are the trunkfuls of music that materialized after him.

Handel was invited to Italy by Gian Gastone de Medici, Prince of Tuscany, whom he met when the music-loving prince was staying in Hamburg. The Italian nobleman and the young German composer had frequently discussed music together. While still in Germany, Handel wasn't impressed with Italian music. The candid young Saxon, in Mainwaring's words, "plainly confessed that he could see nothing in the Music that answered the high character his Highness [de Medici] had given it. On the contrary, he thought it so very indifferent, that the Singers, he said, must be angels to recommend it."[1] The Prince, in turn, insisted to Handel that there was no place outside Italy where he could gain such advantage as a musician. Handel wasn't convinced. "If this were so," he said, he was "much at a loss to conceive how such great culture should be followed by so little fruit." The Prince then promised that if Handel chose to go with him when he returned to Italy, "no conveniences should be wanting."

Despite his low opinion of Italian music, Handel understood that going to Italy would be a wise move. But, ever independent, he was resolved to get there on his own. When he did go, he soon changed his mind about the quality of Italian music. He wholeheartedly adopted Italian-style opera for his own; for many years he would "out-Italian" the Italians with his operas.

According to Mattheson, in Handel's early months in Hamburg he composed, in the German church style he was used to, "very long, long arias, and really interminable cantatas which had neither the right kind of skill or taste." But his Italian sojourn thoroughly cured him of that Germanic habit. Handel picked up and quickly incorporated the influences that would comprise the major elements of his mature style as a composer. He especially developed a facility for writing for voices in a way that would show each solo voice or choral voice-part to best advantage. His vocal and choral music would encapsulate and express a vast range of human emotion in a way unique in the Baroque period.*

The ease with which this assimilation occurred is nothing short of amazing. It points up a quality Handel had in abundance both as a composer and as a person, a characteristic that accounted for his long popularity in his own time: *adaptability*. And it is evident in his ability to compose in a large variety of musical forms, among them anthems, opera, oratorio, odes and serenatas, organ concertos and festive orchestral music.

The young German Lutheran quickly discovered that he could make his living in Catholic Rome through the support of wealthy patrons: several churchmen with opulent tastes and the money to match – Cardinals Pamphili and Ottoboni; and a nobleman who employed a chamber group of players and singers, the Marquis Ruspoli. In thinking of the Italian setting in which the budding Saxon composer worked so successfully despite that setting's religious and initial cultural foreignness to him, it is helpful to remember that at this time there was no "Italy" as we know it. Italian music historian Carlo Vitali concludes that

> this archaic mosaic of political fragments, incomprehensible to a Frenchman, Spaniard or Englishman, perhaps reminded Handel of his German homeland, divided into dozens of principalities, margravates and ecclesiastical or secular baronies, whose rulers clothed themselves in high-sounding titles that a good diplomat had to study very carefully in order not to commit a faux pas. For the sake of his own survival, Handel had to make similar use of his diplomatic skills when he wandered through the Italian labyrinth – especially since the peninsula had for the past five years been the theater of a major military conflict that would ultimately transform its aspect profoundly.

Handel speedily gained a reputation as an exceptional organist and harpsichordist. Vitali notes that early non-musicians' eye-witness accounts refer to Handel as a harpsichordist. In fact, there is a fascinating "dueling keyboards" story in which Handel and highly regarded composer Alessandro Scarlatti (who first met each other at Cardinal Ottoboni's residence) go instrument to instrument, each

---

*Great as Handel was, for "uniqueness" and profundity no one surpassed Bach. Bach was, and is, in a class apart.

playing the harpsichord and the organ. The harpsichord contest may have been a tie, or may have given Scarlatti the edge. But the organ was another matter, says Mainwaring:

> As [Scarlatti] was an exquisite player on the harpsichord, the Cardinal was resolved to bring him and Handel together for a trial of skill. The issue of the trial on the harpsichord hath been differently reported. It has been said that some gave the preference to Scarlatti However, when they came to the Organ there was not the least pretence for doubting to which of them it belonged. Scarlatti himself declared the superiority of his antagonist, and owned ingenuously, that till he had heard him upon this instrument, he had no conception of its powers.

Vitali concludes that, while in Italy, "the image of himself that Handel wished to project was that of a gentleman, not a professional musician seeking employment.... If his prime interest had been opera, he would probably have spent less time in Rome, where the opera-houses were closed, and more time in Venice or Naples." (Handel wrote only two operas while in Italy, *Rodrigo* and *Agrippina*.) In any case, Handel made a fine impression as an already accomplished composer and the gentleman he apparently wished to be.* Grand Prince Ferdinando de Medici wrote to his brother-in-law, the Elector Johann Wilhelm, mentioning Handel's "civility of manners, wealth of honest feelings and a full command of several languages," as if to suggest, Vitali and others have concluded, "that Handel might be engaged in diplomatic activities in the manner of [composer] Agostino Steffani," who was then working at Hamburg's electoral court and carrying diplomatic messages back to Italy. The "wealth of honest feelings" may imply that saying plainly what was on one's mind, as Handel seems to have done all his life, rather than saying what one thought a Prince would want to hear, was a rare quality in the world of the Italian courtiers.

Handel may have considered taking a position as a *virtuoso* at a court or in a noble household, such as composer-violinist Archangelo Corelli held from

---

*Common to the time, Handel was accompanied by a servant, possibly a secretary. Mainwaring notes that, in his independent fashion, Handel turned down an allowance from Fernando de Medici, Grand Prince of Tuscany, initially paying his own expenses (200 ducats). Even so, in Rome, Naples and most other places he traveled, Mainaring says Handel "had a palazzo at command, and was provided with table, coach, and all other accommodations."

Ottoboni, suggests Vitali. However, despite the handful of individual pieces Handel wrote for the Roman liturgy (some of them exquisite, and keenly demonstrating his adaptability), one thing he surely didn't consider at this or any time was a position as the **maestro di cappella** to a church, as the church would have been, of course, of the Roman persuasion.

This was not merely a matter of what he was used to before he came to Italy. It was an issue of serious differences between Handel and his Italian patrons regarding the very nature and means of salvation (and how that was expressed in worship). Each would have regarded the other as heretical. When Mainwaring tells of attempts by some Italian churchmen to convert Handel to Roman Catholicism, and mentions "the road to damnation," he isn't being melodramatic:

> As [Handel] was familiar with so many of the Sacred Order, and of a persuasion so totally repugnant to theirs, it is natural to imagine that some of them would expostulate with him on that subject. For how could these good catholicks be supposed to bear him any real regard, without endeavoring to lead him out of the road to damnation? Being pressed very closely on this article by one of these exalted Ecclesiastics, he replied, that he was neither qualified, nor disposed to enter into enquiries of this sort, but was resolved to die a member of that communion, whether true or false, in which he was born and bred. No hopes appearing of a real conversion, the next attempt was to win him over to outward conformity. But neither arguments, nor offers had any effect, unless it were that of confirming him still more in the principles of protestantism. These applications were made only by a few persons. The generality looked upon him as a man of honest, though mistaken principles, and therefore concluded that he would not easily be induced to change them.

Mainwaring almost certainly got this story from Handel himself, late in Handel's life. It reveals several interesting points. Mainwaring's last sentence implies that Handel openly, easily commented on matters of faith to his Italian patrons and they talked together about these issues. There was nothing unusual about the frequent discussion of faith-related matters at the time, whether in Italy, Germany or England. In such talk Handel revealed his own Lutheran views, an outlook that of course would have differed very strongly on some points from those of these Roman churchmen. Clearly, those churchmen learned that he was no pushover when it came to principle (or anything else). However, devotion to God on the part of these clerics was apparently not a prerequisite for converting "heretics." Debauchery, in fact, characterized Cardinals Pietro Ottoboni and Benedetto Pamphili. There was a gross discrepancy between what these Italian churchmen confessed and their excessive and debased way of life.

Apart from the cardinals' musical patronage, one wonders what young Handel really thought of these supposed men of God. They were wholly unlike the local Lutheran pastors he had known in Halle, some of whom were relatives of his. He may have seen something of their lifestyle and been repelled by it. American musicologist Ellen Harris (*Handel as Orpheus*) interprets a fawning poem which Pamphili wrote in praise of Handel, and which he asked the young composer himself to set to music, as a deliberately homoerotic portrayal of the Orpheus myth indicating the Cardinal's sexual desire for Handel (at this writing, she is the only Handel scholar to have interpreted the poem in this way).

Handel's statement that he was, already then, "resolved to die a member of that communion ... in which he was born and bred," is telling. He kept his word. He did indeed remain a Lutheran for the rest of his life, most of which he would live in England where in the Church of England's Calvinist-infused theology did not differ nearly so radically from Lutheran Christianity as did "papist" views and practice. But though he would regularly worship in the Church of England and would write beautiful anthems for the Anglican service, he never became an Anglican.

But what about that business of remaining in the Lutheran communion *whether true or false*? That may be interpretative license on Mainwaring's part. Or, assuming Handel said just that, it could have been a nod of politeness toward his Italian hosts, and an indication he did not intend to be engaged in serious debate about it. At no time did Handel give any indication that in the few years he had been away from home – or at any later time in his life – he doubted or shrugged off the truth of the Christian faith or of its particular interpretation by Luther. He had a thorough knowledge of the Bible and his own Lutheran Confessions, nurtured in him by his devout parents and by his education. (He would make good use of that knowledge in his choral works.) His own faith proceeded from accepting as true what he had been taught of Scripture and the Confessions.

In catechism Handel would also have been thoroughly grounded in how the Confessions interpreted the Bible. And further, he would have been drilled on the points where Luther differed from the Roman church, and almost surely also on the points where Luther differed from Calvin and the other Reformers). Handel's later statement of gratitude for the freedom he had in England to believe as his heart directed him confirms that his remaining a Lutheran was a matter of belief and conscience to him. Sir John Hawkins, a contemporary of Handel's who wrote a music history about the same time Charles Burney did, says, "He entertained very serious notions touching its [his faith's] importance. These he would frequently express in his remarks on the constitution of the English government; and he would often speak of it as one of the great felicities of his life that he was settled in a country where no man suffers any molestation or inconvenience on account of his religious principles." Of course some people in England – including Catholics and Protestant Dissenters – did suffer "molestation" and "inconvenience" for their religious principles. But on a relative scale, compared to other places in that time, the gist of Handel's remark is true. As a German Lutheran immigrant he certainly experienced it as true.

The fact that Handel spent three and a half years in Italy composing "secular" music for decidedly secular churchmen, and later spent two and a half decades writing Italian opera, is indicative of nothing in regards to his own faith or the ignoring or abandoning of it. The chasm between "sacred" and "secular" that exists in our own time did not exist in his (more about that later). Because there are few sources that mention Handel overtly talking about his faith until late in his life, many modern scholars present him as if he were at best a nominal Christian all those decades, or as if in Italy and then in the opera/theater environment in England he had become either nonchalantly or arrantly secular.[2] This assumption is based on a modern misunderstanding of the nature of Christian life, not on any real evidence that Handel rejected or even ignored his childhood faith until late in life, or even for the rest of his life.

Handel wrote an astonishing amount of music during his three-and-a-half years in Italy – though perhaps less astonishing when considered next to his output during any comparable span in his career. In our own time, Handel's composing of *Messiah* in just three weeks in August-September 1741 is often attributed to his having been especially inspired by the subject. He undoubtedly was, but that thrall wasn't unusual in spurring on his compositional process. He always composed with that sort of facility and efficiency, and sometimes faster.

Due to Pope Clement's ban on opera in Rome, the largest part of Handel's Italian output was not opera but secular cantatas. He composed these mostly in

Rome between 1707 and 1709 and they fall into two main categories: those with orchestral accompaniment (nearly thirty of them); and those with **continuo** accompaniment (almost seventy of them). Handel's Italian church music will be of special interest to listeners who particularly love his English oratorios, as will be his first ventures into Italian oratorio and oratorio-like works: *La Resurrezione (The Resurrection)* and *Il trionfo del Tempo e del Disinganno (The Triumph of Time and Truth)* – the latter which he would rework decades later as his last English oratorio in 1757.

Italian **oratorio** was the only kind of oratorio that existed when Handel sojourned in Italy shortly after the turn of the eighteenth century: it would be 1732 before he himself would begin to "invent" English oratorio. (Handel's first English oratorio, *Esther*, would be publicly inaugurated in 1732. But he had actually written a shorter form of it much earlier, about 1718, for James Brydges, Earl of Carnarvon, later Duke of Chandos – for whom he also wrote his Psalm-based *Chandos Anthems*.) Though *Il trionfo del Tempo e del Disinganno* is often referred to as a "secular oratorio," there was really no such thing at the time. The term *oratorio* properly was applied only to works with non-liturgical "sacred" texts. Its form, however, could vary, as long as it had more than one singer and was longer than one aria or chorus.[3]

In the moral worldview and aesthetic of the eighteenth century, to be considered a worthy composition a piece was required to "instruct" as well as "delight" its audience. *Il trionfo del Tempo* is an allegorical work with a specific moral. But the oratorio of most direct interest and relation to Handel's later English-language biblical oratorios is *La Resurrezione*, because it concerns Christ's resurrection. Handel wrote it for Ruspoli for an elaborate performance on Easter Sunday, 1708, at Ruspoli's Bonelli palace in Rome. *La Resurrezione* musically presents not only the Resurrection, but considers events during the three days Christ is in the grave. A disputation with mortal consequences ensues between Lucifer and an Angel.

Lucifer here might be described as both devil and devil's advocate. He and the Angel verbally battle over whether Christ really has redemptive power. Musically, this dispute occurs in spirited recitatives and brilliant arias. Meanwhile, on flesh-and-blood earth, Jesus's friends and disciples deeply mourn: Mary Magdalene, Mary Cleophas, the Apostle John. After their anguish, they rejoice greatly at the news of Christ's resurrection.

3. A Brave New World in Italy

The soprano who sang Mary Magdalene at this first performance was Margherita Durastante. Later she would travel to England where she would become one of Handel's most enduring and faithful singers. But at this point Durastante's singing sparked a major incident. Pope Clement XI heard of her performance and roundly reprimanded Ruspoli because he had disregarded the edict that women were not to be allowed to sing in public. **Castrati** (eunuchs) were preferred. No matter that the performance was not acted out. From their beginnings oratorios were not dramatized by actors, though they were assumed to be dramatic, and inherently were. *La Resurrezione* was presented with an unusually large orchestra, the timbre and versatility of which must have delighted the young composer. There were twenty-three violins, four violas, six cellos, five contrabassi (in the string bass family), one bass viol, two trumpets, a trombone, and four oboes. The orchestra was arranged in terraced seating and conducted from the podium by the famous violinist-composer Archangelo Corelli. (This was unusual; the harpsichordist – who was often the composer himself – usually conducted, as we've noted). An impressive painted backdrop depicted Christ rising from the dead (amidst flocks of putti and cherubim), an angel announcing the resurrection to the two Marys and John, and demons sinking into hell.

What an opportunity for Handel to exercise his growing dramatic gift in his depicting characters with real human emotion (even in characters who weren't human)! The oratorio seems to have gone over very well with its audience of "many of the nobility and a few cardinals." The one contemporary reference to the event called it "a very fine musical oratorio." That judgment would naturally make people want to hear it again. They got that chance. But after the Pope's reprimand, the second performance used a soprano **castrato** in place of Senora Durastanti.

While in Rome in 1707, Handel also wrote his first music for choir, works for the Catholic liturgy: *Dixit Dominus*, *Laudate pueri* and *Nisi Dominus*. They demonstrate Handel's adaptability in action. His Lutheran tradition contained (and still contains) many choral and congregational riches, and as a child he himself apparently wrote choral music for the Lutheran service under Zachau's instruction. Handel was just twenty-two years old in 1707, but these Latin works seem to have leaped from a mature mind and heart. They wonderfully demonstrate his particular knack for writing for choirs. This he would later demonstrate over and over in England in his Latin peace anthems, the *Chandos Anthems* based on the Psalms, and in the dozens of thrilling choruses in his oratorios.

This brings to the fore an interesting characteristic of Handel's style. As one would expect, he changed and matured as he aged, and his seasoned understanding of human nature and increased musical experience were reflected in his music. But unlike many other composers, Handel revealed no nicely discernible "early" and "late" composition period, with the "late" being considerably more profound. His style right from the start is satisfyingly developed and fully recognizable as his own. This is true of all the genres in which he wrote. His Italian secular cantatas, too, show his exquisite flair for quickly assimilating the style he came to Italy to study, and his Italian duets were never bested.[*]

If Handel was not primarily interested in opera while in Italy, he did, nevertheless, get a chance to write a couple of operas there, and to see them successfully produced (*Rodrigo*, 1707, and *Agrippina*, 1709). He would compose in a huge variety of musical forms in the following decades. Even so, those years would reveal a penchant for opera that would dominate his career in England until he finally left it behind to concentrate on oratorio to the end of his life.

---

[*]As an exquisite example of the Italian cantatas I recommend *Aminta e Filide* ("Arresta il passo," HWV83), a nymphs-and-shepherds story for two voices and strings. At this writing there is still just one recording of this work (Helios CDH55077), released as long ago as 1984, sung by sopranos Gillian Fisher and Patrizia Kwella, with Denys Darlow's London Handel Orchestra. It is hard to imagine a better performance, and the cantata is delectation from start to finish. But its final duet is a truly astonishing movement.

Chapter 4
Rumors of Love, Matters of Character

In late February 1710, just after Handel turned 25, he headed home to Germany with his new-found musical experience. He traveled via Innsbruck and undoubtedly stopped in Halle to see his mother and older sister, Dorothea Sophie; to meet lawyer Michael Dietrich Michaëlsen as his new brother-in-law; and to say hello to his old teacher Zachau, with whom he would have had much to talk about. The traveler's arrival at "home" again after so long would have brought out friends and members of the church community as well. Handel had surely been in contact by letter with his family during his years in Italy. He would have been informed of the joys and sorrows at home which he was forced to experience from a distance. Among those joys was the wedding of his sister Dorothea; foremost among the sorrows was the death of his other sister, Johanne, who was only 19 when she died.

The self-confident twenty-five year old was on the move, ready to pursue the best musical opportunities where he could find them. His growing renown preceded his return to Germany. He made his way to Hanover, seat of Elector Georg Ludwig, who in 1714 would become England's George I. Handel arrived in Hanover at the beginning of June 1710. By June 16 he was the newly appointed *Kapellmeister* (Master of the Chapel), that is, "master" of all the music required in the court chapel. The job was offered despite his telling the Elector that he had promised to travel to Dusseldorf to the court of the Elector Palatine there, and despite an invitation to England as well. In making the appointment, Elector Georg Ludwig agreed that Handel "had leave to be absent for a twelve-month or more, if he chose it; and to go whithersoever he pleased," says Mainwaring, adding, "On these easy conditions he thankfully accepted it."[1]

Elector Georg Ludwig was a true music lover, a fact that would have further impact on Handel when he moved to England. Though Hanover had an opulent opera house known for its capability for impressive stage effects, it had fallen on financial hard times and Georg Ludwig hadn't had the wherewithal to revive it. A *Kapellmeister* did not normally have anything official to do with the opera, but it is possible that Handel's appointment indicated the Elector's intention to revive the opera. On the other hand, the Elector would have known Handel's origins and his grounding in church music.

Handel's duties as *Kapellmeister* seem to have been light and seasonal; the Elector went away for part of the year to his hunting lodge in Göhrde. Besides some composing, Handel was likely expected to entertain the court as a keyboard virtuoso. He got along well with Georg Ludwig's children (his own age), especially Georg August and his wife, Caroline, who would later be his staunch supporters as England's George II and Queen Caroline. A person who eased Handel's way into the Elector's court was court composer Augustino Steffani, whom Handel had known until then only by reputation. (Court composer was a different position than *Kapellmeister*. The officially Lutheran court required a Lutheran *Kapellmeister*, and Steffani was a Catholic: a bishop, in fact.) Steffani's hospitality made a lasting impression. Years later Handel told Sir John Hawkins:

> *"When I first arrived at Hanover .... I understood somewhat of music,"* and, putting forth both his broad hands, and extending his fingers, *"could play pretty well on the organ; he received me with great kindness; and took an early opportunity to introduce me to the Princess Sophia and the Elector's son, giving them to understand that I was what he was pleased to call a virtuoso in music; he obliged me with instructions for my conduct and behavior during my residence at Hanover; and being called from the city to attend to matters of a public concern, he left me in possession of that favour and patronage which he himself had enjoyed for a series of years."* [2]

Despite the easy conditions in Hanover, Handel seems to have grown restless quickly. No sooner was he appointed *Kapellmeister* in Hanover than he prepared for his promised trip to the court at Dusseldorf. Because he intended to be away for some time, he may have first gone in the opposite direction, to Halle once more, though he had been home relatively recently. From Dusseldorf he would continue via The Netherlands to England, his first visit to the British Isles. (Dusseldorf is in west-central modern Germany, not many miles from the Dutch border, directly west, cross country, of Leipzig – from which Halle is not far south. Hanover is north of Dusseldorf and Leipzig, about midway between them, and Hamburg is straight north of that). In London, too, Handel's name had already surfaced as a composer who would be worth listening to. What the young man undoubtedly did not know was that his musical reputation was not the only reputation that had preceded him from Italy.

A titillating bit of gossip had reached the Hanover Court. It linked Handel romantically with the Florentine opera singer Vittoria Tarquini. A few days after his arrival in Hanover, the Electress of Hanover commented in a June 14 letter, "He is quite a handsome man..... Rumor has it that he has been in love with Victoria" (or more accurately, "the lover of Victoria," i.e., "amant de La Victoria"). Mainwaring, in preparing his biography of Handel, published a year after the composer's death, got wind of this story and couldn't resist it, clergyman though he was. But Mainwaring has it the other way around (and has Handel younger than he was). Vittoria was in love with Handel:

> At the age of eighteen he made the Opera of RODRIGO, for which he was presented with 100 sequins, and a service of plate. This may serve for a sufficient testimony of its favourable reception. Vittoria, who was much admired both as an Actress, and a Singer, bore a principal part in this Opera. She was a fine woman, and had for some time been much in the good graces of his Serene Highness. But, from the natural restlessness of certain hearts, so little sensible was she of her exalted situation, that she conceived a design of transferring her affections to another person. Handel's youth and comeliness, joined with his fame and abilities in Music, had made impressions on her heart. Tho' she had the art to conceal them for the present, she had not perhaps the power, certainly not the intention, to efface them.

Two years after first meeting Tarquini, Handel saw her again in Venice, where she sang in his opera *Agrippina*, wrote Mainwaring. Except that she didn't sing in *Agrippina*; nor had she sung in *Rodrigo*, Handel's other opera composed while in Italy. Excluding how "fine" she may have looked, her being a morally "fine woman" would likely have been challenged by even the Italian courtiers, who were accustomed to sexual intrigues that would have deeply shocked the average Christian of Handel's class in Germany or England. What Mainwaring doesn't say (and likely didn't know) is that Tarquini was old enough to be Handel's mother (in 1709, she would have been forty when he was twenty-four); she was married; and she already had a lover, the Grand Prince Ferdinando, who some modern scholars say was bisexual. In Mainwaring's story Tarquini had deliberate designs on Handel, which the latter may or may not have welcomed.

This raises both the nature of Handel's specific relationship with Tarquini and of his sexual morality and "love life" in general. (In the following I assume a traditionally orthodox definition of "sexual morality" as based on biblical teaching and as understood in Handel's time.) In our time, even his sexual orientation is being scrutinized. According to two modern scholars (music historian Ellen Harris and comparative literature/cultural studies scholar Gary Thomas), Handel's previously assumed heterosexuality either *may not* have been or *was not* what it seemed. Because the story about Tarquini arises at this early stage in Handel's career, and because rumors about Handel's personal life are still flying three-hundred years later, this is an opportune place to examine Handel's morality and character in general.

In 1710 Handel was an unmarried man who was already known to be a Christian man of principle. As it turned out, he would never marry. To assume that at any stage of his life his religious principals had nothing to do with his sexual behavior is an indefensible modern assumption. Later in his life he would repeatedly be referred to by his English contemporaries as a person of high morals (Hawkins' word is "blameless"). Handel's contemporaries took his celibacy for granted. Whether that celibacy was life-long is a question ultimately unanswerable, but several points can be noted that lend perspective to the issue. Despite extramarital affairs and sexual hijinks among the monarchs and some of the aristocracy, chastity among the unmarried, and fidelity within marriage, were quite obviously the norm in Lutheran Germany and Anglican England.

Handel was human, of course. About this time he was also a young man on an adventure, and while in Italy was a long way from the faith community that had nurtured him. Yet if he did have a sexual relationship with Tarquini, a married woman whose lifestyle and general amorality contrasted so starkly with what we know of Handel's own life and morality, it would have been out of character -- something he could hardly have tried to morally justify, and which, in the light of a more mature and sober day, surely would have caused him shame. (If he did have a sexual relationship with a woman like Tarquini, one could even speculate that it may actually have even reinforced his later celibacy.)

Many modern Handel commentators find it inconceivable that Handel could have, or would have, remained celibate all of his adult life, or even for part of it. So they assume that he had "discreet" love affairs, relationships that somehow avoided the scrutiny of those who shared his world – people who saw no evidence in him of anything but a life which was consistently Christian, moral and chaste. William Frosch, a music-loving physician who wrote "The 'Case' of George Frideric Handel," is one who makes that assumption. But to take that view is to impose modern values and sexual attitudes on the first half of the eighteenth century, a time which was still the end of the Reformation era in Germany and England, and a time when, as we shall see, a Christian worldview was still society's governing force. After Frosch mentions Tarquini, he calls attention to a "marginal note written into a copy of Mainwaring's 1760 biography ... from the royal library":

> G.F. Handel was ever honest, nay excessively polite but like all men of sense would talk all, and hear none, and scorned the advice of any but the Woman he loved, but his amours were rather of short duration, always with[in] the pale of his own profession.

This refers to Handel during his life in England. If Frosch is assuming that the "amours" and "the Woman he loved" must refer to consummated love affairs, it is an instance of his imposing a modern understanding on eighteenth century language. When a respectable man was unmarried and initiated a romantic relationship, which was presumed to lead to marriage, there was no assumption by others that the lovers were sharing a bed. The assumption, in fact, was that they were not. "Lover" did not mean what it means today. Its primary meaning was "one who is possessed by sentiments of affection or regard towards another; a friend or well-wisher"; or "one who is in love with, or who is enamored of a person of the opposite sex." Of course "lover" could be applied to "one who loves illicitly; a gallant, paramour." But that was not its ordinary meaning, either in French or in English. An *amant* was understood to be a man who had love for a woman, without specific connotation of consummated sexual love. So despite the Electress's letter, and even Tarquini's character and sexual history, there is simply no means of knowing what kind of relationship existed between Handel and Tarquini, or whether there was truly a relationship at all.

Handel's career would bring him into regular interaction with female singers. We know he became fond of several of them and might well have considered them friends. He could have become attracted to a particular singer, gotten to know her and allowed himself to love her and confide in her – if one feels compelled to "justify" that margin note in the Royal Library's copy of Mainwaring. Some of the opera singers Handel worked with had reputations as somewhat less than proverbial paragons of virtue. Most of those singers were married, which neither he nor the great majority of his contemporaries would have easily overlooked.

The primary question of morality aside for a moment, there was also the sheer practical situation. How likely would it have been that someone who became famous so quickly, and who over many decades was constantly in the public eye, could have been "discreetly" bedding the also high-profile women who worked for and with him without even the slightest hint of it escaping to the public, much less to any of his friends? There were no such hints. Charles Burney says:

> Handel, with many virtues, was addicted to no vice that was injurious to society. Nature, indeed, required a great supply of sustenance to support so huge a mass, and he was rather epicurean in the choice of it; but this seems to have been the only appetite he allowed himself to gratify.[3]

Consonant with this description, Sir John Hawkins summed up Handel: "He was a man of blameless morals, and throughout his life manifested a deep sense of religion." According to Coxe's *Anecdotes*, Handel was an emotionally reticent man; but as a young man he did consider marrying. The picture Coxe presents rings true, in line with Handel's character:

> Handel contracted few intimacies, and when his early friends died, he was not solicitous of acquiring new ones. He was never married; but his celibacy must not be attributed to any deficiency of personal attractions, or to the source which Sir John Hawkins unjustly supposes, the want of social affection. On the contrary, it was owing to the independency of his disposition, which feared degradation, and dreaded confinement. For when he was young, two of his scholars [music students], ladies of considerable fortune, were so much enamoured of him, that each was desirous of a matrimonial alliance. The first is said to have fallen a victim to her attachment. Handel would have married her; but his pride was stung by the coarse declaration of her mother, that she never would consent to the marriage of her daughter with a fiddler; and, indignant at the expression, he declined all further intercourse. After the death of the mother, the father renewed the acquaintance, and informed him that all obstacles were removed; but he replied, that the time was now past; and the young lady fell into a decline, which soon terminated her existence. The second attachment, was a lady splendidly related [from an exceptionally "good family"], whose hand he might have obtained by renouncing his profession. That condition he resolutely refused, and laudably declined the connection which was to prove a restriction on the great faculties of his mind.[4]

The possibility that Handel was attracted to those of his own sex had not been seriously considered until a couple of decades ago. In a 1994 journal article

Gary Thomas asked "Was Handel gay?" He answered in the affirmative.[5] In 2001, Ellen Harris published *Handel as Orpheus*, in which she posits "Handel's possible association with same-sex love through his patrons," patrons she believes moved in a secret homosexual culture. (Harris refers to Handel biographer Jonathan Keates's addressing and rejecting the "nagging possibility" that Handel was homosexual; the issue was hardly nagging – it was not raised in the nearly three-hundred years from Handel's time until ours, when Thomas and Harris have led the discussion.) Harris also concludes that Handel's numerous Italian cantatas are full of homoerotic references.

After Harris's book came out, newspapers reiterated the question "Was Handel gay?" Harris links Handel to same-sex love in various ways but can say, a bit disingenuously, that she doesn't herself answer whether he was personally involved in the purported same-sex activities of some of his patrons or friends. Nevertheless, since then, some part of the public has begun to assume that Handel was homosexual, despite the dearth of evidence. He has for some time, in fact, been featured on a "gay heroes" website (along with the Apostle Paul and Joan of Arc, among others).

Harris notes that Donald Burrows' biography, which appeared shortly before Gary Thomas's article,

> depends on a a theory of celibacy, speculating that the death of Handel's father "was so traumatic for the 11-year-old that it produced a psychological insecurity that explains the apparent celibacy of his adulthood," and asserting that homosexual relations would be unlikely in "the life of someone who had probably received a fairly strict Lutheran upbringing in eighteenth-century Germany." Although Handel's sexual activity, if any, remains private, an understanding of the "eighteenth century context" clearly demonstrates that arguments opposing the possibility of homosexuality are themselves based on false assumptions. From the point of view of historical accuracy, these errors need to be addressed.[*]

The assumption of Handel's celibacy is wholly legitimate, as we have seen. Where

---

[*]Harris's expressed concern for historical accuracy becomes peculiar in the context of her book when her theories appear to be based not so much on historical accuracy as conjecture informed by a modern worldview, read into eighteenth century society.

Burrows misses the mark is his looking for a reason at all for an unmarried man to be celibate. The "reason" would have been obvious to the average person in eighteenth century England. The biblical norm that set aside marriage as the relationship in which sexual desires could be given legitimate expression, and that condemned homosexual acts as contrary to creation, was accepted by virtually everyone, and was the basis of English laws against "fornication," adultery, and "sodomy." (Sodomy was considered so unnatural and in defiance of God-instituted moral law that it was still punishable by death in England long after Handel's day.)

The general supposition was that outside of the marriage bond a person must not (and did not) act indiscriminately on his or her sexual desires; such desires were to be curbed by self-control, which had its basis in Christian faith and morality. The immoral actions (whether "heterosexual" or "homosexual") of some portion of the male and female population, especially the aristocratic classes, did not negate the norm. How widespread fornication and adultery were, and sodomy (to use the eighteenth century terms) is difficult to say, though any behavior outside of societal norms was easier to get away with if it occurred among members of the upper classes. Recent historical and church-historical studies of bodies of previously unlooked at sermons, pamphlets, parish records (which were legal as well as ecclesiastical documents), and personal letters and papers from the first half of the eighteenth century in England indicate that the period was far more conventionally, orthodoxly Christian than earlier twentieth century historians have assumed and portrayed – which is not to say that the renewal that John Wesley, George Whitefield and other "Dissenters" worked for was unnecessary.

Burrows's statement (quoting Harris quoting him) that "homosexual relations would be unlikely in 'the life of someone who had probably received a fairly strict Lutheran upbringing in eighteenth-century Germany'" is not as easily dismissable as Harris implies. Burrows at least refers to the heart of the matter, which Harris doesn't address: the relationship of faith to sexual behavior. All human beings were held to be subject to Adam and Eve's Fall into sin. Not surprisingly, some percentage of people violated the norms of chastity and fidelity, some with impunity. But if Handel did not – and his contemporaries say he did not – no one would have seen anything extraordinary in that, nor anything odd or abnormal in his celibacy.

What about other aspects of Handel's character as observed by his contemporaries? "El Sassone" ("The Saxon") was a man who stood out in a crowd, not just musically, but physically and by force of personality. Handel was a big man, both tall and large, and later in life could be described as portly. Coxe draws this comprehensive picture of the composer:

> He was large in person, and his natural corpulency, which increased as he advanced in life, rendered his whole appearance of that bulky proportion, as to give rise to Quin's inelegant, but forcible expression; that his hands were feet, and his fingers toes. From a sedentary life, he had contracted a stiffness in his joints, which in addition to his great weight and weakness of body, rendered his gait awkward; still his countenance was open, manly, and animated; expressive of all that grandeur and benevolence, which were the prominent features of his character. In temper he was irascible, impatient of contradiction, but not vindictive; jealous of his musical pre-eminence, and tenacious in all points, which regarded his professional honour.... His chief foible was a culpable indulgence in the sensual gratifications of the table; but this foible was amply compensated by a sedulous attention to every religious duty, and moral obligation. His understanding was excellent, and his knowledge extensive. Besides the German, his native tongue, he was intimate with the English, and master of the Latin, French, and Italian languages: he had acquired a taste for painting, which he improved during his residence in Italy, and felt great pleasure in contemplating the works of art. His great delight was derived from his attachment to his own science, and he experienced particular satisfaction from religious principles, in presiding at the organ in the cathedral church of St. Paul.... Handel's religious disposition was not a mere display, it was amply productive of religion's best fruit, charity; and this liberal sentiment not only influenced him in the day of prosperity, but even when standing on the very brink of ruin.[6]

We've already noted Handel's early independence, which only deepened as he grew older. Coxe tells the story of Handel's vacationing at a spa ("taking the waters") when the composer heard that the King would be arriving there. Unwilling to be at the monarch's beck and call and have his vacation disturbed, Handel decided to leave before the King arrived.

Several anecdotes which have come down to us about Handel's anger at his singers have given him a modern reputation as arrogant and easily enraged. His contemporaries saw irascibility and stubbornness in him, and recognized that he did not suffer musical fools gladly, but no one who truly knew him called him self-important or ill-tempered. Coxe does say that Handel "perhaps too much" saw his singers as "mere instruments" who were there to give expression to his music. Coxe excuses this to some extent by saying that Handel "possessed the impetuosity and inflexibility of genius."

Some of the singers were male, of course, including the castrati. Handel came to loggerheads particularly with Senesino, a preening and petulant star castrato. The situation is put in better perspective by drawing an analogy from the star opera singers of Handel's day to today's highly paid rock or sports stars. They could indeed be temperamental, keenly competed with each other, and worked to gain factions for themselves among the audience. Many of Handel's singers, however, worked with him for years, notably Anna Maria Strada (fl. 1719-40) and Margherita Durastanti (fl. 1700-34, who, recall, he had first encountered in Italy). Strada stuck with him when almost all of his other singers defected in 1733 to a rival opera company, and Durastanti returned from Italy twice to rejoin Handel's singing cast after the defection. Clearly his most "reasonable" singers did not think him a tyrant. There's ample evidence, too, that he was open to changing arias to better suit singers' needs and desires. There are no stories of trauma between Handel and his English singers during his oratorio period. Whether as he aged he was becoming more mellow (there are reports to that effect) or whether Handel thought his English singers were less temperamental than the Italians we can only surmise.

If Handel could be easily irritated by "fools," he was also quick to forgive. Burney recalls Handel playing the harpsichord while demonstrating to Burney himself as a young man, and to the well-known singer Mrs. Cibber, how the duet "From these dread scenes" from *Judas Maccabaeus* should be performed. Burney hummed along on one part. Handel then asked him to sing it out. Burney did, but Handel grew annoyed and chided Burney for making mistakes, "terrifying" him. Burney describes the scene: "At length recovering from my fright I ventured to say, that I fancied there was a mistake in the writing; which, upon examining, Handel discovered to be the case; and then instantly, with the greatest good humour and humility said, 'I pec your barton – I am a very odd tog.'" ("I beg your pardon; I am a very odd dog"). And then he added, not accusatorily but no doubt with a tongue-in-cheek smile: "'Maishter Schmitt is to plame.'" ("Mr. Smith is to blame" – i.e., J.C. Smith the elder, his copyist.)

Both Handel's essential goodheartedness and the tendency of his flare-ups to present a comical picture are evident in another amusing story about his having "had by much persuasion," and against his better judgment "received under his roof and protection" a delinquent boy whose parents apparently couldn't handle him. The story sounds like an eighteenth century version of a chapter out of Dickens. The boy, said Burney, "had been represented [to Handel] not only as having an uncommon disposition for music, but for sobriety and diligence." Perhaps not surprisingly, the boy "turned out ill, and ran away, no one, for a considerable time, knew whither." Handel "was in the habit of talking to himself, so loud, that it was easy for persons not very near him, to hear the subject of his soliloquies.... During this period, Handel, walking in the Park, as he thought, alone, was heard to commune with himself in the following manner. – 'Der teifel! De fater vas desheeved; – de mutter vas desheeved; – but I vas not desheeved; – he is ein te—d schcauntrel – and coot for nutting.'" ("The devil! The father was deceived! The mother was deceived! But I was not deceived. He is a damned scoundrel, and good for nothing!")

Handel loved gourmet food, and plenty of it. Not surprisingly for someone of his fame, his appetite was periodically the subject of public comment. Again, Burney observed, "Handel, with many virtues, was addicted to no vice that was injurious to society. Nature, indeed, required a great supply of sustenance to support so huge a mass, and he was rather epicurean in the choice of it; but this seems to have been the only appetite he allowed himself to gratify." This comment is interesting for Burney's juxtaposition of the liberal gratifying of culinary appetite with the virtuous controlling of all other appetites; he must have been thinking first of all of sexual appetite. If one is inclined to psychologize about such character habits, modern practitioners have, before now, suggested that sometimes the former can be an unconscious substitute for the latter.

Not all who knew Handel offered moderated criticism. The painter-cartoonist Joseph Goupy was a one-time close friend of Handel's who provided the sets for some of the composer's London opera productions. Goupy published several versions of a nasty caricature of Handel as an excessively bewigged and pig-snouted "Charming Brute." The drawing was accompanied by a vituperative verse asserting, among other things, that "his sole Devotion is – to eat." The cartoon first appeared about 1733 and an engraving reappeared as late as 1754, the latter apparently re-released by the then elderly Handel's aristocratic opera enemies.

Despite Goupy and at least one other contemporary barb mocking Handel's bulk, the composer's taste for large quantities of "epicurean" food, like his rages with his singers, seems somewhat exaggerated. The portraits of him as an older man show him to be large and portly, but by no means grossly overweight; not the "huge mass" of Burney's description. Since Handel was tall and of large frame, and then somewhat overweight (especially in his last decades), he would have been quite a bit larger than the average Englishman or Italian of his day. In addition, painted portraits of Burney show Burney to have been smaller than average, which gives a certain perspective to his seeing Handel as having a "huge mass."

Louis-François Roubiliac's sculptures of Handel at about age fifty, taken from life-casts, reveal a slight double chin but no excessive weight in the face or shoulders. In the Westminster Abbey monument, sculpted from a death mask, Handel has a more decided double chin and is paunchy but not obese. Handel does not appear to have had the health problems which can be associated with years of over-eating and -drinking, though he may have developed some level of arteriosclerosis.[*]

If Handel could be irascible, he was fundamentally kind, compassionate and generous, and had a brilliant sense of humor. His quick wit was a quality that was already integral to his character as a teenager, as Johann Mattheson had noted when Handel and he were friends in Hamburg. Burney describes Handel's penchant for humor and the essentially innocuous nature of his "lively sallies of anger," which were made the more droll by his strong German accent:

> His countenance, which I remember as perfectly as that of any man
> I saw but yesterday, was full of fire and dignity; and such as impressed
> ideas of superiority and genius. He was impetuous, rough, and
> peremptory in his manners and conversation, but totally devoid of ill-
> nature or malevolence; indeed, there was an original humour and
> pleasantry in his most lively sallies of anger or impatience, which, with
> his broken English, were extremely risible. His natural propensity to wit
> and humour, and happy manner of relating common occurrences, in an
> uncommon way, enabled him to throw persons and things into very

---

[*]Handel's serious illnesses are discussed in Chapter 10, and the onset of his blindness (including a theory explaining its cause), in Chapters 15.

ridiculous attitudes. Had he been as great a master of the English language as [Jonathan] Swift, his bons mots would have been as frequent, and somewhat of the same kind.... Handel's general look was somewhat heavy and sour; but when he did smile, it was his sire the sun, bursting out of a black cloud. There was a sudden flash of intelligence, wit, and good humour, beaming in his countenance, which I hardly ever saw in any other.

All these accounts are reinforced by Handel's friends in their letters and diaries. The portrait that emerges is of "a man of firm and intrepid spirit," especially in facing adversity; a man of serious faith and strong principles; witty and good-humored but also capable of explosions of temper and use of expressions considered profane[*]; sometimes irascible, and sometimes given to holding grudges, but a man with no meanness in him; a careful businessman who was fundamentally generous and compassionate to those in need; candidly aware of his musical ability and jealous of his reputation but not arrogant about either, and sensitive to public opinion of him; an honest man whose impulse and preference seemed to be to speak his mind forthrightly even while on a more elemental level being self-protectively wary about revealing to others his deepest feelings – perhaps not only from habit, but a real necessity for one who had become so famous in his own time in a way that few people then were.

----

[*]Several "profane" expressions used by Handel are illustrated by Charles Burney: "damned scoundrel"; "go to the devil"; and in the adjective "damnable." These are always written by Burney in a manner intended to comically imitate Handel's German accent.

Chapter 5
Early Imprints on England

Handel reached England sometime in November or December 1710. On this trip he stayed through the end of the opera season, June 1711. A little of his music was already known in London when he arrived in person. He got to work immediately on an opera; just as quickly he proved with the opulently staged *Rinaldo* that his reputation was justified.

Plays had long predominated on the London stage (Shakespeare had been the greatest of a constellation of great playwrights). Then, gradually English composers began to set English-language drama to music. English operas never really gained a foothold, however. Operas partly in Italian and partly in English began to appear, and after that, opera entirely in Italian and entirely sung (as opposed to containing partly spoken dialogue). Ironically, it would be the German Handel whose Italian-style operas firmly established opera in London.

Mainwaring notes the confused scene in London's opera world before Handel arrived, coupled with a "growing taste for every thing that was Italian":

> *From the account of the commencement of the Italian Opera here, as we find it in the eighteenth No. Of the* Spectator, *it is plain, that, what with the confusion of languages, and the transposition of passions and sentiments owing to that cause, the best Composer could hardly be distinguished form the worst. The arrival of Handel put an end to this reign of nonsense.*[*]

It is safe to say that if Handel had not composed Italian opera as he did in London, he would not have devised *Messiah* and the other English biblical oratorios as he did. The Queen's Theater at the Haymarket would play a role in Handel's life for many years. (It was renamed the King's Theater after Queen Anne's death in 1714 and George I's accession to the throne.) Built in late 1704 by its owner and first manager, John Vanbrugh, the theater was only six years old when Handel arrived in London for this visit. Its main competition was Drury Lane theater managed by John Rich.

---

*The *Spectator* to which Mainwaring refers was an innovative and influential publication run by Joseph Addison and Richard Steele from 1711 to 1714. It was the first daily paper whose subject was not news, but literature and manners. It and its counterpart the *Tatler* speculated about and analyzed aesthetics, literary style and urban life.

Decades later, a friendship between the Riches (John and his second wife, Priscilla) and hymn-writer Charles Wesley would have small repercussions in Handel's life. In 1746-47 he would write tunes for three of Wesley's hymn texts, probably at the request of Priscilla, a Methodist whose daughters would be pupils of Handel during part of the 1740s.

A few years before Handel's first trip to London, Rich and Vanbrugh had agreed that for at least one season (1706-07) Drury Lane would present opera and the Haymarket would present plays. But the next season, Vanbrugh "maneuvered" to reverse that, resulting in the Lord Chamberlain ordering that from then on (January 13, 1708) the Haymarket *must not* present plays and Drury Lane *must not* present operas.[2] (The Lord Chamberlain was the authority to whom play texts and opera librettos had to be sent for approval before they could be presented to the public – a sort of official censor of the realm.) So by the time Handel came to in London in 1710, the Haymarket had already become the home of all-sung Italian-style opera (no speaking parts) in the Italian language.

These opera productions required "star"singers, imported from Italy and paid to match their stellar abilities. So it was immensely expensive to mount even one season of such entertainment. Elaborate costumes and complex, spectacular sets added to the cost. The sets often included mechanized devices to make sets (or parts of sets) move and to add to the spectacle; sometimes live animals added to the pomp. Unlike in earlier years when theater seasons had contained a mix of plays, masques and opera, a mix that helped them survive financially, a season now consisted of just one kind of entertainment. That seriously increased its potential financial liability: the Italian singers knew only the Italian language and sang only Italian opera. In good years, when audiences were plentiful, it was a profitable business; but audiences and patrons were fickle, and the financial wolf was never far from the door, as Handel would find out more than once. This is the environment into which Handel confidently strode with *Rinaldo*, composed in a fortnight and first performed a day after his twenty-sixth birthday, February 1711. (Handel's facility for composition at a furious pace was evident from early on. The librettist Rossi said that Handel "scarcely allowed him time to write the words."[3])

Rinaldo is a love story based on excerpts from Tasso's *Gierusalemme liberata* (*The Liberation of Jerusalem*), set at the time of the First Crusade. The libretto was written by Giacomo Rossi and translated by Queen's Theater manager Aaron Hill. Several decades later, as we'll see, Hill eloquently urged Handel to abandon Italian opera in order to write music set to texts in English, a nudge that would help push him toward English oratorio. But even in 1711, Hill was concerned that Italian opera be adapted to English audiences and their tastes.

At this time Handel also met another person who would play a large role in his musical-entrepreneurial life: John Jacob Heidegger (1659-1749). Heidegger was a director of the Queen's Theater, and one of the many transplanted Germans in London.* Handel would collaborate with Heidegger some years later to produce opera when the composer was being strongly opposed by a group of noblemen producing their own opera.

Rinaldo was a smashing success. It ran for fifteen performances, to the end of the opera season. But a couple of weeks before its premiere Handel had already managed to stage a successful coup of another kind. It was aided by his continental reputation, and probably by a high-placed contact or two met in either Italy or Hanover.

Just before *Rinaldo* appeared, it had been the Monarch's birthday, an occasion always ripe for celebration. At the February 6 festivities in honor of Queen Anne there occurred "a Dialogue in Italian, in Her Majesty's Praise, set to excellent Musick by the famous Mr. Hendel, a Retainer to the Court of Hanover, in the Quality of Director of his Electoral Highness's Chapple." There is now no evidence that reveals what music this was. But it was performed in front of the Queen herself by Nicolini Grimaldi "and the other Celebrated Voices of the Italian Opera," and in the company of "numerous and magnificent ... Officers of state, Foreign Ministers, Nobility, and Gentry." And Her Majesty "was extreamly well pleas'd."[4]

When *Rinaldo* opened to much acclaim a few weeks later on February 24, its printed dedication, written by Aaron Hill, honored Queen Anne. Though the Queen did not then commit herself to becoming a patron of the opera, after Handel moved to England permanently and composed a true birthday ode for her – and his *Utrecht Te Deum* as well – she granted him an annual pension of £200, effective from December 28, 1713. She attached no specific services to that sum but the

---

*The period from 1702 to 1727 was one of German immigration. Up to 50,000 Germans left their native land, many going to the Netherlands, England and the American colonies; 12,000-13,000 arrived in London in the summer of 1708, and a similar number in 1711. Of the latter it is estimated that up to a third were Catholics, the rest Lutheran and Reformed (Vivian Hicks. German History Forum, 1996: Genealogical Exchange, 2001.)

pension no doubt contained the implication that Handel would compose occasional works when the Queen required them. Mainwaring concludes that "this act of the royal bounty was the more extraordinary, as his foreign engagements were not unknown."

As the report of the Queen's birthday music reminded Britons, this young, much admired composer had a job elsewhere, and it was time, high time, he was getting back to it. So Handel returned to Hanover, once again via Düsseldorf (the Elector Palatine there even wrote to Elector Georg Ludwig apologizing for detaining Handel). The composer had technically been in the Elector's employ for a year, but had been away a good part of that time. He did write *some* music for the Elector (the 12 chamber duets), but clearly his heart wasn't in Hanover. Despite that, Georg Ludwig didn't appear to be much upset about his composer's longer-than-intended absence. In fact, he promptly gave Handel permission to make a second trip to England. But before Handel returned to Britain, he went home to Halle for some important family business.

His sister Dorothea's second child, Johanna Friderica, was to be baptized on November 23, 1711, and Handel was to be one of the child's godparents. Dorothea and Michael Dietrich's firstborn, also a daughter, had been born in 1709 and died the next year, shortly after Handel's return from Italy. So this newborn child represented a new beginning. It was customary among German Lutherans for an uncle or aunt to be among a child's three godparents, and for that child to be named after that particular uncle or aunt. The commonality of the custom would not have made it less meaningful for Handel to stand as godfather to this child who was given her middle name in his honor by the sister who was so dear to him.

A little sleuthing is necessary to determine whether Handel was actually present at the baptism, which some scholars doubt. The baptismal register of the Halle Marktkirche names him as a godfather to his niece, and it notes that Frau Händel, his mother, acted as a proxy for one of the two godmothers who was the wife of the Lord Mayor of Zingst and Reinssdorff. If Handel had not been present, he, too, would have needed a proxy, and that substitution, too, would have been noted. But there is no such second proxy listed. So he must have been there.

Because parents play a crucial role in their children's lives, Lutherans naturally saw an obligation to educate their children in the faith, beginning with infant baptism. Baptism was (and is) seen as a means of imparting God's grace to the child. Luther referred to baptism as defining the very nature of the life of faith.

"The Christian life," he said, "is nothing else than a daily baptism, once begun and constantly lived in," whose significance must always be increasingly realized. Lutherans emphasize that the baptized person must then, all his or her life, "constantly grasp and re-appropriate that which baptism has promised to him once for all."[5] As the baptized child grows up, it is the parents' and godparents' duty to help the child do that, until the child can do it on his or her own.

So being a godparent was not merely a social or familial honor. The custom was considered a spiritual necessity. It involved promising to participate in bringing up a child in "the fear of the Lord." It entailed taking responsibility for the child's Christian development in the not improbable event that the child's parents would die before he or she had reached adulthood. In effect, a godparent was a child's spiritual guardian, reinforcing the parents' role.

Baby Johanna Friderica would come to be much loved by her uncle; she would be the last surviving offspring in his immediate family and his primary heir. In the intervening years before that distant time, Handel would take his godfatherly duties seriously. Allusions in letters indicate that he developed a close relationship with her over the years, taking an interest in her spiritual and moral development, as he (and the child's two godmothers) had vowed to do.

Though Handel had already been accustomed to success before his trip to England, his enthusiastic reception in London may have had him thinking about moving to England even as necessity was making him reluctantly return to Hanover. A month after his return he wrote to Andreas Roner, one of the German musicians living in London, telling him that he was studying English. Was it only the memory of that glowing reception in London that made Handel shun his court position in Hanover when he had barely begun it, to go back to London for good by mid-October 1712?

A man could make a living in London in a variety of professions (it was still almost impossible for a woman to make her own living). The middle class was growing quickly. But the city with its nearly one million inhabitants wasn't a pleasant place in some respects: the climate could not compare to Rome or Florence, nor could its art and architecture. The badly cobbled streets were dirty; buildings were sooty from coal-fire smoke; there was poverty; and social and religious inequities. Political chicanery was pervasive. Yet "when considered with all its advantages, it is now what ancient Rome once was; the seat of liberty, the encourager of arts, and the administration of the whole world," wrote an unsigned author later in the century on behalf of the already venerable *Encyclopaedia Britannica.*[6]

That might appear to be merely chauvinistic. But modern evaluation of the city's drawbacks and inequities must be done in light of other parts of the world at that time. And Handel's own statement of gratitude, after years of life in London, for the religious freedom he had in England must be seen in its context. His opinion would not likely have been seconded by Roman Catholics and Protestant Dissenters (nor Jews or other non-Christians). It was born out of his own experience, but he wasn't ignorant of the experience of others in this regard: he would have regular dealings with, and friends among, Catholics, Methodists, Deists and Nonjurors.* Yet in most countries, religious minorities fared far worse at the hands of whoever was in the majority. Compared to other places in the eighteenth century civilized world, England had deeply ensconced freedoms, religious and otherwise, and as a result London attracted numerous visitors and immigrants of diverse nationality and religion (Handel's London circle of friends and acquaintances would also include quite a few German Lutherans in music and related fields). To accommodate its growing population and to try to address some of its problems, London erected hundreds of schools, hospitals, parks and diverse places of worship. In historical context, London *was* the seat of liberty by the time Handel lived there. This was still a lifetime before the American Revolution, and in marked contrast to France, especially.

London would represent liberty to Handel in another way, and perhaps he sensed that during his first visit. We've already noted his penchant for independence and his ability to achieve it through adaptability. In London, Handel would be able to become an entrepreneur. He would set his own course artistically and in business, choosing what he would and would not do, working on what we would call a self-employed contract or commission basis, and investing money during good times to tide him through the bad.

Contrary to what might be supposed, his independence was not negated or even cramped very much by the difficult circumstances he sometimes encountered in

---

*Nonjurors were Protestants who, on principle, refused to take oaths pledging allegiance to the Hanoverian monarchs (George I and II in Handel's time). Nonjurors believed that the Catholic Stuarts, whom the Georges replaced, were the lawful heirs to the British throne. Therefore, no matter how high his social station, a Nonjuror could not be a local magistrate or hold other office. Charles Jennens, *Messiah's* librettist, was a Nonjuror.

the opera world; nor by his periodically composing for England's German-turned-British kings (both George I and George II); nor, soon after his permanent arrival, by his accepting three years of hospitality from Richard Boyle, Earl of Burlington, an art patron and influential amateur architect; nor by the patronage and hospitality from the fabulously wealthy James Brydges, Earl of Carnarvon (later Duke of Chandos), for whom he wrote an oratorio, a Te Deum, a masque and a series of anthems.

Handel always managed to avoid the typical servant-master relationship with a patron, including with the monarchs. For example, at Brydges's estate, he was an honored guest left to his own devices. He often shared company there with the already well-known poet Alexander Pope and with John Arbuthnot, one of the Queen's physicians and also a man of letters who became a personal friend. Throughout his long composing life Handel never held a position that required him to provide music on schedule year after year, for routine events. Even his composing for the monarchs seemed to come mostly from his impetus, not theirs.[*]

To be successful in such a life it was essential that Handel have business savvy along with being the most exceptional and famous composer of the time. (Bach was much better known during his lifetime as an organist than as a composer; his works in church settings — most of his output — were hidden from scrutiny of the world outside Germany.) Handel did have good business sense, though that alone could not prevent financially difficult and emotionally stressful times at several points in his career.

~

Handel returned to England in the fall of 1712. He was twenty-seven years old, and the move was permanent. He immediately wrote another opera, *Il pastor fido* (*The Faithful Shepherd*). It was performed six times (and once later on) — a moderate reception. That told him that pastoral dramas weren't nearly so popular with the English as they were with the Italians. Quickly, he showed his almost uncanny ability to adapt to his audience's tastes. He smoothly shifted setting and

[*]On his permanent arrival in Britain, Handel lived for about half a year in the home of a Mr. Andrews, who lived in Surrey but had a townhouse in London. Handel then appears to have lived at the Burlington estate or used it as a home base from 1713 to 1716. He wrote no music expressly at Burlington's request, as he did for James Brydges, but several of his operas ared dedicated to Burlington (*Teseo*, 1713, and *Amadigi*, 1715); *Silla* is said to have been performed at Burlington House, late 1714 or early 1715.

style to compose a heroic love story set in ancient Athens, *Teseo* (*Theseus*). It fared better, with twice as many performances. Unfortunately, that success was tempered by theater manager Owen Swiney's absconding with the box office take after just two "very full" houses.* Despite con-man Swiney, Handel was now on his way to being seen as London's resident opera composer.

In the meantime, the political landscape was changing in England and well beyond, and events put Handel in an awkward position. During his first stay in London the Tories had come to power in Queen Anne's government. The Tories wanted England to withdraw from war with France (which was part of the larger, ongoing European War of the Spanish Succession) and, in fact, England soon began the peace negotiations that culminated in the Peace of Utrecht on April 11, 1713.

The complicated "peace," signed in the Dutch city of Utrecht, gives an indication of how complex the European political situation had become. There were great consequences for Britain. Most importantly, French king Louis XIV recognized the house of Hanover as the legitimate successors to the English throne and renounced the claims to the French throne of his grandson, Philip V of Spain. Then, French fortifications at Dunkirk were to be razed and the harbor filled up. In the new world, the Hudson Bay territory, Acadia, St. Kitts and Newfoundland were ceded to England. In a commercial treaty, England and France granted each other most-favored--nation treatment. Spain ceded Gibraltar and Minorca to Great Britain and ceded Sicily (exchanged in 1720 for Sardinia) to Savoy. Britain and Spain signed the Asiento, an agreement giving Britain the sole right to the slave trade with Spanish America. The Netherlands and France made their own specific agreements, as did France with Portugal and Prussia, and with Holy Roman Emperor Charles VI.

At this point, twenty-eight-year-old Handel put himself in a bind in two ways: first, officially he was still Elector Georg Ludwig's *Kapellmeister*, though he

---

*A colorful description in Colman's *Opera Register*, Jan. 15, 1713, let opera fans in on the exciting news that Owen Swiny had ordered new "habits" (costumes), "richer than ye former," and had added four new scenes with additional decorations and "machines." But then, alas, "Mr. Swiny Brake & runs away & leaves ye Singers unpaid ye Scenes & Habits also unpaid for. The Singers were in Some confusion but at last concluded to go on with ye operas on their own accounts, & divide ye Gain amongst them." The singers included Handel in the "Gain divided amongst them." (Quoted by Deutsch, p. 52-53).

had no inclination to return to Hanover. (He would have been considered a "servant" of the Elector's, though the job hadn't particularly required him to act like one – which is probably one reason he took it.) He was in danger of direct insubordination to the man who might very well be England's King before long.* Second, he agreed to write music of thanksgiving to mark the peace celebrations (the *Utrecht Te Deum*, completed on Jan.14, 1713). In being associated with the Utrecht Peace through his music, Handel chose to align himself with England and Queen Anne rather than with his homeland and patron-employer, since the Elector opposed the treaty as contrary to Hanover's interests. In addition, Handel's ode for Queen Anne's February 6 birthday, *Eternal Source of Light Divine*, lauds her as a peacemaker.

Though she probably never got to hear it because of ill health, she would no doubt have appreciated it as a stirring anthem reminiscent of the style of Henry Purcell. (Purcell, who died in 1695, was England's last great native composer until the twentieth century.) William Croft was the official court composer. But when Handel wrote, people – even monarchs – listened. And Croft, who a good composer in his own right, was soon influenced by Handel's musical style.

Early in his third year in Georg Ludwig's service, 1713, Handel was dismissed by the Elector. Georg Ludwig told him he could "go wherever he pleased" ... "in a way which he found particularly mortifying," says a June 5 letter written by the Hanover court's diplomatic Resident in London – this despite Georg Ludwig's earlier apparent lack of concern about Handel's absence.[7] Then Queen Anne died on August 1, 1714, and Handel was put in an even tighter bind: Georg Ludwig would now come to England to be crowned King George I. If Handel intended to remain in England, he would owe obeisance to the ruler he had passively (if not actively) eluded and ignored, a ruler who, in the end had not appreciated the affront. Handel did remain in England, of course. A dozen years later, in fact, one of George I's last official duties in the months before his death was signing the Act

---

*The Act of Settlement of 1701 had made Hanover Elector Georg Ludwig, a great-grandson of James I, third in line to the English throne, after the then Princess Anne (who was Queen from 1702-14) and after his mother, Sophia. Sophia would die in June 1714 and Queen Anne would die in August 1714. The Settlement Act ensured a Protestant monarchy in Britain and shut out the exiled Catholic James Edward Stuart, "the Old Pretender," and his son Charles Edward Stuart, "the Young Pretender" (Bonnie Prince Charlie).

that naturalized Handel as a British subject.[*]

Mainwaring is not kind to Handel regarding this situation, no doubt because he believed, as most people would have, that this was no way to treat a ruler to whom one is subject. It is far easier for us at this historical distance to see Handel's behavior as the benign negligence of a young man absorbed in his own affairs and working hard to establish the kind of career for himself to which he felt best suited. Handel was certainly not without conscience. Mainwaring indicates that "he didn't dare show himself at Court because of his negligence in staying so long in England":

> To account for his delay in returning to his office, was no easy matter. To make an excuse for the non-performance of his promise, was impossible. From this ugly situation he was soon relieved by better luck than perhaps he deserved. It happened that his noble friend Baron Kilmanseck [the King's brother-in-law] was here. He, with some others among the nobility, contrived a method for reinstating him in the favour of his Majesty; the clemency of whose nature was soon experienced by greater persons on a much more trying occasion.

That "method for reinstating him" was Handel's composing of the *Water Music* for the King's "party on the water," according to Mainwaring. However, Handel didn't write the *Water Music* until 1717. Mainwaring may be mixing up the situation between Handel and the King in 1714 and a major row between the King and his son George August (the Prince of Wales). The water party was well after that 1714 brouhaha between George Ludwig and George August (and the royal offspring and spouse were not invited to the party).

Donald Burrows sees Handel's being asked to provide music for the water

---

[*]Handel was naturalized in February 1727. If there is irony in this situation, it is also because Handel grew to be more attached to his adopted country than its own monarch was. Though George Ludwig was England's George I from 1714-1727, he never bothered to learn more than a smidgen of English or to familiarize himself with, much less understand English customs and attitudes, he made frequent trips back to Hanover to attend to affairs there, and was in general more concerned with affairs in his native land than he was in the country he ruled as king. George I's preoccupation with Hanover, making him frequently absent from London, created a situation in which Robert Walpole, who was variously Paymaster of the Forces, First Lord of the Treasury and Chancellor of the Exchequer, could become "prime minister" and effectively governed in the King's place when George was away. This situation inadvertently laid the groundwork for the modern roles which the Prime Minister and Parliament play in the British system of government.

party as a "public gesture" that "resolved" Handel's relationship with the British Crown.[8] Handel was not in the King's bad graces by the time of the water party, three years after George I was crowned. In fact, the first Sunday service at the Chapel Royal after the arrival of the new royal family and George's accession to the English throne contained a new *Te Deum* by Handel (the *Te Deum* was later known as the "Caroline" in honor of Princess Caroline, George I's daughter-in-law, whom Handel admired and respected).

Backing up a little, an element of intrigue had entered this whole affair regarding Handel's position at the Hanover court and his relationship with the Elector/King, as revealed in the letter mentioned earlier by Hanover's Resident in London. Even though the Resident went on to "admit ... frankly that Mr. Handel is nothing to me," he nevertheless also admits that he "arranged things so that Mr. Handel could write to M. Kielmansegg to extricate himself gracefully, and I let slip a few words to inform him that, when some day His Highness comes here, he might re-enter his service."

What was the Resident's motive? The Hanover Court imagined it could use Handel to get information about ailing Queen Anne, whom they knew the Elector would succeed in the not-too-distant future, and between whose court and theirs no love was lost. The Resident wrote:

> *The queen's physician* [Arbuthnot], *who is an important man and enjoys the queen's confidence, is his great patron and friend, and has the composer constantly at his house. Mr. Handel could have been extremely useful, and has been on several occasions, by giving me information of circumstances which have often enlightened me as to the condition of the queen's health. Not that the doctor tells him exactly how she is but, for example, when I have been informed by other reliable channels that the queen was ill, he has been able to tell me that on one particular night the physician slept at the queen's residence, and other circumstances of this kind which provide illumination when taken in conjunction with other information. You must know that our Whigs rarely know anything about the queen's health.* [In return,] *since the queen is more avid for stories about Hanover than anything else, the doctor can satisfy her curiosity when he is with her from his own information: you understand the stories to which I am referring.*

Afterwards they are passed on to some serious ecclesiastical gentlemen, and this has a marvellous effect. Perhaps you will not take this seriously, but I do.

Whether Handel provided this information knowingly or whether others deliberately engaged him in what appeared to be "inadvertent" conversation, which was then relayed to Hanover, is an interesting question. It seems highly unlikely that he was aware of the role he was being made to play. First, the nature of the Resident's letter implies that this is so. Then, Handel was a principled man; he could be, and often was, pragmatic when it came to his career and adapting to what audiences wanted, but there are no examples of his "adaptability" involving what might have seen as a duplicitous abandoning of principle.

Handel seems to have made a clear choice early on to cast his lot with the country which would become his adopted home (he had not lived in Germany for more than a few months at a time since his late teen years; how aware he was of the details of European politics is unknown). His commencing English language study as soon as he returned to Germany from his initial English visit indicates that he *did* have moving to England in mind. He was in transition and would naturally have been mulling over his future while he was dipping his feet in the English waters: he had learned what he needed to in Italy but clearly did not want to settle there, he had no desire to be a church musician in Germany, his position at the Hanover court was unsatisfying, and England offered an amenable climate, musically and ideologically. Those things, along with his propensity to be independent would have prevented him from agreeing to being put in such a position had he been asked outright.

At any rate, it had become advantageous to the Elector to have his *Kapellmeister* in London. And after the Elector became King it would be natural, too, that periodically George would prefer to hear music by Handel — music to which the King was quite partial — rather than that by the official court composer. So Handel committed himself to England. But as a German, and a new resident, he would have to tread carefully in regards to his connection to the Hanoverian Court, a Court and King about whom many Britons were dubious.

Chapter 6
A Passion for Opera, a *Passion* for Home

Handel's main preoccupation in 1714-15, his first permanent season in England, was opera. He had already written *Silla,* and now he wrote the much more impressive *Amadigi;* and *Rinaldo* was revived. Though London's opera was not a "court opera," it counted George I among its patrons, and that royal patronage was quite necessary. But attendance that season was off due to "indisposed singers, the King's birthday, the hot summer and Jacobite threats."[1] The next season Handel wrote no new operas and at the end of that season, June 1717, the company closed down amidst a rising political and social rivalry between some of the opera patrons, including the intense family feud between George I and his son, which resulted in the Prince of Wales and Princess Caroline being banned from St. James's Palace and separated from their children.*

Handel made a trip back to Germany about this time (probably late 1716). He went to Hanover and Ansbach, where he met up with Johann Christoph Schmidt (John Christopher Smith), a friend and former fellow student. Handel convinced Smith to go back to England with him. J.C. Smith would, in fact, be Handel's friend, copyist and right-hand man for years; and Smith's son, also J.C., would become essential to Handel near the end of his career, after the composer was blind. Before returning to England, Handel perhaps continued east to see his family.

About this time, Handel wrote his one and only German Passion. It is known to us as the *Brockes Passion* (pronounced "Brock-ess") but carries the lengthy title *Der für die Sünde der Welt gemarterte und sterbende Jesus (Jesus, Martyred and Dying for the Sins of the World).* Handel was long thought to have also written a *Passion According to St. John,* but that work is now considered spurious. Though Handel composed the *Brockes Passion* in England he sent it by post to Hamburg, according to Johann Mattheson in his biographical sketch of Handel.

---

*The royal father and his only son despised each other (for reasons too numerous to go into here). George I could be ruthless, and his son sometimes felt the brunt of it, as George I's own wife had previously: the new King arrived in London with a mistress and without his wife. Just two years after his marriage to Sophia Dorothea in 1682 he had divorced her for alleged adultery (an offense with which he himself was quite personally familiar). He had been keeping her under house arrest in Hanover ever since, and she remained so for the rest of her life – 32 years. In addition, it appears that George's minions (with or without his knowledge) killed the man who he presumed was his wife's lover.

The libretto is a poetic paraphrase by Barthold Heinrich Brockes of the accounts of Christ's Passion from all four Gospels. Latin plainchant Passions existed prior to the Reformation, but the post-Reformation Passion developed as a uniquely German Lutheran Baroque creation, with its text in every-day German. The story of Jesus's last hours as recorded by Matthew is the Gospel lesson for Palm Sunday, and the Passion story from the Gospel of John is heard on Good Friday. The biblical accounts of Christ's arrest, trial, suffering and death are lengthy and heart-rending. A musical setting, especially in the hands of a skillful composer, is capable of uniquely presenting the unparalleled emotion and drama of these events.

Brockes was well-known to music-loving students at the University of Halle around the time Handel was there, and by the time Handel used his Passion libretto Brockes had "impeccable credentials" as a Hamburg councillor, noted poet and musician.[2] Handel was one of a handful of German Lutherans who set Brockes' libretto. So did his friends Telemann, Keiser and Mattheson. So did Johann Fasch and several others; and part of the libretto constitutes some arias in Bach's *St. John Passion* written seven or eight years later. Brockes' libretto seems to have quickly become a standard Passion text.

In London there was no audience or occasion for these works in the German language and Lutheran in conception (but universally Christian in spirit). So Handel's Passion was clearly meant for church services in his native land. It was first performed in Hamburg on April 3, 1719, the Monday of Holy Week, conducted by Mattheson. Telemann's setting was performed at the service the next day. Handel's setting would be heard at least four more times in Hamburg between 1721 and 1724, and once in Lüneberg in 1723.

There is a mystery here. What was the impetus for Handel's setting? Or the reason behind the apparently purposeful choosing by all these composers to set Brockes' text at roughly the same time (roughly the same time, given communication by letter, slow travel in even short distances, the hand-copying of scores and so on)?

Brockes wrote the initial Passion oratorio, using his own libretto; then Keiser set that libretto to music; then Telemann. Was this an informally agreed upon way to produce useable liturgical music even while having some fun comparing notes (literally) with each other? And then Mattheson got involved; and perhaps one of them wrote Handel asking him to submit a version. Maybe Handel wasn't yet too big a wig to turn down such a challenge from old friends! That may not have happened, of course. Yet in the Case of the Many Brockes Passions, there seems to be some thread, now invisible to us, weaving together these young composers, all about the same age, all known to each other, all grounded in the same musical and faith tradition.

The Passions of Keiser and Mattheson have receded into the ether. So has Telemann's: he is known in our time for his orchestral, not his dozens of Passions and church cantatas (which he himself highly valued). Handel's *Brockes Passion* would very likely be far better known were it not for Bach's slightly later, more illustrious Passions according to St. Matthew and St. John. Intriguingly, Bach was familiar with and copied out Handel's score, but not until the 1740s.

Handel's *Brockes Passion* is noteworthy in its own right, but it is also interesting as one of the backdrops for his later development of English oratorio. By the time of Keiser, Telemann, Mattheson, Handel and Bach, the passion as a musical form had become an *oratorio Passion* (or *Passion oratorio*, as it's sometimes called). It uses accompanying instruments, chorales, poetic-reflective texts not taken directly from Scripture, and it reflects the growing influence in Hamburg of Italian oratorio. This uniquely German form had not developed without controversy, the same kind of controversy that would come, for a while, to surround Handel's oratorios in England.

The Saxon Pietists grumbled that this style was too theatrical. One Christian Gerber wrote: "If some of those first Christians should rise, visit our assemblies, and hear such a roaring organ together with so many instruments, I do not believe that they would recognize us as Christians and their successors.'"[3] Keiser the opera composer presented the profound sufferings of Christ just too overtly and dramatically for the sensibilities of some Lutheran listeners – "more emphatically than the Holy Evangelists."

In the 1730s and '40s, when Handel the opera composer would take librettos of biblical stories, combine recitatives, arias and choruses with orchestral accompaniment and mold them into oratorios in the English vernacular of his adopted country – aware while he was doing it of both his native German Lutheran Passion tradition and the secular Italian opera tradition – history would repeat itself. In 1743, a Londoner would object to "the impropriety of [Handel's] Oratorios as they are now perform'd." Handel would have the boldness (if not brashness) to present the biblical texts "together with so many instruments" and singers not in church but in the *theater*. "I ask if the *Playhouse* is a fit *Temple to* perform it in, or a Company of *Players* fit *Ministers* of *God's Word*...?" a concerned London letter writer would ask, assuming his question to be rhetorical. That letter, like that of Christian Gerber, would refer to the historical line and company of believers: "Is God's service less holy now?" than in Old Testament times when "no common Person might so much as touch the *Ark of God*? ... It seems the Old Testament is not to be prophan'd alone [an allusion to Handel's Old Testament oratorios] but the New must be join'd with it [an allusion to *Messiah*]."

This sort of objection from devout Christians to an "unsuitable" style of music used with scriptural texts and to what they saw as "light," even "prophane" performers in an "unfit" place of performance is in a certain way understandable. Separated by a national boundary, by church denominations and by twenty-five or so years, these two writers come to essentially the same conclusion because their primary concern was with maintaining a living, biblical faith. Though many Christians today may conclude (as the great majority eventually did in that time) that this approach sets up a false dichotomy between "sacred" and "secular," the writers' intent was guileless.

Handel apparently never had the opportunity to hear his *Brockes Passion* performed. Nevertheless (and perhaps surprisingly) the work became known to those in his circle in England. Charles Jennens, who would be Handel's librettist for *Messiah*, *Belshazzar* and (presumably) *Israel in Egypt*, obtained a copy of the score. After Jennens and Handel became acquainted, Handel must have mentioned the work to Jennens at some point and piqued Jennens' interest. Jennens would become a collector of Handel's works, but he may have been especially drawn to the *Brockes Passion*. His particular score contained only the music so that he could translate the German text and lay the English translation under the music; but he apparently quit the job when he began to run into translation difficulties.

Jennens was not the only Englishman to eventually get a copy of the score. As was Handel's habit with things he had already composed, he re-used chunks of his Passion in other works: some in the *Chandos Anthems*, some in *Acis and Galatea*, and nine numbers in *Esther* (all of these new works he wrote for James Brydges not long after the *Brockes Passion's* initial composition); later, he used some of the *Passion* in other oratorios of the 1730s. Musicologist Anthony Hicks suggests that "it is likely that the interest taken in it was one of the factors that led Handel to create the new genre of English oratorio with the first version of *Esther*" (1718).[4]

At this time, too, Handel wrote a group of exquisite choral-vocal works for performance at Cannons, near Edgware, just outside London. Cannons was the home of James Brydges (1674-1744), Earl of Carnarvon and soon to be First Duke of Chandos. For "Chandos" Handel composed an early version of his first English oratorio, *Esther*; the delightful English masque *Acis and Galatea*; the *Chandos Te Deum*; and the eleven *Chandos Anthems*.* He also began to make collections of his keyboard music.

Brydges was one of the wealthiest men in England. He had made a huge fortune while Paymaster for the Forces Abroad during the War of the Spanish Succession, by speculating with money he made in that position. (He was to lose some of in the bursting of the South Seas Bubble.) He was the son of a Herefordshire squire (his mother was part of the landed gentry) who rose "by force of personality, administrative ability and the favour of the Duke of Marlborough" to become "one of the most remarkable figures of his age."[5] Since 1713 he had been rebuilding in opulent contemporary style his Jacobean mansion at Cannons, which had been an ancient estate. Brydges' first wife (who was also his cousin) brought the estate to their marriage as a dowry. The home was stuffed with art works and contained a not-yet-finished chapel. Brydges maintained a small orchestra and singers, but since the chapel wasn't complete, Handel's anthems were performed at the parish church, St. Lawrence's, Whitchurch. Handel was part of the Cannons household from August 1717 through sometime in 1718, acting as Brydges' composer-in-residence.

How musically astute Brydges actually was is a question. His hiring of Handel perhaps wasn't a matter of personal judgment but simply of getting the best there was, since he could afford it. German Music historian Deutsch questions "whether Handel was commissioned as a mere implement of grandeur, or chosen from motives of a superior kind..." but then coyly concludes "it is not for us to determine." In any case, his ability to evaluate music was apparently considerably

---

*Readers interested in Handel's oratorios will likely appreciate his 11 *Chandos Anthems*, which he composed for use in the Anglican liturgy at James Brydges' church, St. Lawrence's. The anthems range from deeply spiritually moving to wonderfully exuberant and are based on various Psalms or Psalm verses, taken from Psalms 42, 93, 96, 68, 89, 100, 51, 144, 145, 9, 11, 12, 13, 95. Handel wrote the anthems for just two or three trebles on the soprano part, a tenor, a bass (the solos were sung by any of these singers), one or two violins on each of the two violin parts, organ (played by himself), and one each of oboe, bassoon, cello, double bass. Peculiarly, Brydges had no altos as part of his regular group of singers; altos at the time would have been boys or men rather than women. Alto castrati were opera singers in England and weren't used in church music.

better than his judgment of art works. His biographer, C.H. Collins Baker, notes that "his very nature was incurably credulous and prone to think the best of people: a handicap not altogether unendearing, but of no positive advantage in collecting masterpieces." Even so, out of his vast art collection there were masterpieces, including Grinling Gibbons' famous sculpture of the *Stoning of St. Stephen* (now at London's Victoria and Albert Museum,) and Poussin's *The Choice of Hercules*, now at Stourhead (a subject on which Handel wrote a one-act drama in 1750). Brydges' posthumous glory didn't last long. Within barely four years of his death Cannons was torn down and sold piecemeal.

As for Handel's 1718 version of *Esther* written for Brydges, it consisted of just one act comprising six scenes. And so it was sometimes referred to as a masque rather than an oratorio. But the earliest known score, omitting the title *Esther*, calls it "The Oratorium composed by George Frederick Handel Esquire in London.1718." Whether it was written for a particular occasion or purpose is unknown. Based on the Old Testament book of Esther, the oratorio would become a popular work in Handel's time, and he greatly expanded it in 1732.

Near the end of his time at Cannons Handel encountered another wrenching death in his family: his only remaining and much loved sister, Dorothea Sophie, died on July 28, 1718 – Aug. 8 by the current calendar*. When the news reached him in the slow way of the time, he no doubt took it hard, longing to be there to share the grief with his mother, brother-in-law, his sister's young children and his extended family and church community. The only two surviving children of the five born to Dorothea and Michael Michaëlsen were just seven years old and two years old, and the two-year-old son would live to be just four.

Once again, the funeral sermon (which still exists) gives a meaningful glimpse into the life of the deceased, who was just thirty-one years old, two years her brother's junior. Dorothea Sophie's funeral text was "I know that my Redeemer liveth," a confession from which her pastor said she derived much comfort both in life and in death. Pastor Johann Michael Heineck paints a picture of a devout, spiritually and mentally strong woman not unlike her mother:

---

*"Conservative" England still used the Gregorian calendar (and would until Sept. 3, 1752), while the rest of Europe used the Julian calendar. The continental Julian calender was 11 days ahead of the "Old Style" Gregorian calendar. When Handel wrote to Germany, he appended both dates.

She confirmed by her example the truth of Solomon's words: The
righteous hath hope in his death. Whence comes, however, this
joyousness, since there is no joy at hand? Why does hope flourish, even
if the body, like a flower, withers away? Why does faith not pine away,
even if body and mind pine away? No one can give us better answers
to these questions than the blessed woman, whose voice is henceforth
stilled. She uttered them oftentimes in life, in the words of Job: For I
know that my Redeemer liveth and that He shall stand at the latter day
upon the earth....[6]

Heineck speaks of Dorothea Sophie's "many joys in her only brother, whose quite especially and exceptionally great *Vertues* even crowned heads and the greatest ones of the earth at the same time love and admire, and bestowed on her as well much contentment." The impression is left that Handel's sister talked about him frequently, and no doubt she and her mother gave updates about their famous brother and son to the cousins and church community from Handel's letters. In her "many joys in her brother" their closeness is revealed. It is notable that Dorothea Sophie is depicted as gaining *contentment* from her brother's accomplishments. She (and their mother) obviously understood that the course he was pursuing in the broader world was both making use of his prodigious talent and giving him great satisfaction, which in turn made her content. But her joy and pride in her brother and satisfaction at his success occurred in a fleeting world, and she put all that in realistic, sober-eyed, faith-grounded perspective: "Yet everything must give place to her Redeemer."

As Handel, some hundreds of miles away, was no doubt still mentally adjusting to the idea of never again writing to his sister, and of her being permanently absent from his visits (infrequent as they were), he was also just beginning to have to adjust to a new phase in his life and career. During 1719 he began a renewed focus on opera and would put almost all his energies into it for most of the following two decades. His first new opera would not be produced, however, until the the spring of 1720.

There was now afoot a new attempt by patrons to put together a successful opera company. It took on the name Royal Academy of Musick and was founded with money from its directors, aided by a five-year, £1000-a-year subsidy from George I (as well as the box office). Despite the Academy's name, taken in imitation of the royal opera in Paris (Académie Royale de Musique), it was actually a joint

66

stock company. The directors projected that "the Undertakers will be Gainers at least five and twenty percent upon Twenty percent of the Stock."[7] Though it probably took only a few years for them to understand that they had been much too optimistic, most subscribers weren't sorry they had backed the project, which they did from a genuine love of opera, or as a means to provide the patronage of the arts expected of people of their social station, or both.

Handel and several other composers would provide the music for the new company. If it seems surprising that Handel was not (at first) the Academy's sole, or even primary, composer, we should remember that, despite the degree of fame he had already acquired, he had written only four operas in England in the eight years since his first visit in 1711. There were then several Italian composers in London, notably Giovanni Bononcini, who were the established opera composers. Handel's fame in England at this point was localized within certain upper-societal groups: in the King's circle, based on his providing of royal anthems and the *Water Music*; among Burlington and his friends; among Chandos and his friends, based on the *Chandos Anthems, Acis and Galatea* and *Esther*; and then on the success of the few operas he has already written.

In May 1719 the Academy had sixty-two stock holders ("subscribers"). By the time a royal charter was granted by King George on July 27, 1719, that number had dropped to fifty-eight, but with dukes, earls and various other noble personages were heavily represented. Among that number were people we've already met: Handel's friends Dr. John Arbuthnot, the Duke of Chandos, the Earl of Burlington and John Jacob Heidegger, who was the company manager. Handel was named "master of the Orchestra with a Sallary," but what salary he was given is now a mystery. In exchange for their support, subscribers received two silver admission tickets for a prescribed number of years. That was intended to be twenty-one years, but opera being a precarious and expensive proposition, the company would run out of money in 1728 after nine seasons.

Handel, of course, had hoped to go "home" to visit his mother and brother-in-law after his sister's death. But this new undertaking prevented him. This venture was one on which his livelihood would depend – for a long time, he hoped. Even so, he was eager to get away to Germany and hoped to leave before long. He described the situation to his brother-in-law in a letter dated three days before his thirty-fourth birthday, 1719. Though German was their native language, he wrote in French, the language of international correspondence and business affairs. He was involved, he reported, in "affairs of the greatest moment, on which (I venture to say) all my fortunes depend." The letter makes clear that he had thought the whole business would be off and running by now, and he was much frustrated at the delay. He begs Michaëlsen not to judge his eagerness to see him "by the lateness of my departure." He continues:

> If you knew my distress at not having been able to perform what I so ardently desire, you would be indulgent towards me; but I am hoping to conclude it all in a month from now, and you can rest assured that I shall then make no delay but set out forthwith. Pray, dearest brother, assure Mamma of this, as also of my duty ["mon obeissance"]; and inform me once again of the state of health of yourself, Mamma and all your [dear] family, so as to relieve my present anxiety and impatience. You will realise, dearest brother, that I should be inconsolable, did I not expect very soon to make up for this delay by remaining all the longer with you.

That Handel asks "once again" over the state of the health of those he loves is no polite chit-chat, and his becoming impatient and anxious over a possibly dreadful answer is wholly believable in the context of his own and his family's renewed grief and the horrific mortality rate of the time. In fact, after mentioning some business (he had sent along money for his mother) he returns to the ache of yearning he feels for his family: "I am longing to see you more than you can imagine," he writes. Then he lays the situation, and the grief they all share, in God's hand, believing that God will enact healing: "On my part I trust that the Almighty will shower on you and your beloved family every kind of good fortune and will heal through His precious blessings the painful world which it has pleased Him to make you suffer, and which has pained me no less." He ends by expressing deep gratitude to his brother-in-law for the man's goodness to his sister.*

---

*Handel's letter reveals the view of God's Providence that he held when a boy (expressed in his poem for his father's funeral): there is nothing outside of God's control; he sends us both good and bad, but can, and does, graciously turn our suffering to good. Assumed in this orthodox Lutheran (and Calvinist) view, which the Reformers extrapolated from many Bible passages – is God's utter right to act as he chooses because he is God. Handel ends the letter by asking that his compliments (greeting) be conveyed to "Mr. Rotth and to all my good friends." This was Christian August Rotth, his cousin and good friend with whom he would keep contact over the years.

6. A Passion for Opera, a *Passion* for Home

Three months later Handel finally had the opportunity to leave England. He visited his family and conducted a talent-scouting jaunt on behalf of the Royal Academy in order to acquire top-draw singers for the company. A "warrant" signed by the Lord Chamberlain (Thomas Holles, Duke of Newcastle), governor of the Academy, gave "M͏ͬ Hendel Master of Musick" liberal authority to bring such singers to Britain. Handel stopped briefly in Düsseldorf and the Elector Palatine's court on the way to Halle. Allowing for travel time, he may have stayed in Halle for up to six or seven weeks, and no doubt reveled in this rare opportunity to spend relaxed days with his mother, brother-in-law, the children and his extended family.

~

It was approximately at the end of Handel's time with his family when, from our modern point of view, one of history's most unfortunate missed opportunities occurs. Johann Sebastian Bach traveled down from his home in Cöthen, only nineteen miles north of Halle, in hopes of meeting Handel. But Bach arrived too late. Cöthen, though long a princely seat (at that time belonging to Prince Leopold of Anhalt-Cöthen), was not much more than a village, and rather isolated. So the news that Handel was in Halle undoubtedly took some time to travel to Cöthen.* Bach was familiar with the city of Halle. Three years earlier, in the absence of Halle's most famous son, he (along with Johann Kuhnau and Christian Friedrich Rolle) evaluated the new Christoph Cuncius (Cuntzius) organ at the Church of Our Lady. And during the six years Bach worked in Cöthen he periodically made use of musicians from Halle. Some commentators have concluded that Handel deliberately slunk away, and a few doubt the story altogether. It is not as odd as it might seem that, though Handel's stay was lengthy, by the time Bach received the news (possibly from one of the traveling musicians who showed up from time to time), arranged to be away from his post, then traveled to Halle, Handel had already left.

---

*Bach was *Kapellmeister* for the Calvinist Prince Leopold in Cöthen from 1717-23. Thus, for six years he lived within 20 miles of Halle. An interesting aside: the Prince's father was, many years before, remarried to a woman who was a Lutheran and had allowed her to remain so. So there were two churches in the small town. Bach, and the Prince's widowed stepmother and some other household members attended the Lutheran Agnuskirche; Leopold himself and still other household members attended the Calvinist Jacobskirche. Now and then the two pastors' differences of opinion caused acrimony which seeped into the Prince's household and into the village.

Though we have other evidence that Bach was aware of Handel (for example, his copy of the *Brockes Passion* and the assertion by Bach's son C.P.E. that Handel was among the composers his father highly regarded in his later years), there is no report of how much Handel knew of Bach's music, of his opinion of what he knew, or to what extent he was aware of Bach's magnitude as a composer. It seems unlikely, though, that Handel was unaware of Bach's reputation as an organist, at the very least.

Composer and theorist Friedrich Wilhelm Marpurg (1718-1795), whose knowledge of Bach came from the last years of that unparalleled composer's life, was sure who would come out on top in such a comparison, and he figured Handel knew it too. Some years later, Marpurg asked what he intended to be a rhetorical question: "Did not the great Handel avoid every occasion of coming together with the late Bach, that phoenix of composition and improvisation, or of having anything to do with him?"[8]

Marpurg gives no justification for concluding that Handel deliberately avoided an encounter with Bach, though that interpretation wasn't his alone (and is still favored by some passionate Bach lovers). In November 1756, Jacob Wilhelm Lustig, writing in the *Samensraaken* from Amsterdam, matter of factly said, "Hen[del]... always made a point of avoiding the company of and contact with Bach, that Phoenix in composition and improvisation!" *

There is a fascinating and mostly fair comparison of the two composers which was written in 1788 by an unnamed author. Modern German Bach scholar Christoph Wolf makes a good case for that author having been Bach's composer son Carl Philip Emmanuel. In any case, the author of the comparison quotes Marpurg and recounts the circumstances under which Handel and Bach *could* have met. But he – if he is not being coy – is slightly more kind to Handel than Marpurg was. His conclusion: "So Handel, it seems, was not as curious as J.S.B., who once in his youth walked at least 250 miles to hear the famous organist of Lübeck, Buxtehude.

---

*Lustig (1706-1796) was a native of Hamburg who lived in Groningen (the Netherlands). He was in London in 1734 and met Handel. The two apparently talked extensively, and Lustig naturally wrote about Handel in both his monthly journal *Samenspraaken* and in his book *Inleiding tot de Muziekkunde* (*Introduction to the Art of Music*). He asserted that one would be "absolutely wrong" if he should conclude by Handel's purported avoidance of Bach that Handel was a "bad musician." Lustig implies that Handel simply didn't want to find out whether Bach might be superior to him (as organist, improviser or composer).

All the more did it pain J.S.B. not to have known Handel, that really great man whom he particularly respected."

There was just one performer, the bass Johann Gottfried Riemschneider, who sang under the direction of both composers, though ten years separated the two occasions. (Riemschneider and Handel had been fellow students in Halle, and the singer's father was **cantor** at Halle.) Riemschneider had sung in Bach's Kapelle in Cöthen just the previous year, on Dec. 16, 1718. A decade later he would sing in three of Handel's operas, *Lotario*, *Giulio Cesare* and *Partenope*, at London's King's Theater in the 1729-30 season – Handel's first season on his own after the demise of the now just-begun Royal Academy. How fascinating it would be to have a record of Riemschneider's impressions of both composers, as musicians and men.

~

On leaving Halle, Handel went to Dresden to look for singers, since Dresden had a large opera theater. The city was bustling: it was to be the site of the marriage later that summer of Friedrich August, inheritor of the electorship of Saxony, to Emperor Joseph I's daughter Maria Josepha. Handel came away having signed only the soprano Margherita Durastanti (recall, she sang *Agrippina* for him in Venice). He wrote, on July 26, to the Earl of Burlington (as a representative of the Royal Academy). Handel hoped to conclude negotiations in a few days with Senesino, Berselli and Guicciardi. But Burrows suggests that this didn't happen "perhaps because the Dresden authorities had sniffed out what was going on [and] the Saxon opera pre-empted his negotiations by signing up most of the singers for another year's contract."[9] Later, however, Handel acquired the additional singers he needed (Senesino, Berselli, Salvai and Boschi).

Handel was back in London by sometime in the fall and began composing *Radimisto*, the first of a long string of operas that would occupy him for the next nine years. However, the opening production of that first, shortened season was not *Radimisto* by Handel but *Numitore* by Giovanni Porta. Porta composed operas and church music, and he normally worked in Italy. In general during the Royal Academy's first few seasons, the operas of Bononcini (who then lived in England) were both more prominent and more popular than Handel's.

Handel's *Radimisto* was purposely held back for a night when George I and his newly reconciled son could attend. As such things sometimes went, this "reconciliation" had been brokered. Part of the deal involved bringing Robert Walpole and Viscount (Charles) Townshend back into the government. Walpole, a Whig, had "worked for" George I previously. Both Walpole and Townshend had been leading Whigs during Queen Anne's reign. Walpole had been Secretary at War, and after that, Treasurer of the Navy. Townshend was Secretary of State under George I. But Townshend's "colleague," James Stanhope (First Earl of Stanhope), not only overshadowed him, but undermined his influence with the King and eventually got him dismissed (late 1716). Walpole, who was Townshend's brother-in-law, resigned immediately after Townshend's forced departure (1717). Together, while out of office, they had formed an opposition group within the Whigs, nominally led by the Prince of Wales (George I's son), though the Prince of Wales didn't actually like Walpole and tried (unsuccessfully) to get rid of him a decade later when he (the Prince) came to the throne as George II.

So George I and his son George, the crown prince, attended Handel's opera together. Fortunately, the evening was in all ways a rousing success. Still, in the Royal Academy's first full season (November 1720-July 1721), Handel's *Radimisto* received just seven performances while Bononcini's *Astarto* received twenty-three.

In the fall of that year in London (and Amsterdam, and even Boston and beyond) people were talking about, and deeply concerned with, events other than the new Royal Academy of Music and the supposed reconciliation between George I and his son. The first great stock market crash since the devising of the markets was laying hundreds of people (both aristocrats and those of the middle class) open to bankruptcy and penury, and some them open to fraud charges. The "South Sea Bubble" had burst.

Eight years earlier the South Sea Company had acquired a monopoly on trade to the South Seas. In 1711 it had been anticipated that such trade would expose the wealth of Spain's South American colonies to British investors after a treaty to end the War of the Spanish Succession was signed. (But the Peace of Utrecht hadn't been nearly as advantageous to England as had been hoped.) In return for the government granting the company its monopoly, the South Seas Company had to assume a portion of the national debt which England had incurred during the war.

This scheme was created by Tory Robert Harley as much or more to create a financial institution that could compete with the Whig-run Bank of England (est. 1694) than to conduct South Seas trade (though some trade occurred, including a few slaving expeditions). So the South Sea Company was really a "bank" that used its monopoly primarily to attract investors. But in 1718 when Britain and Spain went to war again, "the immediate prospects for any benefits from trade to South America were nil," as Canadian historian David McNeil succinctly puts it.[10] What mattered was the future, and prospects would presumably soar once again when this new war was over. (The company's directors saw what had been achieved through the Mississippi Company's having been given a monopoly on trade with North America, and they were hoping for the same by "conniving to drive the stock up," as John Law, head of the Mississippi Company had done. Many Englishmen felt it didn't hurt, either, to keep home in England money that was being diverted to France.)

In 1719 the South Sea directors proposed to take on the entire national debt. This offer was accepted on April 29, 1720, amidst bribes to influence the vote (paid in non-existent stock holdings). To make more money for itself the company then quickly began to artificially drive up its stock prices, attracting new subscriptions with pro-trade-with-Spain stories leaving the impression that the stock could only go higher; this brought in Dutch investors as well, and increased the pressure on the "bubble."

All spring the stocks rose steadily. Numerous other increasingly "international" joint-stock companies appeared – some legitimate, many not – to take advantage of the investment climate. Though perpetrating their own scam, the South Sea directors didn't appreciate all this speculation, and pushed to have the Bubble Act passed (June 11, 1720), which required all joint-stock companies to have a royal charter. That gave investor confidence another boost, and the South Sea Company's stock which had been at £175 at the end of February, rose to £380 by the end of March, and stood at £520 at the end of May. It topped the immense sum of £1000 at the end of June. Rumors flew.

More rumors flew. And more and more people, including the directors, sold their stock. The bubble burst. By mid-August, the number of bankruptcy listings in the *London Gazette* had never been higher. Thousands of people lost money; some lost immense fortunes, some their live's savings. By the end of September the stock stood at £135.

David McNeil's summary tells the story's denouement very well:

The last part of the story may be told quickly. Investors scream foul against the South Sea directors. Parliament is recalled and George I hastens back to London. Mobs crowd into Westminster. A committee is formed to investigate the South Sea Company; by early 1721 it uncovers widespread corruption and fraud among the directors, company officials and their friends at Westminister. Unfortunately, some of the key players have already fled the country with the incriminating records in their possession. Those who remain are examined and some estates are confiscated. Robert Walpole then rises to power with some reasonable proposals to restore public confidence. They take effect but the "Bubble" affected the fortunes of several families and remained in the consciousness of the Western world for the rest of the eighteenth century, not unlike our cultural memory of the 1929 Wall Street Crash.

Handel had invested modest sums in the South Sea Company: by 1716 he owned £500 worth of stock and had continued to invest. He probably lost some money, but how the debacle really affected him is not known. A still existing note dated June 29, 1716, to the secretary of the South Sea Company, requests that whatever dividend was owed Handel on £500 of stock "att (sic) the opening of their Books next August," should be paid to a Mr. Thomas Carbonnel, of whom nothing is known. Handel expected to be (and was) in continental Europe when the dividend would be paid. No doubt he, like numerous other middle-class investors, had been advised that the South Sea Company was a good bet, unaware of the nature of the scam being perpetrated.

As it happened, opera was an emotional antidote to these financial woes. The opera was attended by many of the same people affected by the crash. The librettist Rolli wrote to his friend Abbate Giuseppe Riva on September 29, 1720:

My dear Riva, what ruination has the Southsea crash caused. The whole nobility is at its last gasp; only gloomy faces are to be seen. Great bankers are going bankrupt, great shareholders just disappear and there is not an acquaintance or friend who has escaped total ruin. These rogues of Company Directors have betrayed everybody and I assure you the tragic worst is feared.

In an October 22 letter Rolli came back to the subject, writing in his typically sharp-tongued style (though he was no doubt expressing popular opinion): "They ought to be gibbeted these South Sea Directors, who have ruined all my friends – and I very much fear they will in consequence have ruined the Academy.

God damn 'em."*

In 1722, external events once again impinged on the opera. In May, a Jacobite plot aimed to overthrow George I and assassinate various members of the royal family was uncovered. The plot allegedly involved Francis Atterbury (1662-1732), high church Bishop of Rochester, former Dean of Westminster, and a Tory. "Prime Minister" Robert Walpole was able to plausibly convince Parliament that Atterbury was the instigator of the plot – and in the process, Walpole brought down a political enemy. Walpole's decisive dealing with both the South Sea scandal and the Atterbury Plot, as it came to be called, entrenched him even more firmly in his position and gave him strong public support. Whether or not the Bishop actually had a hand in the plot, he *was* a highly influential Tory Jacobite, and his conservative, tradition-prone political views irritated the majority Whigs. In any case, Atterbury paid a price; he was stripped of his ecclesiastical standing and Parliament exiled him from England for life.

An aside here about the Atterbury Plot will sharpen our view of the social-political-religious setting in which Handel lived. The Duke of Norfolk and several others were named in the plot along with Bishop Atterbury. In May 1723, one of them, Christopher Layer, was executed. A month later Atterbury was banished and joined the exiled "Pretender," the Catholic James Edward Stuart, in France. These actions by Walpole and Parliament (and George I) were based on the uncovering of the so-called Norfolk List, compiled in 1721 by a Jacobite agent. The list named twelve Norwich gentlemen who would act on behalf of the Pretender, including some former MPs, five aldermen and Christopher Layer.

Jacobite plots were a grave matter. Jacobites (named for James) refused to acknowledge Britain's accepted monarch as *their* monarch. (Those who refused to take necessary oaths pledging allegiance to the Hanoverian monarchs – e.g., clergy or would-be magistrates – were called Nonjurors.) That refusal was one thing, and

---

*Antonio Rolli was an Italian poet who was living in England. He wrote opera librettos for the Royal Academy of Music for its first couple of seasons, and he taught Italian to Princess Caroline's daughters. In his letters he comes across as gossipy, self-absorbed and hyperbolic. Given Handel's and Rolli's very different personalities (and values), it's not surprising that the two greatly disliked each other, and loathed working together. Handel no doubt thought Rolli a fool and Rolli thought Handel arrogant. Rolli had several none-too-complimentary nicknames for Handel, including "The Savage" ("Il Selvaggio") and "The Alpine Faun" ("L'Alpestre Fauno").

serious enough from the point of view of the establishment. Plotting to bring the Catholic Stuarts back to the throne by overthrowing the current King and his government was another thing: treason.

But support of the Stuarts was also a serious matter – a matter of conscience – for most Jacobites. Not all Jacobites were Catholics, nor were all of them Tories (though especially after the Atterbury Plot, Walpole was able to broadly paint the Tories as Jacobites). The Jacobites and Nonjurors were believers in the "divine right of kings" (a monarch's right to rule is an inherent right granted him or her by God). That right to rule passed down the generations by divine right, a state of affairs that could not be denied or changed by political maneuvering – which is how Jacobites characterized the Settlement Act which gave the British throne to the Protestant Hanovers. (That there had been plenty of maneuvering for the throne for centuries before the Hanovers arrived was apparently a moot point; or seen as a different sort of maneuvering.) The two primary issues involved, then, in the long and frequently bloody controversy between the Jacobites and the Georgians were the origin of the legitimacy of kingly rule, and whether Britain would have, and should have, a Protestant or Catholic ruler. For the average person (including the lower classes) the Protestant-Catholic issue was by far the most potent.

While anti-Catholic feeling was already high ("papists" were seen as apostate, and would thus suffer damnation if unrepentant), these events increased scrutiny and suspicion of all Catholics in England.[*] Composer Bononcini and librettist Rolli – Italian Catholics and friends of each other – lost their jobs with the Academy. Though Handel was also a foreigner he was the "right kind" of foreigner. He was thus put in a position both to compose more frequently and to work with Nicola Francesco Haym, a librettist with whom he was more compatible in personality and outlook.

---

[*] The serious tension between eighteenth century Protestants and Catholics goes back to issues and events that grew from the Reformation in the sixteenth century. If the Reformers considered the Roman church apostate in both doctrine and practice, "Mother Church" considered the Reformers heretics and revolutionaries, and not only excommunicated Reformers but imprisoned and even executed some of them.

Chapter 7
Glory and Grim Reality in the Land of Angels

Mainwaring sums up Handel's Royal Academy years as a period of "musical glory." In his view, Handel's firm grip – the "perfect authority" he maintained over the singers and orchestra – was responsible for the "order and decorum…, union and tranquillity" that Mainwaring saw as rare in musical organizations.[1]

During the Royal Academy years, 1720-28, Handel wrote thirteen of the roughly forty operas he would write in his lifetime (he had written eleven previously).* Conductor and musicologist Christopher Hogwood observes that all but one of the operas of this period were "dynastic, epic and, it is suggested, symbolic of the ruling order, reflecting what one feels as Handel's own desire for stability, hierarchy, and succession." That is true, though the operas of the next period (the Handel-Heidegger collaboration) tend toward the same type.

It might, in fact, be argued that the oratorios are also "dynastic, epic and symbolic of the ruling order"; the difference is that in the oratorios the "dynasty" and "ruling order" are controlled by God and conferred onto his people Israel. (Besides the oratorios' face-value biblical meaning, they were interpreted by Handel's contemporaries in terms of England standing in for Old Testament Israel. To varying degrees they were interpreted politically, too.) The Old Testament characters and events the oratorios portray are certainly "epic," and representative of the countless others in the Old Testament, revealing God's saving acts as part of his "ruling order" (kingdom).

Handel's personality rather freely combined conflicting "conservative" and "liberal" impulses. He exhibited (perhaps to a surprising degree for the time) a desire for personal freedom and self-sufficiency, but that quality combined with an apparently strong need for security and stability – social, financial and emotional. He was a product of the merchant class who coveted respect from noblemen and monarchs (and mostly achieved it); he almost methodically saved and invested

---

*For opera buffs: of Handel's first eleven operas, four were written in Germany, two in Italy and five in London. His Royal Academy operas, 1720-1732, were, in chronological order: *Radimisto*, one act of *Muzio Scevola* (composing duties shared with Bononcini and Amadei), *Floridante, Ottone, Flavio, Giulio Cesare, Tamerlano, Rodelinda, Scipione, Alessandro, Admeto, Riccardo Primo, Siroe* and *Tolomeo*.

money for his future security while freely giving money and time to the poor (as we've seen, his generosity was motivated by the sense of biblical hospitality and charity he inherited from his devout parents, but he may have also had a kind of visceral compassion for the lack of security that poverty brings); he was a cosmopolitan traveler who ached for fellowship with his family; a naturalized citizen of a new country who yearned for his homeland; he wrote music for the Anglican liturgy and worshiped in an Anglican parish but in his heart clung to the Lutheran interpretation of Christianity he learned from his birth, not desiring to or able to take the leap of both faith and emotion that would make him a "real" Anglican; he was both an independent entrepreneur and a faithful servant of the Crown (and as he was a man of principle, it is interesting, though admittedly fruitless, to speculate about his private view of the Hanovers and their governments, to whatever degree he was aware of the political machinations); he could venture into any kind of music he wished to write but had a difficult time making a clean break with the familiar (opera) until he was absolutely sure that the alternative (oratorio) would afford him security.

This was a prosperous and seemingly secure time for Handel. At thirty-eight, he had his appointment as Composer to the Chapel Royal. He had a pension of £400 annually as music master to the royal family. He was music director of the sole opera company in London, and his music was being well-received. All that possibly helped lead him to decide that it was time to establish a home of his own. So in August 1723 he rented a modest house in a new, somewhat less modest neighborhood, Hanover Square, which was being settled by upper- and middle-rank gentry. He would live there for thirty-six years, the rest of his life.* As an alien he could not buy the house, yet when he became a citizen in 1727, he continued to lease it. Perhaps his need to remain as independent as possible played a role in that decision, consciously or not: in the back of his mind, perhaps, he knew that not owning the house would make it easier for him to leave London should he ever need or want to. In fact, in the spring of 1741, when Handel had been having difficulties

---

*Handel's house still stands, in Mayfair, London, at 25 Brook Street. In the 1990s it began to be refurbished, thanks to *New Grove Dictionary* editor Stanley Sadie. In November 2001 it opened as the Handel House Museum (www.handelhouse.org). The museum occupies the upper floors of the connected rooms of 23 and 25 Brook Street. A very different kind of musician, legendary rock guitarist and acid-head Jimi Hendrix, lived at 23 Brook Street in 1968-69.

for some time, there *would be* rumors that he was going back to Germany.

On June 11,1727, an unexpected event precipitated Handel's writing a different kind of music that would have long-term positive consequents for him. The event was the sudden death of George I at age sixty-seven while on a trip to Hanover. The music is the four *Coronation Anthems*.

Though Handel was made Composer of Music for His Majesty's Chapel Royal two days after his thirty-eighth birthday (February 23,1723), it was an honorary title; as an alien, he could not hold an "office of profit under the Crown." However, his naturalization as a British subject occurred in February 1727, so he could then legally provide the music for the coronation of George II. But four months passed between George I's death and the crowning of George II on October 11, and though Handel could *legally* provide the music, William Croft was still the senior composer in the Chapel Royal. That didn't seem to matter. According to the new king's grandson (when he had become George III), George II disliked Croft and "ordered" that Handel write the coronation music and that Handel select the texts himself. Whether that was so or not, it became a moot point when Croft himself died that August. Though Maurice Greene then became the senior composer in the Chapel Royal, Handel was still the favorite (and of course the better composer by far). The soon-to-be George II and Queen Caroline had known Handel in Hanover and particularly loved his music.

Handel relished choosing the biblical anthem texts (as he had with his *Chandos Anthems*). The parameters were stipulated by previous coronation services. Handel knew the Bible very well, of course; but if he had been instructed to select the texts himself, the exalted ecclesiastics involved hadn't been told. Charles Burney tells an amusing story on the subject, and one characteristic of Handel's character:

> *At the coronation of his late majesty, George the Second, in 1727, HANDEL had words sent to him, by the bishops, for the anthems; at which he murmured, and took offence, as he thought it implied his ignorance of the Holy Scriptures: 'I have read my Bible very well, and shall chuse for myself.' And, indeed, his selection of the words, "My heart is inditing of a good matter," was very judicious, and inspired him with some of the finest thoughts that are to be found in all his works. This anthem was sung at the coronation, while the peers were doing homage.*[2]

Handel was indeed "inspired," judging by the results. One of the anthems,

"Zadok the Priest," has been used at every subsequent coronation right down to Elizabeth II's. Handel must have realized how stirring this music is; five years later he adapted almost all of it for his oratorios *Esther* and *Deborah*.) The four anthems are "Let Thy Hand Be Strengthened" (Ps. 89:14-15), used early in the service during the Recognition, and the only one without festive trumpets and drums; "Zadok the Priest" (I Kings 1:38-40) to accompany the anointing; "The King Shall Rejoice" (Ps. 21:1, 5, 3) for the coronation itself; and "My Heart is Inditing" (Ps. 45:1, 10, 12; Is. 49:23) for Queen Caroline's coronation. For the texts of "Let Thy Hand Be Strengthened" and "Zadok the Priest" Handel used a translation from the Latin Bible (which he may have found in copies of pre-Reformation coronation services).

~

Despite the "musical glory" created by Handel's fertile imagination throughout the 1720s, as the decade waned the opera world was falling apart around him. From 1728 onward, opera attendance dwindled. Within the Academy there were problems; and outside the Academy there was a new kind of threat: John Gay's satire *The Beggar's Opera* was staged by John Rich at the Lincoln's Inn Fields Theater from January 29 to the end of the season and was dizzyingly successful. (After this "opera's" immense success, some wags noted that it had "made Gay rich and Rich gay." The great Samuel Johnson immortalized the quip in his *Life of John Gay*.)

Having been in a precarious financial position for some time, the Academy was now broke. Money problems were exacerbated by disagreements between Academy directors, difficulties between the sometimes intractable and always musically demanding Handel and the preening and temperamental star castrato Senesino, and by a fierce rivalry between the leading ladies, Faustina Bordoni and Francesca Cuzzoni and their respective camps. Hawkins tells of a salary squabble. It can readily be transposed to our time and applied to major entertainment or sports figures:

> *The directors, greatly troubled with the dispute, and foreseeing the probable consequence of it, fell upon an odd expedient to determine it. The time for a new contract with each of these singers was at hand, and they agreed among themselves to give as a salary to Faustina one guinea a year more than to her rival. Lady Pembroke and some others, the friends of Cuzzoni, hearing this, made her swear upon the holy*

gospels never to take less than Faustina, and the directors continuing firm in their resolution not to give her quite so much, Cuzzoni found herself ensnared by her oath into the necessity of quitting the kingdom [leaving England]. The following lines were written by Ambrose Phillips on her departure:

Little syren of the stage,
Charmer of an idle age,
Empty warbler, breathing lyre,
Wanton gale of fond desire;
Bane of every manly art,
Sweet enfeebler of the heart;
O! Too pleasing is thy strain,
Hence to southern climes again:
Tuneful mischief, vocal spell,
To this island bid farewell;
Leave us as we ought to be,
Leave the Britons rough and free.[3]

The Beggar's Opera packed in audiences night after night at Lincoln's Inn Fields. Handel's opera Riccardo Primo (Richard the First) competed nicely against it that season – and turned out to be highly appropriate for a season that witnessed the coronation of a new king. Handel's opera saw 60 performances to the end of the 1728 season on June 1, compared to sixty-three of The Beggar's Opera.

But the Beggar's Opera would not die, and the nature of this new form of drama was changing London's theater scene, if not attitudes beyond it. It is really, and deliberately, not an opera at all, but a boisterous, unorthodox play containing songs and incidental music. Forty-one of its sixty-nine airs are broadside ballads that were popular at the time. It lampoons the "good taste" and superficiality of the upper classes, ridicules Italian opera conventions and mocks the high tone and quick happy endings of the opera librettos. That it called itself an opera is part of the satire, and it even helped itself to some of Handel's own music; for example, Gay put his own words to the stirring march from Rinaldo.

Macheath, the "hero," is a cad who is involved in a blatant and unseemly love triangle. He moves in London's criminal underworld of pickpockets and other thieves, fences, jailors, highwaymen and women of easy virtue. Gay alludes to London's social and economical ills through these characters and makes the rogues and gangsters of Newgate types for what he sees as the morally reprehensible politicians and noblemen running the government: Walpole and his friends.

While *The Beggar's Opera* would become the most popular piece of theater in the entire eighteenth century, not everyone found it funny or appreciated its satire. From the outset, Handel's friend Mrs. Pendarves (Mary Granville, later Delany) wrote to her sister Ann Granville: "Yesterday I was at the rehearsal of the new opera [*Siroe*] composed by Handel: I like it extremely, but the taste of the town is so depraved, that nothing will be approved of but the burlesque. The Beggar's Opera entirely triumphs over the Italian one."[4] And Sir John Hawkins lamented Gay's "many acrimonious expressions and bitter invectives against statesmen, lawyers, priests, and others," and asserts — very possibly correctly — that in satirizing "all stations and characters, and, in short, every class of men whose rank or situation of life was above that of the author" Gay was grinding a personal axe, expressing his disappointment in his being denied a preferment at court. (Hawkins saw Gay as a moocher who did as little work as possible: "In the greatness of his soul, [he] preferred ... a life of ease, and servile dependence on the bounty of his friends and the caprice of the town.")

Though *The Beggar's Opera* was more a result of changing tastes and the decline of Italian opera than the cause of its decline, Senesino, Faustina and Cuzzoni saw the handwriting on the wall. All three left the country when the season ended. Heidegger also left for the Continent to look for singers for the next season, even though the Royal Academy of Music was effectively, if not legally, dead.

Heidegger returned empty-handed, or, it might be said, voiceless. Nevertheless, Handel and he decided to carry on. They struck a deal with the ever more spectral Academy, whose directors voted on January 19, 1729, to allow Handel and Heidegger to move forward on their own, making use of the Academy's "scenes, machines, clothes, instruments, furniture, etc."[5] Handel and Heidegger presumably had to raise their own subscriptions, though a letter by Rolli to Senesino (in Venice) says that "Mylord Bingley" (Robert Lord Bingley) would lead the new project and that Heidegger would be given £2200 (per production) "with which to provide the theater, the scenery and the costumes." Handel would get £1000 per production "for the composition, whether it will be by himself or by whomsoever else he may choose." The King would contribute a much-needed £1000. Within ten days of the Academy's decision, it was Handel, this time, who set off to Italy to hunt for singers. From February to the end of June he traveled Europe, searching.

In Italy he went to Venice, Bologna and Rome. On March 11, from Venice, he wrote his brother-in-law in response to a letter he received (he had arranged to receive mail from his family via a Joseph Smith, a banker in Venice and later the British Consul). He urged Michaëlsen to continue to write to him while he traveled in Italy. Once again Handel's letter to his brother-in-law, while not as detailed as several others that survive, is warm and affectionate and exudes yearning for his family and eagerness to see them – he hopes he will be in Halle by July. With his letter to Michaëlsen he enclosed a letter to his mother, which, like all others to her, has been lost.

Michaëlsen had by then remarried, not once but twice, after the death of Handel's sister; his third wife, in fact, was a sister of the second. The death of a spouse due to illness was an all too common occurrence, so such remarriage was also common. Handel's letters to Michaëlsen show no qualms about his former brother-in-law's subsequent marriages. The woman who made them brothers was gone, but that did not loosen the bond between them. Handel continued to address Michaëlsen as "brother," prefaced by "my dear," "very dear," "honored," or "esteemed." He also always asked Michaëlsen to pass on greetings to his wife and the rest of Michaëlsen's family, and to embrace Handel's beloved niece for him. And the former brother- and son-in-law continued to look after Frau Händel and her affairs, at Handel's request.

Handel stopped in Hanover and then arrived in Halle earlier than he expected, but it would be a short visit. This was the visit to Halle during which, according to Bach sources, Handel met composer Wilhelm Friedemann Bach, who, on behalf of his father, Johann Sebastian, invited Handel to come to Leipzig (which didn't happen). This visit, too, would be the last time Handel saw his mother. She died in December the next year (1730) at age seventy-nine. Though she was apparently in reasonably good health when Handel saw her in June 1729, she was elderly and blind, and his trips to Halle were, of necessity, sporadic.

He must have been able to guess that he would not see her again. The visit was a joyful but poignant one for all concerned, but was difficult as it came time for Handel to leave. The effect of that visit on Handel is revealed in part of a letter-in-verse he received some months after his mother's death from his cousin and good friend Christian August Rotth:

It seems to me as though I could still see the kind welcome, when you
so surprisingly brought happiness to my house last year, and

remembered me, as you used to do, in person. The joy of your relatives begin when you entered the town. Everybody wanted to see you, even if they knew you only by name. Your faithful mother wept tears of joy when she felt in the darkness the hand of the stranger. And even today I would not like to mention the word with which she bade you farewell.[6]

As Handel headed back toward England, he stopped in Hamburg, still a fine city for opera. Though we have no record of it, and he moved quickly, it would be peculiar if he did not briefly stop to see his friend Telemann while there. Since 1721, Telemann had been Kantor of the Johanneum and music director of the five main churches in the city. Telemann was then writing mostly church music, but he had also written a couple of operas since he came to Hamburg.

Some of the best singers in Europe were the ones who left the Academy; even so, there *were* other singers around, and in the end this was a productive trip for Handel. He managed to find the seven singers he needed. Only one, the castrato Antonio Maria Bernacchi, had previously sung in London. (The great castrato Farinelli wasn't interested in joining Handel's company.) One of the new singers, Anna Strada del Pò (referred to as Strada), would loyally remain Handel's leading lady for eight years when others eventually deserted to the "Opera of the Nobility."

As Handel prepared for the new, possibly perilous, opera season, his librettist and friend Nicola Haym died (in August). This meant Handel would be forced to reconnect with either the petulant Rolli – the "Papist" threat having passed, temporarily – or with his first London librettist, Giacomo Rossi. Under the new arrangement, Handel was the sole composer. The new season (1729-30) was a mixture of freshly composed operas, a revival of an earlier work, and a **pasticcio** (an often eclectic compilation of music from various sources).* The next season, Senesino was brought back, no doubt much to Handel's chagrin; but he realized it was a necessity. That season and the next proceeded much as 1729 had, some works being quite popular and some disappearing quickly.

Handel's friend Mrs. Pendarves wrote a prescient comment to her sister Ann Granville on April 4, 1730: "Operas are dying, to my great mortification. Yesterday I was at the rehearsal of a new one; it is composed of several songs out of Italian operas; but it is very heavy [compared] to Mr. Handel's [pasticcio

---

*That season included *Giulio Cesare (Julius Caesar)*, now one of Handel's most often heard operas.

Ormisda]."[7] Rolli was of the same opinion about opera dying, though he was hardly "greatly mortified" about it. And he was sure he knew the reason. In his peevish fashion he wrote to Riva: "I shall barely answer you on the matter of that *Coppia Eidegrendeliana* [Heidegger-Handel pair] and their worthless operas. Because in truth they succeed no better than they deserve." Meanwhile, offering some competition at the Little Theater in the Haymarket (though not necessarily assuming to attract the same audience) was a ballad-opera called *The Female Parson, or The Beau in the Sudds*. Like *The Beggar's Opera*, it shamelessly included several tunes by Handel.*

The 1730-31 season was darkened for Handel by his mother's death (December 27, 1730). A letter of his dated February 23/12, 1731 survives, written to his brother-in-law, and mostly in German, not their usual French. When Handel's thoughts go back to his family and childhood home, when he is grieving and writing of matters close to his heart, he writes in his native German – in this case with a scattered couple of words in English and Latin, and with the salutation and closing (formal parts of the letter) in French.

The letter, on black-edged paper and closed with black sealing wax, is a response to his brother-in-law's letter of January 6 (lost to us) in which Michaëlsen described Frau Händel's interment. Handel thanks Michaëlsen for the care he took in seeing to his mother's burial in accordance with her wishes. How Handel must have regretted that he hadn't been in Halle one last time! In his next few sentences we get of glimpse of both the depth of his grief and the depth of his faith:

> *Here I cannot restrain my tears. Yet it has pleased the Almighty, to whose Holy Will I submit myself with Christian resignation. Her memory will, however, never become obliterated for me, until, after this life, we are again united, which may the beneficent God grant, in his grace.*[8]

---

*Those tunes are the gavotte from *Ottone* (first performed January 1723) and a hornpipe in G major. England had a copyright law, but the stringent copyright protections common today were to be a thing of the distant future. Though there had been a licensing act in the latter part of the seventeenth century which legitimized and tried to control what was printed (and made sure it contained nothing blasphemous or treasonous or otherwise hostile to church or state), the first copyright act was passed by the English Parliament in 1709 (the Statute of Anne). It introduced the concept of an author (or composer) being the owner of copyright, and it inaugurated a fixed term of protection (21 years for works already in existence; 14 years for new works, renewable for another 14 if the author was still alive).

Read it at http://www.wikipedia.com/wiki/Statute_of_Anne.

Handel further thanks "my highly respected brother for the continual loyalty and care with which at all times he assisted my dear, blessed mother" ("meiner lieben Seeligen Frau Mutter"). He adds that he "will not declare with words alone but reserve to myself the opportunity of showing my due gratitude." Some scholars have interpreted this as a reference to Handel's intention to make his goddaughter-niece (Michaëlsen's daughter) his heir. This letter reveals more than any other the depth of admiration, affection and respect Handel had for his brother-in-law: Michaëlsen had been both an excellent husband to Handel's sister and a worthy son-in-law, treating his (former) mother-in-law as he would have treated his own mother, and Handel would not forget it. Handel seems to have had difficulty expressing the closeness he felt to Michaëlsen while addressing him outright, so he refers to him in the third person: twice he refers to Michaëlsen as "my beloved brother" and once as "my highly honored brother." Handel thanks Michaëlsen, too, for passing on a "magnificent poem" which, he says, "I shall preserve as a highly treasured memorial" (likely the versified letter written for him by his cousin Rotth).

The letter further reveals Handel's character when he shifts from his own grief to expressing his condolences to Michaëlsen and his wife on the death of Michaëlsen's brother-in-law (presumably his wife's brother). The composer speaks as if he knew the man; if not, the Michaëlsen brother-in-law had apparently been mentioned to Handel on previous occasions. Handel alludes in an unusual way to an account they must have given him of the man's illness and death, apparently a prolonged and painful one which he bore with faith and grace: "And I am particularly edified by his Christian composure." Not "*you* can be edified by his Christian composure," as a private issue of theirs, but "*I* am *particularly* edified" by it. Then he prays for them all, including himself: "May the Almighty fulfil for us all his wishes[,] full of consolation," ending by commending Michaëlsen and his family to "[God's] omnipotent care."

There is nothing platitudinous about Handel's references to submitting to God's will or finding comfort in God's care. Every source in which Handel makes reference to God demonstrates that he believed and had experienced God to be an ever-present, gracious and compassionate God whose care for human life and all of his world is always ultimately for the benefit of that life and world, however much it may sometimes look otherwise. It is interesting to note that in Handel's letters, such references often occur in the context of grieving, a time when what a person truly believes (or doesn't) often becomes most obvious.

Rotth's poem reaffirms Handel as a man of deep Christian faith – in his middle age at the height of his opera career, and not just when he was a child or what he might be as an old man. Rotth shared that faith, and he naturally appeals to it to comfort his cousin-friend. He clearly knew Handel well and shows deep empathy for his famous cousin. After the lingering delight of Handel's still rather recent visit,

> now all that pleasure has suddenly vanished, for Death has flung you into pain and grieving. Hope for such pleasant hours is gone, and so your soul must bleed. Through Heaven's will you, the last of her nearest and dearest, have lost a most faithful mother, and this, after the loss of two sisters, leaves you alone. No one can be so without feeling as not to understand that to bury one's mother is the richest of woes. Even though she was so well advanced in years, yet a pious son could never forget her who first loved him; in the midst of his daily occupations he could not forget those prayers which brought to him her life's blessing. This son has ever shown such piety—the last time in a letter which clearly revealed his tenderness. In it he bade us shelter her in life, by all means to succor her, to hold off death as long as possible, and to help her by word and deed.... Blessed be she who has earned for herself so much praise from all in this world; who died in such blessedness and whose spirit has conquered with such honor.... Your great heart also knows that her blessing rests on your head, and that it behooves us, who remain behind, to do God's Will. May God give you long life, many years, as many as those with which he favored her, and may the New Year be gracious to you. With that I end this poem of condolence which I have felt compelled to write. Do not shed upon it further tears—like you, your mother is now in the land of angels.*

While Handel's opera *Poro* was playing at the King's Theater, his *Utrecht Te Deum and Jubilate* and two of the *Coronation Anthems* were being rehearsed in St. Paul's Cathedral the day after his birthday, February 24 (1731), for a service and festive gathering the next day. The service with Handel's music was part of the annual meeting of the a charity called the Sons of the Clergy, and Handel's music

---

*Rotth puns on the word "England": "Engelland" = "angel land."

would attract more people than an event without music (or with other composers' music) would have. Collections would be taken for the Sons of the Clergy, the first of countless times Handel's music would assist a charity to raise money.[*]

By the early eighteenth century a large majority of Church of England clergy were university educated. The Sons of the Clergy paid for that education for sons of needy ministers (and also helped their widowed mothers) so that they would be able to follow in their fathers' footsteps. This was not merely a helpful gesture. Though incomes were gradually rising, there were a surprising number of needy ministers in the Church of England. Records from Queen Anne's Bounty five years later classify an astonishing 5,638 clergy as poor (worth a meager £50 annually, or less), those in the north and west being poorer than those in the south and east, reflecting conditions in English society generally.[**] Shockingly, almost twenty percent of these poor clergy made less than £10 a year, and neither of these figures reflects the plight of curates, i.e., "unbeneficed" clergy who had no "livings" of their own and who therefore assisted vicars or rectors.[9] The social structure of the Church of England and its place in and influence on English society at this time were complex; there is in our time considerable difference of opinion as to the spiritual state of the church and how Christian "Christian England" was during the long eighteenth century.

---

[*]Founded in 1655, the Sons of the Clergy was granted a royal charter in 1678. The organization still exists. Today its stated purpose is "for helping clergy of the Anglican Communion in the UK, Eire and Anglican missionaries abroad, providing they are sponsored by a UK-based missionary society..., widows and widowers of such clergy, their separated or divorced wives, and the dependent children of any of the above. Help can also be given to unmarried daughters of pensionable age [and] ordinands may be eligible for a book grant." <sonsoftheclergy.org>

[**]In 1703 the "Bounty" was established by Queen Anne, the titular head of the church, as a perpetual fund of "first-fruits" and "tenths" to augment the livings of the poorer clergy. First-fruits and tenths had existed since before the Reformation, in those days as part of the revenue paid by the clergy to the papal exchequer. First-fruits were the first year's profit of a clergyman's entire income; tenths were tithes: one-tenth of a clergyman's annual profits after the first year. The income derived from first-fruits and tenths was annexed to the revenue of the crown in 1535 by Henry VIII. In 1703 Queen Anne surrendered that revenue, and granted the Bounty a royal charter – her personal but official charity, as it were. Anne was a devout Anglican who opposed her Catholic father James II; she thus supported the "Glorious Revolution" of 1688 which deposed him and brought her Calvinist brother-in-law, William. III (the Dutch William of Orange) and Mary II to the throne.

At the Sons of the Clergy rehearsal a collection of "above £200" was taken (rehearsals of concerts, operas, and later the oratorios were generally open to the public). At the service itself, an additional £203 9s 6d was collected, "very near double what has been given in any other Year." And at the "feast" after the service, which closed that year's gathering, another £476 was collected. The donors included "a great Appearance of Persons of the first Rank and Figure," as the *Daily Courant* described those who attended the rehearsal; and at the festival itself "there was a nobler Audience, and a more generous Contribution to the Charity than has been known." So Handel's *Utrecht Te Deum and Jubilate* began to be heard at the Sons of the Clergy annual festivals at St. Paul's in 1731. Various of his works would continue to be heard at these gatherings year after year; and benefit concerts of these and other of his works (notably, but by no means only, *Messiah*) would be mounted for the rest of his life – and well beyond.

Handel clearly believed in the good of the causes his music would benefit, and seemed to have emotional ties of various kinds to those causes. His affinity for the Sons of the Clergy is understandable. Though the church situation was somewhat different in Germany, he grew up in a setting in which excellent education for pastors was considered crucial to their calling as ministers of the Gospel. The many pastors on his mother's side of the family familiarized him with that way of life and no doubt created in him an empathy for the unique problems they faced.

Burney concluded that the combined strength and sublimity of Handel's music make it particularly suitable for raising money to support charitable work, and not incidentally, also helped to keep the music itself alive even after his death:

> *The most honourable eulogium that can be bestowed on the power of Music is, that whenever the human heart is wished to expand in charity and beneficence, its aid is more frequently called in, than that of any other art or advocate: as the delight it affords in exchange for superfluous wealth, is not only the most exquisite which the wit of man can supply, but the most innocent that a well-governed state can allow. Indeed Handel's Church-Music has been kept alive, and has supported life in thousands, by its performance for charitable purposes: as at St. Paul's for the Sons of the Clergy; at the Triennial Meetings of the Three Choirs of Worcester, Herford, and Gloucester; at the two Universities of Oxford and Cambridge; at the Benefit Concerts for decayed Musicians and*

their Families; at the Foundling-Hospital; at St. Margaret's Church for the Westminster Infirmary; and for Hospitals and Infirmaries in general, throughout the kingdom, which have long been indebted to the art of Music, and to Handel's Works in particular, for their support.[10]

Chapter 8
A Novel Species of Entertainment

Throughout Handel's life, February – his birth month – seemed to be a seminal time. While the 1731-32 opera season was proceeding (Handel's *Sosarme* was successfully running at the Haymarket, and another of his operas, *Poro*, had crossed the Channel and was being performed in Hamburg) a noteworthy event occurred on his forty-seventh birthday, February 23, 1732: his Cannons oratorio, now referred to as *Esther*, was heard in three private performances beginning on the 23rd at the Crown and Anchor Tavern.

It was not uncommon for large taverns to have a room, often furnished with a harpsichord, in which tavern patrons could amuse themselves musically, or in which performances were held for the entertainment of those gathered or specifically invited. The *Esther* performances were instigated and directed by the Master of the Children of the Royal Chapel, Bernard Gates, with the help of the Philharmonic Society and the Academy of Ancient Music, Gates' Chapel Royal children (boy choristers), and adult male singers from St. James's and Westminster Abbey. (*Acis and Galatea*, another of Handel's works written for the Duke of Chandos, had been resurrected the previous year on March 26, 1731, at Lincoln's Inn-Fields by John Rich: *its* first public performance, presumably with Handel's consent.)

Esther at the Crown and Anchor occurred against a backdrop of animosity between Gates and Maurice Greene. Greene was, recall, William Croft's successor as the Chapel Royal's senior composer; he was also the organist at St. Paul's Cathedral. About a year before Gates's presentations of *Esther* there had been a dispute, which became public, over the authorship of a madrigal by the Italian composer Antonio Lotti. Greene had presented the madrigal to the Academy of Ancient Music (then the Academy of Vocal Music) as the work of Bononcini, who was a friend of his and still living in London. When Greene was proven wrong (with the implication that he had deliberately presented the work as by Bononcini, knowing that it wasn't), he left the Academy and his supporters left with him; the remaining members re-formed as the Academy of Ancient Music (the Academy of Vocal Music had been made up of singers from the Chapel Royal, Westminster Abbey and St. Paul's Cathedral). Gates had also been responsible for an Academy program in January 1731 which presented the contentious Lotti madrigal as well as Handel's *Utrecht Te Deum and Jubilate*.

Gates may have been promoting Handel's music "in an attempt to outface or annoy Greene": the newspapers presented that January 1731 Academy performance as news, not as an advertisement.[1] When Handel arrived in England he and Greene got along cordially; Greene showed him around town and made the organ at St. Paul's available to Handel whenever he wished. But Handel was a favorite of the King's and had become a competitor in Greene's eyes. While Greene was competent, everyone knew he wasn't Handel's equal. Whether that frustrated him or was a cause for bad feeling towards Handel is not known. In the next year, Handel would write an oratorio using a subject that Greene had already set: *Deborah*; and later, two others, *Jephtha* and *The Judgment of Hercules* (Handel's setting is *The Choice of Hercules*).

Handel attended one of Gates's *Esther* performances, likely the one on his birthday – which may have been presented in honor of his natal day. At that point in his life it was a novelty for him to listen to his own music without being involved in performing or directing it. Though he didn't realize it then, these performances of *Esther* would be the catalyst that set him on the road away from opera toward oratorio – though a rather long and often arduous road it would be.

Viscount Percival wrote after hearing *Esther*: "From dinner I went to the Music Club, where the King's Chapel boys acted the *History of Hester*, writ by Pope, and composed by Hendel. This oratoria (sic) or religious opera is exceeding fine, and the company were highly pleased, some of the parts being well performed." (Note Percival's spelling of Handel's name; even after Handel had lived in England for twenty years, this was common, indicating that it was still often pronounced as it was in German, with an umlaut "a").

Percival says the boys "acted": the Crown and Anchor performances were apparently staged, at least to some extent (which would become an issue later). If Percival was more impressed with the music itself than with the consistent quality of the performance, when Princess Anne (who thought very highly of Handel and was, recall, a favorite music student of his) got wind of *Esther* she wanted to see for herself. She asked Handel to produce it at the King's Theater, again with stage action. But before Handel could respond, the *Daily Journal* announced a performance of this "oratorio or Sacred Drama" "Never Perform'd in Publick before" at the Great Room of the York Buildings, April 20th – the Crown and Anchor performances had been by invitation and thus were not "public." Who initiated or performed in this un-authorized production is a mystery.

Handel's music had, before then, been used in a few instances without his involvement, though usually with his consent. But this was the first time he would be competing head-on with his own music, and quite unexpectedly: just the day before this announcement appeared in the *Daily Journal*, his opera *Flavio* opened at the Haymarket. He reacted quickly, enabled by his nimble ability to compose and revise with remarkable speed. Within twelve days, another *Esther* appeared, and it was a substantially different work. This time the *Daily Journal* reported that

> at the King's Theater in the Hay-Market, on Tuesday the 2d Day of May, will be performed, The Sacred Story of ESTHER: an Oratorio in English. Formerly composed by Mr. Handel, and now revised by him, with several Additions, and to be performed by a great Number of the best Voices and Instruments.

The "several additions" were twelve extra numbers!* In his unique fashion, Handel borrowed from himself to compete with himself — with the help of librettist Samuel Humphreys, who provided some needed text. Humphreys had been writing the English translations for the wordbooks of Handel's Italian operas, so it was natural Handel would turn to him for some bits of libretto. For *Esther* reborn, Handel chose and revised music from *La Resurrezione*, the *Ode for the Birthday of Queen Anne*, *Zadok the Priest* and a second *Coronation Anthem*; then he added newly composed material. He re-orchestrated some of it for bigger forces, including instruments he didn't have available at Cannons.

Modern music lovers accustomed to hearing *Messiah* with four soloists may be surprised to know that Handel used eight soloists for *Esther* (there was no doubling of roles): three English singers in addition to his five Italian opera singers. Among the latter were Strada as Esther, and the castrato Senesino, for whom Handel adapted the male role of Ahasuerus (Senesino was a soprano).

---

*Further to Handel's fast composing: though many composers at the time composed quickly, and had to, Handel was a particular speed demon. In fact, on his first trip to England, having composed *Rinaldo* in two weeks, Handel was the subject of an acerbic jibe from poet Joseph Addison, editor of the *Spectator* (No. 5). Addison, not having heard *Rinaldo*, assumed that music so fleetly written couldn't be worth much. Burney takes Addison to task for that attitude, saying "Had this writer and critic, so admirable in other respects, been possessed of judgment and feeling in Music equal to his learning and taste in literature, he would have discovered that to compose an entire opera in less time than a copyist could transcribe it, and in a more masterly and original style than had ever before been heard in this, or perhaps, any country, was not a fair subject for sarcasm.." Burney then adds a jibe of his own: "All Music seems alike to Addison, except French Recitative, for which he seems to have a particular predilection" (Burney, *Sketch of the Life of Handel*, p. 10).

Heard by six audiences, *Esther* in its fresh guise as a full-length English oratorio met with "vast Applause," said the *London Magazine, or Gentleman's Monthly Intelligencer* of May 1732. The Prince of Wales and his three eldest daughters were among those who attended more than once. In our day of recorded music, twenty-four-hour radio, and Internet streaming it is easy to overlook the obvious fact that in that age the only way to get to know a work was to repeatedly attend live performances of it. And after that, to buy a copy of the score as soon as it was published, and to attempt to play and/or sing it at home.

When Handel reused his music or made use of other composers' music, almost none of it would have been recognized from its previous incarnations. Very few in the audience at *Esther* would have been present at George II's coronation, none would have known Handel's Italian oratorio *La Resurrezione*, and no one had ever heard the *Ode for the Birthday of Queen Anne*. In a sense, Handel was democratizing his music with such reuse. Further democratization would take place as the oratorio audiences gradually came to include the middle class. The issue of Italian-style opera being sung in the Italian language was becoming an increasing impediment to its enjoyment for many. "English opera" was a subject for discussion and was gradually being attempted more frequently by some composers (but not by Handel).

The fact that *Esther* was in English surely helped to increase its popularity. As did the fact that its audience would have been acquainted with this story from the Bible. *Esther* was profitable for Handel. After the third performance, he was able to invest the large sum of £700 in South Sea Annuities, a South Sea Company now appearing in renewed and presumably incorruptible form.

These performances were not staged, despite Princess Anne's wishes. Charles Burney intimated that the reason lay with the Bishop of London, Edmund Gibson. This issue still comes up frequently among Handel scholars and aficionados. Until quite recently, Handel scholars have continued to blame Gibson's "narrowness" (Winton Dean's term) for the tradition of non-acted Handelian oratorios, presuming that Handel, being a dramatist at heart, would have preferred them to be performed as opera, with costumed actors on a set.* But as earlier noted,

---

*The now elderly Winton Dean is the dean of those Handel scholars. (See his *Handel's Dramatic Oratorios and Masques*, London, New York: Oxford University Press, 1959, especially pp. 34, 37, 122-123). Quoting Mainwaring's argument that the oratorios should be staged, Dean blames the "Puritan anti-theatrical

in the Italian tradition oratorios were not acted; nor were the German Passions, which also brought influences to Handel's English oratorio. Another British Handelian, Anthony Hicks, says that "the public staging of biblical drama as drama had long been forbidden in Britain and the bishop would merely have confirmed the position."[2]

Bishop Gibson (and a number of other clergy) had adamantly opposed the masquerades in the 1720s, so it is often assumed that he must have had moral objections to theatrical productions. Interestingly, it was Heidegger who had introduced London to the masquerades, and who produced them from 1717 into the 1720s. But these two forms of entertainment were quite different entities. Opposition to the masquerades, held at first in theaters, did not necessarily mean opposition to the theater (to opera or plays).

There were specific reasons most clergy opposed the masquerades. Often referred to as "the World Upside-Down," masquerades invited attendees into a carnival-like world lavish with music, food, drink, gambling and an element of intrigue because of the disguises worn. Masks and costumes disguised the attendees' identities. While there was supposed to be a strict code of verbal behavior governing questions asked about masqueraders' identities, the eating, drinking, and gambling were often "unrestrained" and frequently the sexual tension was high. There was some degree of male-female role reversal as well as intermingling of the social classes of a type which many critics thought would reverberate with negative repercussions into every-day life. The mask and disguise could not only detach the masquerader from his or her own identity and the identity of others, but from traditional morality and social conventions.

In the historical context it is not so difficult to see why a movement opposing the masquerades developed, and why that movement might especially have involved bishops and other clergy who were concerned about the spiritual welfare of their parishioners. The opponents' attitudes also have to be seen in their eighteenth century social context. Along with their legitimate moral interest they were concerned

---

party" for "submerging this point of view" and for "at one time [coming] near to suppressing oratorio *altogether.*" His work has been highly influential. It helpfully uncovered much about the oratorios that had been forgotten or unknown by the first half of the twentieth century. But it also reveals a quite blatant anti-Christian bias. Dean dismisses the importance of Christian faith in Handel's life and sees Christianity's role negatively in English society at the time. That results in missing much of the essence of the oratorio librettos.

with the masquerades' overturning of what they saw as necessary social conventions. They viewed masquerades as an indecent European import from more "lascivious" (and in their minds not incidentally, Catholic) countries such as Italy and France. Bishop Gibson was, therefore, of the opinion (and stated it in a 1724 sermon) that the custom had been devised by France to "enslave true Englishmen by encouraging in them Licentiousness and Effeminacy." This was fairly typical, and not particularly "conservative" for the time.

So Gibson's opposition to the masquerades did not necessarily mean that he was an enemy of the theater. Still, Gibson allowed the boy choristers of the chapel choir to sing in *Esther* but they were not to take part if it were acted. Burrows speculates that Gibson's objections were "administrative" – the boys would have been prevented from carrying out their regular duties. However, it's not clear how dramatizing the oratorios with singing actors would have made much difference in terms of the boys' time: they would still be the choristers, not the role-playing soloists. It's possible that, though Gibson didn't object to theater productions *per se*, he was uncomfortable with Scripture-based stories being acted out in theaters. As we shall see, this was, and would become, be an important issue for quite a few people in London (not just clergy).

Whatever the case, *Esther* proved to be "a novel species of entertainment," as William Coxe labeled it. It newly and uniquely combined these elements: an English-language text based on biblical characters and stories (or poetic versions of those accounts), the recitative and aria style of Italian oratorio and opera (and the German Passion), and a chorus style partly newly wrought and partly based on Handel's own English church-anthem style. This "novel species" was to develop as the English oratorio, a musical form that will forever be associated with the name George Frideric Handel.

The success of *Esther*, though a catalyst for oratorio, did not set Handel on an immediate and easy road to further fame and fortune via composing biblical oratorios in English. In fact, it took him some years – almost a decade – to figure out that he really ought to abandon opera altogether and concentrate on this "novel species" he had hit upon. When he finally did that, he would be in his mid-fifties. While that decision would certainly hinge on his need to continue to make a living, it also seemed to include personal and spiritual (and probably emotional) factors.

Within a couple of weeks of Handel's performances at the King's Theater, which were his answer to the *Esther* pirates, another set of pirates went to work:

Thomas Arne this time, along with his singing daughter, Susanna.[*] The newspapers announced that *Acis and Galatea* would be presented at the Haymarket's Little Theater, right across the street from where Handel's operas were playing. Round 2: Handel responded in the same way he did regarding *Esther*.

Again, in a couple of weeks (by June 10) he had a new version of *Acis and Galatea* ready, a combination of a cantata he had written years earlier in Naples featuring these pastoral-mythological characters, the work he had written at Cannons, and some bits of his music from elsewhere. The result was a serenata that used a libretto in both English and Italian, a bilingualism odd to us but not uncommon then. It had the same positive affect on audiences that *Esther* had, and Handel would further revise this work in the next four years.[**] In retrospect, these works have significance in the broad scheme of Handel's composing life. But at the time, they appeared as musical flashes in the pan. Handel turned once again to writing a new opera (*Orlando*), which was ready in January 1732, while in the meantime the 1732-33 opera season progressed with a couple of revivals and a pasticcio.

Also meanwhile, unknown to Handel, a new generation of aristocrats was working on a scheme for their own opera company that would feature another composer. They would be known popularly as the Opera of the Nobility and would cause Handel much grief, both personal and financial. Ironically, the pasticcio Handel put together for that current season contained some music by Nicola Porpora, the primary "other composer" who would soon be working for the opposition.

Handel was still also getting opposition from across the street, where a work not only in the English language but celebrating England – *Britannia* – was

---

[*] This Thomas Arne was the father of the composer Thomas Augustine Arne. Susanna Arne became the famous (or infamous) Mrs. Cibber, whose singing Handel admired. (She married one Theophilus Cibber and her marriage broke up amidst a well-publicized adulterous scandal.) She sang a small role in *Deborah*, Handel's next oratorio, then focused on an acting career for a while. She later sang the alto arias in the first Dublin performances of *Messiah*, and two further oratorio seasons for Handel.

[**] This version carried the Italian title *Acis, Galatea e Polifemo*. The story comes from the pastoral tradition of ancient Greece. Acis and Galatea are a shepherd and shepherdess in love, They are thwarted by the cyclops Polyphemus, who kills Acis. The English version is a splendid example of Handel's "secular" vocal-choral works; there is much delightful and compelling music in it.

playing. A second irony: it was written by another transplanted German, John Frederick (Johann Friedrich) Lampe. Handel countered by rerunning *Acis and Galatea*, though a good part of it was still in Italian. Gradually more works with English texts were playing in London, pleasing audiences who were growing tired of having to read a wordbook in order to comprehend a plot. It was during this period that Aaron Hill, who had been the manager of the (then) Queen's Theater when Handel first came to town and translated the wordbook of *Rinaldo*, wrote a straightforward letter to Handel (December 5, 1732) to try to persuade him to cast aside Italian opera and develop English opera.

That theater works should communicate in English so that audiences could understand them was obviously a subject close to Hill's heart. But there was still a question in the minds of many educated people about whether English was really the kind of language that could properly combine with music to not only please the senses but carry lofty sentiments for the betterment of its listeners – which **sublime** music was supposed to do. That the English language had long been doing this in plays and poetry was apparently considered a different kettle of linguistic fish. English was "strong," but some wondered whether it was also "soft" enough.

Hill thanked Handel by letter for the gift of some opera tickets and used the occasion as an excuse to raise the opera-in-English issue. Hill thought Handel had already taken "considerable steps" towards that goal, but he urged Handel to "deliver us from our Italian bondage." Hill was convinced that

> *male and female voices may be found in this kingdom, capable of every thing, that is requisite; and, I am sure, a species of dramatic Opera might be invented, that, by reconciling reason and dignity, with musick and fine machinery, would charm the ear, and hold fast the heart, together.*[3]*

Whether Handel answered Hill in writing we don't know. Probably not. But when he did respond a couple of months later, it was to write another English oratorio,

---

*Handel had given Hill a "silver ticket" allowing him to bring two guests. Hill and two of his daughters, "both such lovers of musick," gladly used them. It was hard to say which girl was more "charm'd by the compositions of Mr. Handel," Hill told the composer. Hill had nine children: it's no wonder he didn't have an opera subscription, though he was a great lover of music, literature and the arts in general, and of Handel's music in particular. It wasn't financially difficult for Handel to give a silver ticket to a man he knew well by that time and whom he may have considered a friend, yet it is another small example of Handel's generosity.

Deborah. Yet Handel still didn't abandon Italian opera, despite declining audiences.

The opera-versus-oratorio situation is described in a fascinating pamphlet which was published in the form of an open letter to "A- - -H- - -.Esq." (presumably Aaron Hill). Entitled "See and Seem Blind: Or A Critical Dissertation on the Publick Dversions, &c," it was written sometime in 1732 after the public performance of *Esther* in May. The writer attended *Esther* expecting it to be staged as an opera. He concluded that he would appreciate oratorios only *if* they were staged (he chastised himself for being so "wicked" as to prefer one opera to twenty oratorios). He spoke his mind in a slightly sardonic, comically exaggerated manner:

> *I left the Italian Opera [Handel's opera], the House was so thin, and cross'd over the way to the English one, which was so full I was forc'd to croud in upon the Stage. This alarm'd H—l, and out he brings an Oratorio, or Religious Farce, for the duce take me if I can make any other Construction of the Word, but he has made a very good Farce of it, and put near 4000£ in his Pocket, of which I am very glad, for I love the Man for his Musick's sake.**
>
> *This being a new Thing set the whole World a Madding; Han't you be at the Oratorio, says one? Oh! If you don't see the Oratorio you see nothing, says t'other; so away goes I to the Oratorio, where I saw indeed the finest Assembly of People [aristocratic people of*

---

* "Religious farce" is a puzzling phrase here – apart from it giving the writer an opportunity to play on words. A "farce" was understood in the eighteenth century as a dramatic form intended to excite laughter. Proceeding from that came the definition we know: something ludicrously futile or insincere, a mockery. It may seem surprising, then, that the word also had liturgical connotations, and before that, a culinary meaning. "Farce" (or "farse") goes back to the thirteenth century, when it came from Old French and Latin (*farsa, farsia*), "force-meat" or "stuffing." In France and England it then rather quickly came to be used metaphorically in a liturgical context, applied to the words or phrases interpolated ("stuffed") between "Kyrie" [Lord] and "eleison" [have mercy] and other liturgical forms, e.g., "Kyrie, *genitor ingenite, vera essentia*, eleison"). Charles Burney uses the word in a liturgical-music context in his *History of Music* (II, p. 256). From its liturgical meaning, "farce" went on to be applied to the extemporaneous amplification and interludes of "impromptu buffoonery" which the actors in morality plays and other biblically based dramas began to "stuff" into their texts. The pamphlet writer calling Handel's oratorio a "religious Farce" may be combining a vague understanding of both the word's dramatic and liturgical meanings. *Esther* was not a farce in either sense, but he doesn't quite know what it was. The writer's intent and breezy style do not make him appear to be someone of strict views who would have thought *Esther* a farce in the sense of mockery of Scripture. *That* issue – related to the oratorios being performed in theaters – arose most acutely with *Messiah* because Christ himself is its subject.

"consequence"] I ever beheld in my Life , but, to my great Surprize, found this Sacred Drama a mere Consort [concert], no Scenary, Dress or Action, so necessary to a Drama; but H—l was plac'd in Pulpit, (I suppose they call that their Oratory), by him sate [the soloists] in their own Habits [clothing]; before him stood sundry sweet Singers of this poor Israel [i.e., British choral singers], and Strada gave us a Halleluiah of Half an Hour long; Senesino and Bertolli made rare work with the English tongue you would have sworn it had been Welsh; I would have wish'd it Italian, that they might have sung with more ease to themselves, since, but for the Name of English, it might as well have been Hebrew.

...I like one good Opera better than twenty Oratorio's: Were they indeed to make a regular Drama of a good Scripture Story, and perform'd it with proper Decorations, which may be done with as much Reverence in proper Habits, as in their own common Apparel; (I am sure with more Grandeur and Solemnity, and at least equal Decency) then should I change my Mind, then would the Stage appear in its full Lustre, and Musick Answer its original Design....[4]

Chapter 9
A Matter of Degrees

Deborah, Handel's second biblical oratorio, was first performed in mid-March 1733 with large forces: "near a hundred performers," said Viscount Percival. And the orchestra was at least three times bigger than the choir! The result: "It is very magnificent."[1] If there were about twenty-five choir members, plus soloists – or very possibly, including soloists – the orchestra must have consisted of seventy to seventy-five instrumentalists: far larger than the numbers we associate with the "Baroque orchestra." That choir-to-orchestra ratio has not been tried by historically informed performance advocates in our day; it is one that would certainly not work using modern instruments. It would require the mellower, softer sounds of "period instruments," and no doubt an adjustment of our aural expectations for this music.*

Like *Esther*, *Deborah* was partly newly composed and partly adapted from previous compositions: excerpts from the *Brockes Passion* and from the two *Coronation Anthems* Handel hadn't used in *Esther*. As with his other extensive borrowing (especially when borrowing from himself), the reworking and inserting in no way adversely affects the music's quality. However, Handel – or perhaps Heidegger, or both – did make a crucial and inexplicable mistake. In any case, Handel was naturally blamed because it was his music: they doubled the ticket prices, which made the performance quite expensive. And those who held "season tickets," as we would call them, were asked to pay an additional fee. Understandably, many people balked, and some number even entered the theater without the paying extra fee. A letter by a Lady Irwin to Lord Carlisle (March 31, 1733) says that Princess Anne encouraged Handel to believe that *Deborah* merited higher ticket prices. (As Viscount Percival did, Lady Irwin took note of *Deborah's* "vast number of instruments and voices." But her verdict was different: "Tis excessive noisy." Handel's music was periodically criticized as "excessive noisy.")

---

*Modern stringed instruments – and old instruments revamped for use in modern orchestras or quartets – have steel (or steel and nylon) strings strung under higher tension, on a larger bridge, than the gut strings of Handel's day were. The high tension strings, also played with a different bow than Handel knew, allow the volume needed to fill today's large concert halls (and to offset the power of modern brass instruments). Modern strings consequently produce a bigger sound and less mellow tone quality than Baroque strings produced. Comparing, say, a concerto grosso by Handel played by a modern-instrument symphony (or even chamber orchestra) with that same concerto played by one of today's many "Baroque" or period-instrument orchestras will immediately reveal the differences.

There was a further backlash. A scathing diatribe was printed in *The Craftsman* (also called *The Country Journal*), a paper radically opposed to Robert Walpole and his government policies. The attack, ostensibly against Handel, has been interpreted by historians as a parable aimed at Walpole. It was vitriolic and mean-spirited in the extreme if aimed at Handel (or any individual), and rather nasty even if aimed at politician Walpole and his Whigs. It was signed "P–lo R–li": Paolo Rolli. Handel's former librettist indeed still bore a grudge against the composer and could be meanly critical of him. However, as Deutsch points out, Rolli had never opposed Handel publicly, and there are no signs in the piece that it was written by a person who was using English as a second language.

The writer asserts that Handel had "grown so insolent upon the sudden and undeserved Increase of both [Power and Fortune] that he thought nothing to impose his imperious and extravagant Will." After a section elaborating on the theme "no music but *his own* was to be allowed," readers are told how this "Excess and Abuse of Power soon disgusted the Town [and] his Government grew odious and his *Opera*'s grew empty." Then the piece goes into detail about how he "form'd a *Plan*"– and that, "without consulting any of his *Friends* (if he has any)" – which he would make known when he was ready to, and which involved oratorio instead of opera, and at hefty prices "for his *own Benefit.*"

The article then recounts the opposition that rose against the "*insolent and rapacious Projector of this Plan*," opposition that "succeeded so well" that "the *Projector* had the Mortification to see but a very thin audience in his Oratorio." That, "they say, has thrown Him into a *deep Melancholy*, interrupted sometimes by *raving Fits*"... and "it is much question'd whether he will recover." If he were to recover, "it is not doubted but He will seek for a Retreat in his own *Country* from the general Resentment of the Town." Anthony Hicks puts this growing opposition from the elite in this perspective:

> *Handel's position as the effective controller of opera performances, with no body of aristocratic directors to govern him, appeared presumptuous in an age when musicians were regarded as servants; and the fact that he owed this position primarily to the king allowed him to be seen as a symbol of the corrupt Whig government, making him a natural focus of hostility for the new opposition groups cultivating Frederick [Prince of Wales] as a future "patriot king." [2]*

That helps explain the nature and depth of the opposition. The group of aristocrats who were then busy forming the Opera of the Nobility in competition with Handel were doing so not only because they decided they were tired of Handel's music and would prefer music from somebody else. John West, Earl of Delaware, wrote to Charles, Duke of Richmond, in January 1733 about the new opera company being contemplated, saying that "there is a Spirit got up against the Dominion of Mr. Handel." He was talking about both the man and his music, and Handel's growing musical influence, which was gradually having social repercussions.

Handel surely saw or heard about the piece in *The Craftsman*. He must have known, or his true friends pointed out, that the attack was intended for others as well as himself. But that would not have blunted the blow very much, and the wound to this man whom his friends, including the King, experienced as "so generous and so good-natured" must have gone deep.[*]

The rival opera party was headed by Frederick, Prince of Wales, who had never been in Handel's camp, partly because his father the King, whom he hated, was; and partly to spite his sister Anne, who had as much respect and affection for Handel as he did for her. That, according to John, Lord Hervey. He wrote in his *Memoirs*, "Another judicious subject of his [Frederick's] enmity was her [Anne's] supporting Handel, a German musician and composer ... against several of the nobility who had a pique to Handel, and had set up another person to ruin him; or, to speak more properly and exactly, the Prince, in the beginning of his enmity to his sister, set himself at the head of the other opera to irritate her, whose pride and passion were as strong as her brother's (though his understanding was so much weaker), and could brook contradiction, where she dared to resist it, as little as her father."

---

[*]In his *Memoirs*, 1734, Handel's contemporary Lord (John) Hervey attributes this description of Handel to King George. Hervey was a close friend of Queen Caroline's and Princess Anne's, thus his "recollections" sometimes appear to have motives in their favor. In this passage Hervey is describing, rather humorously, the intense support of the Royal Family for Handel (especially Anne, but generally excepting Frederick), and recalls conversations among them about Handel. Hervey portrays the King trying to stay out of it: "He took no other part in this affair than subscribing £1000 a year to Handel." But then George II can't resist adding this jibe about his son Frederick's attitude towards Handel: "He did not think setting oneself at the head of a faction of fiddlers a very honourable occupation for people of quality." And about Handel the King says: "The ruin of one poor fellow so generous or so good-natured would not do much honor to the undertakers, whether they succeeded or not; but the better they succeeded in it, the more he thought they would have reason to be ashamed of it."

Despite the Monarch's and Princess's support for Handel, the Prince's support for the opposition added to Handel's difficulties. When the rival company was actually formed it must have stunned Handel to learn that five men who had been his supporters as directors of the Royal Academy of Music were among the directors of the new company. These even included Richard Boyle, Earl of Burlington, in whose home Handel had lived. It was no doubt gratifying that the Duke of Chandos was not among them. Later, handbills announcing Handel's operas were torn down as fast as he could have them put up. That had to have happened with the consent of *someone* in the rival company.

When we read the contemporaneous accounts of the opposition Handel began to face, Hicks's interpretation of it as a class struggle rings true. But there was another element imbedded in those let's-put-the-man-in-his-place feelings: over and over Handel was referred to as a "foreigner" or a "German," long after he had become a naturalized citizen, and as if he were not a citizen. The embarrassing irony that a German had become the preeminent "English" composer of the age was not lost on observers, nor appreciated by some of them. And there was resentment that Handel the German could count on support from Britain's German king.

Handel faced another difficulty near the end of this 1732-33 musical season. Once again, relations between him and Senesino broke down and he fired the castrato. When the papers got wind of this, they were not sympathetic to Handel. One wrote: "The World seems greatly ASTONISH'D at so unexpected an Event; and that all true Lovers of Musick GRIEVE to see so fine a Singer dismissed, in so critical a Conjuncture." Senesino had already been negotiating with the Opera of the Nobility for some months, so he did not need to kowtow to Handel (as he saw it). In fact, all of Handel's singers except Signora Strada would go over to the competition at the end of the 1733 season when the Opera of the Nobility began to offer subscriptions.

Handel was by no means forsaken by all of his supporters. Before he could worry about what he would do in the fall season, his attention was diverted to Oxford and its university, where he was offered an honorary doctorate. Oxford's "Public Act," which included a degree ceremony and also a commemoration of benefactors, a church service and various musical performances, was reinstated in 1733 after a hiatus. Handel was asked to participate; he did, very successfully. In fact, word was out that he would receive an honorary doctorate from Oxford during the Public Act celebration.

Handel wrote his third biblical oratorio, *Athalia*, for presentation at Oxford University's Sheldonian Theater (the only Handel concert venue that still exists today, essentially unchanged). *Athalia* received two performances, along with two of *Esther* and one of *Deborah*. (One audience also heard *Acis and Galatea*, and churchgoers' worship was enhanced by Handel providing music for three Sunday services on July 8.)

Athalia, with a libretto again by Samuel Humphreys, was newly composed throughout; a pamphlet described it as "a spick and span new Oratorio." Considering the setting and circumstances in which it would be performed, Handel concluded that this occasion, of all times, was not one to reuse old material. The subject matter, based on 2 Chronicles 22 (duplicated in 2 Kings 11) and on French playwright Racine's *Athalie*, is unusual in that its main character is not a "hero of faith" but an apostate queen of Israel whose willful defiance of the LORD and attempt to wipe out the royal family and young crown prince Joash who remained faithful to the Lord results in her destruction.

The audiences were "most noble and polite," and *Athalia* was met with "utmost Applause"; it was "esteemed equal to the most celebrated of that Gentleman's Performances."[3] But once again Handel's status as both a foreigner and a mere musician became relevant. Dr. Thomas Hearnes, a tradition-bound Oxford don, noted in his diary that some players (comic actors) had been denied a venue at Oxford by the university's Vice-Chancellor, "tho' they might as well have been here as Handel and (his lowsy Crew) a great number of forreign fidlers...." The day before, Hearnes had also referred to Handel in his diary as "a forreigner (who, they say, was born in Hanover)."

Handel, of course, was not born in Hanover, but it is significant that Hearnes thought he was. (Hearnes was described as a "staunch Jacobite," one of numerous Jacobites at Oxford). As a Jacobite, Hearnes was no friend of the Hanoverian George II, and his prejudice against Handel was undoubtedly seated in both the composer's presumed Hanover connection and because of his social status: in Hearnes's mind that status was the same as his working-class "lowsy crew" of "fidlers." Hearnes said that an old man who had seen previous Oxford Acts observed to him that this Act was "the very worst that ever was." Hearnes agreed. He concluded that the Vice-Chancellor was to be commended for re-instituting the

Act, "tho' not for bringing Handel & his Company from London."[*] And Hearnes
and the old man weren't the only ones of that opinion. A pamphlet about the
Oxford Act published the following June (1734), billed as "a particular and exact
Account of that Solemnity," noted that

> one of the Royal and Ample had been saying, that truely, 'twas his
> Opinion, that the Theater was erected for other-guise Purposes, than to
> be prostituted to a Company of squeeking, bawling, outlandish
> Singsters, let the Agreement be what it would.

What was that "Agreement"? And what about that honorary doctorate?
Handel declined the degree. He wrote in a later letter, "I neither could nor would
accept the Doctor's degree, because I was overwhelmingly busy."[4] Surely Hearnes
would have found *that* an affront. Hearne's diary says only that the Vice-Chancellor
offered "encouragement" to Handel by allowing him "the benefit of the Theater
both before the Act begins and after it." Donald Burrows interprets this to suggest
that the degree issue was a red herring to get Handel to participate and "brighten
up the Act."

Dr. William Holmes was the university Vice-Chancellor (and president of
St. John's College) who initiated Handel's Oxford visit. If Burrows's interpretation
is true and Holmes got Handel to come to Oxford on that pretext, Holmes was
using Handel. He would then seem to have been fairly cynical, the more so if he was
behind floating the story to the press. (If Handel agreed to come – which he did,
of course – it would make Holmes look good.) There is no official record among
university archives of a degree being either offered or refused, so some modern
scholars have concluded that Handel wasn't actually offered the degree. Because
Handel's cryptic statement about his refusal seems a lame excuse, and the rest of the
letter is unknown, the statement is often discounted. It certainly gives the feeling that
there was more to the story, perhaps something as follows.

---

[*]Hearnes likely didn't know that Handel had worked for George I when George was Hanover's
Elector. Or if he did know, it only reinforced Handel's suspect connection to Hanover. Hearnes noted each
oratorio performance in his diary – and, each time, the cost of the tickets, which ranged from three to five
shillings. He also noted that Handel provided a Te Deum and anthems on Sunday for the service at St. Mary's
Church. And he remarked on how much money Handel is said to have made: "'Tis noted that 'twas computed,
that Mr Handel cleared by his Musick at Oxford upwards of 2000£" – probably an exaggeration, considering
ticket prices and estimated audiences. The *Norwich Gazette* also thought it important to keep its readers
informed about Handel's "take" from Oxford (reports of July 14 and July 21).

The degree ceremony was, as its very name said, a highly public act. An institution such as the University of Oxford would never risk the public embarrassment of a well-known person openly declining an offered degree in front of a distinguished audience. The university, then, would surely not offer a degree to any such person without prior discussion with the intended recipient over the circumstances of its being offered and accepted. Sometime in the spring Handel was probably approached by the university with such intent. Word got around (far more likely spread by someone at the university than by Handel himself) and various papers reported it. For example, the *Bee*, June 23, 1733, wrote: "Great Preparations are making for Mr. Handel's Journey to Oxford, in order to take his Degree of Musick; a Favour that University intends to compliment him with, at the ensuing Public Act." But when Handel told the university representatives that he had no interest in receiving the degree (whatever his reasons), the matter would have been quietly dropped. His music would still be welcome to "brighten up the Act," but no doubt he ruffled feathers with his impertinent independence, as his "betters" perceived it. (Incidentally, Maurice Greene had accepted a doctorate from Cambridge and went there to teach. Handel did not have great respect for Greene and may have questioned the basis or wisdom of that action by Cambridge University. But it is impossible to draw any real connection between his possible feelings about Green's doctorate and his own supposed rejection of a degree from Oxford.)

Seen that way, Handel's "I'm-too-busy" statement actually saved the university from public chagrin and himself the need to explain further. It also accounts for the stories about the offer and decline of a degree but no university records mentioning either one. Such a circumstance also would explain why some sources close to Handel mention it and some do not.

William Coxe, whose *Anecdotes*, as we've noted, came primarily from his stepfather John Christopher Smith Jr., who knew Handel well and worked closely with him in his last decades, said Handel was offered the doctor of music in Oxford but declined to accept it. Mainwaring says that "by this journey the damages he had suffered in his fortune were somewhat repaired, and his reputation more firmly established" (not entirely true, despite Handel's good reception, since his troubles with his opera rivals were just beginning). Hawkins mentions the Oxford Public Act and the performance of *Athalia*, the "considerable" profits from which help "in some degree to repair the damage his fortunes had sustained in that dreadful conflict in which he was then engaged," but nothing at all about a doctorate offered. Burney, too, mentions the Public Act and *Athalia*, "where he opened the organ in such a manner as astonished every hearer."[5]

Christopher Hogwood has this theory about the incident:

Could it be that Athalia *(despite its choruses in eight parts) was not considered academic enough as an Exercise, and that Handel refused to submit some dry display of counterpoint? For the rest of his life he is referred to stubbornly as "Mr. Handel" except, curiously enough, in the subscription list of Telemann's 1733* Musique de Table, *for which he was the only English subscriber and from which he borrowed wholeheartedly,where he is "Mr. Hendel, Docteur en Musique, London."*

The composer being "referred to stubbornly as 'Mr. Handel'" for the rest of his life also fits the theory put forward here about the pre-Act discussions with Handel, his refusal, and the consequent irritation that this would have caused to some among that educated elite. It is not unreasonable to make a connection from attitudes like those expressed by Hearnes and the "Royal and Ample" personage mentioned in the 1734 Oxford Act account pamphlet, to the Oxford situation that Hogwood surmises or the more general one of my theory, to the opposition of the London aristocrats behind the Opera of the Nobility.

Such attitudes came from similar social and psychological impulses. Political attitudes probably played a part as well, as Hicks suggests regarding the "Nobility" who opposed Handel. Oxford in Handel's day was a bastion of Tory Jacobites, and Handel was a Hanoverian and presumed Whig (he voted Whig in the one election of which there is still a record). Many Oxonians were Jacobites not because they were Catholics. They weren't, of course; no known Catholic, never mind Protestant Dissenters, could teach at Oxford. Rather, they were conservative supporters of the historical status quo: the divine right of the previous Stuart regime to rule (which is not to say that there was no true conviction behind their view, or at least the views of some of them). They refused to recognize the legitimacy of the kings George. Vice-Chancellor Holmes was a Tory *Hanoverian* and in Handel's camp, musically and otherwise (despite the "red herring" theory). Despite his exalted position at the university, he presumably needed at least some backing regarding offering Handel the degree. He may have had that, but he also obviously had some opposition.

Class-based attitudes infused English society and all European societies and their colonies in one way or another, as those societies were based on a hierarchical class system. It is next to impossible for modern North Americans who live in a deeply individualistic society in which money talks louder than any other voice to fully understand Handel's eighteenth century communal and class-based world. The system worked well only when people knew, and kept to, their particular inherited place. Despite some social fluidity, there could be unpleasant consequences for not measuring up to, or ignoring or stepping outside of one's class or the expected social norms. And the increasing number of people who were nudging their self-reliant way into the "better" classes would, later in the century and in the nineteenth century, cause great dis-ease among the upper classes. The inequities which stemmed from the class system would eventually cause revolts, most notably in France.

Handel's circumstances put him in an ambiguous social position. He was no individualist in the modern definition. Nor was he either ignorant of or contemptuous of proper social behavior, but his independent bent and the circumstances of his profession allowed him a personal freedom greater than most men of his class, further aided by the fact that he had no responsibility for a wife and children. This was bound to breed the contempt of some of those "above" him.

There were many people, however, who continued to delight in both the man and his music – eventually to a degree that he could never have expected or dreamed. As part of the Commemoration of Donors program during the Public Act there were orations. One of these – eleven stanzas in Latin – was about sacred music, specifically praising Handel's ability, as demonstrated in *Deborah*, to "woo pure Ears" with a "holy theme" that expresses itself in both "thunder[ing] forth Harmonious Tumult" and "a softer Variance." Handel was probably present to hear the poem recited. Translated, the last stanza says:

> But Handel's Master Touch now comes to play
> On Ears expectant. Forward Muse, be still!
> For Vic'tries, Triumphs, Pomps
> No Bard can sing so well.
> No Bard can sing so well.[6]

Once back in London, Handel had to look to the new opera season which was almost upon him, and to his new competition. In August, unable to go to Halle for a visit to his brother-in-law, niece and other relatives, he had to content himself with hearing news from them in a letter from Michaëlsen, which he answered on August 13 (in German once more). Michaëlsen updated Handel regarding matters still related to his mother's death. Michaëlsen enclosed materials from Handel's relatives in Gotha (possibly additional condolences and funeral poems) and accounts of expenditures related to his mother's estate, her tombstone and the house she left.

Michaëlsen had suggested that it might be necessary for Handel to come there himself and inspect the house, with an eye to deciding how to dispose of it. But Handel realized that that was not going to be possible any time soon. Besides, a relative – referred to as "Frau Händel" – was now living in the house and paying six Reichsthalers-a-year rent for it. The woman in question was likely the widow of Handel's nephew Georg Christian Händel (son of his half-brother Karl). She was apparently not well off, and Handel responded in kindness and compassion to her situation. He allowed her to live there rent-free as long as she liked. "I could wish that in the future she might be absolved from paying such, as long as she likes to remain in occupation," he told his brother-in-law. And after the widow's death, Handel remembered her son in his will.* Once again, this letter reveals Handel's generosity and his obvious desire to maintain contact with his extended family.

Handel managed to assemble the singers he needed for 1733-34, including Anna Maria Strada (who did not defect to the other opera group), Margherita Durastanti (who sang for him years earlier in Italy), and Giovanni Carestini (an excellent new castrato who would be a direct competitor for Senesino). Heidegger, by now an old man, was still in the picture as co-manager. Though Handel was preoccupied early in the summer with his Oxford trip and then with gathering singers, he managed to compose a new opera (*Arianna in Creta*). But to start the season on October 30 he presented pasticcios and a revival of *Ottone*, which he had written fourteen years earlier. If it seems odd that Handel would use pasticcios instead of his own newly composed operas, he may have done so because they contained the music of composers writing in the "modern" style, the style with which Porpora – writing for the Opera of the Nobility – was associated. And two of Handel's singers had sung the leading roles in the original Italian productions of *Semiramide* and *Arbace*, so Handel was giving the London audience an up-to-date taste of what was being sung in Italy.[7]

For two months there was no competition: the Opera of the Nobility didn't

---

*The will, drawn up June 1, 1750, refers to Christian Gottlieb Händel as a "cousin." Born in 1714, he lived in Copenhagen. Handel bequeathed him £100, and later an additional £200. But Handel outlived him, so the £300 intended for Christian Gottlieb he transfered to the man's eldest sister, and designated the same amount for a second sister.

open its season until December 29, at Lincoln's Inn Fields, a smaller theater. When they did open, Porporo brought out an opera (*Arianna in Nasso*) based on the same characters as Handel's new opera, which wouldn't be heard until January 26. It seems they may have had at least one spy in Handel's camp. This rivalry would be a serious one. However, Handel's *Arianna in Creta* was well-received, *Deborah* was successfully revived, Carestini held his own against Senesino, and in general Handel survived this first season of competition in good shape.

Meanwhile, each February, Handel's music was still benefitting the Sons of the Clergy, heard at their annual festival. Collections of Handel's music were also being published periodically by John Walsh of London, who was becoming Handel's exclusive publisher. Two such collections came out on Handel's forty-ninth birthday: "The Favourite Songs in the Opera, call'd Ariadne; also the Favourite Songs in Arbaces; with their Symphonies in Score" and "The celebrated Te Deum and Jubilate for Voices and Instruments; as it was perform'd at St. Paul's" (at the Sons of the Clergy festival). A month later, the marriage of Anne, Handel's favorite princess and now his friend, to Willem, Prince of Orange, was also an occasion at which his music shone.

About this time Mary Pendarves wrote a comment to her sister describing an oratorio she heard by Porporo, *Davide e Bersabea (David and Bathsheba)*, with a libretto by Paolo Rolli. An ardent Handel supporter, and his friend and neighbor, Mrs. Pendarves was obviously checking out the competition. She wrote on March 28, 1734; Handel's *Deborah* was not revived until April 2, so she couldn't specifically comment on it:

> Yesterday in the afternoon Phil and I went to the oratorio at Lincoln's Inn, composed by Porpora, an Italian, famous for church music, who is now in England: it is a fine solemn piece of music, but I confess I think the subject too solemn for the theater. To have words of piety made use of only to introduce good music is reversing what it ought to be, and most of the people that hear the oratorio make no reflection on the meaning of the words, though God is addressed in the most solemn manner; some of the choruses and recitatives are extremely fine and touching, but they say it is not equal to Mr. Handel's oratorio of Esther or Deborah.[8]

Mary Pendarves's correspondence confirms her as a thoughtful woman who took faith seriously. She counted it important to reflect on an oratorio's biblical words and was disturbed that many people around her seemed not to engage in such reflection, an issue that would become very important for *Handel's* oratorios. The libretto was in Italian, but the story of David and Bathsheba would have been thoroughly familiar to audiences. If the audience Mrs. Pendarves described could be assumed to be typical, that many people did not seem to consider the meaning of the story shouldn't be surprising at this early stage of oratorios in England. They were not used to doing that, being accustomed to operas in Italian whose mostly unintelligible texts they had learned to ignore while simply enjoying the music.

While Handel spent most of his time composing and professionally engrossed in music in one way or another, music also offered recreation for him. He and Mattheson as young men in Hamburg had played organs at all hours, in their shirt sleeves; or Handel would play after evening services at St. Paul's for his own pleasure (though usually acquiring an audience) then retire with some of the gentlemen of the choir to the pub a few hundred yards from the cathedral.

An interesting, if brief, picture of Handel in a social and recreational-music setting also comes from Mary Pendarves. Writing to her sister Ann in the spring of this first season of "dueling operas," Mary described a gathering at her home when Handel was one of the guests. It presents an appealing glimpse of Handel in a setting in which we rarely get to see him and provides a miniature portrait of home-grown entertainment and social life among upper-middle-class friends in 1730s London, and of a close sibling bond between two sisters and a brother in that era:

> *I must tell you of a little entertainment of music I had last week; I never wished more heartily for you and my mother than on that occasion. I had Lady Rich and her daughter, Lady Cath. Hanmer and her husband, Mr. and Mrs. Percival, Sir John Stanley and my brother, Mrs. Donellan, Strada and Mr. Coot. Lord Shaftesbury begged of Mr. Percival to bring him, and being a profess'd friend of Mr. Handel (who was here also) was admitted; I never was so well entertained at an opera! Mr. Handel was in the best humour in the world, and played lessons and accompanied Strada and all the ladies that sang from seven o'clock till eleven. I gave them tea and coffee, and about half an hour after nine had a salver brought in of chocolate, mulled white wine and biscuits. Everybody was easy and seemed pleased, Bunny [Mary and Ann's brother, Bernard] staid with me after the company was gone, eat a cold chick with me, and we chatted till one o' the clock.* [9]

112

The odd habit – which Mary Pendarves demonstrates in this letter – of writing to one's sister or brother about another sibling or one of their parents, and referring to the other sibling or parent as *my* brother (sister) or *my* mother (father) instead of *our* brother, *our* mother, was not uncommon in the eighteenth century. Handel's friends the Harrises do the same in their letters.

Mary had told her sister ahead of time that she intended to have this party, and that "if Lady S. [Judith, Countess of Sunderland] would lend her harpsichord, then Lady S. would also be at the party." (If Lady S. refused, we might wonder whether she would have been disinvited.) Almost all the guests were musicians, professional or amateur. Strada, of course, was Handel's loyal opera singer. Most of the others were amateurs: Philip Percival played viola and composed; Lady Catherine Hanmer sang and played the harpsichord; "her husband," Sir Thomas Hanmer, played violin. He was a former Speaker of the House of Commons, a Tory but a Hanoverian, who later became known as the editor of a Shakespeare edition (note that Mary Pendarves doesn't mention him by name).

Lord Shaftesbury, was the Fourth Earl of Shaftesbury. He would become a solid friend of Handel's and an enthusiastic public supporter – not to be confused with his father, the Third Earl, the philosopher and proponent of "natural religion" (they were both named Anthony Ashley Cooper). Mrs. Donellan was a personal friend of Mary Pendarves' and a relative of the Percivals. (Handel would leave her fifty guineas in his will). Mr. Coot was an Irish gentleman, also a friend of Mary's. (After Mary married Rev. Patrick Delany in 1743 they moved to Ireland. Delany was made Dean of Down through the interest of relatives of Mary's first husband, Alexander Pendarves. Jonathan Swift described his friend Delany to Alexander Pope [letter, Jan. 7, 1737] as "one of the few men not spoilt by an excess of fortune," and praised his "hospitality and generosity which often left him without money as before.") Mary would regret the move to Dublin from the point of view of no longer hearing Handel's music so regularly and under his own direction. The Delanys would return to London periodically, however, and whenever they did Mary attended whatever oratorio was being performed. Sir John Stanley was Mary and Ann's uncle – the person who introduced Mary to Handel when she was a girl, in 1711. (He was a customs commissioner, not the composer John Stanley.) Mary and Ann's brother "Bunny" was Bernard Granville, who would also become one of Handel's close friends and faithful supporter in the coming years. The "lessons" Handel played would have been some of his harpsichord pieces, which had already been published (though he undoubtedly played them from memory).

Two-and-a-half weeks later in another letter of Mary Pendarves expressed concerned with London's declining interest in Handel's operas. She reported to her sister that that very evening she would attend for the second time "an opera of Mr. Handel's and a charming one [a revival of *Sosarmes*], yet, I dare say it will be almost empty! 'Tis vexatious to have *such music* neglected." A year later Mary would be telling the famous writer and divine Jonathan Swift, "Our operas have given much cause of dissension; men and women have been deeply engaged; and no debate in the House of Commons has been urged with more warmth." She would mention contentious disputes about the merits of the composers and singers, and feared it would be the death of the art form.[10]

At the close of that current season (1733-34), the five-year agreement that allowed Handel to use the sets and costumes and the King's Theater came to an end. Heidegger, seventy-five years old, then disengaged from his connection with Handel. The Opera of the Nobility quickly took over the King's Theater, but Heidegger remained at the theater as manager, and so began to work with Handel's rivals. Undaunted, at least outwardly, Handel moved over to John Rich's theater at Covent Garden, which was more or less newly built, having opened in December 1732. Rich then ran plays three nights a week alternating with two nights of Handel opera. The Opera of the Nobility, meanwhile, had managed to snag Carlo Broschi as their star. Broschi, known as Farinelli, by most accounts was considered the greatest castrato anyone had ever heard. To maintain an audience, Handel needed to counter with something unusual. For the 1735-36 season he engaged the French dancer Marie Sallé and her troupe to provide ballet music for some of the operas.[*]

In February, Handel's long-time friend Dr. Arbuthnot died at age sixty-seven. Samuel Johnson described this exceptional man as

> *estimable for his learning, amiable for his life, and venerable for his*
> *piety. Arbuthnot was a man of great comprehension, skilful in his pro-*

---

[*]Madame Sallé was well known in France (Deutsch notes that Voltaire dedicated some verses to her). Her costume, which would now be perfectly ordinary now for a ballet dancer, was unusual, even sensational, in 1734 London: "She ventured to appear without skirt, without a dress, in her natural hair, and with no ornament on her head. She wore nothing in addition to her bodice and under petticoat but a simple robe of muslin arranged in drapery after the model of a Greek statue." (London correspondent of the *Mercure de France*, March 15, 1734, quoted in the *Grove Dictionary of Music*, 1st ed., Deutsch, p. 387).

fession, versed in the sciences, acquainted with ancient literature, and able to animate his mass of knowledge by a bright and active imagination; a scholar with great brilliancy of wit; a wit, who, in the crowd of life, retained and discovered a noble ardour of religious zeal.[11]

It would be easy to understand Handel mourning the loss of such a man and such a friend.* Just having passed his own fiftieth birthday, and now having to constantly readjust to audience whims, Handel may have experienced some moments when, with Ecclesiastes' Preacher, he began to wonder if all is vanity. If so, he could console himself with assurances from his own current oratorios that God never abandons his people. As *Athalia* confesses in its final chorus: "His chosen people are His chosen care." Or from *Esther*, expressing the assurance Handel himself had confessed more than once when confronted with death: "Thus pleas'd is th' Almighty to dispense,/ In ways unknown to us, His providence."

Because the theaters were closed to plays and opera on Wednesdays and Fridays during Lent (and all during Holy Week), Handel now turned to the three Old Testament oratorios he had already written (*Athalia* had not yet been heard in London), which he presented on those Lenten Wednesdays and Fridays. As he gradually abandoned opera he was also moving away from using castrati as soloists (they sang male roles, but in the soprano or alto range). Castrato roles were normally associated with heroic mythological characters, and the castrati were Italian, and thus sang most comfortably, or only, in their native language. The tenor voice, so valued today, was not accorded as much esteem at that time. In fact, before Handel's oratorios, arias written for tenor soloists were rare. However, during this 1734-35 season, the fine tenor John Beard became one of Handel's regular oratorio singers, and Beard would sing in Handel oratorios for the rest of the composer's life.

An added attraction during the Lenten oratorio concerts was another "novel species" Handel invented: the organ concerto. In them, the organ rather than one of the instruments of the orchestra takes the role of soloist. Handel began to devise these concertos and present them during the intermissions between the parts or acts of the oratorios. Naturally, he himself was the organist, and improvised much of the concertos' solo parts.

---

*Arbuthnot (with Alexander Pope) is thought to have provided Handel with the libretto for the initial version of *Esther*.

115

Though Handel wrote nearly every type of music current in the first half of the eighteenth century (even while being preoccupied much of the time with his operas and oratorios), he always maintained his personal love of the organ, the instrument that played so vital a role in his boyhood, early adulthood and Lutheran heritage. There are many amazed remarks by Handel's English contemporaries about his organ playing. Hawkins describes Handel's playing of the concertos:

> When he gave a concerto, his method in general was to introduce it with a voluntary movement on the diapasons, which stole on the ear in a slow and solemn progression; the harmony close wrought, and as full as could possibly be expressed; the passages concatenated with stupendous art, the whole at the same time being perfectly intelligible, and carrying the appearance of great simplicity. This kind of prelude was succeeded by the concerto itself, which he executed with a degree of spirit and firmness that no-one ever pretended to equal.

> Such in general was the manner of his performance; but who shall describe its effects on his enraptured auditory? Silence, the truest applause, succeeded the instant that he addressed himself to the instrument, and that so profound, that it checked the respiration, and seemed to controul the functions of nature, while the magic of his touch kept the attention of his hearers awake only to those enchanting sounds to which it gave utterance.[2]

Most English organs at this time had no pedals, so the English style of organ composition and playing was quite different than that in Germany and the Netherlands, and necessarily not as complex (if written out, most of it is sight-readable by a competent organist). English audiences were unaware of the organ's greatest exemplar – Bach – and even people like Burney and Hawkins seemed to have no had real conception of German organ playing in general, much less of Bach's astonishing organ mastery. In the already cited 1788 comparison of Bach and Handel (probably written, as noted, by Carl Philip Emmanuel Bach), the author reacts to this statement in Burney's account of the Handel centennial celebration in Westminster Abbey, 1784 (a year early): "In [Handel's] full, masterly, and excellent *organ-fugues* ... he has surpassed ... even Sebastian Bach and other of his countrymen...." C.P.E. Bach argues for his father's superiority as a composer of organ fugues, and for his superiority as an organist (which we can't judge except from contemporaneous descriptions and by relating the ability needed to play Bach's music to the music itself).

C.P.E argues that because the pedals are such an essential part of organs in Germany, and German organ music makes integral use of them, the pedal parts always being independent of the manuals, "an Englishman can have no clear conception of the true and essential qualities of an organist." He asserts that in Handel's organ music "everywhere the pedal lets its cards be trumped [that is, it does no more than strengthen the bass] and everything can be played on the manuals alone without any weakening of the effect." He asks (rhetorically, from his point of view): "Should not Handel have disposed at least one piece among his organ works in such manner that the masters across the sea, too, could tell that he measured up to their higher art? Should he not have written and left behind in Germany a single work worthy of the German organ?"

~

Despite the fertile diversity of Handel's imagination that produced the embarrassment of riches which flowed from his pen, either audiences were becoming blind (or deaf) to it, or they simply had too many diversions to choose from.[*] Attendance throughout that performance season fluctuated drastically. While there were still heartening successes in individual works, the enterprise as a whole – continuing to focus on Italian opera, with or without ballet – just wasn't paying, for Handel or for the Opera of the Nobility. Near the beginning of that 1734-35 season (November 2), Lord Hervey had written to a friend enumerating London's theaters, telling him that "Heidegger had computed the expense of these shows, and proves in black & white that the undertakers must receive 7600 odd pounds [per season] to bear their charges, before they begin to become gainers." The season's losses for both opera companies were huge: Handel's were estimated at £9000, and the Opera of the Nobility's at £10,000.

---

[*]London then had five theaters. They accommodated plays, operas, and plays in French: the King's (Haymarket), Covent Garden, Drury Lane, Goodman's-Fields, the Little Theater at the Haymarket. Lincoln's Inn Fields was no longer in use.

Chapter 10
So Great a Shock: Palsy, Lunacy and Recovery

A rumor circulating in spring 1736 flew all the way to Paris:

Mr. Handel...had undertaken to keep his theater going in face of the opposition of all the English nobility. He flattered himself – unjustifiably – that his reputation would always bring him a sufficient audience; but deprived of this support he has incurred so much ruinous expense and so many beautiful operas that were a total loss, that he finds himself obliged to leave London and return to his native land."[1]

It is unlikely that Handel seriously considered a permanent return to Germany, but he may have intended to visit his relatives after the end of that dismal season. Two English papers reported: "Mr. Handel goes to spend the Summer in Germany, but comes back against Winter, and is to have Concerts of Musick next Season, but no Opera's." They were right (more or less) about the coming season, but not about how Handel would spend his summer: he "took the waters" at Tunbridge Wells, a common means of relieving stress and "curing"ailments.

Meanwhile, he turned down Johann Mattheson's second request for biographical material; he had declined the first request sixteen years earlier. He now wrote Mattheson, "To put together events of any period of my life...is impossible for me, since my continual application to the service of this Court and the Nobility keeps me from any other business." This July 18/29, 1735, letter is often seen as a brush-off – presuming that Handel no longer saw Mattheson as a friend and could not be bothered to contribute to his *Grundlage einer Ehren-Pforte*; and because it is the second time Handel said no. The first time (February 24, 1719) he had pleaded "many pressing affairs," but said he'd do it when he was "a little freer" so that Mattheson would "be assured of the esteem and consideration" in which Handel held him. In the context of that letter, this seems more than mere politeness, and Handel did take the time to write on a musical matter Mattheson had asked about.

Forward to 1735: Handel's increasingly precarious financial/social position and growing stress were preoccupying him. Understandably, he was not in a frame of mind to take a careful, time-consuming look back at his life to that point in order to write a professional memoir for Mattheson. He tells Mattheson that he regrets his inability to comply, even while assuring his friend that he has "every esteem for your great talents." Mattheson did have great talent as a music theorist and writer on music; still, this could be interpreted as flattery, spurred by a guilty conscience sixteen years in the making. But Handel was more straightforward than that; if anything, his forthrightness sometimes got him into trouble and he appeared "rough" by English standards (Burney's word). Handel was writing to someone he had known well, to a fellow German of the same social class, someone to whom he would not likely prevaricate. And apart from Handel and Mattheson's ultimately harmless teenaged duel, there's nothing to indicate that the friends had had a falling out. They had likely just drifted apart, as long-distance friends often do. Their camaraderie had been based on each having a fellow musician to talk and socialize with, but it likely did not consist (at least in Handel's perception) of a profound meeting of the minds, compatibility of personality and depth of affection such as Handel and Telemann shared. Thus, alas, we have no detailed auto-biography of Handel's career as set down by Mattheson.

Also that summer of 1735, and significantly for Handel's trek down the road to oratorio, he received from Charles Jennens the libretto for an oratorio Jennens hoped Handel would write. No, not *Messiah* (not yet). It was probably *Saul*, though Handel's reply doesn't mention it by name.* However, Handel wouldn't get around to writing the music for *Saul* for another three years (September 1738). Jennens was a devout Anglican, an upper-middle-class lover of music, literature and art who read widely, collected books and music for his library and was an excellent Shakespeare scholar. He was also an acute student of the Bible. He lived 120 miles northwest of London in Gopsall (county of Leicestershire). He had a townhouse in London so that he could attend the annual concert seasons, a common practice among those who could afford it. He was a connoisseur of Handel's music, and a friend, if a periodically troublesome one.

Since Handel was unable to continue with another season as ambitious as

---

*Handel's letter to Jennens will interest language buffs. In both spelling and construction it stands up to many letters of the period by native English-speakers but it shows some grammatical peculiarities. Nouns were often capitalized in eighteenth century English (as they were, and are, in German) and spelling fluctuated (Dr. Johnson had not yet written his dictionary). There are three "logical" spelling irregularities: "extreamly"; "Direktion," (a Germanization); and "allways." Handel's punctuation is faulty (a habit of native English writers also). Several times he uses a comma when he should have used a period, but his English subject-verb agreement and word order are flawless. His sense of musical economy didn't extend to his usage of English: even by the verbose standards of the time he could be accused of run-on sentences. Yet his one very long sentence of four clauses (two independent, two dependent) has a kind of lilting rhythm. There are nine surviving letters to Jennens, more than to any other single correspondent.

the one he had just mounted, he was forced to modify his approach for 1735-36. That is the sense in which the newspapers were right about his plans. He would wait to start his season until what would have normally been the second half of the musical "year." He would concentrate on English-language works (*Alexander's Feast*; *Esther*; *Acis and Galatea*) with singers who were available, adding some orchestral works, concertos and an Italian cantata. Then, when the opera season in Italy finished, he would be able to contract with some additional Italian singers to continue his season with several operas, both new (*Atalanta*) and revived (*Ariodante*).

The newly composed *Alexander's Feast* was the unusual work in this group and was another important step down the road to English oratorio full time, though Handel probably still wouldn't have recognized that. *Alexander's Feast* is not an oratorio but an exuberant ode to the patron saint of music, Cecilia, with a text by one of Britain's greatest poets, John Dryden (1631-1700). It has elements that characterize Handel's oratorios, especially stirring choruses.

A January 24, 1736, letter from Lord Shaftesbury to James Harris after Handel paid the Earl a visit at his London home shows Handel to have been exuberant about *Alexander's Feast*, which he had just finished. He was "in high spirits," a phrase Mary Pendarves used of him also, and a refrain in the letters of the Shaftesbury/Harris circle when Handel was engaged with his music or planning a concert season and not being harassed by the opera faction. Handel played and sang through "almost his whole new peice [sic] which is not yet transcrib'd from his own hand," marveled Shaftesbury as Handel's audience of one. "Handel was so eager to play over his peice to me, I had hardly any discourse with him."[2]

The idea for *Alexander's Feast* came from Newburgh Hamilton, who would be the librettist for several of Handel's future oratorios: *Samson*, the *Occasional Oratorio*, and probably *Joshua*.* Hamilton by now knew what Handel could do with the English language, and how inspiring his choruses were. Hamilton felt that Handel was the only one "capable of doing it [i.e., English] Justice; whose

---

*The author of the libretto for *Joshua* has long been unknown. Ruth Smith notes in *Handel's Oratorios and Eighteenth Century Thought* (Cambridge: Cambridge University, 1995) that in conversations with her, Merlin Channon "has persuasively conjectured that it was Newburgh Hamilton" (p. 410, n1). Hamilton was steward to the Earl of Strafford and his family.

Compositions have long shewn, that they can conquer even the most obstinate Partiality, and inspire Life into the most senseless Words." Hamilton as librettist divided Dryden's text into recitatives, arias and choruses, and added an ending that goes beyond Dryden's poem. (Handel may have known that two previous composers had set Dryden's famous ode of 1697: Jeremiah Clark, in the same year Dryden wrote it, and Thomas Clayton, in 1711).

With his own twenty-eight-line ode, Hamilton dedicated his libretto "to Mr. Handel, On his Setting to MUSICK Mr. *Dryden's* "FEAST OF ALEXANDER." Much of what Hamilton said about the effect of this specific piece Handel's audiences would apply to the oratorios as well. And there would be numerous other poems addressed to and about Handel that marvel at the sublimity of his music. Hamilton said, in effect, that ordinary music – the stuff that charms nature – could be left to others, but Handel's music can "improve the heart":

Be ever Yours (my Friend) the God-like Art,
To calm the Passions, and improve the Heart;
The Tyrant's Rage, and Hell-born Pride controul,
Or sweetly sooth to Peace the mourning Soul;
With martial Warmth the Hero's Breast inspire,
Or fan new-kindling Love to chaste Desire.[3]

~

Handel himself attended at least one of the operas staged by the Opera of the Nobility in the 1735-36 season, in November, before his own season began. In Lord Hervey's view, his presence "seemed in silent triumph to insult this poor dying Opera in its agonies" (the opera was *Adriano in Siria* by Francesco Maria Veracini, libretto by famous and ubiquitous Pietro Metastasio). The experience was a "yawning four hours" of the "longest and dullest Opera that ever the enobled ignorance of our present musical Governors ever inflicted on the ignorance of an English audience," quipped Hervey. However, he had harsh words for Handel too, calling him "as great a fool for refusing to compose, as Veracini had shown himself by composing, nobody feeling their own folly, though they never overlook other people's...."[4] Lord Hervey apparently also thought Handel a fool for not starting the season as normal, and thereby giving the Opera of the Nobility immediate competition (obviously Hervey didn't know Handel's plans for his season). And perhaps he felt Handel was foolish for not composing in English (*Alexander's Feast* hadn't been heard – or completed – yet), providing even better competition.

Hervey continued:

That fellow having more sense, more skill, more judgement, and more expression in music than anybody, and being a greater fool in common articulation and in every action than Mrs. P—t or Bishop H—s, is what has astonished me a thousand times. And what his understanding must be, you may easily imagine, to be undone by a profession of which he is certainly the ablest professor, though supported by the Court: and in a country where his profession is better paid than in any other country in the world. His fortune in music is not unlike my Lord Bolingbroke's in politics. The one has tried both theaters, as the other has tried both Courts. They have shone in both, and been ruined in both; whilst everyone owns their genius and sees their faults, though nobody either pities their fortune or takes their part.

Henry St. John, Viscount Bolingbroke (1678-1751) was a Tory and Deist, a notorious libertine, vehemently anti-Whig and anti-Dissent, an erstwhile Member of Parliament and Secretary of State who moved in and out of political favor. He was exiled to France by George I for his role in peace negotiations with France and his intrigues with the Jacobites. He was as contemptuous of Roman Catholicism as he was of Protestant Christianity; when he supported the Jacobites it was for political reasons. He was a superb orator and an excellent writer and political analyst, but no profound philosophical thinker. While mounting campaigns against Robert Walpole's corruption, he was himself morally unprincipled and gained a reputation for treachery. He was pardoned in 1723; he returned to England but never recovered his peerage and seat in the House of Lords. He went back to France from 1735-42, then came to England once more. In England Bolingbroke wrote anti-Whig political pieces for *The Craftsman* (the publication whose nasty attack of Handel, described earlier, was also an attack on Walpole). Bolingbroke's best-known work is *The Idea of a Patriot King* (the "Patriot King" idea is apropos to some of Handel's oratorios.) His *Letters on the Study of History* were a no-holds-barred attack on biblically orthodox Christianity. Typical of Deists, he believed in a God so vastly distant, omniscient and omnipotent as to be *incommunicado* and essentially unknowable. Thus, he believed, the Bible does not reveal God in any real way, prayer is useless, Jesus is not divine, and none of this adds anything to what can be discovered by Reason. Bolingbroke wrote his Diest views in while France but when they were published in England posthumously (1754) they caused widespread controversy and dismay. Such ideas, and Deism in general, were thoroughly unacceptable to the great majority of the population.

No person of integrity would have wanted to be compared to Bolingbroke. In comparing Handel and Bolingbroke, Hervey was noting a superficial similarity in circumstances summed up in his line: "Everyone owns their genius and sees their faults, though nobody either pities their fortune or takes their part." Whether or not some other aristocrats saw Handel like that, his contemporaries in general did not. Handel would later commit what was considered a grievous *faux pas* that further offended his antagonists among the nobility. Handel's foolishness, in Hervey's view, may additionally have consisted in his unorthodox refusal to submit to the desires of those influential noblemen and -women.

During this 1735-36 season the use of Handel's music for charitable purposes began to expand. On March 31, for the first of many annual performances, the "distressed Sick Poor" treated by Mercer's Charitable Hospital in Dublin benefitted from Handel's music. For a half guinea each, audience members were admitted to St. Michan's Church to hear the *Utrecht Te Deum and Jubilate* and one of the *Coronation Anthems*, never before performed in Dublin. Back in London, Handel's *Water Music* was also doing benefit duty. The *London Daily Post* of March 27, 1736, reported that a "Company of Comedians" (comic actors) would present a tragedy and a farce that day at Covent Garden to benefit one of their members, "the Whole concluding with Mr. Handell's Water-Musick."*

April of 1736 witnessed the marriage of Frederick, Prince of Wales, to one of his German cousins, and Handel provided an anthem for the occasion: *Sing unto God* (HWV 263).** Despite Frederick's heading the other opera camp, he was, after all, the Crown Prince in the Royal Family whose "servant" Handel technically was. Even so, when Handel's new opera *Atalanta* opened two weeks later on May 12, Frederick made a show of *not* being there on opening night.[5] Even while

---

*The tragedy (*Abramule, or Love and Empire* by Joseph Trapp) and farce (*A City Ramble, or, The Humours of the Compter* by Charles Knipe) were both immensely popular and had been running for years: since 1704 and 1715, respectively.

**The "HWV" designation is attached to all of Handel's works as a way of identifying them. It stands for *Handel Werke Verzeignis*: Handel Works List.

Frederick was at least the nominal head of the opera competition group his household accounts show that he was giving Handel financial support. He appears to have been trying to play both sides of the court (figuratively and literally).

The 1735-36 season wasn't any more successful than Handel's previous season was; nor was the Opera of the Nobility thriving. In May 1736, one Benjamin Victor wrote to a singer friend of Handel's in Dublin with this glum prediction: "The two opera houses are, neither of them, in a successful way; and it is the confirmed opinion that this winter will compleat your friend Handel's destruction, as far as the loss of his money can destroy him."[6]

That summer, at least briefly, Handel was afforded the opportunity to think of something else, something pleasurable. Johanna Friederika Michaëlsen, his dearly loved twenty-five-year-old goddaughter and niece, was to marry. The groom would be Dr. Johann Ernst Flörcke, a law professor at the University of Halle. Handel's brother-in-law wrote, not merely to inform him, but to ask his approval of the marriage as Johanna Freiderika's uncle and godfather. As Johanna's father, Michaëlsen was the only one who needed to agree to the marriage, strictly speaking, but his gracious gesture is an indication that the esteem in which Handel held Michaëlsen was reciprocated by Michaëlsen towards Handel. Handel happily answered Michaëlsen's letter on August 17/28 (he returns to writing in French):

> As I now have no nearer relative than my dear niece and have always loved her particularly, you could not apprise me of more welcome news than that she is to marry a person of such distinguished character and attainments.... The sound upbringing which she owes to you will assure not only her own happiness, but also afford you some consolation; and you will not doubt but that I shall add my voice thereto to the best of my ability.[7]

His approval was accompanied by a substantial wedding gift. He was unstintingly generous despite his increasingly shaky financial situation: for the bride, a solitaire diamond ring with a stone "of the first water" weighing "a little over $7^{1/2}$ grains"; and for the groom, a gold watch and chain by Delharmes and two seal rings, one of amethyst, the other of onyx.

~

For the next nearly five years Handel would appear to straddle the fence between opera and oratorio, until in 1742 *Messiah* would change his life (and ours). Despite positive audience reaction to every English-language work he had yet written, he still seemed uncomfortable relying on English oratorios and other English works to make a living. He wrote new operas, revived old ones. He rejuvenated an Italian serenata, presented a pasticchio, reran an English ode and reprised *Esther* (performed with the addition of several Italian arias!). He even revised and enlarged his first Italian oratorio, written as a young man in Italy, *La Resurrezione*. These newest operas were not his best work. He even experimented with inserting arias by other composers into one of his own operas. For a time, the bad feeling between the Opera of the Nobility and Handel subsided somewhat. Perhaps they both felt, though refused to acknowledge, that they were on the same sinking ship.

In all this, Handel was not recommitting himself to Italian opera. He was looking for whatever ways he could find to please audiences – except going to all-English fare. Meanwhile, Briton's English-born composers were presenting biblical works in English. William Boyce's *David's Lamentation Over Saul and Jonathan* was presented at the Devil Tavern. When Handel heard about it, he joked, "De toctor Creen is gone to the Teufel" ("Dr. Greene [has] gone to the Devil.")[*]

One chilly night in November 1736 while having dinner together, Mary Pendarves and her brother Bernard Granville compared notes on what the Opera of the Nobility was offering and what Handel was offering, and Mary critiqued the singers on both sides. There was no doubt in her mind who had the far superior season, and her description is amusingly to the point:

> They have Farinelli, Merighi, with no sound in her voice, but
> thundering action – a beauty with no other merit; and one Chimenti, a
> tolerable good woman with a pretty voice, and Montagnana, who roars
> as usual! With this band of singers and dull italian operas, such as you
> almost fall asleep at, they presume to rival Handel – who has Strada,
> that sings better than ever she did; Gizziello, who is much improved
> since last year; and Annibali who has the best part of Senesino's voice
> and Caristini's, with a prodigious fine taste and good action![8]

Mrs. Pendarves also wrote of Handel being at her house again: "He was here two or three mornings ago and *played to me both the overtures* [to his new

---

[*]This remark was not recorded until the nineteenth century, by Charles Knight in London, published 1841-1844. Despite that, the anecdote rings true of Handel, both for its wit and for the use of the phrase "gone to the devil," which Handel used frequently in various forms (cf. Burney).

operas *Arminio* and *Giustino*], which are charming." Mary Pendarves and Handel seemed to know each other well enough now for him to drop by periodically (her letter sounds as if the visit was impromptu).

Within five weeks, Bernard Granville would also live in Handel's and Mary's neighborhood. After Bernard moved in, Mary jested to Ann about "going home with my neighbor Granville" after being "regaled with Mr. Handel's new opera" at its rehearsal that morning.[9] But just three months later, Mary informed her mother, "Mr Handel will not compose any more!" She meant that Handel would not compose any more operas. (It turned out she wasn't entirely right about that.) In the same written breath she said, "Oratorios begin next week, to my great joy, for they are the highest entertainment to me."

It may seem odd to some readers that Mary Pendarves would call works with biblical texts "the highest entertainment." In saying that, she was of course not disparaging the oratorios as incapable of being **sublime** works. Rather, her being a woman of faith was why she found them the highest entertainment: for her as a Christian listener they consisted of biblical truth given exquisite musical tangibility by Handel. She was responding to the oratorios' ability to address and move her spiritually, emotionally and intellectually. And she voiced a view and experience with the oratorios which many Christians from then to now thoroughly understand. Her letters often expressed delight in the beauty of Handel's latest opera (though occasionally she isn't impressed, particularly not with *Lotario*), but she never referred to any of the operas in the particular way she praised the oratorios. In the same letter she had just said, "Music is certainly a pleasure that may be reckoned intellectual." All three elements – spiritual, emotional, intellectual – were important to her, and she felt them all particularly embodied by Handel's oratorios.

The mixed bag of music Handel was then offering in his attempt to please audiences seemed to reveal a double mind in him. Mulling over what looked like a shaky future was likely robbing him of sleep. His continued outward confidence did not betray that the growing uncertainty of his situation was creating an apprehensive tension in him that was about to painfully, shockingly manifest itself.

Handel was a strong man, physically and emotionally, but stress was taking its toll: in April 1737 he suddenly lost the use of his right hand and arm through paralysis. The paralysis came on without warning, according to Handel's friend Shaftesbury. On April 26, by which time Handel must have been afflicted for some days, Shaftesbury told his cousin James Harris, who was also a friend of Handel's:

"'Tis his right arm that is struck[,] which was taken ill in a minute."[10] Shaftesbury's account to Harris is the earliest mention of Handel's 1737 illness. Shaftesbury worried about what it would mean for the composer's future:

I was near an hour with Handel yesterday[;] he is in no danger upon the whole though I fear or am rather too certain he will loose a great part of his execution so as to prevent his ever playing any more concertos on the organ.

If Handel was inwardly anxious about his condition he was sanguine about it with Shaftesbury; he accepted his situation calmly and appeared in good spirits. Shaftesbury noted Handel's "exceeding" gratitude (to God) for the fact that his condition was not much worse or ill-timed:

He submitts to discipline very patiently & I really believe will be orderly for the time to come[,] that this unhappy seisure may possibly at last be the occasion of prolonging his life. Handel is in excellent spirits & is exceeding thankfull his desorder[,] which is rhumatick palsie[,] did not attack him till he had done writing.*

Shaftesbury's assumption that Handel would be "orderly" in the future and that this experience would "at last be the occasion of prolonging his life" refers to the habit Handel must have gotten into of composing at all hours of the day or night, disrupting normal sleep times, and probably normal eating and social patterns as well. It also made him sedentary. The paralysis episode forced him to leave off these bad habits. Shaftesbury thought the illness would prevent Handel from further sacrificing his life for his art.

Whatever habits Handel had and hours he kept, Hawkins could still call his lifestyle "regular," by which he meant that Handel lived a quietly moral life and had no mistress. If Hawkins' conclusion that Handel's "social affections were not very strong" somewhat misinterprets the composer's personality, Hawkins was undoubtedly correct in saying that Handel's having a small number of intimate friends (and no wife and family to support) was advantageous to his life as a

---

*This picture of a Handel who could bear serious illness and possible permanent and career-ending paralysis with cheerfulness, submitting "very patiently" to "discipline" and "rough medicines" with their implied unpleasant side-effects (see the next quote of Shaftesbury), provides high contrast with the stereotype of the quick-tempered, self-centered, arrogant though witty genius which is part of the popular picture of the "secular Handel" in our time. The film *Farinelli* is an obvious example of the latter.

composer: "A temper and conduct like this, was in every view of it favourable to his pursuits; no impertinent visits, no idle engagements to card parties, or other expedients to kill time, were suffered to interrupt the course of his studies. His invention was for ever teeming with new ideas, and his impatience to be delivered of them kept him closely employed."[11] Burney said essentially the same thing: "He knew the value of time too well to spend it in frivolous pursuits, or with futile companions, however high in rank. Fond of his art, and diligent in its cultivation, and the exercise of it, as a profession, he spent so studious and sedentary a life, as seldom allowed him to mix in society, or partake of public amusements." The opposite side of that studious, constant-work coin – it's ill-effects on Handel's health – was what was concerning Shaftesbury.

By April 30, the first public report of Handel's illness appeared in the *London Daily Post*. He was said to have "rheumatism."[12] In fact, the paper suggested that he was "in so fair a way of recovery" that it was hoped he would be able to accompany *Giustino* (i.e., conduct it from the harpsichord) on May 4. On the day of that *Daily Post* report, Shaftesbury further told James Harris:

> *Mr Handel is surprizingly mended[;] he has been on horseback twice[.]*
> *Parry was with him two hours the day before yesterday & he tells me*
> *by his vast strength of constitution which is able to bear all the rough*
> *remedies they have given him[,] he will recover again presently.*[*]

However, by May 14, Handel had had a relapse, and there was worse to come. The *London* Evening Post asserted that he was "very much indispos'd, and it's thought with a Paraletick Disorder, he having at present no Use of his Right Hand, which, if he don't regain, the Publick will be depriv'd of his fine Compositions."

About the same time or not long after, he was affected mentally, enough so that it was commented upon by those who knew him, and was made worse for him by the fact that he himself was aware that the mental affliction was affecting his behavior. "His disorder was so deeply rooted, that by several particulars in his behaviour ... he discovered that his mental powers were affected; and, to complete his distress, one of those hands, which had frequently administered such delight to

---

*Parry was apparently a doctor. This is not the only contemporary reference to Handel's unusually strong constitution. He was now fifty-two years old, had rarely been ill to that time, and was the only survivor in his immediate family of parents, three siblings and six half-siblings. This reference to Handel riding a horse seems to be to recreational riding – a sign that, for the moment, he felt better and could use both hands.

others, was now become useless to himself."[13] Thinking of the implications of a useless right hand (as Shaftesbury had privately and the press now did publicly) must at last have become profoundly disquieting to Handel. To what degree he became mentally unhinged is hard to say; the written comments about it were so discreet as to be uninterpretable, but the mental effects were almost certainly part of the ailment rather than a reaction to it.

In the meantime the opera season went on, but barely. *Bernice* ran for only four nights in mid-May, but Handel wasn't – couldn't be – involved in its production. If he had anything to look forward to it was relief that the competition was folding: the Opera of the Nobility closed shop, early and for good, on June 11, 1737. The renowned castrato Farinelli had a cold, couldn't perform and left the country. Without their star, the Opera of the Nobility couldn't expect to continue successfully. And they were already in as dire financial straits as Handel was. Handel may have wondered, just then, if the fortunes of his competition would ever matter to him again. His own season ended with a tinge of unpleasant irony : a final performance of *Alexander's Feast*, his fine ode to Cecilia, patron saint of music.*

Mainwaring gives a lengthy, poignant description of Handel's illness:

> *The observation that misfortunes rarely come single, was verified in Handel. His fortune was not more impaired, than his health and his understanding. His right-arm was to become useless to him, from a stroke of the palsy; and how greatly his senses were disordered at intervals, for a long time, appeared from an hundred instances, which are better forgotten than recorded. The most violent deviations from reason, are usually seen when the strongest faculties happen to be thrown out of course. In this melancholic state, it was in vain for him to think of any fresh projects for retrieving his affairs. His first concern was how to repair his constitution. But tho' he had the best advice, and tho' the necessity of following it was urged to him in the most friendly manner, it was with the utmost difficulty that he was prevailed on to do what was proper, when it was in any way disagreeable.*

---

*Two years later Handel would write another piece honoring St. Cecilia, the *Song for St. Cecilia's Day* (Nov. 22). This now frequently heard piece is often referred to as the *Ode for St. Cecilia's Day*, but Handel called it a "song."

This seems to contradict Shaftesbury's observation about Handel's compliance, but it may refer to a later stage, by which time his patience was likely wearing thin. He may at last have tried – not entirely successfully – to fend off the vile boluses and medicinal drafts urged upon him. But by autumn, when whatever good effects of those strong and disagreeable medicines had dissipated, he agreed to go for a cure to the hot springs ("vapor baths") of Aix la Chapelle (Aachen). That treatment was quite painless and would restore the balance of the "humors."

In language typical for the time, William Coxe referred to Handel's ailment as "a violent illness, and even attended with fits of lunacy." Sir John Hawkins would have recoiled from associating Handel with lunacy at any time. His more socially delicate description is set in the context of Handel's increasing professional difficulties, which deeply affected his person:

> *After a contest which lasted about three years, during which time he was obliged to draw out of the funds almost the whole of what in his prosperous days he had there invested, he gave out; and discovered to the world of that in this dreadful conflict had had not only suffered in his fortune but his health. To get rid of that dejection of mind, which his repeated disappointments had brought on him ... he was prevailed upon, but with great difficulty, to resort to Aix la Chapelle; accordingly he went thither....*

Looking back, twenty-three years later, Shaftesbury also connected the illness to "great fatigue and disappointment" – the cumulative affect of what we would call stress, perhaps accompanied by serious depression:

> *Great fatigue and disappointment, affected him so much, that he was this Spring (1737) struck with the Palsy, which took entirely away, the use of 4 fingers of his right hand; and totally disabled him from Playing: And when the heats of the Summer 1737 came on, the Disorder seemed at times to affect his Understanding. His Circumstances being in a manner ruined, he entered into an Agreement to Compose, for the Gentlemen at the Hay Market (And from this time, there was never any Contest between M' Handel and any Sett of Gentlemen), and by the advice of his Physicians went to the Baths of Aix-la-Chapelle.*

Being as well known as he was, Handel's illness was very soon "discovered to the world." Naturally, Handel's friends were disturbed by the news, as were all who loved his music. When Shaftesbury informed his cousin James Harris about the composer's distressing condition, Harris wrote back:

> Y^r $Lord^{p's}$ [Your Lordship's] information concerning Mr Handel's Dis-
> order was y^e first I received – I can assure Y^r $Lord^p$ it gave me no Small
> Concern – when y^e Fate of Harmony depends upon a Single Life, the
> Lovers of Harmony may be well allowed to be Sollicitous. I heartily re-
> grett y^e thought of losing any of y^e executive part of his meritt, but this
> I can gladly compound for, when we are assured of the Inventive, for tis
> this which properly constitutes ye artist, & Separates Him from ye Mul-
> titude. It is certainly an Evidence of great Strength of Constitution to be
> so Soon getting rid of So great a Shock. A weaker Body would perhaps
> have hardly born ye Violence of Medicines, wch operate So quickly.*

The symptoms totally vanished while Handel submitted to the vapor baths. As we shall see, they would return nearly six years later (April 1743) and again two years after that, related to two more acutely stressful periods.

Since the nineteenth century there has been much speculation about just what was or was not wrong with Handel during this period. Among the cross-temporal diagnoses have been stroke (cerebral thrombosis), a muscular disorder, cervical arthritis and a peripheral neuropathy or saturnine gout – the gout having been induced by lead poisoning.[14] Dr. William A. Frosch has speculated that Handel may have become afflicted with saturnine gout from regularly drinking high-lead-content port that had become contaminated from the brandy with which it was fortified, brandy distilled "presumably" using "piping reinforced with lead." The port would have come from Portugal, its original home.

Port was by then a common drink in England, and there's one indication that Handel drank it: a note Handel scribbled (ca. 1735) on a sheet containing a figured and unfigured bass line is apparently a shopping list: "12 Gallons Port. /12 bottles French[,] Duke Street, Meels."[15] Despite this possibility, the consequence of intense stress seems to have been was the key factor in Handel's condition.

Whatever the exact medical cause, Handel's removing himself for six weeks

---

*Harris of course regretted any loss any of Handel's intellect, but especially hoped that his inventive power was in tact: *that* made him the great artist he was. (Deutsch interprets the "executive part of his meritt" to refer "certainly to his organ and harpsichord playing, implying the management of the Opera," p. 434.) James Harris was himself a musician; he would found and conduct a concert series in Salisbury which for many years featured Handel's music.

from the controversy and stress of his life in London while submitting daily to "such sweats...as astonished every one," as Hawkins put it, in the sauna-like baths at Aachen worked wonders. Said Mainwaring:

> His cure, from the manner as well as from the quickness with which it was wrought, passed with the Nuns for a miracle. When, but a few hours from the time of his quitting the bath, they heard him at the organ in the principal church as well as convent, playing in a manner so much beyond any they had even been used to, such a conclusion in such persons was natural enough.[16]

If Mainwaring (himself a Church of England clergyman) shows mildly paternalistic anti-Catholicism in telling of the nun's readiness to believe Handel's cure to have been a miracle, those nuns might well have considered Mainwaring's faith rather too earth-bound had they known his attitude. The nuns weren't the only ones who imputed Handel's cure to the Almighty. Hawkins wrote a similar story; or the same story in slightly different guise: "In a few hours after the last operation he went to the great church of the city, and got to the organ, on which he played in such a manner that men imputed his cure to a miracle."

In any case, it is not unlikely that many friends and music lovers had prayed for Handel's recovery, as perhaps had his parish church at St. George's, Hanover Square, and that Handel himself had privately pleaded with God from an anguished spirit for the recovery of his weal and wits.[*]

---

[*]The offering of prayers for the healing of ill parish members or clergy was an important part of church life, then as now. W.M. Jacob in *Lay People and Religion in the Early Eighteenth Century* (Cambridge, 1996, p. 201) cites prayers at the Abbey in Bath as including both public intercession for the sick and thanks for returned health. Bath had its own nearby "waters," but this was not an isolated practice. The 1662 edition of the *Book of Common Prayer*, still the current one in Handel's time, contained prayers for the sick intended to be prayed by the congregation (as does today's edition). The practice of Christian believers praying for each other (and the world), in and out of formal worship settings, goes back to the New Testament. If St. George's Hanover Square prayed for sick parishioners, the well-publicized illness of Handel, its best-known member, would hardly have escaped notice within the church.

Chapter 11
Another Direction to His Studies

Late in October 1737, Handel returned to London "in perfect health," according to Hawkins. Now, we might suppose, he would be without competition from either the opera or oratorio front. The Opera of the Nobility had died, and the periodic English-language operas and oratorios presented by others held no candle to Handel's own unique and far superior brand of biblical oratorio. But the Opera of the Nobility was, so to speak, undead; or rather, its backers were. Not willing to lie down and concede the victory to Handel (however pyrrhic that victory looked in light of what Handel had just suffered) they managed to pull together several pasticcios in order to begin an opera season in October while Handel was still away, and out of the way.

We might also expect that having been through what he had, Handel would make a conclusive move to oratorio; or that he would abandon that experiment altogether and stick wholly with Italian opera – one or the other. By November 15 he was hastily scratching out another opera (*Faramondo*), so it looked as if he couldn't abandon opera, despite the ongoing pressure to provide works in English. He and the "other party" now shared the King's Theater, and thus weren't, strictly speaking, competing against each other.

But just five days later both Handel and they were caught up short by an untoward event, one that once again affected Handel personally: on November 20, 1737, Queen Caroline died at age fifty-four. Besides knowing Caroline as the Queen, Handel had known her as Caroline of Brandenburg-Ansbach. He had tutored her and composed for her since, as a young genius, he had arrived back from Italy with an already established reputation and accepted a position at her father-in-law's electoral court in Hanover. She, in turn, had offered him strong support. Like her husband, she was fond of him personally and was committed to his music. She was apparently also committed to her Lutheran Christian faith in substance as well as ceremony.

To observe a period of mourning, all theaters closed until the beginning of January 1738. On December 17, almost a month after Caroline's death, her nearly three-and-a-half-hour long funeral was held in Westminster Abbey. On December 7, George II had requested that Handel write the music for the Queen's funeral. No doubt he would have written something without having been asked, given his friendship with Caroline. So Handel put aside writing *Faramondo* to work on music for the funeral, which he finished with just four days to rehearse. He produced a quieting and moving forty-five-minute anthem, "The Ways of Zion Do Mourn," using a text compiled by the sub-dean of the cathedral from a variety of Bible books and the Apocrypha: Lamentations, Samuel, Job, Ecclesiasticus, Philippians, Wisdom and Psalms 103, 112. (The anthem's title comes from Lamentations.)

The Duke of Chandos, writing to his nephew, described the work as "exceeding fine, and adapted very properly to the melancholy occasion of it."[1] Chandos added, "But I can't say so much of the performance." As with some past royal occasions (notably, George II's coronation), though the piece itself was splendid, the initial performance left something to be desired, most likely because of short rehearsal time. The Bishop of Chicester said the anthem "is reckoned to be as good a piece as he ever made."

In the anthem Handel calls to mind the Queen's (and his own) Lutheranism and German roots in several ways: first, he makes prominent use of a Lutheran **chorale**. In the opening movement he uses it as a *cantus firmus* (the pre-existing tune around which are woven other parts), presenting it in **chorale prelude** style. Second, he alludes to ancient Germanic funeral music by quoting from a sixteenth century motet by Jacobus Gallus.[*] Given the melodic allusions to both Lutheran congregational song and choral motets, it is appropriate that the work is entirely for choir. (The handful of recordings of the *Funeral Anthem* present several of the movements sung by soloists rather than choir. The anthem was printed in that manner in 1795, and has been performed so ever since.) Handel would make use of a chorale tune again shortly, in a pasticcio oratorio, and later in an ode and in several of the Old Testament oratorios.)

His periodic use of chorale tunes has more significance than has so far been granted by writers in English. It gives us clues to his faith and his thinking, so the subject is worth discussing at this point. Donald Burrows believes that, in using German and Lutheran elements in the *Funeral Anthem*, Handel may have been "moved by the thought that Queen Caroline had been brought up in the same Lutheran culture as himself," spurred by recent contact with German church music

---

[*]The motet was *Ecce quomodo moritor justus.* Gallus was of Slovenian descent, a Catholic composer of motets and masses who worked in Austria and Bohemia most of his short life (1750-91). His original name was Petelin ("rooster"). Jacobus Gallus is the Latin equivalent of the name, and it's diminutive equivalent in German is, interestingly, "Handl."

during his recuperative trip to the Continent. Burrows concludes that the "'chorale element" is "of technical interest" but is "only one feature of a rich work that draws upon many categories of musical idea...."[2]

The *Funeral Anthem* is certainly a rich work, and the "chorale element" isn't so blatant as it is in, say, the last chorus of *L'Allegro, il Penseroso ed il Moderato*, which pointedly quotes both *Jesu, Meine Freude* ("Jesus, Priceless Treasure") and *Erhalt' uns, Herr, bei deinem Wort* ("Lord, Keep Us Steadfast in Your Word").* But in the handful of times Handel introduces chorale tunes or fragments of them into his music, he's doing more than fondly remembering (alone or with others) his Lutheran "culture," of which his recent trip reminded him.

The aim of any composer in quoting chorales – which until Handel's usage was always done in church – was to get listeners to mentally call up the text associated with the tune they were hearing (congregations knew the chorales from memory) so that they could meditate on the text and be spiritually affirmed and even instructed. Even if only a fragment of the tune is quoted or alluded to, the beauty of this method is that the whole tune, and thus the gist of its text, emerges from the allusion anyway. That spiritual purpose was the intent of the hundreds of chorale preludes written by the dozens of German Lutheran composers throughout the Baroque period, a form of composition that Handel heard every Sunday of his life until he left for Italy at age twenty-one, and in which during his years of musical training he had had a thorough grounding from Zachau.

At Caroline's funeral and in the other instances of Handel's chorale usage, he wasn't musically addressing a church congregation, as such. But given the deeply ingrained tradition of chorale usage just described, it is hard to believe he would have pulled this feature out of his musical hat without intending it to signify anything, or for vague "cultural" reasons; or that he "borrowed" these tunes simply because he needed melodic material in those instances, and the chorales would do as well as anything else. Rather, when Handel uses chorale phrases or fragments in an anthem (or, later, in an oratorio chorus) he's overlaying an additional, unsung-but-very-

---

*The title *L'Allegro, il Penseroso ed il Moderato* is almost never translated. Handel wrote this work between Jan. 19 and Feb. 4, 1740. The text comes from John Milton's poems *L'Allegro* ("The Merry Man") and *Il Penseroso* ("The Thoughtful [pensive] Man"). The addition of *Il Moderato* ("The Moderate [balanced] Man") was Handel's own suggestion and was written by Charles Jennens, who supplied the *Messiah* libretto the following year. *L'Allegro* is discussed further below.

much-present textual meaning to the concretely audible English words and meaning. But almost none of his English listeners would have recognized those German Lutheran chorale quotations or have known their texts; those listeners did not have the key to opening that supplementary meaning. So why *did* Handel put it there?

Handel included the chorale phrases essentially for himself and his own edification. Little did he know that he also did it for future generations of listeners who *do* hold that key – since those chorales have, in the intervening centuries, been translated, disseminated cross-denominationally, sung and memorized throughout many parts of Christendom. An observation by Hawkins is apropos: "At the same time that he labored to please his hearers, he seems not to have been unmindful of his own gratification." While some things he composed hastily, "it is no less true that there are others which must be supposed to have been produced under the influence of the strongest enthusiasm, when the brightest illuminations irradiated his fancy, and he himself felt all that rapture which he meant to excite in others."[3]

While that can apply in a general way to Handel's personal pleasure in composing, he must have drawn particular pleasure (and comfort) from inserting, in specific instances, small, biblically based elements of his German Lutheran faith heritage into his also biblically based English-language works. This assessment agrees with present-day German musicologist Friedhelm Krummacher's: "More important than the understanding of others must have been Handel's own reflection, which was directed inward and needed no public."[4]

There *are* clearly discernible theological/faith-based connections that Handel was making in choosing specific German chorales to use with specific English texts. The chorale tune he used in the *Funeral Anthem* is "Du Friedefürst Herr Jesu Christ" ("Thou Prince of Peace, Lord Jesus Christ"). This tune is evident in the movement "She deliver'd the poor that cried," set as a slightly ornamented *cantus firmus* for sopranos, with the altos harmonizing in thirds below them. The text of the chorale focuses on Christ as both Prince of Peace and Judge. He is a strong helper to those in need, in every situation, "in life and in death" ("im Leben und im Tod"). This chorale was well-known to Handel and Bach and their fellow German Lutherans, known to musicians and ordinary churchgoers. (It's 1601 text is by Jakob Ebert.) It is not surprising that Handel would have thought of this clear-eyed but comforting text in a funeral context – and perhaps also in light of his own recent harrowing troubles of body and mind.*

A fact we've already seen evidence of can be emphasized here: Handel's ties to his homeland consisted of far more than nostalgia for his family and the Lutheran "culture" of his boyhood. Aided by regular correspondence and occasional visits with his extended family and friends (including Telemann), he maintained a lively interest in, and ongoing contact with, his devoutly Lutheran roots in Germany – and devout they were, as we've seen. The small amount of this correspondence that does survive shows that those roots continued to nourish him. He never ignored, much less renounced, those roots. Another statement by Hawkins is relevant, both in regards to Handel's personality and in regards to his faith and his considering himself a Lutheran even after decades in London (part of which we've already quoted in another context):

> Such as were but little acquainted with Handel are unable to characterize him otherwise than by his excellencies in his art, and certain foibles in his behaviour, which he was never studious to conceal: accordingly we are told that he had a great appetite, and that when he was provoked he would break out into profane expressions. These are facts that cannot be denied; but there are sundry particulars that tend to mark his character but little known, and which may possibly be remembered, when those that serve only to shew that he was subject to human passions are forgotten. In his religion he was of the Lutheran profession; in which he was not such a bigot as to decline a general conformity with that of the country which he had chosen for his residence; at the same time that he entertained very serious notions touching its importance. These he would frequently express in his remarks on the constitution of the English government; and he would often speak of it as one of the great felicities of his life that he was settled in a country where no man suffers any molestation or inconvenience on account of his religious principles.[5]

It is likely a significant factor in the close and life-long friendship between

---

*Bach composed a complete cantata on this text (BWV 116) and used it in two other cantatas (BWV 67 and 143). He used the tune for an early organ chorale prelude (BWV 1102), part of the late eighteenth century Neumeister collection discovered in 1985 in the music library at Yale University.

Handel and Telemann that they shared a faith heritage. Telemann remained deliberately immersed in it all his life, engaged in an occupation – composing church music – which he believed to be of more than just material importance. For the time, Handel trips back to Germany and specifically to his family were reasonably frequent, allowing him periodic in-the-flesh contact with his extended family and the friends and church community of his youth.

In the two weeks after Queen Caroline's funeral, Handel readied his new opera, which he completed on Christmas Eve. When the theaters reopened after their nearly six-week black-out, *Faramondo* debuted on January 3 with mostly new singers; it saw eight well-received performances. When Handel reappeared in public on January 3 for the first time since his illness, he was "honour'd with extraordinary and repeated Signs of Approbation," said a London newspaper the next day. But on January 15 he was confronted with another death: that of librettist Samuel Humphreys. In the future, several of Handel's oratorio librettists would become friends as well as colleagues of his, but we have no information to indicate how well he knew Humphreys apart from their professional relationship, or to what degree this death affected him emotionally.

Contrary to what we might expect, Handel still did not choose one musical path and unwaveringly stick to it. His season was again a conglomerative affair. At our historical distance we can see this period as one embodying Handel's inexorable move toward oratorio, but his thinking on this matter is difficult to discern; and of course for him it wasn't a mere academic discussion. Though he saw the plain signs that the public was tiring of opera's "senseless tyranny," he was still reluctant to abandon, once and for all, his long attachment to it. He understood, though, that he could not obstinately hang on to Italian opera only because of a long personal association with it and fondness for it. But he may also have thought it unwise to surrender opera to history just yet.

Was he afraid that what he had to replace it with – oratorios and odes in English – would not, in the end, stand up? He had always scorned second-rate music, such music as comes from second-rate composers. The English oratorio is a musical form that he essentially invented, whereas Italian opera had an already long and mostly successful history. Despite his awareness of the unusual nature of his own abilities, was he hesitant to base his future livelihood on musical forms he himself devised? What if he couldn't produce the kind of music in these genres that would be necessary, quite possibly for the rest of his life – during which time opera would no doubt die a final death and not, at last, be subject to resurrection. He had been forced to start seriously thinking about this a few years earlier at about age fifty. Despite his recent paralysis and mental affliction, and the generally fleeting nature of life in that still medicinally dark age, a man of his constitution could live a rather long life. So just what would he be committing himself to if he out-and-out abandoned opera?

Did Handel reason in this manner? Undoubtedly not. He is not known to have shown doubts about his own prodigious abilities. His heterogeneous now-this-thing, now-that approach wasn't the prolonged limping between two opinions that it appears to have been. There was something else behind his approach. He had extraordinary aptitude for quick thinking and even swifter writing. And he had, all his life, been versatile; from early on he had that knack for adaptability, personal and musical; he had already composed more music, in more forms, for more combinations of voices and instruments, than virtually any other composer living or dead (Telemann being the major exception).* Even if this wasn't the choice he had initially preferred, why should he not present a combination of musical works of now contrasting, now complementary types that would cover a broad range of tastes – and that would satisfy his own musical, emotional and spiritual desires in the process? That appears to be what Handel did with his 1737-38 season, and what he continued to do until *Messiah* (1741), that irresistible musical Hound of Heaven that set him on another course to the end of his life.

According to Hawkins, Handel recognized, about the time of his last three operas, that he should give "another direction to his studies": he should write oratorios. Not the least reason for the change was that setting biblical texts is

---

*Of necessity, we have to pass over almost all of it here. Over a roughly fifty-year career Handel wrote Italian oratorios and operas, cantatas, duets and trios, and individual arias; German operas, a Passion and individual arias, some with devotional texts; Latin liturgical works (canticles); English church anthems and ceremonial works, odes and oratorios, hymn tunes and songs with devotional texts; orchestral suites, concertos grosso and concertos for individual instruments (organ, harp, oboe); individual orchestral movements (overtures, sinfonias, marches, gigues and other dance movements); music for winds; solo instrumental sonatas (for violin, recorder, oboe, flute, viola da gamba); instrumental (not organ) trio sonatas; suites, partitas, preludes, toccatas and fugues for harpsichord (or organ), and numerous individual movements; music for mechanical clocks; exercises for students. Two of the most readily available sources of works lists of Handel's music are the *New Grove Dictionary of Music and Musicians* (2ⁿᵈ ed., 2001), available online as well as in print, and Donald Burrows' *Handel* biography.

better suited, as he himself used to declare, to the circumstances of a man advancing in years, than that of adapting music to such vain and trivial poetry as the musical drama is generally made to consist of. This resolution led him to reflect on that kind of representation, the Concerto Spirituale, so frequent in the Romish countries, and which, by the name of the Oratorio, is nearly of as great antiquity as the opera itself, and determined him to the choice of sacred subjects for the exercise of his genius.[6]

Those who love Handel's operas, and who see Handel as primarily a "secular" composer (and man), may doubt that Handel felt this way, much less that he actually said it, and said it more than once (the repetition implied in "used to declare..."). He did, after all, write more than three dozen operas, and did seem to have a hard time putting opera aside. Yet the statement is undoubtedly true (though Handel may have come to see this more in hindsight than while he was in the midst of his meandering course-change to oratorio; he referred to it in conversations with Hawkins well after his opera career was over). The view that setting biblical texts was a more substantive and worthy pursuit (a pursuit of the *sublime*) than was setting "trivial" opera texts would have been disputed by very few people in Handel's day, even by those who loved opera. While there were also practical reasons Handel would do better with oratorio (it was far cheaper to produce), there is also implicit in this statement Handel's increasing awareness of his mortality as he aged, and his realization that he would be called to account someday soon for how he had used his talents.

Faramondo, Handel's last opera in the traditional heroic style, ran for only eight nights. He then presented a pasticcio and another new opera, the essentially comic *Serse* (*Xerxes*). It ran for only five nights, but is by modern standards one of his best late operas and in our time is extremely popular.[*] Still in debt from audiences' earlier tepid responses, Handel just wasn't making any money. In order

---

[*]Handel's operas are regularly being heard again in live performances – usually in Italian, sometimes in English – by both the large, traditional opera companies and by companies specializing in Baroque opera. Unintelligible texts are no longer a problem, since most companies electronically project surtitles above or below the stage, allowing audiences to read the libretto in their own language as the opera progresses. Year by year, more recordings of the operas are being produced and many are also available in video formats. The oratorios are also increasingly being performed in concert , and are sometimes also staged; all are available on CD.

to bring in some additional income, he had more of his music published. And he agreed to a benefit concert on his own behalf, on the Tuesday of Holy Week, March 28, 1738: "It was at this time that his friend with great difficulty persuaded him to try public gratitude in a benefit, which was not disgraced by the event."[7]

Such concerts for individuals were not uncommon; just two-and-a-half weeks before Handel's benefit there had been a benefit at the Swan Tavern in Cornhill for a Mr. Adcock, a trumpet player, at which the last part of Handel's Coronation Anthem "Zadok the Priest" was performed.

The benefit for Handel featured another pasticcio of sorts, but not an opera pasticcio. This time he turned to church music and oratorio (some of it in Italian), forming a pasticcio of biblically based music that he called simply "An Oratorio." The evening was most helpful to him – financially, to his musical reputation and no doubt to his spirits. It reportedly brought him £1000 and was attended by "near 1,300 persons besides the gallery and upper gallery."

The "Oratorio" was put together from a revised version of his *Chandos Anthem* "As Pants the Heart," arias from *Deborah*, the Coronation Anthem "My Heart is Inditing" and other arias and duets. As part of the revision of "As Pants the Hart," Handel newly composed a strong chorus that once again makes use of a Lutheran chorale tune: he took the great German Easter chorale, Luther's own "Christ lag in Todesbanden" ("Christ Jesus Lay in Death's Strong Bands"), and used it blatantly: it is woven into a sung chorale prelude in which tenors and basses present the tune as a **cantus firmus.**[*] Though Handel omitted the melodic repetition of the chorale's opening phrase, and slightly truncated the closing phrase, the tune is easily recognizable. He wrote and compiled this "Oratorio" during Lent, when he and all Christians were both contemplating Christ's Passion and looking forward to Easter (two weeks after the benefit).

Handel's personal meditation during this season may well have brought him back to this best-known of the Lutheran Easter chorales, putting it in mind for ready

---

*This chorale text and tune were both adapted from the eleventh century sequence *Victimae paschale laudes.* When the chorale was first published in Johann Walther's 1524 *Geystliche Gesangk Buchleyn,* Walther (a younger contemporary of Luther's) was credited for the tune arrangement. But Luther himself is thought to have had a hand in it. Handel would not have known Bach's now famous settings of the chorale: three for organ; the basis of Cantata BWV 4 (composed 1707/8 and performed in Leipzig in 1725, and possibly 1724); and used again in Cantata BWV 158.

use in his "Oratorio." "Christ lag in Todesbanden" would have been chief among the Easter chorales Handel grew up singing in Germany. He would have known it further from the numerous organ works based on the tune, some of which he must have encountered with Zachau. Nor is it improbable that, given both Queen Caroline's and Samuel Humphreys's recent deaths, he was still inwardly consoling himself periodically with this and some of the other comforting chorales deeply imbedded in his memory. "Christ lag in Todesbanden" emphasizes Christ's conquering of death, breaking Satan's power and victory over evil: "Christ Jesus lay in death's strong bands, for our offenses given; but now at God's right hand he stands and brings us life from heaven. Therefore let us joyful be, and sing to God right thankfully loud songs of alleluia! Alleluia!" (stanza 1).

The text Handel used with this chorale tune is Psalm 42:4: "For I went with the multitude, and brought them forth into the house of God." It seems obvious that he deliberately chose this particular chorale, and saw a link from it to Psalm 42. The English psalm text and the implied German Lutheran chorale text work in tandem. The sung psalm text presents the exiled psalmist – a musical and/or liturgical leader in Israel – poignantly remembering what it used to be like to "go with the multitude," leading the procession to the temple to worship. This occurs in the psalm's context of crying with longing out of the depths of depression and oppression by evil to a God who seems silent. Despite the psalmist's isolation and affliction, he chides himself for being downcast, and never loses faith that God will hear and sustain him. The implied chorale text alludes to the same evil, but celebrates Christ's triumph over evil after a "strange and dreadful strife when life and death contended" (stanza 2). Thus, the chorale and the psalm express the same hope in God's rescue, with the chorale tune/text pointedly alluding to the fulfillment of that hope.

~

Handel's troubles with the nobility and temperamental singers aside, over his two-and-a-half decades in England to this point he had gained a reputation as a *sublime* composer – the adjective almost always applied to his mostly biblically based English-language choral music. His serious illness, recovery and return to London, culminating in the successful benefit concert with its heartily accepted "Oratorio," indicates that the esteem in which the man and his music were held had not diminished; and perhaps it shows a positive change of opinion on the part of some who had earlier felt differently.

Concrete evidence of this high regard was revealed in late April 1738 in a remarkable statue of Handel erected in Vauxhall Gardens. It was sculpted by a gifted young Frenchman, Louis-François Roubiliac (also spelled Roubillac), commissioned and paid for by Jonathan Tyers, owner of Vauxhall Gardens since 1732. The *London Daily Post* (April 18, 1738) reported that Tyers paid Roubiliac £300 for this unusual tribute to Handel. The gardens, previously part of a nobleman's estate, were "filled with large trees, laid out in shady walks."[8] They were filled with music, too: for on summer evenings Tyers would hire "a band of excellent musicians, he issued silver tickets for admission at a guinea each; and, receiving great encouragement, he set up an organ in the orchestra" – which sometimes played Handel's music.[*]

The statue was set up in "a conspicuous part of the garden," said Hawkins. The *London Post* reported that Tyers had the statue placed "in a grand Niche, erected on Purpose in the great Grove" because he thought it proper "that [Handel's] Effigies should preside there, where his Harmony has so often charm'd even the greatest Crouds into the profoundest Calm and most decent Behaviour" (an acknowledgment of the sublimity of Handel's music).

The statue, now in London's Victoria and Albert Museum, is exceptional in two ways: first, for its existence: it was unusual for a *public* statue to be erected in honor of a living subject who was not a monarch, nobleman or war hero; second, for its unusual execution: Handel is posed informally; he is casually dressed, wearing slippers, a banyan (a loose, near floor-length robe) and a turban, not his ubiquitous wig. He is represented as the lyre-plucking Apollo, ancient Greek head of the

---

[*]Handel wrote one piece specifically for Vauxhall Gardens: "Hornpipe compos'd for the Concert at Vauxhall, 1740." In 1833 a Rev. J. Fountayne would tell this amusing story: "My grandfather...was an enthusiast in music, and cultivated most of all the friendship of musical men, especially of Handel, who visited him often, and had a great predilection for his society. This leads me to relate an anecdote, which I have on the best authority. While Marylebone Gardens were flourishing, the enchanting music of Handel...was often heard from the orchestra there. One evening, as my grandfather and Handel were walking together and alone, a new piece was struck up by the band. 'Come, Mr. Fountayne,' said Handel, 'let us sit down and listen to this piece; I want to know your opinion of it.' Down they sat; and after some time the old parson, turning to his companion, said, 'It is not worth listening to – it is very poor stuff.' 'You are right, Mr. Fountayne,' said Handel, 'it is very poor stuff; I thought so myself when I had finished it.' The old gentleman, being taken by surprise, was beginning to apologize; but Handel assured him there was no necessity, that the music was really bad, having been composed hastily, and his time for the production limited; and that the opinion given was as correct as it was honest" (*History of the Parish of Marylebone*, quoted by Hogwood, *Handel*, p. 150).

GEORGE FRIDERIC HANDEL

Muses, representative of order, harmony and even all of civilization. (Some assumed the illusion was to Orpheus, that other Greek mythological creature associated with music, but Roubiliac intended an association with Apollo.)

Roubiliac's Handel-as-Apollo is no distant mythological music maker. He is also Handel the *man* of music, in a vigorous, uncannily lifelike and intimate cast, looking directly at the viewer. He looks fit and well, revealed especially in the set of his facial features. If Handel had sat for Roubiliac for a life-cast in the previous months or half-year, it would have been so not long after the composer's health-restoring visit to Aix-la-Chapelle; the sculpture leads to the conclusion that Handel had lost weight during his prolonged illness and "waters" regimen.

Roubiliac would later sculpt several other likenesses of Handel, including copies for Handel's friends the Harrises and Shaftesburys for their personal enjoyment.* One, the next year, was a bust in which Handel's facial contours and expression, outlined by a firmly set jaw, exude strength of character. (Handel is also wearing a turban in this bust, though a more compact one than in the Vauxhall sculpture.) After Handel's death, Roubiliac also provided the most viewed likeness of Handel: the monument that still so strikingly marks the composer's grave in Westminster Abbey. In that life-sized statue, Handel – much older and somewhat paunchier – is again casually dressed, but bareheaded; that is, in his own hair, which was apparently naturally wavy. Here too, the sculpture commands a presence that makes its subject seem almost capable of clambering down from his pedestal to engage the viewer in discussion over a glass of port. Hawkins, who knew Handel late in life, said, "The most perfect resemblance of him is the statue on his monument, and in that the true lineaments of his face are apparent."[9]

There is also a report of people who had seen the Vauxhall Gardens statue but who were personally unacquainted with Handel; having then met him in the

---

*In a letter, April 16, 1741, Roubiliac tells James Harris in Salisbury that the "busto" of Mr. Handel is ready. Roubiliac wants to know if he should leave it white or "put a colour upon it" (i.e., a patina). Roubiliac informs Harris that he has also "made after life" busts of Pope, Milton and Newton, implying that Harris might like to buy one or more of those also (none of these was on public display). Thomas Harris, meanwhile, gets a first look at the Handel busts – there was one for James Harris, one for the Countess of Shaftesbury and one for Charles Jennens (who was a friend of theirs as well as Handel's). Thomas explains to James that the color would be a "light dun colour," which looks "handsomer" than the white plaster) and which (Roubiliac told him) "will keep clean better" (letter from Thomas to James Harris, April 21, 1741, Harris Papers, p. 114).

street, they recognized him immediately and were astonished at the likeness. Hawkins describes Handel's features as "finely marked and the general cast of his countenance placid, bespeaking dignity attempered with benevolence, and every quality of the heart that has a tendency to beget confidence and insure esteem." In contrast, Hawkins judged the paintings of Handel as far inferior to the sculptures: "Few...are to any tolerable degree likenesses.... In the print of him by Houbraken, the features are too prominent; and in the mezzotinto after Hudson there is a harshness of aspect to which his countenance was a stranger."

In the grave monument sculpture, a scroll rests partly against Handel's left arm (which is bent at the elbow) and partly against a backdrop, and is kept unfurled by the grip of Handel's right hand along its bottom edge. The scroll bears the text of Job 19:25 and the tune to which Handel set it in *Messiah*, making it, since then, the most frequently repeated Christian confession of hope in the resurrection, one with which Handel will forever be associated: *I know that my Redeemer liveth, and that He shall stand at the latter day upon the earth.*

Chapter 12
Maggots and a *Faux Pas*

There is no account of Handel's reaction to being honored with the Vauxhall Gardens statue, though surely it must have cheered, and possibly amazed, him. At about the same time as the unveiling of the statue, his own financial affairs having eased a little, he was among the founding members of a new charity. The Fund for the Support of Decayed Musicians and Their Families held its first meeting April 23, 1738, at the Crown and Anchor. This site of Bernard Gates's 1732 *Esther* performance that had nudged Handel ever so slowly toward oratorio was a common and congenial meeting place for musicians and music lovers. Handel was now spurred to charitable action when he learned that the children of one of his former oboists were destitute. As with the Sons of the Clergy, his music became a mainstay in helping to raise money for the fund.

John Jacob Heidegger, still alive and functioning at age seventy-nine, was now trying to rouse support for a new opera season to begin during the fall of 1738. But by July 25 he announced that he had failed to get that support or to come to agreements with the singers. At last, Italian opera appeared to be dead in London. Still, Handel seemed to be again leaning toward presenting his own season of mixed treats, possibly with some opera at the end of the season, when Italian singers would be available after finishing their season in their homeland. Two days before Heidegger's announcement, Handel had begun work on a new oratorio, the *Saul* libretto, which is what Charles Jennens presumably sent him in 1735. It would be one of his most significant oratorios.

The birth of *Saul* wasn't an easy one. Handel worked on it for a month then put it aside, oddly enough, to start another opera (*Imeneo*). He did that knowing he didn't have the resources to perform the opera. So he put it aside too. He went back to *Saul*, spurred by a meeting with Jennens.

Jennens, in a September 19 letter to Lord Guernsey, his second cousin, described his meeting with Handel and what Handel was up to. Jennens knew the value of Handel's music but did not hold him in awe. Jennens freely criticized and made recommendations; his critiques were usually astute, if frequently exasperated or even ill-tempered. Handel's and Jennens' correspondence shows a close working relationship between composer and librettist. Though Jennens' future bald and relentless criticism of *Messiah*, for example, would hurt Handel and even cause him severe stress, he listened to Jennens' advice.

Many scholars – going back to Samuel Johnson in the latter part of the eighteenth century – have not been kind to Jennens. Dr. Johnson is said to have thought Jennens a vain fool and called him "Solyman the Magnificent." But that sobriquet and the story that its origin lay in Jennens leading an extravagant and ostentatious life come from George Steevens. Steevens was an unscrupulous man who saw Jennens as a rival at editing Shakespeare, and who attacked him at every opportunity. Steevens was "a byword even among his friends for professional jealousy and malpractice."[1]

The truth is that Jennens was an immensely able man in a variety of areas. His editions of Shakespeare, which he started late in life and of which he finished only five volumes, were careful and innovative. According to Brian Vickers, foremost among modern historians of Shakespeare criticism, Jennens' Shakespeare editions were the first "which approach anything near modern standards in textual criticism, and vastly more scholarly than anything that had yet appeared." Steevens reviled Jennens on account of those Shakespeare editions; Steevens knew he himself was capable of no such brilliance. Jennens' Shakespeare is good precisely because he was capable of a "rigid exactitude," according to Gordon Crosse in his essay "Charles Jennens as Editor of Shakespeare." Says Crosse, "He perceived, as some editors of that age did not, that it was no part of his business to improve on the poet."

"Rigid exactitude"was a characteristic whose importance for editing literature was not then recognized – and was one of Jennens' characteristics which caused Handel grief, though it probably also resulted in improvements to the oratorios on which Jennens and Handel collaborated.* The quality of Jennens' librettos for Handel has sometimes been overlooked; what has instead been emphasized is his tendency to appear (from his letters) self-important and quick to criticize, even while being too pious. That view of his piety as excessive is a modern one. Jennens was an Anglican (and Nonjuror) who seems to have understood what St. Paul calls "developing the '*mind* (my emphasis) of Christ.'" He was concerned with living his faith and spreading the Gospel, though depression sometimes got in way, altering his behavior and outlook.

Jennens' September 19, 1938, letter told Lord Guernsey that Handel's

---

*The Handel-Jennens collaboration was on *Messiah*, *Saul* and *Belshazzar* (and likely *Israel in Egypt*).

head was full of "maggots," by which he meant crazy ideas.* Handel's musical ideas weren't really so crazy, just a little unorthodox. First, Handel had gotten hold of "a very queer instrument," a carillon, which he intended to use "to make poor Saul stark mad."[2] The carillon Jennens describes has a tone "like a set of Hammers striking upon anvils" and "is played upon with keys like a Harpsichord." As is obvious from Jennens's description, this "carillon" was not the tower-bells sort of carillon which most readers will think of when they hear the word, nor the set of horizontally hanging rectangular metal plates, struck by hammers, used in the modern orchestra. It was played via keyboard like a celesta (interior keys strike metal bars rather than strings), and sounded like a glockenspiel (a table-top set of graduated metal bars mounted on a wooden frame, played with mallets).

Handel's second "maggot" was the commissioning of a chamber organ for use during his oratorios, costing £500. He "so contriv'd that as he sits at it, he has a better command of his Performers than he used to have; and he is highly delighted to think with what exactness his Oratorio will be performed by the help of this organ: so that for the future instead of beating time at his Oratorios, he is to sit at the Organ all the time with his back to the Audience." Jennens quipped that Handel commissioned the organ "because he is overstocked with money." If Jennens meant to be sarcastic rather than funny, he surely could have described himself with the same words.

Handel intended, of course, to use this organ far more often than for a few performances of *Saul* that season. Since opera did not require the use of an organ, his having committed the substantial sum of £500 for such an instrument indicates that he was already seriously contemplating writing more oratorios, and playing organ concertos during their intermissions. The organ was installed in the Covent Garden Theater, where Handel used it for the rest of his life and bequeathed it to theater manager John Rich.

Handel's third "maggot" was again related to *Saul*, and to a different conception of its climax than Jennens had. Handel thought *Saul* needed a "grand," majestic ending, and so composed a "Hallelujah" chorus as its climax. Jennens

---

*Lord Guernsey was the heir to Jennens' large collection of music manuscripts known as the Aylesford Collection. Jennens was godfather to Guernsey's son.

bluntly called this "nonsensical." Not only that, Jennens insisted that if the oratorio's conclusion wasn't "Grand enough," it was Handel's own fault: "The words [Jennens's words!] would have bore as Grand Musick as he could have set 'em to." Where the oratorio really needed a "Hallelujah," Jennens fumed, was at the end of its first Chorus (the end of Scene 1), and Handel had refused to put one there "on a pretence that it would make the Entertainment too long." In most circumstances, Handel's intuition for what was appropriate where was unerring, but Jennens also had an excellent instinct for the spiritual, emotional, and dramatic impact of setting Scripture and scriptural stories to music. Jennens's sensing where the "Hallelujah" would be most appropriate was correct, and in the end Handel saw the wisdom of it. He moved the "Hallelujah," creating an exultant ending to a magnificent chorus (based on Psalm 8) in which Israel praises God for delivering them from Goliath and the Philistines: "How excellent they name, O Lord, in all the world is known! Above all Heav'ns, O King, ador'd, How hast thou set thy glorious Throne! Hallelujah!"

Within eight days of the date of Jennens's letter Handel had the oratorio finished. It is a gripping work and quite different from his previous three oratorios and the pasticcio, including requiring a large orchestra with unusual instruments in it. Thanks to Jennens's libretto, and no doubt his advice as well, *Saul* tells a cohesive story, and by modern standards does so in a more dramatic way than do *Esther*, *Deborah* or *Athalia*. *Saul* allowed Handel to exhibit his operatic talents – his uncanny ability to musically draw and probe characters, aided by his intimate understanding of the human voice and how best to write for it, alone or in chorus. And it demonstrated his talent for making instruments "speak" as well.

Handel's autograph for *Saul* shows numerous revisions. Winton Dean interprets this as a sign of what he calls the "convulsive struggle that brought the oratorio to birth."[3] However, it may not indicate anything so dramatic or troubling. It is more likely evidence of Handel's close (and at this point, unusual) collaboration with Jennens: there are comments and changes on the manuscript in Jennens's handwriting, and the Jennens-Handel correspondence gives evidence of that cooperation. Donald Burrows goes so far as to say that Handel and Jennens "act upon each other as reciprocal artistic stimulants."[4]

Handel gave himself a three-day break after completing *Saul*. But on October 1 he began another new oratorio, *Israel in Egypt*, which he finished in exactly a month. (On October 4, meanwhile, more of Handel's music appeared in print: six "concertos for harpsichord or organ.")

Israel in Egypt is a wholly different musical animal than *Saul*. It consists almost entirely of choral music. Instead of using recitatives and arias to move the story forward and the chorus to comment on the action, Handel has the chorus (or double chorus) tell the story: of the Ten Plagues, the Exodus from Egypt and Pharoah's drowning in the Red Sea. In his previous oratorios Handel had used the chorus as a "character" in the drama, representing either the Israelites as a nation and God's people, or some part of them, for example, the Levites or priests. A chorus might also embody one of the pagan nations or their priests. Here Handel goes farther.

Israel in Egypt, as Handel first wrote it, has a Part 1 consisting of the re-used *Funeral Anthem for Queen Caroline*, which no more than a handful of people in his oratorio audiences had heard before. He transformed the Queen's *Funeral Anthem* into an extended lamentation over the death of Joseph. He had intended to use some or all of the *Funeral Anthem* in *Saul*, for the elegy at Saul and Jonathan's death, but Jennens provided new text for the elegy and Handel used it.

The unnamed librettist for *Israel in Egypt* was almost certainly Jennens. The libretto comes straight from Scripture. Of all Handel's oratorios, the only other one which does this is Messiah, – libretto is also by Jennens. And later Jennens said that *Messiah* was the second "Scripture Collection" he compiled for Handel. Donald Burrows suggests a plausible scenario: when Handel and Jennens met to discuss *Saul*, they also talked about and outlined *Israel in Egypt*. The *Funeral Anthem* would make a good Part 1 to a choral oratorio, balanced by Part 3, "Moses' Song," from Exodus 15, which Handel began working on while Jennens completed the compilation of Old Testament passages for Part 2.

Israel In Egypt contains some of Handel's earliest and most explicit word-painting in the oratorios: jumping frogs, buzzing flies, rattling hailstones raining down while "fire, mingled with the hail, ran along upon the ground"; thick darkness covering the land, the waters of the Red Sea overwhelming the frenzied Egyptians, Pharaoh and his hosts sinking to the depths "as a stone."

Saul and *Israel in Egypt* were the two new works for Handel's 1739 season (not the 1738-39 season because Handel's shortened concert season did not begin until January 16, 1739). On January 16, 1739, *Saul* was first heard at the King's Theater, where it met with "general Applause by a numerous and splendid Audience," said the *London Daily Post* the next day. The increasingly reclusive widowed King himself was there, along with his children who still lived at home. Besides sublime music there were elements of novelty: a large orchestra, including three trombones, harp, theorbo (a lute-like plucked stringed instrument), flutes, solo organ, carillon and military kettle drums borrowed from the Tower of London. The cast consisted of an unprecedented twelve soloists: three sopranos, one countertenor, four tenors and four basses.

The initial reaction to *Israel in Egypt*, which premiered on April 4, was also a different story from *Saul's* reception. "Lukewarm" would describe it. It is now assumed that the reason for the tepid response was that *Israel in Egypt* consists almost entirely of choruses, a musical form that Handel's audiences were not at all used to. Italian opera, which they *were* used to, is made up almost entirely of recitatives and arias, and showcases virtuoso soloists from start to finish. With a few exceptions among Handel's operas, the "choruses" in them offer a chance for those star soloists to sing together, still doing their star turns (and bringing the plot to a happy conclusion); such choruses are ensemble pieces, not inherently choral works written to be sung by a choir.

It is possible, even probable, that some in Handel's audiences felt the choral nature of *Israel in Egypt*, coupled with its direct quoting of Scripture, to be particularly church-like and worship-oriented, making them uncomfortable about hearing *Israel in Egypt* in the theater. We first saw this issue years earlier related to the Passion oratorios in Germany. In England the theatrical performance of biblical texts and stories was also an issue and would come to a head with *Messiah*, because Christ himself is its subject matter. The main issue was this: a carefulness to maintain a proper atmosphere and attitude of reverence for God and the Word of God, and how and where that God's name and Word were used. The issue was not that faith was considered to have no place in the theater. There was no cavernous gulf between "sacred" and "secular." The gap was still rather narrow, in fact. Because that is not the case in modern European-based society it is important to understand that there was an easy blending of sacred and secular in Handel's world.

Life at the time was still primarily communal rather than individual. There was much less differentiation between what we now consider private life and public life. The Christian worldview that undergirded British society in the first half of the eighteenth century was still assumed to guide all of life. Neither faith nor the morality that proceeds from it were considered a private and individual matter, divorced from one's life and work in the world. There was a natural merging of the individual and communal, the social and political, the "sacred" and "secular."

One of the most obvious examples of this can be seen in the co-mingling of church and state, which arose centuries earlier out of a worldview that understood that faith naturally touches every area of life ("Out of the heart come the issues of life," as Proverbs 4:23 puts it). But a gradual misunderstanding of how faith-imbued life should manifest itself in the state and in the institutional church, fueled by the human tendency to turn legitimate stewardship into power struggles, often caused both church and state to overstep their boundaries.* A partial course-correction occurred as one of the results of the Reformation, and there were strong vestiges of that Reformation view left in Handel's England.

W.M. Jacob in *Lay People and Religion in the Early Eighteenth Century* addresses how a Christian worldview still permeated that society:

> *The parish was the basic local unit of government. The forum of government was the [church] vestry.... Its responsibilities, in modern terms, were both spiritual and secular, though this is not a distinction that would have been real in the early eighteenth century. The relationship between Church and State was not distinguished at national or at local level. It is not the case that the Church was an agent of the State, exploited by politicians for their own ends, or that the clergy were trying to subvert the political system to their own ends. It was an expression of a particular form of Christianity, in which citizenship and Christianity were coterminous and in which, perhaps because death in one's prime was an ever-present reality, most people had a concern for their own and other people's eternal salvation. The generality of people accepted the spiritual disciplines of the Church because they wished to safeguard their future hope. Of course people fell short of their hopes for themselves, and there were many who gave up hope, and seem to have abandoned themselves to lawlessness, but they were not the majority. For the majority the Christian religion was real and was a central, perhaps the central, focus in their lives.*[5]

---

*The term institutional church refers to the church as it developed and spread historically and organized itself into specific institutions, East and West and, post-Reformation, into denominations. The biblical usage of "church" (*ecclesia*) has another meaning: the "called" people of God. In biblical terms, the gathered *ecclesia* form the institutional church.

What we would call personal identity did not exist in the modern way, either. To the extent that it did, the person was formed in terms of, and in the bosom of, the community, at the center of which was the church, the corporate embodiment of individual and communal faith and social life. That's why "offences against moral and spiritual standards had social significance," to use Jacob's words. Besmirching someone's good name, for example, was not only un-Christianly uncharitable; it disrupted the local peace. In the same manner, extramarital sexual conjunctions were both sinful and a threat to the community's peace because of the resulting strained or broken familial and community relationships they caused. Such sexual activity might have economic consequences as well, not only for the parents (especially mothers) of illegitimate children produced, but for citizens of the parish who had to support them via assessed parish tithes. Numerous writings and documents of the period demonstrate that scriptural moral standards and general social attitudes coincided, and were generally enforced by the Church courts, which had legal standing. Not incidentally, published collections of sermons were the most popular reading material of the period. Catholics and Protestant Dissenters fell outside the official Church of England government-sanctioned and supported parish life, but tended to develop their own alternative means of living in community, to the extent they were allowed to do so.

The prevailing orthodox worldview was questioned by a small minority of people (libertarians and "free thinkers," for example, including Deists and Unitarians) who rebelled against this system they perceived as too vigilant, and morally or philosophically confining. As the century wore on, that minority grew, and the communal, biblically based worldview was very gradually supplanted by talk of individual rights in a pluralistic society no longer minutely watched over by a God who is both Creator and Savior and both merciful and just. Even as the Enlightenment was dawning, our modern age's absolutizing of the individual, compartmentalizing of religion and relativizing of truth (with its rejection of "natural law") would have been incomprehensible to Handel, his friends and audiences.[*]

---

[*]Jacob sets out a great deal of evidence using parish records, court records, personal writings and other contemporaneous sources. He concludes this about the evidence: [It] "demonstrates that in general in England in the first half of the eighteenth century religion was embedded in all aspects of human life. The view that by 1700 England was a secularised society is untenable. By 1700 religion was not [yet] being 'confined to ever fewer areas of life.' Religion was not 'only part of culture'; nor was it marginalised and easier to ignore. There is little evidence that the 'English form of Protestantism ... is a secularising religion' wanting to 'separated

Being aware of that context helps to understand Handel and his oratorios, and why he himself, with his robust view of Providence and of Scripture, had no qualms about devising biblical works for the theater in the first place.

~

After three performances of *Israel in Egypt*, Handel decided to cancel it because of lack of audience interest. But he relented and added an additional performance after he received private encouragement from friends and public praise for the oratorio from several letter writers to the *London Daily Post* (April 13 and April 18, 1739). Both letter writers assert how sublime the oratorio is; they marvel, especially, at how well Handel fashions his music to the libretto's words from Scripture, a constant refrain among listeners to the oratorios. Rumor had it, however, that Handel was working on another opera. Odd as it may seem, the rumor was true (more or less). Handel finished *Jupiter in Argos* on April 24. His singers – one of whom was a soprano castrato newly arrived from Italy – would have just under a week to rehearse for a May 1 performance. There was just one more performance after that, and then *Jupiter in Argos* disappeared for two centuries. Despite its English title, this work is an Italian-style opera, in Italian, though not quite a full-fledged opera. A pasticcio with a handful of new numbers from the unfinished *Imeneo*, it was referred to in its newspaper announcement as a "Dramatical Composition ... intermix'd with Chorus's, and two concertos on the Organ." The oratorios are also "dramatical compositions"(usually called "sacred dramas"), but unacted. So *Jupiter in Argos* is what we might call a concert opera, an interesting species for Handel to insert in the midst of an ever more steady diet of oratorios, which can be seen as biblically based concert dramas.

In spite of the disfavor in which most Londoners now held Italian opera, and the general success of Handel's oratorios to that point, there was a die-hard group who still craved opera. So a new opera company was formed once again, this one by the twenty-seven-year-old Charles Sackville, Earl of Middlesex, who had just returned from Italy. (He was, perhaps not incidentally, a good friend of Frederick, Prince of Wales.) This group quickly mounted four performances of a work by

----

religion from other aspects of life – for the sake of purifying religion.' (C. John Sommervile, *The Secularization of Early Modern England: From Religious Culture to Religious Faith*. NY, 1992. pp. 5-17). Two centuries after the English Reformation religion was still the basis of English society."

Italian composer Giovanni Battista Pescetti, but Middlesex was primarily trying to gather opera subscriptions for the upcoming season (1739-40). Middlesex was only modestly successful, not enough to warrant a season at the King's Theater at the Haymarket, which was a large theater. Nor did Handel use that theater in 1739-40. He went to Lincoln's Inn Fields, while Middlesex's company rented the Little Theater at the Haymarket.

There were those outside London, as well as in this new London opera faction, who still wanted to see Handel's reputation damaged. In mid-November 1739, Shaftesbury reported to James Harris a story Handel had just related to him about an incident said to have happened in August or early September, in the English Channel-side town of Southhampton:

> There is an unaccountable report spread to the great detriment of our friend Handel & it is this. That Handel was very surly at South-[ampton] & call'd out as he was playing on the organ[,] "Shut the doors or I will leave off instantly.["] You know the falsity of this – yet it has hurt Handel. He is now in the room & tells me, he shall perform the Ode & a new short one twice...."[6]

Shaftesbury's slightly ambiguous wording and punctuation imply that Handel had just spoken to him about both Southampton and about his new season ("the Ode" is *Alexander's Feast*; the "new, short one" is the *Ode for St. Cecilia's Day*). Shaftesbury's assertion to Harris that "You know the falsity of this" could mean that Harris was present in Southampton, and knew that the incident didn't happen. But there's no record of Harris having been there. More likely Shaftesbury meant: You (and I) know this is untrue, because Handel wouldn't do something like that.

Why was Handel upset in November about an alleged incident from the previous summer? It's probable that the story about his supposedly ill-tempered and arrogant behavior in Southampton had just been concocted by his enemies, timed to coincide with the beginning of his music season; or the story had been flying around since late summer and Handel had just then finally heard about it. This fits the tactics used by those who wanted to denigrate Handel. It is unlikely that the story had made the rounds in the summer, Handel heard it at the time and was still troubled by it two-and-a-half months later; he wasn't a brooding man. In any case, Handel was wounded by the story, as he was meant to be.

Later that November Handel's concert season began, consisting only of works in English, though it would take just a little longer for him to decide to present only oratorios. The new piece on the docket was another English ode, *Song for St. Cecilia's Day*, an affecting, anthem-like work. The night after the season opener Lord Shaftesbury hosted an evening of reading and music, to which he naturally invited Handel, whose mind and heart perhaps still needed diversion. Shaftesbury was ebullient:

> *I never spent an evening more to my satisfaction than I did the last —*
> *Jemmy Noel read through the whole poem of [Milton's] Samson*
> *Agonistes and whenever he rested to take breath Mr. Handel (who was*
> *highly pleas'd with the peice [sic]) played I really think better than ever,*
> *& his harmony was perfectly adapted to the sublimity of the poem. This*
> *surely ... may be call'd <u>a rational entertainment</u>.*[7]

Two years later, Handel would begin writing his oratorio *Samson*, based on *Samson Agonistes*. Handel no doubt had keen memories of that evening of poetry and music which he had spent so happily with Milton's classic poem and with friends. Perhaps he vowed to himself then that he would some day use Milton's work to bring the Samson story to musical life.

Meanwhile, in November 1739 and the subsequent winter months, Handel had an additional, unusual opponent: the weather. London's winter was far colder than its moderate climate normally produces, and it started early. Normally, a gathered audience would raise the temperature of the theater somewhat. But that couldn't be relied upon that winter. When the first concert was announced, the potential audience was assured that "particular Preparations are making to keep the House warm; and the Passage from the Fields to the House will be cover'd for better Conveniency."[8] Nearly three months later, patrons of an early February concert were still being told, "Particular Care has been taken to have the House survey'd and secur'd against the Cold, by having Curtains plac'd before every Door, and constant Fires will be kept in the House 'till the Time of Performance." On the day of that performance (February 14) the *London Daily Post* announced, not surprisingly, that "two chief Singers being taken ill, the Serenata ... that was to be perform'd this Day ... must therefore be put off performing a few Days longer, whereof Notice will be given in the London Daily Post, and Daily Advertiser." The concert occurred on the same day a week later. During that week Handel wrote an organ concerto (op. 7, no. 1).

In mid-January Handel had started writing another new English choral-vocal work, again working with Charles Jennens. In his usual speedy style, he finished the work by February 4. It takes its Italian title, *L'Allegro, il Penseroso ed il Moderato*, from two poems by John Milton, "L'Allegro" ("The Merry Man") and "Il Penseroso" ("The Thoughtful Man"), with the added *Moderato* section written by Jennens, at Handel's urging. The suggestion for a piece based on these Milton poems came from Handel's and Jennens's friend James Harris (who had, during Handel's illness, lamented the possible loss of his music to himself and the world). Handel's finished product is an engaging and important work – and it pointedly makes use of several Lutheran chorales.

The piece presents the peculiarities of two opposing kinds of personalities and spirits, alternately holding to light the characteristics of one, then the other. Harris did the initial work on the libretto and Jennens worked on it further. But Handel himself wanted the work to have a decided conclusion and an overall moral design, so "Moderation" (an advocate of Reason) gets the last word in a verse written by Jennens. The piece consists of nine verses, divided like this: accompanied recitative; aria; accompanied recitative; chorus; aria; recitative; aria; duet; final chorus.

Adding the *Moderato* section became somewhat controversial. Jennens's verses couldn't compete *as poetry* with the verses of Britain's greatest poet, and some critics said the work is better off without the resolution of Moderation, as some critics still say. But the *Moderato* section effectively does what Handel wanted it to do. Perhaps bowing to pressure, for a 1743 revival Handel dropped the *Moderato* (no doubt much to Jennens's annoyance), giving Allegro the last word. He also recast some of Penseroso's music which had been for soprano, giving it to an alto who he had available. Always practical, Handel frequently and readily adapted his music to specific soloists for specific performances.

In typical eighteenth century style, the virtues are personified. *Moderato* is a "divine grace," a gift of God to save "mad mortals" from themselves (second aria). Many benefits accrue to Moderation; among his (or her) "serene company" are Sweet Temp'rance, Contentment, Frugality (a "fast friend" of Bounty), and chaste love ("by Reason led secure, With joy sincere, and pleasure pure..."). For the penultimate verse, set by Handel as a lovely soprano-tenor duet, Jennens borrowed from Shakespeare's *The Tempest* (Act V, Scene 1, Lines 64-68). In it, Allegro and Penseroso are joined in harmony, musical, philosophical and spiritual. Then, as the followers of *Moderato* are having the last word in the final chorus, Handel pointedly introduces two chorale tunes which are still in many hymnals today: "Jesu, meine

Freude" ("Jesus, Priceless Treasure") and "Erhalt uns, Herr, bei deinem Wort" ("Lord, Keep Us Steadfast in Your Word").

Once again, his use of chorales, and these chorales in particular, cannot be random; their texts are confessionally and theologically related, and he beautifully and seamlessly weaves the chorale tunes into his final chorus. There are just two short lines of text in the final chorus: "Thy pleasures, Moderation, give,/In them alone we truly live." Handel begins the movement by stating this text once, forthrightly, to the opening musical phrases of "Jesu, meine Freude" – a tiny prelude, which segues immediately into a "fugue." The fugal subject is the opening measure of "Erhalt uns, Herr, bei deinem Wort," which Handel then expands slightly. At two points he returns to fragments of "Jesu, meine Freude," making the fragments of the two chorales utterly inseparable.

The texts of those fragments, and the entire stanzas from which they come, flood into the mind of any listener who knows these chorales. The interwoven chorales provide a subtle spiritual counterpart to the moral conscience of Milton's poems and Jennens's addition. Thus, while the chorus is singing about the pleasures of moderation – real living and enjoyment of life come via moderation – the implied chorale texts are positing a far deeper wellspring of life: "Jesus, Priceless Treasure, source of purest pleasure." That chorale talks of the vanity of earthly treasure, paralleling Moderato's point that pleasure for its own sake will ultimately fade. The speaker in the chorale (Christian in Bunyan's *Pilgrim's Progress* comes to mind) banishes the temptations of this world's treasures, but without sadness, because Jesus, "Lord of gladness, enters in."* Almost simultaneously, the second chorale Handel uses reinforces the thoughts brought to mind from "Jesu, meine Freude" by imploring Christ to "keep us steadfast in your Word" ("Erhalt uns, bei deinem Wort"). But here, the message is broader. The speaker who was the individual but universal Christian is now a chorus made up of the entire Body of Christ on earth, and the focus which was on the individual's struggle is now a communal battle of cosmic proportions: "Curb those who by deceit or sword would wrest the Kingdom

---

*The thought of *Pilgrim's Progress* here is not inappropriate. The chorale is German Lutheran, but the Christian taking refuge in Christ and struggling against the assaults of "sin and hell," "pain or loss or shame or cross," is universal to Christian faith. Bunyan's Puritanism was not unlike the Lutheran Pietism which flourished around Handel during his youth. And, in fact, the text of "Jesus, meine Freude" is by Johann Franck, leader of the Halle Pietists.

from your Son and bring to naught all he has done." This chorale again refers to Christ as being of priceless worth, comforter, sender of peace and unity, and support in "our final strife" who will "lead us out of death to life." In Handel's "private" use of these chorales in the summation of L'Allegro..., he can be seen to be confessing Christ as the source of all virtue (cf. the biblical fruits of the Spirit) and prays, with the second, dominant chorale, to be kept steadfast in following that Way and Word.

L'Allegro, il Penseroso ed il Moderato was performed on February 27. The program was filled out with Handel's new organ concerto and two **concerti grossi.** At this time as well, John Christopher Smith (the younger) – son of Handel's friend and copyist J.C. Smith the elder, a student of Handel's and eventually Handel's right-hand man and "successor" – presented his own biblical oratorio, *David's Lamentation over Saul and Jonathan.* The Younger Smith's work did reasonably well, having six performances from February 22 to April 2.[*]

In March, Handel himself again offered a benefit concert for the Fund for the Support of Decay'd Musicians and Their Families (the music was *Acis and Galatea* and the *Ode for St. Cecilia's Day*). He continued to offer his opera-patrons-cum-concertgoers an astonishing variety of music. In the spring of that freezing 1739-40 season he presented revivals of *Saul, Esther, Israel in Egypt* and *L'Allegro.* All these concerts also included a concerto grosso and an organ concerto. That cold winter of 1740 at last subsided into spring and early summer. In May, Handel provided wedding – or rather betrothal – music for one more of George II's offspring, Princess Mary. (The circumstances were peculiar: the groom was the Prince of Hesse-Cassel. He had refused to come to England to marry, and George II had refused to allow his daughter Mary to leave England unmarried. So a low-profile ceremony of espousal was held in the Chapel Royal – at which Handel's music was heard – and Mary was then shipped to Germany to join her groom.[9])

Yet Handel was experiencing more winter, metaphorically speaking. Thomas Harris, James's brother, mentions in a May 10 letter having been with

---

[*]William Boyce had set the same text (by the poet John Lockman) in 1736. Smith's oratorio was presented at Hickford's Great Room, one of a series of works by him held there. Donald Burrows notes that "there were very few clashes of dates" of Smith's concerts with Handel's concerts, suggesting there was a spirit of co-operation rather than competition. (Had the younger Smith disregarded Handel's concert dates he would have been in conflict with his father's interests as well, as his father worked for Handel.) Burrows, *Handel*, p. 207.

Handel and Jennens the day before. But just a week later Thomas had bad news about Handel for James: "Handel is soon going to Aix-la-Chapelle [Aachen], having lately found a weakness in his hand."[10] This time, Handel appears to have recognized the early-warning signs of paralysis. He no doubt concluded that the waters which once seemed so beneficial would be again. As before, he didn't let the situation get him down: "But he was in good spiritts yesterday and played finely on the piano-forte."

Of interest here, besides Handel's returned ill health, is the reference to him playing the pianoforte. The piano was still a fairly novel instrument, particularly in Britain. In fact, Charles Jennens was the owner of the first one in London, which he had had imported from Florence in 1732. It is unfortunate that we don't know Handel's reaction to this new instrument which was destined to replace the harpsichord; but he apparently didn't go out of his way to play it more frequently. There is just one other reference to Handel playing the piano; it occurs in Thomas Harris's brother George's diary, May 29, 1756, when Handel was seventy-one years old.

After Thomas Harris's letter, we don't hear anything else about Handel or his trip to Aachen until mid-July. The word was that Handel had set off for Germany.* By September he was in Haarlem, the Netherlands, where he tried out the new organ there "in the large church. "The large church" was built in the fifteenth century as St. Bavo Kerk and converted to the Reformed "Groote Kerk" in 1578. Its now famous organ was just two years old when Handel first played it. The organ was built in three years (finished in 1738) by Christian Müller as a three-manual, sixty-two-stop instrument, including a thirty-two-foot pedal stop. At the time, and for many years, it was the largest organ in the world. It has a singularly beautiful casework, fashioned in the intensely ornamented high-Baroque style. Mozart would play this organ in 1766 when he was ten years old, and Mendelssohn

---

*On July 19, 1740, John Robartes (shortly to become the Fourth Earl of Radnor), told his friend James Harris that Handel had set out the previous Thursday "in company with Goupée" (Joseph Goupy). "Therefore [I] have little hopes of his amendment" (Harris Family Papers, p. 100). Burrows and Dunhill note that Robartes himself "was severely disabled by attacks of gout" (p. 101). That no doubt made him careful not to over-indulge in food and drink, and may have increased his concern for Handel, who, all his friends knew, was particularly fond – too particularly fond, they thought – of good food and drink.

would also play it.*

Handel is said to have intended to travel from Haarlem to Berlin. It seems likely that he may have intended to go to Halle as well, but we have no evidence that he did, or even that he did go to Berlin. By early October, he was back in London, looking "perfectly well"and like his travels had "done him great service." For the new 1740-41 season Handel made what seems to be yet another inexplicable move: he went back to Italian opera. He finally finished *Imeneo* in October 1740. That both Charles Jennens and Thomas Harris refer to *Imeneo* as an "operetta" may say something about their judgment of its lightweight character – and about the fact that after all this time, Handel had written only two acts for it. (He doesn't appear to have been particularly committed to *Imeneo*, though he himself did not call it an operetta.)

That fall, in Handel's native Germany, Johann Mattheson's biography of musicians, *Grundlage einer Ehren-Pforte* (*Basis for an Honor Roll*), was finally published (the German title alludes to a triumphal arch). Handel never did contribute to the book after declining the second of Mattheson's two widely dispersed requests, and Mattheson took Handel's declining to participate hard and personally. (Bach also declined, incidentally.) In informing his readers that "several great princes of art" had been negligent in sending him information, Mattheson compared "the praiseworthy Telemann" to those "dilatory" princes Keiser and Handel. Keiser had died in the meantime, and "the other has put the matter aside." Mattheson bluntly asserted, "They have both broken faith with me" – a most ungracious introductory comment to the account of Handel's professional life which Mattheson finally wrote himself.[11]

Not surprisingly, Mattheson gives himself a prominent role in the first part of Handel's story. But his work shouldn't be discounted. He does provide stories about Handel of which he is our only source, and he corroborates other information. On the whole, his musical-biographical sketch is not unkind to Handel. A cynic might say that Mattheson knew very well that Handel was still alive to read what he had written. However, Handel was also alive to read that unflattering introductory

---

*The organ underwent extensive work in 1866 when it was romanticized according to then current tastes. It was again altered in 1904. In 1961 it was restored to Müller's original specifications, and still attracts organists and visitors from around the world.

For photographs and a stop list see <www.xs4all.nl/~twomusic/christine/bavo/Muller.html>.

comment. Was Mattheson hoping Handel would feel chastised by it? There are indications that Mattheson was writing with the thought of Handel reading it. He appears to want readers to know, without doubt, that he was (would he have put it in present tense?) a close friend of the great man. As some have said, Mattheson's biographical sketch of Handel reveals nearly as much about Mattheson as it does about Handel.

Also that fall, from October 27 to November 20, Handel wrote one last opera, his forty-second: *Deidamia*. The reliable Mrs. Pendarves tells her sister Ann (now Mrs. Dewes, for she had married earlier that year): "Mr. Handel has got a new singer from Italy. Her voice is between Cuzzoni's and Strada's – strong, but not harsh, her person miserably bad, being very low, and excessively crooked. Donellan [a mutual friend] approves of her...."[12] (Mrs. Pendarves' comments on Monza apply to her physical person – a handicap – not her character.) The singer was Maria Monza; in fact, Handel had two new Italian singers, the other being the castrato Giovanni Battista Andreoni, who had sung for Middlesex the previous season.

Handel's return to Italian opera in the 1740-41 season is usually interpreted as a stepping into the breach: Middlesex's company had already disintegrated and would not offer competition.

This move by Handel has also been seen as a last-ditch, stubborn effort to cling to a musical form he loved. If it was a "stepping into the breach," it was a limited one; not a return to Italian opera, as such, nor a renewed, impassioned embrace, but an inclusion of Italian opera, creating another season of mixed delights. It was an inclusion that looks reactionary, but one that made practical sense (theoretically, anyway); and despite occasional appearances otherwise, Handel was an eminently practical man. Offering *some* opera would draw Middlesex's obdurate opera lovers in his direction (many of them, his own former patrons). Handel didn't – and surely didn't intend to – offer an opera season; rather, he offered some opera and some oratorio, the latter with a degree of Italian-language accommodation to his two Italian singers.

In that mixed season, the February 10 presentation of *Deidamia* is significant in that it was the last opera performance Handel was ever involved in. That may be more important for us in retrospect, however, than Handel considered it to be when it occurred in the middle of his 1740-41 season.[*]

There was more going on near the end of this season (spring 1741) than Handel's concert schedule indicates, and once again it caused him deep distress. He committed what was considered a serious *faux pas*, and consequently reaped ridicule and disdain from his social betters. The matter is referred to during the season's final week by a letter writer to the *London Daily Post* who signed himself "J.B." (he has not been identified; by his own word, he was not someone who knew Handel personally). We learn of Handel's social mistake from J.B., but he doesn't vilify the composer. In fact, he mounts a compassionate and heartfelt defense of Handel in light of, and in spite of, what he calls "a *faux Pas* ... a single Disgust" committed by him.[13] What did this entail? There has been much speculation about it for the last two centuries, and about whether the rather sparse number of performances in the 1740-41 season was a result of it.

The mistake Handel made or "disgust" he caused was seen in that era as a serious social transgression, or at least one that seriously offended some of the powerful nobility. It is quite likely, as in the earlier situation with the Opera of the Nobility patrons, that it was an incident in which he refused to bow to their social status or concede to their wishes related to the opera, and Middlesex may well have been involved in some way. But it is hard to imagine, from the distant perspective of our egalitarian age, what Handel could have done that so annoyed, even disgusted, his "betters." It has been suggested that it may have been connected with Handel's renewed (and to some, arrogant) opera promotion. The language of the letter writer refers to the *faux pas* as a single, specific incident to which the parties who took offense responded with something akin to fury. J.B. mentions their "interely [entirely] abandoning" Handel, it having "become a Fashion to neglect him." J.B.'s

---

[*]Donald Burrows suggests that Handel may have continued, as a point of honor, to offer opera this long because technically he had obligations under the twenty-one-year charter of the Royal Academy of Music, though (as with more things about Handel's life and work) there exists "no documentary evidence to illuminate the connection." Burrows points out that the twenty-one years was actually up in July 1740, "but Handel might have interpreted the period as beginning from the first Academy season in April 1720" (*Handel*, p. 213). Fulfilling such a perceived obligation would have been consistent with an eighteenth century gentleman's sense of honor, especially a man like Handel. On the other hand, the charter didn't actually restrict Handel to opera. It called for "opera And to Exhibit all other Entertainments of Musick within any house built ... where [they] can be best fitted..." (Judith Milhous and Robert D. Hume , "New Light on Handel and The Royal Academy of Music in 1720," *Theater Journal*, v. 35, no. 2 [1983], p. 149, in Burrows).

purpose in writing the letter was to remind his countrymen of the musical riches Handel had been providing for them for so many years. J.B. wanted those who felt wronged to reconsider. If the *faux pas* was the slighting of certain noblemen or - women by Handel – a specific ignoring their musical wishes, and thus, their persons – those exalted persons may well have considered such a thing the willful, arrogant act of someone acting beyond his station in life.

Whatever the details were, the unpleasantness related to the incident was severe enough to begin rumors once again that Handel was going to leave the country, implying he would go back to Germany permanently. J.B. is sure that Handel's offense was unintentional, and that it was a matter of pride, or old age or infirmity – all causes which could, or should, excuse the act (Handel was then fifty-six years old. Many people lived well beyond that, but it was a more advanced age then than we would consider it to be.) J.B. wants to

> *persuade the Gentlemen who have taken Offence at any part of this great Man's Conduct (for a great Man he must be in the Musical World, whatever his Misfortunes may now too late say to the contrary:) I wish I could persuade them, I say, to take him back into Favour, and relieve him from the cruel Persecution of those little Vermin, who, taking Advantage of their Displeasure, pull down even his Bills as fast as he has them pasted up; and use a thousand other little Arts to injure and distress him. I am sure when they weigh the Thing without Prejudice, they will take him back into Favour; but in the mean time, let the Publick take Care that he wants not: That would be an unpardonable Ingratitude; and as this Oratorio of Wednesday next is his last for this Season, and if Report be true, probably his last for ever in this Country, let them, with a generous and friendly Benevolence, fill this his last House, and shew him on his Departure, that London, the greatest and richest city in the World, is great and rich in Virtue, as well as in Money, and can pardon and forget the Failings, or even the Faults of a great Genius.... I heartily wish, that all the polite Part of his disgusted Friends, may do him the Honour of their Attendances; in which Case, I doubt not but he will have the Fate of the Swan, who, just under the Knife of the Cook, was saved by the Sweetness of his last melancholy melodious Song.*

J.B. concludes by asking those offended to consider what ill effects their displeasure – the displeasure of "So many Gentlemen of Figure and Weight" so openly expressed – was having upon Handel's person and career. He asserts poignantly, "I'm sure ... that they will reflect upon the Frog in the Fable, who, whilst the Boys wantonly pelted him with Stones, cry'd out to them in his Hoarse Voice, Good Gentlemen forbear, it may be Sport to you, but it is Death to me."

On the day of the last performance of the 1740-41 season, four days after J.B.'s letter appeared, the *London Daily Post* carried an announcement of the concert that evening. Appended to the announcement was a notice from Handel himself. It is mostly informational, but from it we can infer that J.B.'s letter (no doubt the buzz of London in the previous few days) had some effect – if not on the disgusted noblemen, on others who wanted to hear this last concert of Handel's (probably his last ever in London, if they believed the rumors). Handel seems wary of causing further offense:

> *This being the last Time of performing, many Persons of Quality and others, are pleas'd to make great Demands for Box Tickets, which encourage me (and hope will give no Offence) to put the Pit and Boxes together, at Half a Guinea each. First Gallery 5s[shillings]. Second Gallery 3 s. To begin at Half an Hour after Six o'Clock.*[14]

Handel clearly did have friends among the nobility. "All the fashionable people were there," observed Mrs. Pendarves's friend Miss Donellan from her own seat at the concert.

That summer Handel stayed in London. The Fourth Earl of Radnor (John Robartes), still concerned about Handel's health and his possible succumbing to gout (whose pains he himself knew well), informed James Harris:

> *Mr. Handel instead of goeing to Scarborough to drink the waters, drinks wine with Mr. Furnes at Gunsbury[,] and I fear eats too mutch of those things he ought to avoid. I would fain methinks preserve him for a few years longer.* *

---

*Burrows and Dunhill identify "Furnes" as MP Henry Furnese, whom Handel knew as a subscriber to the Royal Academy of Music in 1723 and to his own (and Heidegger's) opera enterprise in 1728, and as a director of the Opera of the Nobility. Furnese also subscribed to Handel's Op. 6 concerti grossi. Further, "a letter of 9 April 1739 from Giambattista Gastaldi to Prince Antioch Kantemir suggests that Furnese paid the theater rent, and possibly other expenses, for Handel's season of performances at the King's Theater in January-May 1739, perhaps on account of his admiration for [the singer] Francesina" (Harris Papers, p. 117). In a July 25 letter, Radnor had already told Harris that "Mr. Handel has dined with me but twice this summer but is mutch with Mr. Furnes in this neighbourhood."

Chapter 13
The Subject is *Messiah*

Having done his best to rid himself of the memory of the previous, emotionally difficult season, Handel now wrapped himself in oratorio writing, which would, finally, be the primary occupation of the rest of his life. If this decision was practical, it also offered him spiritual solace. He knew how well the "sublime passages" which abound in Scripture lend themselves to musical setting, and he received "high gratification" from providing these settings.[1] By now, given his numerous anthems and previous oratorios, he could also readily recognize that he had a particular knack for effectively setting English-language Scripture and Scripture-based texts to music. Hawkins said, "He was well acquainted with the Holy Scriptures, and was sensible that the sublime sentiments with which they abound would give opportunities of displaying his greatest talents."

Charles Jennens, for one, was quite happy about Handel's writing oratorios. It was Jennens's *Messiah* libretto that Handel took in hand late in the summer of 1741. (Strictly speaking, in the case of *Messiah* Jennens was a compiler, as he did no writing of his own but selected and ordered passages from Scripture. This was no small task, however, and one he did expertly.) In July, Jennens told his friend the Classical scholar Edward Holdsworth that he had hoped to persuade Handel to

> set another Scripture Collection I have made for him, & perform it for
> his own Benefit in Passion Week. I hope he will lay out his whole
> Genius & Skill upon it, that the Composition may excell all his former
> Compositions, as the Subject excells every other subject. The Subject is
> *Messiah*.[1]

Jennens succeeded, and Handel wrote *Messiah* between August 22 and September 14, 1741, a span of twenty-four days.

In the nineteenth century and most of the twentieth, much has been made of Handel's feat of writing a three-part, fifty-three-movement, three-hour long oratorio in three weeks and three days. Christians have often pointed to this as an indication of his enthralled commitment to the Subject of *Messiah*, and the inspiration he took from writing an oratorio with Christ himself as its center. Handel surely *was* committed. It should be clear by now that all his life Handel embraced the Christian faith on which he was nurtured, and that he was expressing his own faith when he wrote *Messiah*. But we also noted earlier that Handel's exceedingly swift composition of *Messiah* was not so unusual for him. (Nor was very quick composition unusual for other composers of the time. Handel's friend Telemann could compose so fast that Handel himself said of him that he could complete a piece in the time it would take most people to write a letter.) With only a couple of exceptions in Handel's entire output of hundreds of works, he wrote speedily. Even among the exceptions, it wasn't so much that he composed them slowly, but that he laid them aside uncompleted to work on other things, then came back to them later.

Messiah's twenty-four-day composition time can best be put into perspective by comparing to the time it took Handel to write his other oratorios. All of the oratorios are substantial works; many are about the length of *Messiah*, a few are shorter, some are longer. A representative sample of the dozen-and-a-half oratorios: *Saul* is a behemoth, having eighty-six movements; Handel composed it from July 23 to September 27, 1738 – a span of thirty-six days.* *Joshua*, sixty movements, is approximately the length of *Messiah*. Handel wrote it from July 19 to August 19, 1747 – thirty-two days. *Israel in Egypt* was completed between October 1 and November 1, 1738 – thirty-two days – though its entire first part had been previously composed and only needed adapting *Solomon*, in just over sixty movements, was composed between May 5 and June 13, 1748 – forty days. In that context, So Handel's composing of *Messiah* in twenty-four days is not quite so astonishing. However, he did complete it in somewhat less time than any other oratorio of comparable length.

There is anecdotal evidence that Handel was intensely affected by the act of setting *Messiah's* libretto to music. One often quoted example comes to us from Sir John Hawkins's daughter, Leatitia, on the authority of Dr Allot, Dean of Raphoe. Upon completing the "Hallelujah" Chorus, Handel is said to have exclaimed, "I did think I did see all Heaven before me – and the great God himself!"

Most modern scholars dismiss this quotation as a later fabrication, since there is no discernable historical source to tell us who might have overheard Handel say this, or confirming that he told someone of his experience afterwards; and few scholars today believe such visions possible. While there is have no source verifying

---

*The number of movements in each oratorio, including *Messiah*, is somewhat fluid, since Handel frequently rewrote and substituted movements according to the circumstances and soloists of a given performance, and a particular oratorio may have been performed with a combination of original and reworked or substituted movements.

that Handel said the specific words attributed to him, or if he did, what exactly he saw and felt while composing *Messiah's* "Hallelujah," the thought that he himself was profoundly, spiritually affected while composing *Messiah* is wholly plausible, and a quite natural assertion. Given the oratorio's intense spiritual as well as musical effect on vast numbers of people in the subsequent two-and-a-half centuries, would *Messiah* not have, first of all, profoundly effected its creator?

Despite that effect, Handel could not know then how intricately and intimately this new, unique oratorio would inhabit the rest of his life; nor, of course, could he immediately know how profoundly its sound would go out into the world (to appropriate the words of one of its choruses). It would be March of the following year, 1742, before anyone but the composer himself would hear *Messiah* in performance. There is justice in the fact that those who would hear it first, and unfeignedly embrace it, would not be the "Quality" English who had been, and still were, such a consistent thorn in Handel's side, but the nobility in Dublin: Irishmen and -women whose acceptance and hospitality the composer would so come to value. That's because two months after finishing *Messiah*, Handel set out for Ireland at the invitation of the Lord Lieutenant William Cavendish, and he took *Messiah* with him.

He went well-prepared. Not only did he have *Messiah* in hand, but quite literally a trunkful of other music, including a second, still unfinished oratorio, *Samson*, which he had started but then laid aside two weeks after *Messiah* was done. (Perhaps he intended to finish it in any spare time he had.) He also shipped over his own organ, and several of his London oratorio soloists would travel to Dublin to sing for him there. The tables were turned in another way. Only a night or two before he left, Handel spent the evening at the opera, as a spectator for once. He confessed to a certain glee that the opera he saw was as bad as it was. "It made me very merry all along my journey," he forthrightly admitted in a letter to Jennens.[2]

On that trip Handel was given unexpected time to rehearse *Messiah*. He and the other passengers who were to sail across the Irish Sea by packet boat were grounded in the medieval English city of Chester for some days waiting for the wind to change. The young Charles Burney met Handel there for the first time and "very well remember[ed] seeing him smoke a pipe, over a dish of coffee, at the Exchange-Coffee house." But Burney most particularly remembered that first-ever rehearsal of some movements of *Messiah*. Handel "applied to Mr. Baker, the Organist, my first music-master, to know whether there were any choirmen in the cathedral who could sing *at sight*," says Burney, "as he wished to prove some books that had been hastily transcribed, by trying the choruses which he intended to perform in Ireland."[3] One of those recommended was a bass named Janson, a printer and amateur musician.

A time was fixed for this private rehearsal at the Golden Falcon, *where HANDEL was quarter'd; but, alas! On trial of the chorus in the Messiah, "And with his stripes we are healed," – Poor Janson, after repeated attempts, failed so egregiously, that HANDEL let loose his great bear upon him; and after swearing in four or five languages, cried out in broken English, 'You shcauntrel! Tit not you dell me "dat you could sing at soite?" " – "Yes, sir," says the printer, and so I can; but not at first sight."* *

The packet boat arrived in Ireland in the third week of November. But when Handel arrived he experienced a situation which modern air travelers who have had luggage lost will relate to: "His cloaths & organ were not yet come," Shaftesbury reported back in England.[3] Dublin was a city with a thriving musical and theatrical establishment to which performers from London traveled periodically for a change of scenery. The city had two theaters and a new concert hall on Fishamble Street where Handel's music would be heard (large music halls devoted specifically to concerts, as opposed to spoken-word drama and opera, were a rather new thing).

From December to April, an ebullient Handel remained in Dublin providing a variety of his music for Dubliners – but not yet *Messiah*. At his arrival, his reputation had preceded him. "I needed not sell one single Ticket at the Door," he told Jennens in his December 29 letter. "The Nobility [who] did me the Hoñour

---

* Burney's frequent mimicking Handel's German accent in print sometimes exaggerates for effect, as also seems to he true with Handel's "swearing" – which consisted of phrases like "damned scoundrel," and jocular references to going to the devil (which, much more serious then than now, was a polite way of telling a person to go to hell). Handel was a proficient in German, English, Latin, French and Italian (re: the "swearing in four or five languages"). His life-long German accent, combined with his knowledge of these other languages and his native wit, often had his listeners smiling. Hawkins said, "Among other particulars in his character that rendered his conversation very pleasing, one was a talent that enabled him to tell a story with all the circumstances that tend to enliven it." And: "Of the English also he had such a degree of knowledge, as to be susceptible of the beauties of our best poets; so that in the multiplicity of his compositions to English words, he very seldom stood in need of assistance in the explanation of a passage for the purpose of suiting the sense with correspondent sounds. The style of his discourse was very singular; he pronounced the English as the Germans do, but his phrase was exotic, and partook of the idiom of the different countries in which he had resided, a circumstance that rendered his conversation exceedingly risible."

to makes amongst themselves a Subscription for 6 Nights, which did fill a Room of 600 Persons." For all the subsequent concerts, too, subscriptions were sold in advance, and newspaper announcements warned that "no Single Tickets will be delivered, or Money taken at the Door." As was the custom in London also, the tickets were in most cases sold under the auspices of Handel himself, from the house in which he was staying.

Handel was joyous. His singers, he told Jennens, "please extraordinary," the chorus was singing "exceeding well," and the orchestra, whose concertmaster he had brought from London, was "really excellent." (After his comments about the soloists Handel refers to "the *rest* of the Chorus Singers" – evidence of the then common practice of the soloists singing an entire oratorio, choruses as well as their own recitatives and arias.) He was also happy with the acoustics of the new Fishamble Street music hall: "The Musick sounds delightfully in this charming Room." Altogether, it put him "in such Spirits (and my Health being so good) that I exert my self on my Organ with more than usual Success" (playing the organ concertos at the intermissions, as he did in London). He concluded:

> *I cannot sufficiently express the kind treatment I receive here, but the Politeness of this generous Nation cannot be unknown to you, so I let You judge of the satisfaction I enjoy, passing my time with Honnour [sic], profit, and pleasure.*

Handel's faithful friend Lord Shaftesbury again passed the good word on to James Harris, quipping, "Handel is like to come home a considerable gainer, if the great hospitality shown him does not kill him with good living."* Then, at last, on March 27, 1742, Faulkner's *Dublin Journal* informed the city:

> *For the Relief of the Prisoners in the several Gaols, and for the Support of Mercer's Hospital in Stephen's Street, and of the Charitable Infirmary on the Inns Quay, on Monday the 12th of April, will be performed at the Musick Hall in Fishamble Street Mr. Handel's new Grand Oratorio, call'd the MESSIAH, in which the Gentlemen of the*

---

*In a December 29 letter to Jennens, Handel had asked Jennens to "insinuate my most devoted Respects to My Lord and my Lady Shaftesbury, You know how much Their Kind Protection is precious to me." Besides Jennens, Shaftesbury, James Harris, Thomas Harris and Lord Radnor all passed around information about Handel while he was in Ireland, some of which came directly from Handel via Jennens, the rest of which came from Perceval, another friend of theirs.

> *Choirs of both Cathedrals will assist, with some Concertoes on the Organ, by Mr. Handell.*[4]

Tickets were half a guinea each; buying a ticket also entitled the buyer to attend the public rehearsal on April 10.** The first performance was postponed a day, to April 13, "at the desire of several Persons of Distinction," reported Faulkner's *Dublin Journal*, demonstrating that in Ireland too, when the nobility spoke, people listened.

The rehearsal alone was an "event," causing excited anticipation of Handel's new, unusual oratorio. The *Dublin News-letter* of April 10 noted that "Mr. Handel's new sacred Oratorio, ... in the opinion of the best Judges, far surpasses anything of that Nature, which has been performed in this or any other Kingdom." *Messiah*, even in its first full rehearsal, was heard to the "entire satisfaction of the most crowded and polite Assembly." Faulkner's *Dublin Journal* said much the same, adding: "The sacred Words [are] properly adapted for the Occasion" – a point considered debatable (and contentious) when Handel brought *Messiah* home to London.

As the enthusiastic reaction to *Messiah*'s public rehearsal made clear, there would be a great number of people attending the performance and the hall would be crowded. That being so, the *Dublin Journal* carried this most civil and now famous request regarding that first performance, which was to begin at noon on Tuesday, April 13, 1742:

> *Many Ladies and Gentlemen who are well-wishers to this Noble and Grand Charity for which this Oratorio was composed, request it as a Favour, that the Ladies who honour this Performance with their Presence would be pleased to come without Hoops, as it will greatly encrease the Charity, by making Room for more company.*

On the day of the performance there was a counterpart request for the gentlemen:

**The guinea was a gold coin whose worth had been set in 1717 at 21 shillings. The English crown was worth five shillings; a pound was made up of 20 shillings and there were 12 pennies to a shilling. The shilling (not the pound) was the principal medium of exchange A shilling was a fair day's wage for most workers, though highly skilled workers might make more than twice that much, and unskilled workers and farm laborers less. Wages and prices were complicated by the social stratification. This puts into perspective the cost of opera and oratorio tickets, whose usual price was half a guinea (nothing extra was charged in the case of a benefit concert). The cheapest theater seats in the gallery generally cost a shilling. Calculating the modern equivalent worth of this money isn't a straightforward task, but to get a general idea, multiply eighteenth century pounds by 100 (Allen Grove, professor of eighteenth century literature, Alfred University, Alfred, NY).

not to take up extra room, they were "desired to come without their Swords." In the event, 700 people crammed into the Music Hall, which normally held 600.

The report on the concert, which ran in three Dublin papers on April 17 (there was an independent report in a fourth publication), summed up *Messiah's* powerful effect on its first audience:

The Sublime, the Grand, the Tender adapted to the most elevated, majestick and moving Words, conspired to transport and charm the ravished Heart and Ear.

It is an effect that all subsequent *Messiah* audiences down the years have come to know. Reinforcing the moral sublimity of the music, its composer "generously gave the Money arising from this Grand Performance" to the three charities named in the concert announcement of March 27, and the gentlemen of the choir and the soloists did as well, being "satisfied with the deserved Applause of the Publick, and the conscious Pleasure of promoting such useful, and extensive Charity," reported the *Dublin Journal.*

Messiah was performed again on June 3, the last of Handel's concerts in Ireland. Since it was now essentially summer, at that last Dublin performance in *Messiah's* debut year, "in order to keep the Room as cool as possible, a Pane of Glass [would] be removed from the Top of each of the Windows" of the Music Hall, prospective concertgoers were assured.

Handel's intensely gratifying and immensely successful Dublin concert season over, he remained in the city until mid-August (1742), no doubt simply enjoying himself, thankful for his great success and luxuriating in the warmth of his Irish hosts. A few days before he left Dublin he reportedly attended a performance of *Hamlet* featuring the great actor David Garrick. Dubliners had had the opportunity to attend fifteen concerts of Handel's music (mostly choral music). They heard, interspersed with organ concertos, *Acis and Galatea,* the *Ode for St. Cecilia's Day, Alexander's Feast; L'Allegro, il Penseroso ed il Moderato, Imeneo* (performed as a serenata, not an opera); *Esther* and *Saul* (specially requested); and – in its first two performances of thousands in the roughly 260 years since – *Messiah.* In addition, *Utrecht Te Deum and Jubilate* and the *Coronation Anthems* were performed at church-services-cum-benefit-concerts for Mercer's Hospital.

Handel had not intended to stay nearly so long, but early on found it necessary to ask the permission he needed from King George to remain in Dublin in order to present more – and more – concerts. (Handel was still receiving several

Royal pensions. These carried certain stipulations, one of which, apparently, required him to get Royal permission to be away for any substantial length of time.) He hoped to see Charles Jennens at Gopsall on his way home, to give him a word-of-mouth account of "how well Your Messiah was received" in Ireland, "that generous and polite Nation."[5] That didn't work out. He eventually saw Jennens in November, after Jennens had moved to London for the winter musical season.

In the meantime Handel wrote a letter to Jennens, enclosing comments about *Messiah* by the Bishop of Elphim, Edward Synge. Handel talked about his future plans:

> *The report that the Direction of the Opera next winter is comitted to my Care, is groundless. The gentlemen who have undertaken to middle with Harmony can not agree, and are quite in a Confusion. Whether I shall do some thing in the Oratorio way (as several of my friends desire) I can not determine as yet. Certain it is that this time 12 month I shall continue my Oratorio's in Ireland.*[6]

It has been suggested (by Deutsch) that Handel's reference to "the gentlemen who have undertaken to *middle* with Harmony" is a pun on the name of Lord Middlesex. That fits Handel's lively sense of humor and ability to produce puns and *bon mots* in various languages. Or, more mundanely (and less likely, given his knowledge of the language), Handel mistook "middle" for "mettle."

Once again, his manner in writing to Jennens is easy and rather informal, as friends who, at base, share musical and spiritual values. He is so eager to see Jennens and fill him in on his almost eight months in Ireland that he says, "I think it a very long time to the month of November next when I can have some hopes of seeing You here in Town." Then he urges Jennens, "Pray let me hear meanwhile of Your Health and Welfare."

It is easy to see why Handel wanted to return to Ireland, but surprising that he says that he hadn't really determined if he was going to concentrate on oratorio for the next season (and beyond). On the other hand, he surely had lingering doubts about how he would be received again in his adopted country, just what he should offer critical London audiences, and how and when he should offer it.

Not long after Handel's return from Dublin, he told Radnor (John Robartes) that he was "goeing somewhere into the country." He no doubt needed some solitary time to consider his future. A week later that was confirmed: "Mr. Handel intends soon to visit Wilton for some time" (Wilton House, near Salisbury, was the home of the Earl of Pembroke). In mid-October Handel paid Radnor a visit. Radnor wrote to James Harris on October 21:

> *He tels me he does not intend to leave town this season, neither is he employd by the directors of the opera. I believe he wil give us some oritorios after Christmus, for I understand by him he has voices enough at command for that purpose.**

So Handel had decided that he would, indeed, present oratorios in London in the New Year, and that he would not return to Ireland. Working toward that end, he plunged back into the still unfinished *Samson*.

~

That was how the situation stood prior to the London debut of *Messiah* on March 23, 1743. Four days before *Messiah's* appearance in London the issue of the appropriateness of biblical oratorios being performed in the theater was again publicly raised, this time by a writer to the *Universal Spectator* who signed himself "Philalethes" ("lover of truth"). The magazine's editor acknowledged that the letter might be, for many of his readers, "too rigid a Censure on a Performance which is so universally approv'd," but he felt he should publish it because "there is so well-intended a Design[,] and pious Zeal runs through the whole, and nothing derogatory said of Mr. Handel's Merit."[7] Many subsequent critics have not been that understanding.

Philalethes described himself as a music lover and "one of the few" who never deserted Handel. Unlike an earlier writer who had said that a place is hallowed (or profaned) by the action that takes place there, and not the action hallowed or profaned by the place, Philalethes believed that the oratorios' performance in theaters by singers whose lives were (or were presumed to be) less than Christian, for the purpose of "diverting" a less-than-devout audience was a "prophanation" that would hinder the Gospel:

> *An Oratorio either is an Act of Religion, or it is not; if it is, I ask if the Playhouse is a fit Temple to perform it in, or a Company of Players fit Ministers of God's Word, for in that Case such they are made.*
> *Under the Jewish Dispensation, the Levites only might come near*

---

*Burrows and Dunhill (Harris Papers) interpret this as Handel not going to the country after all. But it may refer to his not going back to Ireland as he had hoped and intended.

to do the Service of the Tabernacle, and no common Person might so much as touch the Ark of God: Is God's Service less holy now?

In the other Case, if it is not perform'd as an Act of Religion, but for Diversion and Amusement only (and indeed I believe few or none go to an Oratorio out of Devotion), what a Prophanation of God's Name and Word is this, to make so light Use of them? I wish every one would consider, whether, at the same Time they are diverting themselves, they are no accessory to the breaking the Third Commandment. I am sure it is not following the Advice of the Psalmist, Serve the Lord with Fear, and rejoice unto him with Reverence: How must if offend a devout Jew, to hear the great Jehovah, the proper and most sacred Name of God (a Name a Jew, if not a Priest, hardly dare pronounce) sung, I won't say to a light Air (for as Mr. Handel compos'd it, I dare say it is not) but by a Set of People very unfit to perform so solemn a Service. David said, How can we sing the Lord's Song in a strange Land; but sure he would have thought it much strange to have heard it sung in a Playhouse....

As to the Pretence that there are many Persons who will say their Prayers there who will not go to Church, I believe I may venture to say, that the Assertion is false, without Exception; for I can never believe that Persons who have so little regard for Religion, as to think it not worth their while to go to Church for it, will have any Devotion on hearing a religious Performance in a Playhouse. On the contrary, I'm more apt to fear it gives great Opportunity to prophane Persons to ridicule Religion at least, if not to blaspheme it; and, indeed, every Degree of Ridicule on what is sacred, is a Degree of Blasphemy....

The writer wondered how this impiety would appear to later ages – to us. He even wondered what a "Mahometan [would] think of this, who with so much Care and Veneration keep their Alcoran [Koran]?"

What must they think of us and our Religion? Will they not be confirm'd in their Errors? Will not they be apt to say, that surely we ourselves believe it no better than a Fable, by the Use we make of it; and may not the Gospel, by this Means (as well as by the wicked Lives of Christians) be hinder'd from spreading? A Thing of no small Consequence, and which ought to be consider'd by us who have the lively

Oracles committed to us, and are bound by all the Ties of Gratitude and Humanity, as well as Honour and Conscience, to endeavour to enlarge that Kingdom of Christ, which we pray should come.

Philalethes had, not surprisingly, heard about *Messiah*, and that it would very soon be performed in London. That distressed him because of its subject, though he wisely didn't say anything beyond that about the work because he didn't know anything about it at that point. Given the seriousness of his criticism, at first glance it seems amazing that he didn't direct any of it at Handel himself. Philalethes criticized Handel's "company of players" and his audiences but not Handel himself, though Handel had spent two and a half decades in the theater (not, however, setting *biblical* texts for theatrical performance during most of that time). But Handel was, after all, as the creator of these biblically based "diversions" and therefore was responsible for their being performed in theaters, and for choosing the performers. (He couldn't, of course, control who was in his audiences, what level of devotion they had, or with what intent they attended the oratorios.)

For all Philalethes' own genuine concern regarding the oratorios' performance and audiences, perhaps he didn't criticize Handel because his love of Handel's music predisposed him in favor of the composer. Yet given the serious nature of his argument, it is doubtful that love of Handel's music *per se* would have prevented him from criticism of the composer himself if he felt it was warranted. So what exempted Handel from criticism in this context? Handel's irreproachable personal reputation seems to be the answer. While those who knew him knew his foibles, there are no stories of immorality or other scandalous behavior that accrued to him, as there are regarding various other figures of the period attached to both the spoken and musical theater. On the contrary, he was known, publicly and privately, as a sincere and generous Christian whose creating music based on Scripture was seen – even by Christians as "rigid" as Philalethes – as congruent with his character. Burney saw Handel as "having been *always* [my emphasis] impressed with a profound reverence for the doctrines and duties of the Christian religion." Burney also noted,

Fond of his art, and diligent in its cultivation, and the exercise of it, as a profession, he spent so studious and sedentary a life, as seldom allowed him to mix in society, or partake of public amusements.[8]

And William Coxe (or J.C. Smith speaking through him) said:

Handel's religious disposition was not a mere display, it was amply

> *productive of religion's best fruit, charity; and this liberal sentiment not only influenced him in the day of prosperity, but even when standing on the very brink of ruin.*

As already mentioned, Hawkins also confirmed in Handel an obvious sincerity of faith and "regularity" and morality of lifestyle (excepting gastronomic indulgence).

Among the Harris Papers, unearthed by Donald Burrows and Rosemary Dunhill and published for the first time in 2002, there is a comment by George Harris to his brother James that seems to indicate that Philalethes's reservations about biblical oratorios in the theater was much more widely shared than is now usually assumed. George Harris wrote from London to his brother at home in Salisbury:

> *I am told there was a prodigious croud at the Foundling Hospital this morning to hear the Messiah. —There were more tickets disposed of than the chappel would contain;—two or three bishops were there; so that I hope, in a little while, the hearing of oratorios will be held as orthodox.* [9]

What is especially notable about this is that George Harris was writing in May 1750, *seven* years after *Messiah* made its debut in London, and eighteen years after *Esther* first appeared in public and Bishop of London Edmund Gibson was presumed (by some) to have prevented it from being acted for theological and moral reasons. Harris's remark indicates that the appropriateness of biblical oratorios being sung in theaters, by singer-actors, was, even then, an ongoing issue. The remark implies that there were enough critics who worried about the Word-of-God-in-the-theater issue and had concluded that the oratorios (and thus their listeners) were biblically unorthodox that some number of people had stayed away from the oratorios all this time, and still were staying away for fear of branded unorthodox.

George Harris hoped that the presence of Church of England bishops at *Messiah* would correct this situation. But he may have been overlooking the fact that this performance which the bishops attended was in the Foundling Hospital *chapel*. Even without the presence of the bishops, some critics undoubtedly considered the chapel performance an improvement over the theater. The fact that it was a charity performance may also have helped – though those who objected to the presumably free-living opera singers pouring out biblical words that concentrated on the Savior were likely not assuaged by this change of setting. If George Harris's perception was true at this time, it cannot be assumed that the main objections were coming mostly from "conservative" Methodists, Baptists and other evangelical Dissenters. Though increasingly influential, they were a relatively small minority compared to the Church of England. And George Harris was a Church of England clergyman, so his view of the scene was surely from the point of view of its Anglican leaders and members.

On the same day that Philalethes's argument appeared in the *Universal Spectator*, Handel's advertisement for *Messiah* appeared in the *Daily Advertiser*. It is not possible that he had already seen Philalethes' letter (unless *Spectator* editor Henry Baker had specifically shown it to him before it went to press). But Handel was cautious: he was aware of the issue because it had been raised previously. He knew that especially a directly scriptural oratorio centered on Christ himself might draw criticism in London. So his announcement omits any reference to *Messiah* as the oratorio's name. It informs the public of "A NEW SACRED ORATORIO. With a *Concerto* on the *Organ*. And a Solo on the Violin by *Mr. Dubourg*."

Philalethes's letter, naturally, brought responses from those who believed that where an oratorio is performed, and who performs it, does not corrupt its biblical message. After three performances of *Messiah*, the *Daily Advertiser* of March 31 contained a verse "wrote extempore by a Gentleman, on reading the *Universal Spectator*." Those three performances had given Londoners an opportunity to judge *Messiah*, and many reacted warily. At issue were precisely the points Philalethes raised about where and who performed it at issue, including an uneasiness about Christ being the oratorio's subject and its words being taken directly from Scripture. No one (except Jennens!) criticized the quality of the music.

The "Gentleman" defended *Messiah*, arguing that it is not the place that profanes one's praise but the praise that sanctifies the place:

Cease, Zealots, cease to blame these Heav'nly Lays,
For Seraphs fit to sing Messiah's Praise!
Nor, for your trivial Argument, assign,
"The Theater not fit for Praise Divine."

These hallow'd Lays to Musick give new Grace,
To Virtue Awe, and sanctify thePlace;
To Harmony, like his, Celestial Pow'r is giv'n,
T' exalt the Soul from Earth, and make, of Hell, a Heav'n.[10]

Philalethes responded, partly also in verse, reiterating that it wasn't the "heav'nly Lays" of "Handel's Art" that he was finding fault with.

Given the ongoing nature of this public discussion, there was undoubtedly talk of it in private circles as well. Jennens had intended Handel to present *Messiah* in London during Lent of 1742, when it would have been most appropriate, and when other theatrical entertainment would not have competed with it. (Handel's trip to Ireland, with *Messiah*, had materialized without Jennens's knowledge.) *Messiah*'s debut in London finally occurred during Lent of 1743 (in March). But given the nature of the objections, the fact that it was presented during Lent may only have exacerbated the negative reaction of those who were of the same mind as Philalethes.

The point of the librettos being in English, of course, was that the texts as well as music can be understood and reacted to. Philalethes and those of his opinion were not the only listeners to take seriously the spiritual effects of the oratorio librettos. (We've already seen Mary Pendarves' response.) While an adjustment in this regard — learning to heed the texts — was required by some portion of the former opera audience, the fact that the oratorios are "an Act of Religion" was immediately obvious to many in Handel's audiences. (That did not mean, however, that they agreed that such "acts" should not be conducted in a theater.)

The difference between the English audiences' chilly reception and the Irish audiences' warm embrace of *Messiah* (which was at that moment repeating itself in the Dublin 1743 musical season without Handel himself) seems to have weighed heavily on him. England was, after all, his adopted home. If he now envisioned with trepidation a re-experiencing of his earlier desertion by audiences of "Quality," and if he felt like the biblical prophet without honor in his own country (which also described the Messiah), it would not be surprising. In fact, he was ill again soon after *Messiah*'s London debut — a recurrence of the paralysis and mental disturbance that had afflicted him in 1737.

Nothing like *Messiah* had ever been composed before, by anyone — not for church use, and certainly not for concert use. No Latin or English church music can be compared to it. Even in Handel's own German Lutheran tradition, where there were musical "histories" of Christ's birth, Passion and resurrection (such as Heinrich Schütz's *Historien der Geburt und Auferstehung Jesu Christ — History of the Birth and Resurrection of Jesus Christ*), there was nothing approaching the scope or intent of *Messiah*. Jennens's libretto does far more than present the story of Jesus's life on earth, set to nicely suitable music by Handel. It "preaches" the entire gospel by presenting the biblical story of salvation, from the Old Testament prophecies of the Messiah's coming to the fulfillment of those prophecies in Christ's birth, death and resurrection, to the Savior's finished work and cosmic and eternal reign.

Beyond the stated objections, part of the initial negative reaction by London audiences may have been that *Messiah*, properly heard, indeed requires an "Act of Religion." Handel's eighteenth century Christian and nominally Christian audience had little, if any, notion of the modern secular practice of ignoring the biblical message of *Messiah* while attempting to glean from it general humanistic truths. (The Old Testament oratorio performances drew some of London's Jews, but it is logical to assume that that was not the case with *Messiah*.) No one but a Deist (in whose view Christ is not divine) could have easily been able to shuck aside the oratorio's textual content to concentrate on the music alone. In the instance of *Messiah*, that undoubtedly unnerved some audience members who had been accustomed to doing just that when listening to Italian opera, whose unintelligible librettos required nothing of them as listeners. In *Messiah's* case, its peculiar combining of "Church-Musick" with the "Airs of the Stage," as Newburgh Hamilton defined oratorio, may have initially made nervous even some *Messiah* listeners who easily accepted Handel's previous oratorios.*

But when the strangeness and novelty of the subject matter had finally been accepted and assimilated, the immense emotional and spiritual power of Handel's musical treatment of it were obvious. And so *Messiah's* unique place in history began to be molded. No one, least of all Handel himself in the spring of 1743, predicted the vast change in its reception in England within the last decade of Handel's life, nor the eventual place *Messiah* would be accorded by audiences worldwide and across the centuries.

If some of Handel's critics complained of *Messiah* on theological and moral

---

*As indicated earlier, the numbers of Deists in Britain were then few and confined to the educated upper classes. Their ideas of course later took root in other guises, and spread. Those ideas – e.g., God is a distant, impersonal and largely impotent entity; human reason is morally autonomous and consequently humankind needs no salvation – were worrisome to the greater part of English society and were adamantly opposed in tracts, sermons and numerous publications. The free-thinking Voltaire, in commenting on the church and various Christian groups during his three-year stay in England (1726-29), was of the opinion that the Deist thinkers didn't stand a chance of having their ideas take hold. He asked, rhetorically and sardonically: "Is it not whimsical enough that Luther, Calvin, and Zuinglius, all of them wretched authors, should have founded sects which are now spread over a great part of Europe, that Mahomet, though so ignorant, should have given a religion to Asia and Africa, and that Sir Isaac Newton, Dr. Clark, Mr. Locke, Mr. Le Clerc, etc., the greatest philosophers, as well as the ablest writers of their ages, should scarcely have been able to raise a little flock, which even decreases daily?" (*Letters on the English. [Lettres Philosophiques]* Harvard Classics, Vol. 34, Part 2, Letter vii.– On the Socinians, or Arians, or Antitrinitarians.)

grounds, others did so on social grounds. *Messiah's* mediocre reception was, according to both Burney and Hawkins, due to a new bout of ill-will on the part of some of the nobility. Hawkins says,

> *He had a slight return of that disorder which had driven him to seek relief from the baths of Aix-la-Chapelle; and, to add to this misfortune, an opposition to him and his entertainment was set on foot by some persons of distinction, who by card assemblies, and other amusements, at that time not usual in the Lent season, endeavoured to make his audiences as thin as possible. The effects of this association he felt for a season or two, in the course whereof he frequently performed to houses that would not pay his expenses; but at length a change of sentiment in the public began to manifest itself; the Messiah was received with universal applause....*[11]

The deliberate sabotaging of Handel's oratorios by certain aristocrats who held card parties and other social gatherings on concert dates would become all too common in the next years. Burney suggests that they still held a grudge because of Handel's firing of the castrato Senesino:

> *During the first years of his retreat from the Opera stage, the profits arising from the performance of Oratorios were not sufficient to indemnify his losses; and it would remain a perpetual stigma on the taste of the nation, if it should be recorded, that his MESSIAH, that truly noble and sublime work, was not only ill-attended, but ill-received, on its first performance in 1741 [sic], were its miscarriage not to be wholly ascribed to the resentment of them many great personages whom he had offended, in refusing to compose for Senesino, by whom he thought himself affronted, or even for the Opera, unless that singer were dismissed; which inflexibility being construed into insolence, was the cause of powerful oppositions that were at once oppressive and mortifying.*

Though the trouble with Senesino occurred much earlier, and Burney's dating of the first London *Messiah* performance is two years early, his drawing a connection between resentment of Handel by some of the nobility and the "ill-attended, ill-received" *Messiah* is corroborated by Hawkins. That resentment affected attendance at the other oratorios also. All this time there were still efforts to keep Italian opera going, and Handel's oratorios were now taking audiences away from the operas. Two months before *Messiah* debuted in London, Horace Walpole had written unhappily to Horace Mann, "Handel has set up an Oratorio against the Operas, and succeeds." Walpole, a die-hard opera lover, included a sarcastic barb about both Handel's singers and his music:

> *He has hired all the goddesses from farces and the singers of* Roast Beef *from between the acts at both theaters, with a man with one note in his voice, and a girl without ever an one; and so they sing, and make brave hallelujahs; and the good company encore the recitative, if it happens to have any cadence like what they call a tune.* *

A week later Walpole wrote Mann again, quipping, "The Oratorios thrive abundantly – for my part, they give me an idea of heaven, where everybody is to sing whether they have voices or not."

There were those determined to ruin Handel's oratorio success, and they would go some way towards that goal. That summer Middlesex and his friends attempted to get Handel to compose for them. According to a lengthy letter from John Christopher Smith the elder to Shaftesbury, Handel was approached by Middlesex and others to compose two new operas for them, for which he was promised the fine sum of a thousand guineas, even though Middlesex's company was nearly bankrupt. Handel expressed interest, and possibly agreed to provide the two operas the next season, if his health permitted. Later he changed his mind, which even the Prince of Wales couldn't turn back. Middlesex then put pressure on Smith to put pressure on Handel, warning that if Handel refused, "my Lord [Middlesex] would have some of his old operas performed without Him and to let the Publick know in an advertisement, what offers was made to Mr. Handel, and that there was

---

* "Roast Beef" is the song "Roast Beef of Old England," by playwright-novelist Henry Fielding, set to music and popularized by singer-songwriter-actor Richard Leveridge in 1735 (*Grub Street Opera*. Act iii, Sc. 2). It quickly became ubiquitous, from music halls to Royal Navy ships, in the latter where it became part of the tradition of calling officers to dinner. The song is both self-deprecating and anti-French, decrying the "dwindling" of the English since Queen Elizabeth I's day caused by France's softening ("vapouring") influence. Eating roast beef is a metaphor for masculinity and strength, contrasted with the dainty-morsel-eating, effeminate French. Satirical artist William Hogarth alluded to the song and its anti-French message in his 1749 painting "Calais Gate" or "O the Roast Beef of Old England" (Tate Gallery, London). Hogarth added an anti-Catholicism which the song doesn't specifically voice, but which can easily be read into it: France's Roman Catholicism was generally assumed to be the cause of its (perceived) degeneration and its bad influence on Protestant Britain.

no possibility to have any thing from Him."[12] That fall it was still an issue, and in fact Handel felt the repercussions for the next two seasons. Smith told James Harris on Oct. 4, 1743:

> *I could wish Mr. Handel had agreet with Lord Middelsex [sic] to compose for the opera's this winter[;] it would turn vastly to his advantage, for you can't imagine how the Quality—& even his friends[—] resent it, to refuse such offers, they have made him.*

The resentment came from Handel's temerity in refusing a request from his "betters." Middlesex's "request" that Handel compose for them may have been an actual command. As noblemen they considered themselves to be inherently superior to those beneath them on the social ladder, and therefore in a master-servant relationship with them. Most people accepted that view, though not always without resentments of their own. A true gentleman, of course, would not have issued a "command" in such circumstances which would force the recipient to comply; nor would a gentleman threaten ruin of the other's reputation if the other man did not comply.

If Handel had indeed firmly promised to provide the operas, going back on that promise would have been a serious breach of integrity in an age when a person's word was binding and verbal promises were expected to be honored. Breaking a firm promise would have been out of character for Handel. He was fastidious about providing music commissioned from him, and about payment of his musicians; his personal honor in such dealings had never been questioned. Handel may not have done more than show interest, and the by then desperate and not very honorable Middlesex imputed more to Handel's interest than the composer intended. Smith told Shaftsbury "it seems that Handel promis'd my Lord Middlesex...." Smith got that information from Middlesex, not Handel. It is also possible that Handel made the promise and felt he couldn't fulfill it because of his health. Or that he did provide some music they could adapt or use as they wished.

Such incidents, including Middlesex's threat to blackmail Handel, were the stuff over which duels were fought. Smith was still fretting about this in a second letter to James Harris a week later; clearly Smith didn't have the moral courage or independence of spirit Handel had:

> *[I] think he is very ill adviced as to fly in the Prince of Wales's and the Quality's face as he has done; I am sorry to see it & wish him heardily well, and dont doubt but all his friends do the same.*

Ironically, *Messiah's* librettist was also a thorn in Handel's side at this time. Jennens critiqued *Messiah* and found it wanting. As we've seen, Charles Jennens was devout, intelligent, competent, well-educated and well-read; but he had his faults. Among those were a streak of arrogance, a sometimes untoward need for recognition and a lack of empathy. He also suffered from serious depression, possibly from what we would call bipolar disorder or manic-depression. Such depression can affect the sufferer's thinking, judgment and social behavior in ways that can cause serious problems (and embarrassment).[13] Whatever Jennens's exact ailment, it did affect his outlook, judgment and behavior. Later evidence of a memory difficulty, also related to Handel, is another symptom of manic-depression. Musicologist Ruth Smith calls Handel's music "Jennens's only bulwark against recurring depression" – a great irony given his frequent lashing out at that music's composer, his friend.

Jennens' first reaction to Handel's setting of *Messiah* was that the music wasn't good enough for his libretto; he felt Handel was too lazy to do a better job! The day after *Messiah's* first London performance on March 23, Jennens wrote to his friend Edward Holdsworth that the oratorio is "in the main, a fine Composition, notwithstanding some weak parts, which [Handel] was too idle & too obstinate to retouch, tho' I us'd great importunity to perswade him to it."[14] Since Jennens had just heard *Messiah* for the first time the night before, his importuning Handel to change it had occurred after reading the score, not from actually hearing it.

That autumn, again writing to Holdsworth, Jennens was still concerned that Handel make changes to *Messiah*. Handel did then incorporate some of Jennens' suggestions. Jennens's harsh criticism was painful to Handel; Jennens had become a friend. Jennens, in fact, actually acknowledged to his friend Holdsworth, with a blunt lack of compassion, that his prodding contributed to Handel's recurred illness:

> *I don't yet despair of making him retouch the Messiah, at least he shall suffer for his negligence; nay I am inform'd that he has suffer'd, for he told Ld Guernsey, that a letter I wrote him about it contributed to the bringing of his last illness upon him; & it is reported that being a little delirious with a Fever, he said he should be damn'd for preferring Dagon (a Gentleman he was very complaisant to in the Oratorio of Samson) before the Messiah. This shews that I gall'd him: but I have not done with him yet.*

Jennens' malignant attitude bothered Holdsworth, and angered him; he was friend enough to Jennens to tell him so in a letter. He begins, however, with a diplomatic directing of his anger at the bad influence of Jennens' environment (Leicestershire), not at Jennens himself:

> *Pardon my speaking so freely of Leicestershire; but in truth I am angry with it. You have staid too long there already; it has had an ill effect upon you, and made you quarrel with your best friends, Virgil & Handel. You have contributed, by yr. own confession, to give poor Handel a fever, and now He is pretty well recover'd, you seem resolv'd to attack him again; for you say you have not yet done with him. Pray be merciful: and don't you turn Samson, & use him like a Philistine.*[*]

Both Handel's showdown with Middlesex and the Jennens-Holdsworth exchange indicate that his ailment was again stress-related. This time the result wasn't so intense. Common to stress-related conditions and depending on one's circumstances and state of mind, Handel's symptoms seemed to have appeared erratically, coming, subsiding and returning over several months.

---

[*]It is noteworthy that Holdsworth refers to Handel as Jennens's best friend (along with Virgil's writings), his own esteemed position in Jennens's life notwithstanding. He must have said that based on observing Jennens' relationship with Handel or from hearing Jennens talk of Handel. In a slightly different reading, when Holdsworth names Virgil as Jennens's best friend along with Handel he may be acknowledging his own place as Jennens's friend, as he was a noted Virgil scholar. Some time after Holdsworth's death in 1746 Jennens erected an elaborate, carefully thought-out memorial monument for him, which combines symbols representing both Christianity and the Classical world of Virgil and bears biblical inscriptions and the phrase associated with Constantine's conversion vision: "By this sign [the cross] you shall conquer." (For a detailed description of the monument and its "temple," and several photographs, see Ruth Smith's "The Achievements of Charles Jennens," pp. 176, 178-181).

Chapter 14
Grand Chorusses – Ineffectual Labours

After Handel's return from Ireland, that fall of 1742 he reverted to working on *Samson*. By October 12 it was to his liking, but it wasn't performed until Lent 1743, a year after Londoners first heard *Messiah*. *Samson's* libretto, prepared by Newburgh Hamilton, is based on the great blind Milton's epic *Samson Agonistes*, with added stanzas from short poems by Milton. Milton's poem and the oratorio center on the willful and tragically blinded Israelite judge whose story is told in Judges 13-16. It is in the preface to *Samson's* wordbook that Newburgh Hamilton's subsequently famous definition of *oratorio* occurs: "A musical Drama, whose Subject must be Scriptural, and in which the Solemnity of Church-Musick is agreeably united with the most pleasing Airs of the stage."*

When *Samson* was first heard on February 18, 1743, it was immediately embraced. A private letter from London, publicly printed in Faulkner's *Dublin Journal*, described audience reaction. After the enthusiastic reception of Handel's music in Dublin, and especially *Messiah*, the public was no doubt especially interested in his affairs – thus the public printing of an extract of a private letter:

> *Our Friend Mr. Handell is very well, and Things have taken a quite different Turn here from what they did some Time past; for the Publick will be no longer imposed on by Italian Singers, and some wrong Headed Undertakers of bad Opera's, but find out Merit of Mr. Handell's Composition and English Performances: That Gentleman is more esteemed now than ever. The new Oratorio (called SAMSON) which he composed since he left Ireland, has been performed four Times to more crouded Audiences than ever were seen; more People being turned away for Want of Room each Night than hath been at the Italian Opera....*[1]

The response to *Samson* would perhaps slightly buffer the negative reaction to *Messiah* soon to come. *Samson* remained highly popular for the rest of Handel's life. After two more performances in February and five in March (*Messiah* debuted in London on March 23), *Samson* warranted revival the next year and in

---

*The first phrase of Hamilton's sentence – "as Mr. *Handel* had so happily introduc'd here *Oratorios*" – makes clear that he is assuming this to be a general definition of oratorios, and is not referring to *Samson* only.

1745, -49, -52, -53, -54, -55 and -59. At the end of 1743 when London first heard *Samson* and *Messiah*, novice oratorio attender Miss Catherine Talbot would write to Mrs. Elizabeth Carter not only of her delight with *Sampson*, but about the positive moral and spiritual effects of the kind of "entertainment" provided by Handel's oratorios:

> *I will own having been highly delighted with several songs in Sampson, and especially the choruses.... Having never heard any oratorio before, I was extremely struck with such a kind of harmony as seems the only language adapted to devotion. I really cannot help thinking this kind of entertainment must necessarily have some effect on correcting or moderating at least the levity of the age; and let an audience be ever so thoughtless, they can scarcely come away, I should think, without being the better for an evening so spent. I heartily wish you had been with me when I heard it.*[2]

Handel and Middlesex apparently went head to head in June (1743). Handel stood his ground, but the situation agitated him, and once again he must have seriously wondered about his future and his ability to continue to support himself. On June 18, Thomas Harris reported that he and Lord Radnor "mett Handel lately in the park, whose head does not seem so clear as I could could wish it to be"– an indication of a return of the mental confusion he had previously suffered.[3] Handel's symptoms subsided somewhat after that, and he immediately plunged into his work again.

By July 4 he had completed *Semele*, a mythological work worlds away from *Messiah*. It is a "musical drama" (Handel's own term), based on a text by comedic playwright William Congreve (1670-1729) which the latter provided for an opera by John Eccles that was never performed. *Semele* is the closest Handel ever came to writing English opera, though – like his oratorios – it is a drama not intended to be acted. In fact, in the twentieth century it was often referred to as an oratorio. But *oratorio*, as Handel and his contemporaries used the word, refers only to works with "sacred" texts.

After *Semele*, Handel wrote two new ceremonial-liturgical works, the Dettingen Te Deum and *Dettingen Anthem* ("The King Shall Rejoice"), which honored George II's June 27 defeat of the French at Dettingen, where the King himself had led the English troops.* Then Handel began work on a new oratorio, *Joseph and His Brethren*. Meanwhile, more of his music was published.**

On September 13, 1743, George Harris reported having seen Handel a few days earlier, "in appearance very well, airing him self on foot in the park." (Handel finished *Joseph* on September 12.) It is possibly noteworthy that George Harris specifically mentions seeing Handel on foot. The most common alternative would have been a carriage (a closed carriage would have prevented occupants from being easily recognizable). It might be taken as a good sign that Handel, despite his recurred illness that summer, was able and willing to be out walking rather than riding in a carriage. But perhaps Handel was used to riding horseback in the park. The reference by Shaftesbury to Handel's having been on horseback as he was recovering from his previous illness stated the fact as if it marked a certain natural point of return of normal activity by Handel. If Handel rode periodically for pleasure, the fact that he was now on foot could relate to his not having yet recovered the coordination or balance necessary to ride. Harris's next statement reinforces that; he indicates that Handel was not completely well. He also implies that Handel, and especially his eating and drinking habits, were the subject of discussion and speculation among the Harris circle and their friends (and quite probably in circles beyond):

> *I am told, that he would probably recover his health again, were he not so much of the epicure, that he cannot forbear going back to his former luxurious way of living, which will in the end certainly prove fatal to him.*[3]

By November 22, Shaftesbury relayed better news about Handel to George Harris's

---

*The battle at Dettingen was part of the ongoing War of the Austrian Succession, ca. 1740-48, which had varying participants and goals. In the main war, Britain was allied with Austria, fighting the French for the recognition of Maria Theresa's throne. France, allied with Bavaria, Saxony and Spain, wanted Charles Albert, Elector of Bavaria, to be emperor. Britain was interested keeping France in check, which would help maintain Britain's commercial and colonial empire.

**"Six Overtures for Violins, &tc. In eight Parts, from the Operas and Oratorios of Samson, the Sacred Oratorio Saul, Deidamia, Hymen and Parnasso in Festa" (*Daily Advertiser*, July 19, 1743). And "the entire Masque of Acis and Galatea, in Score, as it was originally compos'd" (*Daily Advertiser*, Aug. 24, 1743).

brother James. As Shaftesbury wrote, he was interrupted by a visit from Handel himself, who

> is better in spirits than ever I saw him; and what is still better, I believe will succeed: for we have great reason to expect, his number of subscribers will be more than sufficient, to defray all his expences in performing.

The new *Dettingen Te Deum* and accompanying anthem were heard in November in the Chapel Royal after the King returned to Britain safely and victorious. Mrs. Pendarves, by then Mrs. Delany (having married Rev. Patrick Delany), was at the well-attended public rehearsal and thought the music "excessively fine," as did her husband.[4] The *Daily Advertiser*, too, commented on the music's sublimity, as well as on Handel himself, who, though then almost fifty-nine years old and having been frequently been laden with stress, mental and physical, did not appear to be showing signs of ill health, age or waning imagination. The *Te Deum* and anthem were "so truly masterly and sublime, as well as new in their kind," said the *Advertiser*, "that they prove this great Genius not only inexhaustible, but likewise still rising to a higher Degree of Perfection."

In mid-December Handel once again used Shaftesbury as an audience for his newest work, *Joseph and His Brethren*. Shaftesbury relished it; he looked upon Handel, his accomplishments and fortitude in amazement:

> I had a noble entertainment this morning in hearing Handel play over the oratorio of Joseph. I will not pretend to describe the beautys of this excellent composition. The last of his is always the best. He played too the overture of Semele, which is a delightfull thing. I think (if possible) Joseph is more pathetick than any of his former pieces. I must confess, I can't help, after hearing such a performance, looking at Handel with surprise and admiration. He is perfectly well in health and spirits.[5]

The year after *Messiah's* inglorious appearing in London, Handel again offered biblical oratorios during Lent. Within that framework, *Semele*, which opened the 1744 season, was an odd kettle of Lenten fish because of its subject matter. Mary's husband, Patrick Delany, referred to *Semele* as "a profane story." He meant "profane" not as blasphemous or even ribald, but as distinguished from "sacred," and the "sacred dramas" of Handel's biblical oratorios.

The story is one of the many mythological tales that involve Greek gods cavorting with human beings. It depicts an adulterous relationship between Jupiter and Semele – treachery, jealousy and improper grasping for immortality. In seventeenth and eighteenth century guise it is a cautionary tale, but the "medicine" goes down easily, and there are elements of humor in it. Because at least some of *Semele's* audience members seemed to overlook its "moral," and talked instead about the rather juicy plot details, and because Delany was a Church of England minister, he thought it best not to attend.

It seems to have been generally well-received, though according to Mary Delany's forthright comments to her sister, it had "a strong party against it, viz. The fine ladies, petit maîtres, and *ignoramus's*."[6] (The beautiful, now popular aria "Where'er you Walk" is from *Semele*.) Some of those Mrs. Delany is referring to were apparently among the aristocrats. They were undoubtedly some of the same people who had long been wishing for Handel's musical demise, and therefore stayed away to spite him. Presumably, *Semele* would have been the type of work Italian opera lovers would appreciate; no doubt, that's what Handel thought as well.

Charles Jennens's reason for staying away from *Semele* was different. Though *Semele* ends with the "guiltless pleasures" of marriage being celebrated as the proper expression of sexual desires, the plot in general apparently made Jennens uncomfortable. The fact that he was unmarried himself, was extremely shy around women, and had no sisters and no women friends or any substantial contact with women may have played a role in his discomfort with or embarrassment at this subject. He passed judgment without having heard *Semele*, probably from having read the libretto or having seen the score (as with *Messiah*). Jennens seems to have missed its point; or more probably, he didn't appreciate the road it took to get to its point. *

When Handel offered *Semele* again the next year (1744-45), Jennens recounted to James Harris that when he (Jennens) sent someone to subscribe on his

---

*Ruth Smith has noted: "The sermon preached at [Jennens's] funeral describes him as being acutely shy in mixed company – and ardent connoisseurship and enlightened patronage must have filled some of the place of family life for him" ("The Achievements of Charles Jennens," p. 170). That sermon was by Rev. George Kelly, with the title *The Blessedness of those who Die in the Lord: considered in a Sermon preached at Twycross, in the County of Leicester, on the Death of the Late Charles Jennens, Esq; of Gopsall; on Sunday, January the Second, 1774.* (The sermon was published "by Desire," i.e., by request.) Handel, of course, was also unmarried. But he had had a strong, intelligent mother and sisters, women friends, worked with women all his life, and was used to setting to music love stories of all sorts; he suffered from no such acute shyness in mixed company.

behalf to Handel's season, excluding *Semele*, Handel – apparently affronted – refused to sell him *any* tickets. Jennens may have been taken aback by that (though he didn't let on). He apparently tried again to get tickets for Handel's season; he then told Harris, "I have since given him a second dose." Nevertheless, Jennens still seemed irritated with Handel, and took peevish delight in his friend's reportedly small audiences. "*Deborah* has been performed twice to very thin audiences," he told Harris, "and *Semele* comes forth tomorrow, I hope to thinner."

In January Handel began to sell subscriptions to the twelve performances he planned for his 1744 Lenten season. (He would revive *Samson* and then present his new oratorio, *Joseph*.) But the opera faction had not forgiven him. Shaftesbury urged his cousin James Harris to subscribe as soon as possible, because "the sooner people who wish well to Handel, subscribe — the better. For the subscription becoming numerous at the beginning will draw in more folks to follow."[7]

Others had the same thought: Handel got 156 subscribers on the second day of ticket sales. Though he seemed to be doing well, "the Opera people take incredible pains to hurt him," Shaftesbury told Harris. In addition, Handel had just been deprived of £200 of the £600 in Royal pensions he had been getting for some years as music teacher to the royal princesses. But he was loathe to admit it. Handel seems to have been embarrassed by the withdrawal of part of his pension, but Shaftesbury found his embarrassment at this inexplicable. Shaftesbury relayed this bit of information immediately after saying that the opera people were taking great pains to hurt Handel, and he followed it with, "He has[,] poor man[,] very powerfull enemies" – meaning to imply, it seems, that one or more of those powerful enemies was responsible for convincing the Court to stop that part of Handel's pension.

One of the frustrations for modern music historians and music lovers when piecing together Handel's life is the lack of surviving historical detail about various events and circumstances. However much we might like to know the particulars about Handel's powerful enemies and the "incredible pains" they took in their campaign against him, we can only guess. Beyond reports of their scheduling their own social events on Handel's concert night, bad-mouthing his music, of being complicit in tearing down his concert posters, and a high placed enemy's possible role in depriving him of his pension, details haven't come down to us. Or, if they still exist, they haven't yet been uncovered.

With *Joseph and His Brethren*, Handel worked with a new librettist, James

Miller. Miller was a Church of England clergyman who was also a playwright. His libretto begins with Joseph in prison in Egypt (Genesis 39) and ends with Joseph reuniting with his brothers many years after they sold him to a caravan of Ishmaelites going to Egypt. The story of famine inducing ten of Jacob's sons to travel to Egypt for grain, their uncomprehending encounter with Joseph, his eventual insistence that they bring their youngest brother back with them, and, finally, his revealing his identity to them and his ultimate reunion with their aged father makes for one of the most poignant human dramas in all of Scripture. Both Handel and Miller recognized this, as did previous writers and painters (and not only English writers and painters). In fact, for Handel's oratorio Miller adapted and expanded the libretto of an Italian oratorio about Joseph – *Giuseppe* by Apostolo Zeno, set to music by Antonio Caldara in 1722. The text of *Giuseppe*, in turn, had been based on a popular French play, *Joseph*, written by the Abbé Genest in 1711.

For a long time modern musicologists dismissed *Joseph and His Brethren* for having a confused and uninspired libretto and as being (therefore) substandard Handel, too.[*] Handel would be perplexed at such a critique, as would his audiences. *Joseph* was well received, earning a spot in the top four most popular Handel oratorios, gauged by the number of its performances during Handel's lifetime. (*Joseph's* popularity was exceeded only by *Messiah, Judas Maccabaeus* and *Samson*). Joseph Chisholm, who helped rehabilitate Miller in the late 1980s when he uncovered the sources Miller used, thinks "Handel must have found the figure of Joseph appealing" because "he too was a foreigner with some power in a strange land, and at various times had been the victim of plots. He may well have meditated on 'The People's Favour, and the Smiles of Pow'r.' The melancholy and reflective character of Joseph's music may indicate a deeply personal element."[8]

That may well be true. The primary stress Handel felt, which precipitated his bouts of paralysis and confusion, was caused by his aristocratic enemies' attempts to bring him down. It is also true that the story of Joseph has immense spiritual resonance for Christians in general (as for Jews first). Not only is it full of touchingly human drama, but it is a powerful reminder of God's care in the midst of adversity, and of his blessing on and care for those who trust him, especially in affliction. Given

---

[*]Especially Paul Henry Lang in his Handel biography and Winton Dean in *Handel's Dramatic Oratorios and Masques.*

what Handel had been subject to, he likely needed and savored such a reminder as he began work on *Joseph and His Brethren*.

He collaborated with Miller on only this one oratorio. Miller died on April 27, 1744, having lived just long enough to hear *Joseph's* first performance on March 2. Once again, we have no indication of how this death affected Handel personally. His oratorios, however, were no doubt a source of joy. Mary Delany told Ann on March 10, "The oratorios fill very well, not withstanding the spite of the opera party."[9] And at the beginning of April, a Salisbury friend of James Harris's, Mary Smith, told Harris:

> *I rejoice very much at the defeat of Handel's opposers, & should be heartily glad, if he could get a large quantity of money in the oratorio way, but should be realy grieved if Italian operas again took place. There seems to a fair opportunity at present, of throwing aside all foreign nonsense, & resolving, to seek our own good from ourselves.*

The context of Mary Smith's remarks indicates that Handel's "opposers" – who were *still* drumming for the revival of Italian opera – were seen as having been defeated because Handel's oratorios were succeeding. Though Middlesex's season wouldn't end until mid-June, the opera company was in such financial trouble that the word was already out that another season would not be attempted. So Mary Delany and Mary Smith rejoiced for Handel because his oratorios were succeeding. They hoped, as Aaron Hill and others had years earlier, that finally they would be rid of the unintelligible "foreign nonsense" of Italian opera librettos.

Handel was now doing his best to oblige the many listeners of like mind. He turned to Jennens again for a libretto, which Jennens mentioned to Edward Holdsworth on May 7: "Handel has promis'd to revise the Oratorio of Messiah, & He & I are very good Friends again. The reason is he has lately lost his Poet Miller, & wants to set me at work for him again."[10] Jennens letter, once again, doesn't reveal much regard for Handel's feelings – the loss he may have felt over Miller – but Jennens *was* concerned for his own place as Handel's librettist. Very soon he would "set to work again" for Handel, providing the libretto for *Belshazzar*.

Belshazzar's story comes from Daniel 5 about the downfall of the apostate Babylonian king who was a successor (and possibly grandson or other descendent) of Nebuchadnezzar. Jennens expanded on the biblical story by using material from the ancient Greek historians Herodotus and Xenophon, both of whom confirm the sort of profane banquets described in the biblical account. But *Belshazzar* would not be heard until the next season (1745).

Jennens wasn't the only one who wished to be Handel's librettist (despite his periodic protestations). Mary Delany thought *she* would enjoy that distinction. In the same letter mentioned above she tells Ann that she had been occupying her time with writing a libretto "to give Mr. Handel to compose to." (In our time, Mary Delany is known as an excellent painter.) Since she intended her libretto for the very best composer, she refused to enlist just any minor poet or insignificant tale to lean on: she went right to the top poetically as well. She chose *Paradise Lost*, Milton's *sublime* telling of human creation, fall and redemption. The libretto, she said, "has cost me a great deal of thought and contrivance." Her pastor-husband had encouraged her, which gave her "some reason to think it not bad, though all I have had to do has been collecting and making the connection between the fine parts." She began with "Satan's threatening to seduce the woman, her being seduced, and it ends with the man's yielding to the temptation." Above all, she didn't want "a word or a thought of Milton's altered," so she hoped to persuade Handel to set it without reversifying any of it; reworking Milton's great work would "take from its dignity."

A couple of weeks later, Handel was a dinner guest of the Delany's, along with Mary's brother Bernard Granville and her friend Anne Donellan. We might suppose that Mary was anxious to discuss her developing libretto with Handel. If she did, we can only surmise what they talked of or how he went about declining her wishes: there is no setting by Handel of John Milton's *Paradise Lost*. That, despite the fact that Mary Delany wasn't the only one who suggested such a project to Handel. James Harris and Jennens also worked on a *Paradise Lost* libretto which they hoped he would set. And so did John Upton, a clergyman and close friend of James Harris's. But Handel managed to elude them all. It would be fascinating to know his reasons, and whether they had to do with the subject itself, with Milton's poetic setting, with the types of librettos he was shown, or with more practical or logistical matters, such as the difficulty of effectively condensing its huge length.

Despite the libretto issue, the Delanys' dinner with Handel must have been a pleasant affair. Beforehand, Mary had "ardently wished" that Ann and their mother could be there too, because not only was Handel coming to dine, but he would earn his supper, so to speak: they would be "entertained with Handel's *playing over Joseph to us.*"[11] This brief sentence sets up an arresting mental picture of Handel sitting at the harpsichord, informally surrounded by agroup of four

194

friends, playing through his oratorio *Joseph*, singing some of the recitatives and arias to his own accompaniment, quite probably moving from one soloist's part to another, and even to the choruses, and exchanging conversation about the oratorio as well.

~

Though Handel did write several more non-biblical "musical dramas," he was now fully committing himself to writing oratorios. For Lent 1745 he went well beyond what he had offered in the presvious several years. Instead of twelve performances, he planned to double that number, since the Middlesex opera group was near defunct. It had been taking what seemed to be last gasps, but by the end of the 1744 season it was, at last, truly dead. Seeing that coming, Handel abandoned Covent Garden and engaged the King's Theater which Middlesex would no longer be using.

Was this as a deliberate move by Handel to be seen by the public as the substitute for opera? Donald Burrows calls it "perhaps the one aggressive competitive gesture of [Handel's] career: he wanted those who had undertaken to 'middle with harmony' not merely to be beaten but to be seen to be beaten."[12] But the long competition with the opera party had ended earlier, in Handel's favor, and he knew it. It would be natural for him to want to gain many of the opera subscribers; but the planned twenty-four performances instead of twelve for 1745 couldn't have been entirely connected to the absence of opera performances. There weren't many opera subscribers at this point and some were bound not to be interested in biblical oratorio. Once again, though, he would offer one work based on a mythological subject, this time, *Hercules*. This may have been for the benefit of the part of the opera audience who *would* come to the oratorios. Handel had done the same thing the previous year with *Semele*, and before that with *Alexander's Feast* and *Acis and Galatea*).

It would be natural for Handel to assume that additional performances, with greater numbers of works presented per season, would be successful. He probably reasoned that he had had several successful oratorio seasons, but they had been short seasons by any account, and far shorter than normal opera seasons were. The extra concerts would also allow him to better fill his time, and of course to create more income.

All his life he had been accustomed to, and even seemed to relish, a rigorous composing schedule. Though he was getting older, most of the time he was still in good health and he still wrote quickly, so he had time on his hands. Doubling the number of performances *was* an unusual move, and risky, but he obviously thought it was the right one.

After a few-weeks holiday in the country, on July 19 he began to compose for the new season. The *Hercules* libretto is by Thomas Broughton, who, like James Miller, was a minister in the Church of England and had previous writing experience. Also like Miller, Broughton would provide only one libretto for Handel.*

Before Handel left London for his holiday he initiated what would be a series of letters between himself and Charles Jennens about the new oratorio for the season: *Belshazzar* – the only oratorio for which we have such specific correspondence. The letters allow us a detailed look at how Handel and Jennens collaborated and gives further evidence of their friendship. Despite their both being opinionated, and Jennens' periodic grumbling to Holdsworth about Handel, the two worked well together, judging by the exceptional results (*Saul, Messiah, Belshazaar* and presumably *Israel in Egypt*).

Handel opened the correspondence on June 9, 1744, just after Jennens arrived at his summer home in Gopsall. Jennens must have been ill and had recently recovered: the first thing Handel does is express his pleasure that Jennens had arrived safely in Gopsall and that his health was much improved. Handel spends his whole first paragraph on Jennens' health – an important preoccupation at the time, as we've seen, thus not merely a polite formality. Handel then fills Jennens in on his plans for his 1745 oratorio season, telling him about having engaged the "Opera House at the Haymarketh" and about the singers he will need. (Incidentally, one of these was tenor John Beard, a former chorister in the Chapel Royal under Bernard Gates when Gates brought out *Esther* in 1732. Beard would sing for Handel for

---

*Broughton used Ovid and Sophocles as his source materials. Mythological gods are hardly eternal or omnipotent, especially when it comes to love. The part of the myth Broughton used ends in Hercules' tragic death, which inadvertently results from his marriage problems with his wife Dejanira. Dejanira believes Hercules has been unfaithful; in order to win him back she sends him a gift: a robe (a "rich embroidered vest" in the libretto). Unknown to her, the robe has absorbed the blood of Nessus, a centaur Hercules has killed. Hercules, in turn, is killed by the robe, consumed by poison imbedded in it. The libretto's "point" – there is always a Christian "moral" which might enlighten and improve listeners who pondered it – is the corrosively destructive power of jealousy. *Hercules* contains powerful if somber music. Indeed, there's not much in the story to provide joy, or even moderately lighthearted relief, and Handel set it accordingly, including the startling aria "Where Shall I Fly," in which the emotionally unhinged Dejanira believes she is being chased by snakes and scorpions.

twenty-five years, to Handel's death, longer than any soloist.) Lastly Handel gets down to what he needs from Jennens:

> Now should I be extreamly glad to receive the first Act, or what is ready of the new Oratorio with which you intend to favour me, that I might employ all my attention and time, in order to answer in some measure the great obligation I lay under. this [sic] new favour will greatly increase my Obligations.[13]

The "obligations" Handel felt towards Jennens, though expressed in the typically polite and formal language of the time, were surely real. How could he not be grateful for the previous excellent librettos Jennens had written for him, despite Jennens's temperamental insistence on "corrections" to *Messiah*?

Jennens obliged Handel with new material, and after Handel was back in London, a July 19 letter from him assured Jennens:

> I immediately perused the Act of the Oratorio with which you favour'd me, and, the little time only I had it, gives me great Pleasure. Your reasons for the Length of the first act are intirely Satisfactory to me, and it is likewise my Opinion to have the following Acts short. I shall be very glad and much obliged to you, if you will soon favour me with the remaining Acts.

In the midst of this correspondence about *Belshazzar*, Jennens again pressed Handel to make changes to *Messiah*. This is clear from Handel's side of the correspondence when he adds graciously – or perhaps in private exasperation – "Be pleased to point out these passages in the Messiah which You think require altering."

On August 21 Handel wrote Jennens again:

> The Second Act of the Oratorio I have received Safe, and own my self highly obliged to You for it. I am greatly pleased with it, and shall use my best endeavours to do it Justice. I can only Say that I impatiently wait for the third Act....

Since Handel was now finished with *Hercules* and had the first two parts of the *Belshazzar* libretto in hand, he began the new oratorio two days after this letter to Jennens. Meanwhile, throughout the summer his music was being heard here and there in London, led and performed by others.

After being immersed in *Belshazzar* for some three weeks, Handel told Jennens on September 13:

Your most excellent Oratorio has given me great Delight in setting it to Musick and still engages me warmly. It is indeed a Noble Piece, very grand and uncommon; it has furnished me with Expressions, and has given me Opportunity to some very particular Ideas, besides so many great Choru's [Choruses]. I intreat you heartily to favour me Soon with the last Act, which I expect with anxiety, that I may regulate my Self the better as to the Lenght (sic) of it. I profess my Self highly obliged to You, for so generous a Present....

We see here further evidence of Handel's careful study of his librettos. He considered their meanings and how his music might best enhance those meanings, also taking care to preserve whatever literary form the librettos exhibit. He and Jennens must have discussed their overall approach to *Belshazzar* (as with *Messiah* and *Israel in Egypt*, presuming the latter was provided by Jennens): perhaps the general length and approximate breakdown of each act, but probably without any great detail at that point.

When Handel had received just part of the libretto, he simply began to write; he wrote on as he received more text. Jennens replied forthwith to Handel's letter of September 13, enclosing the third act as requested. But Handel thought Act 3 was too long. He wrote back to say so on the second of October, and also told Jennens about the singers he intended to use. As Handel was writing arias, in almost every case he had in mind the particular singers who would sing them. And when a singer left and a new one took his or her place – or, in the case of a later revival of a work, when arias were performed with different singers than had originally sung the work – Handel changed the arias to suit the new singers. This is why it is sometimes hard to say there is a definitive version of a particular oratorio. *Messiah* is perhaps the best case in point. Now that *Messiah* is frequently performed in its entirety once again there has developed in our time a "definitive" version, with a few minor variations. But during Handel's lifetime he did quite a bit of re-composing – redistributing, revising, shortening – of arias to suit the singers he had for particular seasons: "Rejoice Greatly" (meter change making it easier to sing); "Thou Art Gone Up on High" (versions for three different singers); "But Who May Abide" (three versions; the original is for bass, substantially different from the aria now sung); "Why Do the Nations Rage" (shortened); "How Beautiful Are the Feet" (the original for soprano; a version for alto; a version for alto duet and chorus); "Their Sound is Gone Out" (originally a chorus; version two is a short tenor aria).

198

When Handel initially wrote an oratorio he also wrote for the kind of orchestra he knew he would have or specifically wanted, sometimes including unusual instruments, as in *Saul*. Or he scored it lightly in the presumed absence of a normal complement of players, as in *Messiah*, probably because he knew he would be taking it to Dublin.

In Handel's October 2 response to Jennens he wrote (with eccentric punctuation):

> *I received the 3ᵈ Act, with a great deal of pleasure, as you can imagine, and you may believe that I think it a very fine and sublime Oratorio, only it is rely too long, if I should extend the Musick, it would last 4 Hours and more.*
>
> *I retrench'd already a great deal of the Musick, that I might preserve the Poetry as much as I could, yet still it may be shortned. The Anthems come in very properly. but (sic) would not the Words (tell it out among the Heathen that the Lord is King) [be] Sufficient for one Chorus? The Anthem (I will magnify thee O God my King, and I will praise thy name for ever and ever, vers). the Lord preserveth all them that love him, but scattreth abroad all the ungodly. (vers and chorus) my mouth shall speak the Praise of the Lord and let all flesh give thanks unto His holy name for ever and ever Amen.) Concludes the Oratorio. I hope you will make a visit to London next Winter. I have a good Set of Singers. S. Francesina performs Nitocris, Miss Robinson Cyrus, Mrs. Cibber Daniel, Mt Beard (who is recoverd) Belshazzar, Mr Reinhold Gobrias, and a good Number of Choir Singers for the Chorus's. I propose 24 Nights to perform this Season, on Saturdays, but in Lent on Wednesday's or Fryday's. I shall open on 3ᵈ of Novermbʳ next with Deborah. I wish You heartily the Continuation of Your health....*

In keeping with Handel's habit of throwing away letters sent to him, Jennens' side of this entire exchange has been lost, though much can be inferred from reading Handel's side. Jottings on Handel's autograph (original) score in Jennens' hand-writing also indicate the extent to which they conferred and discussed changes after Handel had initially completed *Belshazzar*. Jennens agreed on the solution to the third act being too long: some of the text would not be set to music, but all of it would nevertheless appear in the *Belshazzar* wordbook accompanying the first performance during Lent 1745 (March 27). This was not uncommon; the unsung sections were marked as such.

During this time, Jennens's letters to Holdworth indicate that he felt pressure from Handel's requests for the next act. Jennens wanted more time to complete the libretto. That's not surprising, since not everyone was able to work at the furious pace that was second nature to Handel, much less produce the same sterling results.

As Handel told Jennens he would, he began this new twice-as-long season with a revival of *Deborah* on Saturday, November 3, 1744. He was able to deposit £500 in the bank as *Deborah* opened, but his plan for a long season ran into trouble almost immediately. Two days later the *Daily Advertiser* carried this notice: "As the greatest Part of Mr. HANDEL'S Subscribers are not in Town, he is requested not to perform till Saturday the 24th...."[14] However, subscriptions would still be taken at Handel's home, at Walsh's (his music publisher) and also at White's Chocolate-House. (A chocolate house was not just a store which sold chocolate but a "coffee house" which, instead of coffee, served primarily drinking chocolate, a popular beverage in the eighteenth century.)

Meanwhile, Handel's music was being heard increasingly outside London. Early that summer of 1744, *Alexander's Feast* was presented at Ruckholt House in Essex. Those wanting a music-filled holiday were assured that "proper Cooks are provided every Day in the Week, and Plenty of Fish; and the Doors free, except Monday." A day's events began with a 10 a.m. breakfast, continued with afternoon vocal performances and evening "Entertainments" starting at 4 p.m. "A Book of the Entertainment" would be given to each person; lest they have to spend a few extra pence, "the Gates at Hummerton and Temple-Mills will be Toll-free."[15]

On August 25, "Mr. Handel's grand Chorusses out of several of his Oratorios" were heard at Cuper's Gardens, performed by the Widow Evans' Band of Musick, who were "by the best Judges allow'd to be inferior to none." The gardens, which had been built by Cuper Boyder, circa 1690, had become a rival to Vauxhall Gardens some six years earlier when Ephraim Evans began concerts there in 1738, and Evans's widow introduced Handel's music there. On August 28 the Coronation Anthem *Zadok the Priest* was used to conclude a concert of vocal and instrumental works at Lord Cobham's Head, Cold-Bath-Fields.

In Dublin, Handel's music was still benefiting Mercer's Hospital. In Manchester, a subscription series featured the *Water Music* and overtures from several oratorios and operas. In Germany, a musical treatise, *Critischer Musikus*, was published in Bach's home of Leipzig. It said that Handel "manifested all the time a great understanding and a powerful deliberation, and assuredly has shown in all his pieces how refined and delicate his taste in the arts must be." And before the end of the 1745 Handel was elected as the first honorary member of the Societät der musikalischen Wissenschaften in Leipzig – the Society of Musical Science.

One of Handel's foremost singers, Mrs. Cibber, became ill that season. But there was far worse trouble to come, already perhaps making this planned "long season" feel interminable to him. Once again some of the nobility, who now had no opera to divert them, were riled. They were affronted by Handel's move back to the King's Theater and his plan to provide a season of twenty-four concerts. Lady Brown, wife of the British Resident in Venice, led a boycott of the performances, with the help of others (she seemingly didn't have enough of merit to occupy her in London while her husband was in Venice). Mainwaring refers to her without naming her (he's almost two years early in his chronology) :

Indeed in the year 1743, he had some return of his paralytic disorder; and the year after fell under the heavy displeasure of a certain fashionable lady. She exerted all her influence to spirit up a new opposition against him. But the world could not long be made to believe that her card-assemblies were such proper entertainments for Lent, as his Oratorios.[16]

Jennens mentioned various "ladies" who opposed Handel's season of performances in a letter to Holdsworth, well into the season, in February 1745. But Charles Burney had no scruples about naming Lady Brown as an instigator against Handel. And in a private letter to James Harris, Handel's publisher, John Walsh, mentioned her by name as part of a "strong party against [Handel]."

It was probably unwise of Handel to deviate from a Lenten oratorio scheme that had been working, so he had to bear at least part of the blame for his "thin" audience. Jennens was of this opinion. He told Holdsworth:

I believe it is in some measure owing to his own imprudence in changing the profitable method he was in before for a new & hazardous Experiment. For the two last years he had perform'd Oratorios in Covent-Garden Playhouse on Wednesdays & Fridays in Lent only, when there was no publick Entertainment of any consequence to interfere with him: & his gains were considerable, 2100£ one year, &

1600£ the other, for only 12 performances.

Still, Handel cannot be judged for the nastiness of those who mounted up against him. Lady Brown and her "noble" friends did their damage and it looked as though Handel's season would all but fall apart. Shaftesbury wrote to James Harris of the first disastrous performance of *Hercules*:

> *A lady bespoke fifty places (one Miss Matthews) at Drury Lane, in order to hurt Handel.* Unfortunately Mrs. Cibber was taken violently ill, that she could not perform: so Waltz was obliged to read a few lines here and there of recitatif to carry on the sense of the drama. He had such a miserable hoarseness, that he was hardly able to utter a word. This produced a little laughter and a faint hiss from the audience.*

Handel would soon not be able to support his financial losses. Nor would he be able to offer nearly the number of concerts he promised; clearly this distressed him. He wanted to make amends. He must then have thought very carefully about how to respond. When he did, it was with a public notice that is gracious and generous (while expressing perplexity, mortification and sorrow that his "labours" have become "ineffectual"). The affecting notice was carried in the *Daily Advertiser* (addressed to its editor), the paper which carried notices of so many of his concerts:

> *Sir,*
>
> *Having for a Series of Years received the greatest Obligations from the Nobility and Gentry of this Nation, I have always retained a deep Impression of their Goodness. As I perceived, that joining good Sense and Significant Words to Musick, was the best Method of recommending this to an English Audience; I have directed my Studies that way, and endeavour'd to shew, that the English Language, which is so expressive of the sublimest Sentiments is the best adapted of any to the full and solemn Kind of Musick. I have the Mortification now to find, that my Labours to please are become ineffectual, when my Expences are considerably greater. To what Cause I must impute the loss of the publick Favour I am ignorant, but the Loss itself I shall always lament. In the mean time, I amassur'd that a Nation, whose*

---

*That is, she reserved 50 tickets for her friends for a theater performance on the same night as Handel's *Hercules*.

Characteristick is Good Nature, would be affected with the Ruin of any Man, which was owing to his Endeavours to entertain them. I am likewise persuaded, that I shall have the Forgiveness of those noble Persons, who have honour'd me with their Patronage, and their Subscription this Winter, if I beg their Permission to stop short, before my Losses are too great to support, if I proceed no farther in my Undertaking; and if I intreat them to withdraw three Fourths of their Subscription, one Fourth Party only of my Proposal having been perform'd.

I am, sir, Your very humble Servant,

G.F. Handel

Attendance will be given at Mr. Handel's House in Brook's Street, near Hanover-Square, from Nine in the Morning till Two in the Afternoon, on Monday, Tuesday, and Wednesday next, in Order to pay back the Subscription Money, on returning the Subscription Ticket.

Lady Brown's boycott and the inevitable aspersions on Handel that accompanied it, had their practical effect and took their emotional toll. Yet ultimately there was no great depth to the erosion of Handel's support – which he couldn't know while in the middle of it. Those who loved Handel's music loved his music. Period. They were not about to desert it or him so easily. The oratorios were also gradually drawing middle-class concertgoers who lived and moved outside the goings-on among the nobility, and who seemed better able and willing than at least some of the nobility to appreciate the biblical oratorios for what they are, textually and musically.

The day after Handel's announcement, the *Daily Advertiser* carried a lengthy, friendly response in verse, addressed to Handel. It was not so friendly to Handel's adversaries. The writer drew parallels between the noblewomen opposing Handel and the Thracian women who, in opposing that great mythological musician Orpheus, "despis'd all Music but their own," and who "in rage the sweet Musician slew." The proverb in Latin from Virgil's *Aeneid* with which the anonymous writer preceded his verse summed up his message to Handel: *Tu ne cede malis, sed contra audentior ito* – "Don't surrender to adversity, but face up to it all the more boldly."

In the same paper there was a satiric epigram by a second writer, who also made classical allusions. He wrote it "after reading Mr. Handel's Letter to the Public in this Paper on Thursday last" (January 21, 1745):

Romans, to shew they Genius[e]s wou'd prize,
Gave rich Support; and dead, did Bustos rise:
But wiser we, the kindred Arts to serve.
*First carve the Busts; then bid the Charmers starve.**

Handel evidently received many private expressions of support as well, and his subscribers refused his offer to compensate them for the concerts they would not hear. On January 25 the *Daily Advertiser* carried another announcement from him, this one quite different, but just as poignant:

The new Proofs which I have receiv'd of the Generosity of my Subscribers, in refusing upon their own Motives, to withdraw their Subscriptions call upon me for the earliest Return, and the warmest Expressions of my Gratitude; but natural as it is to feel, proper as it is to have, I find this extremely difficult to express. Indeed, I ought not to content myself with bare expression of it; therefore, though I am not able to fulfil the whole of my Engagement, I shall think it my Duty to perform what Part of it I can, and shall in some Time proceed with the Oratorios, let the Risque (sic) which I may run be what it will.

After this exchange in the newspaper, as a means of helping Handel, the Duke of Grafton (the Lord Chamberlain, and therefore the person responsible for approving theater productions) actually offered to refuse granting a license to the opera; that would have presumably provided Handel some emotional satisfaction as well. Also, opera patrons might then attend the oratorios for lack of something else to do (though probably not in a frame of mind open to the oratorios' spiritual *sublimity*). But Handel refused to take advantage of this proposed bending of the rules on his behalf. He declined to do to others as they had done to him: "After thanking his Grace, [Handel] desired he might not obstruct any bodys (sic) entertainment, and for his own part trusts to the kindness of his patrons."

---

*The ancient Romans demonstrated that they prized genius by richly supporting those who showed this extraordinary artistic ability, and by continuing their appreciation after the artists were gone by means of raising posthumous statues ("Bustos") to them. But we, says the writer, being wiser than the Romans, have a better way to serve the arts: we carve the appreciative statues first and then allow those geniuses who have given us pleasure to starve. The writer no doubt intended his readers to consider the statue of Handel which still stood in Vauxhall Gardens, and how things had fared for Handel since that statue had been erected a decade earlier.

In the end, Handel presented sixteen of the twenty-four concerts he first intended, not a bad ratio for the circumstances, and four more than he had produced the previous year. From March 1st onwards audiences had a chance to hear *Hercules* (once), *Samson* (twice), *Saul* (once), *Joseph* (twice), *Belshazzar* (three times) ,and *Messiah* (twice, both during Holy Week, which became a tradition as the season-ender). Also, Handel's music was still being heard at benefit concerts and services in London; there were concerts and benefits in other English cities and in Dublin; and his music was not unknown in other countries. In January, publisher John Walsh offered *Hercules* in score, for which there was evidently a market.

Handel's troubles brought out other supporters who publicly voiced – or rather, versified – their support for him. One of these supporters, upon hearing *Saul*, waxed poetic about Handel's exceptional talent (as displayed in the oratorios) being a foretaste of heaven. For those of classical- mythological bent, the writer referred to Pythagorus's theory that spirits "transmigrate from Age to Age" inhabiting different bodies. Though the writer didn't believe that unorthodox doctrine, he said (no doubt smiling as he wrote) that he was "convinc'd by [Handel's] sweetly-magic Strains" that perhaps in Handel's case that theory was actually true: Orpheus was, in their time, embodied as Handel.[17]

Most of this twenty-two-line verse specifically addresses a Christian audience (the writer clearly assumes he is addressing Christians) who long for the joys of heaven, yearning to join the angels, stars and all nature in exultant praise. Handel's music, with its power to dispel grief, is the appetizer – the "Antepast" (which we would call antipasto) of heaven's harmony:

> *Ye purer Minds, who glow with sacred Fire;*
> *Who, to th' eternal Throne, in Thought aspire;*
> *For Dissolution pant, and think each Day*
> *An Age, till You th' Aetherial Climes survey;*
> *Who long to hear the Cherubs mingled Voice*
> *Exult in Hymns, and bid the Stars rejoyce;*
> *Bid universal Nature raise the Theme*
> *To Boundless Goodness, Majesty supreme:*
> *O listen to the Warblings of his Shell,*
> *Whose wondrous Power can fiercest Grief dispell!*
> *O to his Sounds be due Attention given*
> *Sweet Antepast of Harmony in Heaven!*

Chapter 15
A Blast of Hell: Civil War, Personal Pain

A couple of months later, in the spring of 1745, there appeared "An Ode, to Mr. Handel." It is a major work of thirty-seven four-line stanzas that was published as a pamphlet, and also by the *Daily Gazetteer* on May 2. It was published anonymously, but may have been written by one Joseph Warton, who wrote a series of odes on various subjects. As in so many eighteenth century odes and shorter verses, including previous verses about Handel, there are again references to classical antiquity. This author also refers to the mythological pastoral tradition, including a nod to *Acis and Galatea*; and to Handel's setting of Dryden's *Alexander's Feast* and *Ode for St. Cecilia's Day*; and to *L'Allegro* and *Il Penseroso*.

In one stanza he alludes to Handel's role in providing the *Coronation Anthems*, in another to the *Dettingen Te Deum*. These references are included within one monumental, many-claused fourteen-stanza sentence.

The other twelve stanzas (plus a thirteenth) refer to the oratorios, to the mighty works of God they portray, the nature of God demonstrated by his works, the praise of God they elicit, and Handel's sublime portrayal of it all in music. After this exposition, the author wonders what Handel would do next (in light of the criticism against him), and the final three stanzas address the "dim-eyed form of Folly" which appreciates and derives "senseless glee" from much more trivial music. The writer labels the malicious, envious spirit set to ruin Handel nothing less than a "blast of Hell" – one that loves "with venom'd breath" to taint the composer's merit.

The writer alludes to several of the oratorios specifically, not by name but by some of their musical/textual content. Part of his reference to *Israel in Egypt* reads:

> ...*Speaks the God*
> *Whose Vengeance widely spreads*
> *The Darkness palpable,*
> *And kindles half the storm, with thunder hail,*
> *Hail mixt with Fire; divides the deep Abyss,*
> *And to the vast profound*
> *The horse and rider hurls;*

And of *Messiah* he wrote:

> *Tremendous theme of song! The theme of love*
> *And melting mercy HE, when sung to strains,*

> *Which from prophetic lips*
> *Touch'd with ethereal fire,*
> *Breath'd balmy Peace, yet breathing in the charm*
> *Of healing sounds; fit prelude to the pomp*
> *Of choral energy,*
> *Whose lofty accents rise*
> *To speak MESSIAH'S names; the God of Might,*
> *The Wondr'rous and the Wise – the Prince of Peace.*
> *Him, feeder of the flock*
> *And leader of the lambs,*
> *The tuneful tenderness of trilling notes*
> *Symphonious speaks: Him pious pity paints*
> *In mournful melody*
> *The man of sorrows; grief*
> *Sits heavy on his soul, and bitterness*
> *Fills deep his deadly draught – He deigns to die –*
> *The God who conquers Death,*
> *When, bursting from the Grave,*
> *Mighty he mounts, and wing'd with rapid winds,*
> *Thro' Heav'ns wide portals opening to their Lord,*
> *To boundless realms return'd,*
> *The King of Glory reigns.*
> *Pow'rs, dominations, thrones resound HE REIGNS,*
> *High Hallelujah's of empyreal hosts,*
> *And pealing Praises join*
> *The thunder of the spheres.*[1]

Though Handel presented three-quarters of the concerts he first intended that long season, attendance at some performances was meager. Handel's enemies had yet another trick to play. There were hints disseminated to the socially conscious that being seen at the oratorios was "not quite the thing." However, those who did attend could count on being not only delighted but edified.

A private letter by Mrs. Elizabeth Carter refers to both this perceived "unfashionableness" and to how affecting the oratorios are:

> *Unfashionable that I am, I was I own highly delighted the other night*
> *at his last oratorio. 'Tis called Belshazzar, the story [of] the taking of*

Babylon by Cyrus; and the music, in spite of all the very bad performers could do to spoil it, equal to any thing I ever heard. There is a chorus of Babylonians deriding Cyrus from their walls that has the best expression of scornful laughter imaginable. Another of the Jews, where the name Jehovah is introduced first with a moment's silence, and then with a full swell of music so solemn, that I think it is the most striking lesson against common genteel swearing I ever met with.

Two years later (1747), the Countess Shaftesbury would also use the word "unfashionable" to describe herself for not attending the opera. Lady Shaftesbury's and Elizabeth Carter's self-effacing comments about their own unfashionable tastes reflect the power the aristocratic opera crowd had to set social-artistic fashions. But that power was not strong enough to inhibit these two intelligent, independent-minded women – one an aristocrat herself, and one middle-class – from attending works they enjoyed and felt they would benefit from. Further, and as we've previously seen, Mrs. Carter's drawing a "moral" from an oratorio (against swearing, in this case) was a common response among Handel's listeners. Lady Shaftesbury, too, offers proof that eighteenth century thinking people assumed that art should have a moral purpose and "improve" its audience, and that art was lacking if it only entertained. Handel's music did enlighten, but, she wrote, "I [went] to see the new farce [David Garrick's *Miss in her Teens*] which I think has neither wit nor spirit but its merit consists in the representation and may be look'd upon as one of those entertainments which divert some minds but are far from being an improvement to any."

It was impossible for the upper classes to entirely ignore Handel. A remark by Horace Walpole indicates, in fact, that however unstylish some of them found attending Handel's oratorios to be, it was perfectly fashionable to argue about Handel among themselves:

The Master of the House [Walpole's brother Edward] plays extremely well on the bass-viol, and has generally other musical people with him.... He is perfectly master of all the quarrels that have been fashionably on foot about Handel.[2]

When the difficult 1744-45 season ended, Handel wisely left London to take a holiday. He began his well-earned vacation with the family of the Earl of Gainsborough at Exton in Rutland, Leicestershire – the same general area of England where Jennens lived. There is a revealing letter by Gainsborough's brother,

James Noel, to Shaftesbury (who was Noel's brother-in-law) that gives a picture of the homegrown entertainment they engaged in, ably aided by a pleasant, most obliging Handel. The household, including Handel, thoroughly enjoyed themselves:

> As Handel came to this place for Quiet and Retirement we were very loath to lay any task of Composition upon him. Selfishness however prevail'd; but we determined at the same time to be very moderate in our Requests. His readiness to oblidge soon took off all our apprehensions upon that account. A hint of what we wanted was sufficient and what should have been an act of Compliance he made a voluntary Deed. We laid our plan accordingly and reserved his Musick for an Eclat at this close of the entertainment. We likewise intermix'd the Poem with several of his former Compositions, as your Lordship will see by the copy I have sent you, which I think gave it great Life and Beauty. The whole scheme was concerted and executed in five Days; and that I believe your Lordship will allow was good Dispatch. It was intended to have been performed in the Garden, but the weather would not favour that design. We contrived however to entertain the Company there afterwards with an imitation of Vaux Hall: and, in the style of a newspaper, _the whole concluded_ with what variety of fireworks we could possibly get.[3*]

Handel left the Earl of Gainsborough's household and intended to return there briefly after a visit to the Shaftesburys at St. Giles House in Scarborough. As Shaftesbury was a relative of the Gainsborough clan, the Gainsboroughs amiably accompanied the composer on the trip to St. Giles. There, too, Handel was not averse to providing music for his friends. He wrote a sarabande for keyboard whose score carries a note indicating that he composed it extemporaneously and was desired to write it down.

Handel's holiday was pleasant, but the very real uncertainties about his future and his place in London society, musically and socially, struck forcefully upon his return home. The situation would require immediate action — which, it turned

---

*The piece that Handel composed for their entertainment was *There in the Blissful Shades* (HWV 44), a short version of Milton's *Comus*, based on a libretto by John Dalton for composer Thomas Arne (Burrows, *Handel*, p. 285, n1).

out, he was unable to take. In fact, according to an October letter by Jennens, Handel was already showing signs of mental perturbance during his holiday.

According to Rev.William Harris (another of the Harris brothers, and the chaplain and secretary to the Bishop of Salisbury), Handel looked well at that time; but he was not well. As he grew older (he was by now sixty), physical and mental symptoms of stress seemed to affect him more frequently, probably aggravated by having too much time alone to think and worry, no spouse to provide encouragement, no children to divert him, and few or no opportunities to unabashedly and immediately discuss the situation with a trusted confidant. William Harris met Handel on the street at the end of August, and his brief account of the encounter suggests that Handel was eager to talk with a trusted and sympathetic ear:

> *I met Handel a few days since in the street, and stopped and put him in mind who I was, upon which I am sure it would have diverted you to have seen his antic motions. He seemed highly pleased, and was full of inquiry after you and the Councillor. I told him I was very confident that you expected a visit from him this summer. He talked much of his precarious state of health, yet he looks well enough. I believe you will have him with you ere long.*

By sometime in the fall Handel was showing serious signs of the kind of mental and emotional distress (though apparently not the paralysis) that he had suffered twice before. A letter from Charles Jennens to Holdsworth, dated October 16, 1745, indicates the severity of Handel's current illness. Jennens actually wondered whether Handel would succumb to madness:

> *I am sorry to hear of M.' Handel's illness, & heartily wish his recovery; but he has acted so mad a part of late, I fear voluntarily, that I don't at all wonder if it brings a real unavoidable madness upon him, of which I am inform'd he discover'd some very strong Symptoms in his travels about the Country this last Summer.* [4]

Eight days later (October 24), Shaftesbury encouragingly reported to his cousin James Harris after just having seen Handel, "Poor Handel looks somewhat better." Shaftesbury, too, of course, expressed a wish for Handel's complete recovery, "though he has been a good deal disordered in his head."

Not only was "poor Handel" having grave difficulties in the autumn of 1745; so was the country. On July 21, the "Young Pretender," Charles Edward Stuart (Bonnie Prince Charlie) had sailed over from exile in France, leading an invasion into Scotland, gathering around him Jacobites, latent and blatant, as he marched south to England against very little opposition. By September 17 he entered Edinburgh with about 2,400 men; by early November, with well over twice that many, he was in England and steadily marching his way toward London. Britons who supported King George II (the large majority of them) were either deeply troubled or terrified, or both, by Charles's agile advance. A groundswell of patriotism inevitably arose in response.

Handel's public contribution to this response was the *Song for the Gentlemen Volunteers* of the city of London, "Stand round, my brave boys," which was performed as part of a what might be called a "variety night" of drama and music at the Royal Theater in Drury Lane on November 14. The song was published and offered to the public the next day and saw a repeat performance at Drury Lane on November 26. Besides a couple of Italian duets that Handel wrote on August 31 (the purpose of which is not known) the song for the volunteers was the only composing he did in the latter half of 1745. The "entire" recovery Shaftesbury wished for him was a long time in coming.

Bonnie Prince Charlie couldn't muster much real support from his Scottish and English Jacobites; nor from France, which was supposedly backing him. He advanced as far as Derby, 130 miles from London. But owing to dissension among his followers and the prospect of facing an army of 30,000 of King George's troops, he then retreated to Scotland, and his support dissipated over the next few months. On April 16, 1746, he was defeated in the bloody, now infamous, rout at Culloden Moor by William Augustus, the twenty-five-year-old Duke of Cumberland, the younger of George II's two sons.* Charles Stuart, who was also only twenty-five, at the time, slipped away and spent five months evading his English pursuers before escaping back to France in September 1746. He died in Rome in 1788, having become an alcoholic drifter.

By November 1745 Handel was once again his old self. But having been

---

*The Duke of Cumberland is a detested figure in Scottish history, while the English named a flower after him (Sweet William). The defeat at Culloden, the last battle on British soil, not only dashed the dream of returning a Scot to the English throne but began the disintegration and clearance of the highland clans. Cumberland earned the nickname "Butcher" from the Scots as his order to give no quarter was zealously carried out by his men. Cumberland's army killed the wounded and mercilessly hunted down Jacobites who had escaped.

burned so frequently he was now cautious about presenting *anything* to the public. Thomas Harris told his brother James on November 2:

> *I have seen him, and he is making some new chorus's but I don't know what they are; he says it is for his amusement only & that he has no thoughts of attempting any performance this winter.*

This is confirmed by Shaftesbury. On November 7 he wrote James Harris:

> *Mr. Handel is entirely recovered. His in now engaged for his amusement only in composing chorus's[,] some of which he has played me over himself. His fingers move as nimbly as ever, and I believe you'l easily credit me, when I say the chorus's are really excellent. They are rather in more parts than commonly they us'd to be. His genious after such an illness especially appears prodigious.*

The work with which Handel was "amusing" himself was the *Occasional Oratorio*. Unlike almost all of Handel's other music, it carries no specific date, only Anno 1746.) It was not until January 31 that his plans were publicized in the *General Advertiser*, and even then by hearsay rather than via the normal direct announcement from Handel himself:

> *We hear, that Mr. Handel proposes to exhibit some Musical Entertainments on Wednesdays and Fridays the ensuing Lent, with Intent to make good to the Subscribers (that favoured him last Season) the Number of Performances he was then not able to complete in order thereto he is preparing a New Occasional Oratorio, which is design'd to be perform'd at the Theater-Royal in Covent-Garden.*[5]

The "occasion" of the *Occasional Oratorio* hadn't yet occurred: the final defeat of Charles and his Jacobites after many "Rebellions," which would provide for the continuing succession of the Hanoverians. Or, the "occasion" can be seen as Charles's fallback to Scotland and impending defeat. Either way, this was viewed in the context of deliverance by God from an enemy, not unlike David's deliverance from *Saul* (Charles's supporters, of course, didn't for a moment see it that way). There was never any real chance that the Catholic Charles would march triumphant into London and snatch the throne from George II. But the fact that this long-time, near pagan enemy of Britain – as he was perceived by the majority – was still "out there" in January 1746 was disheartening and disquieting to them, despite ongoing dissatisfaction by some with King George II and the dissatisfaction of many more with his male offspring. (Among those dissatisfied Frederick, Prince of Wales was seen to be a philandering, conniving fop, and William Augustus, Duke of Cumberland, sadistic and shallow. Frederick would die in 1751 at age forty-four, saving the country the need to honor him as their King. Frederick's eldest son would become King George III in 1760 when his grandfather George II would die at age seventy-seven.)

The new oratorio by Handel provided some salve to the public (except to his personal enemies). Apart from any political context, it undoubtedly provided personal salve for the composer, who could intimately relate to its heartfelt cries (in rhymed paraphrases from Milton) from Psalm 3 ("O Lord, how many are my foes!") and Psalm 5 ("Jehovah, to my words give ear,/My meditations weigh!/The voice of my complaining hear,/To thee alone, my God and King, I pray"), and to much else in its libretto by Newburgh Hamilton.

Handel created the oratorio from a combination of old and new material, the old taken from mostly from *Israel in Egypt*. That older oratorio, not incidentally, also celebrates God's deliverance, and Handel's re-use of it in this context is ironic if Jennens was the librettist of *Israel in Egypt*. As a Nonjuror, he could have taken no pleasure in the disintegration of Charles Stuart's cause. So he had no desire to hear the *Occasional Oratorio*. To Holdsworth he grumbled irritably – understandable in light of his political views, but quite unkind to Handel as a friend, if he still considered the composer a friend when he wrote that this oratorio is "transcribed from Milton & Spencer, but chiefly from Milton, who in his Version of some of the Psalms wrote so like Sternhold & Hopkins [versifiers of the Psalter] that there is not a pin to choose betwixt 'em." He continued in a a more malignant vein:

> *The Oratorio, as you call it, contrary to custom, raised no inclination*
> *in me to hear it. I am weary of nonsense and impertinence; & by the*
> *Account Ld. Guernsey give me of this piece I am to expect nothing else.*
> *Tis a triumph for a Victory not yet gain'd, & if the Duke does not make*
> *haste, it may not be gain'd at the time of performance. [The libretto is]*
> *an inconceivable jumble of Milton & Spencer, a Chaos extracted from*
> *Order by the most absurd of all Blockheads.*

The extreme peevishness of Jennens' response to this oratorio he had not heard may, once again, have arisen from his ongoing depression. On the other hand, the Harrises and Shaftesburys (and many other listeners), felt the oratorio "extremely worthy of [Handel], which you will allow to be saying all one can in praise of it," to use William Harris's words. Harris noted that "the words of his

Oratorio are scriptural, but taken from various parts [of the Bible], and are expressive of the rebels' flight and our pursuit of them." Then he made a salient point: "Had not the Duke carried his point triumphantly, this Oratorio could not have been brought on."

To commemorate the actual defeat of Charles Stuart, Handel wrote only *A Song on the Victory Obtained Over the Rebels by His Royal Highness the Duke of Cumberland* (published by Walsh in May 1746). The song is set to five stanzas by Thomas Lowe, who was also a singer – the tenor who sang in Handel's first performances of *Samson*. Other composers responded as well. Maurice Greene (at the time still officially composer of the Chapel Royal) wrote a Te Deum related to the victory. And John Frederick Lampe wrote *Musick on the Thanksgiving Day*, which was performed in the Savoy Hospital chapel by the "Churchwardens and all the Gentlemen belonging to the German Lutheran Church ... in their native language." (The German Lutherans who lived in Britain were just as happy about the victory as the majority of native Britons were, since the continued succession of Britain's Hanoverian monarchs was now assured.) But the royal celebrations were subdued. Despite the many years the Stuarts had been thorns in the side of the Hanoverian monarchs, whom most Britons agreed were their legitimate rulers, the victory was, after all, one that involved "the king's army killing the king's subjects," as Donald Burrows puts it.

As summer came on, Handel was feeling well, had increased in strength, and remained well for some time – six months later, just after the New Year 1747, Shaftesbury described him as "now in perfect health and I really think grown young again."[6] In July he began to compose his next oratorio, *Judas Maccabaeus*, and completed its three parts in a span just like his old timetable – about a month (on August 11). It figured in his plans for that year's Lenten oratorio season. With *Judas Maccabaeus* he began working with a new librettist, Rev. Thomas Morrell, yet another Church of England minister. Handel seemed comfortable working with Morrell: this was the first of four librettos Morrell would provide, along with an adaptation of a fifth.[*]

---

[*]Besides *Judas Maccabaeus* they are *Alexander Balus*, *Theodora* and *Jephtha*. The adaptation is Handel's last work, *The Triumph of Time and Truth*, an extended version of his 1737 Italian oratorio *Il trionfo del Tempol e della Veritá*.

Despite the demise of the Middlesex opera company, those who loved opera continued to conjure it where they could, and Middlesex was still involved. In fact, the next great opera composer before Mozart, Christoph Willibald von Gluck (1714-1787), had recently been in London – though he didn't stay long. In January 1746 his opera *La caduta de' giganti* ("The Fall of Giants") was presented in the midst of the alarm and fervor aroused by the situation related to Charles Edward Stuart. The Duke of Cumberland was in the audience, and Handel may have been too. How ironic that the opera crowd now turned to another German to provide them with Italian opera! However, Gluck produced just two operas in London, presented two glass harmonica concerts, met Handel, and moved on.*

Handel wasn't impressed with Gluck's fugue-writing abilities; but Handel had grown up with a generation of German Lutherans to whom the fugue – and counterpoint – was their musical lifeblood, and Gluck was of the younger generation for whom melody, laid over a subservient harmony, was just the thing – part of the new and fashionable *gallant* style. (No doubt Bach would not have appreciated Gluck's counterpoint either, had he heard it.) According to Burney, Handel made the now infamous comment that his cook knew more about counterpoint than Gluck did. That is not quite as quirky or hyperbolic as it sounds, and, in fact, is a small example of Handel's sense of humor: the cook, Gustavus Waltz, was a professional musician; Handel hired him as a bass for operas beginning in 1733.

Thus, at mid-century in London, opera was not doing well, despite the assumption and assertion by its backers that gentlemen and -women of style would, of course, want to support this fashionable entertainment. As we've seen, not all aristocrats agreed, and certainly Handel's friends among them did not. In January 1747, Lord Shaftesbury called the current incarnation of the opera "absurd and ridiculous," and informed James Harris (in Salisbury, outside London's social orbit) that it was "not likely to meet with success." Because that was true, Handel was "delighted," and would continue, unabashed, to stay clear of opera and present

---

*The glass harmonica as Gluck used it was a set of twenty-six drinking glasses filled with varying amounts of water to produce different pitches, played by rubbing a wet finger on the rim of each glass. Gluck was said to have invented the tuned glasses as a playable instrument. Deutsch notes that an Irishman presented such a concert in Dublin several years before Gluck (May 3, 1743). A more sophisticated, self-contained version of the instrument was used later by both Mozart and Beethoven.

oratorios during Lent. Shaftesbury concluded with a sarcastic little skewer of this latest attempt at opera, praising Handel simultaneously: "We shall have a little *music* in Lent."

If Handel's delight in the assured failure of yet another attempt at opera reveals a very human glee in the discomfort of those who had spitefully used him, his response is easy to empathize with: he was reacting to people who had long treated him as a foe and had repeatedly, deliberately tried to engineer his downfall. Ironically, the opera group was about to resurrect *Rossane*, the work which was adapted from Handel's *Alessandro*, which he gave Middlesex after his refusal to directly compose for Middlesex's group.

The new oratorios that Shaftesbury so looked forward to met with an obstacle before they even began, but an obstacle of an unusual kind. The trial of Scottish nobleman and Jacobite conspirator Simon Fraser, Eleventh Baron Lovat, began two days before *Joseph and His Brethren* was to have been heard on March 18. (*Judas Maccabaeus* was to debut soon after.) Fraser's case would prove to be high-profile, if amazingly short by modern standards. Many Londoners who normally would have attended *Joseph* were preoccupied. Shaftesbury explained to James Harris:

> *The trial interrupts our harmonious system extremely. To-morrow Handel has advertised 'Joseph,' though I hope he will not perform, for nothing can be expected whilst the trial lasts. The week after, we flatter ourselves that 'Judas' will both give delight to the lovers of harmony and profits to the fountain whence it flows. However, I am not certain 'Judas' will be performed next week.[7]*

Fraser was the kind of man tabloid news gatherers in any age crave: his political fortunes intertwined murkily with his love life and he was notoriously unprincipled in both. He appears to have been a Jacobite, then a Hanoverian, then a Jacobite again. He was just as mercenary in "love," having eloped with a cousin whom he assumed would be inheriting her father's title, which would pass to him. When that didn't happen, he put her away and forced her mother (his aunt and recent temporary mother-in-law) to marry him. He eventually received his title and its accompanying lands, though he didn't have long to enjoy them. By the time of his 1747 trial he had already been impeached by the House of Lords. The trial was quite literally the end of the line: he was hanged after being declared guilty of treason.

Joseph was postponed, but by only two days; it was performed on the 20th and repeated on the 25th. Then *Judas Maccabaeus* made its first appearance April 1. Its plot, at face value, centers on the Israelite leader of the title who lived in the biblical intertestamental period, whose story is told in the Apocryphal books of the Maccabees. Judas is one of five sons of a God-fearing priest. He and his brothers lead a revolt in about 167 B.C. against the Seleucid king, Antiochus IV Epiphanes, who has taken over Jerusalem. (Antiochus was a descendent of Ptolomy, one of the five Greek generals who divided Alexander the Great's empire upon his death.) Antiochus burns parts of Jerusalem, strips the temple, builds an idol altar within it, kills some number of the people, carries off ten-thousand more into captivity, erects a citadel and plants a garrison of Macedonians there to keep the Israelites in line. Judas, his brothers, and the army they raise manage to recover Jerusalem. They rededicate the temple and rebuild the city wall.

The oratorio's story of the conquest of Israel by an apostate usurping power, and the rise of an heroic Israelite who routs the God-denying conquerors, struck consonant chords with Britons, and this oratorio, too, became a celebration of the "deliverance" from Charles and his Jacobites by the Duke of Cumberland. Morell, in fact, dedicated the wordbook to the Duke.[*] Though that was the case, and the oratorio was clearly associated with the victory over the Jacobites, *Judas Maccabaeus* is not the simple war-glorifying patriotic rant it has gained a reputation for being. The war with the (mainly Scottish) Jacobites was a civil war, and grievous in the peculiar way that civil wars are. While that war involved political and social issues, like all wars, it is difficult for us at this chronological, social, and ideological remove to grasp the nature and depth of the Anglican-Catholic antipathy involved, an antagonism that was initiated in the first place when James II became a Catholic, but whose foundation had been laid much earlier in the aftermath of what became the Protestant Reformation. Those Protestants who took the faith seriously (not only in England, but elsewhere) were disturbed by much of the theology and practice of Roman Catholicism at the time, with its superstition arousing extra-biblical fiats and requirements, a deep obscuring of Scripture, and a too intimate and opulent

---

[*]The dedication calls William Augustus "a Truly Wise, Valiant, and Virtuous Commander." The bloody details of the battle at Culloden and its aftermath would almost surely not have been general knowledge then. Even so, the battle was of course viewed very differently by the English than by the Scots.

affiliation with the temporal, material powers of this world. This became for them not just a matter of debate but one of life and death: salvation or damnation. And the Holy Mother Church, embodied by its popes, was just as adamant that the Protestants were heretics.*

So eighteenth century (Protestant) Britons equated their country and its future with the people of biblical Israel as God's peculiar people, who deserved and received God's blessing: England had superceded the biblical Israelites as God's people and supplanted the nations, particularly France and Italy, who still clung to an apostate Roman Mother Church. This view uses as its starting point the biblical teaching by Paul and the other apostles that all who are grafted into Christ are God's people. It moves precarious steps farther, however, in ignoring the word "all" and equating that "peoplehood" with British nationhood. They could point to plenty of biblical promises that *nations*, as well as persons who fear God and pursue justice and righteousness, will be blessed. But equating one's own nation with the biblical Israelites whom God chose for a unique purpose and direct relationship with himself at a specific point in human history is wrought with pitfalls – which Britain did not escape.

Judas Maccabaeus "went off with very great Applause" and remained among Handel's most popular oratorios, from then to now.[8] Librettist Thomas Morell, writing years later (circa 1779-80) described his collaboration with Handel on *Judas Maccabaeus*, and like the Handel-Jennens correspondence regarding *Belshazzar*, it reveals something of the mundane yet fascinating process of Handel's oratorio composing.

Handel approached Morell about the latter supplying him with a libretto, and Morell confirms how adeptly and quickly Handel worked:

> *Upon this I thought I could do as well as some [librettists] that had gone before me, and within 2 or 3 days carried him the first Act of* Judas Maccabaeus, *which he approved of.* "Well," *says he,* "and how

---

*The Roman Catholic Church was not the only church that was often too much "of the world." The Church of England was not guiltless in the manner in which it wielded temporal power. Also apropos: Anglicans were not the only anti-Catholic Protestants. Most Dissenters were just as unyieldingly so because of a particular aversion to high-church hierarchy and liturgy, coupled with what they saw as grossly erring theology. From the Roman Church side there was, equally, no love lost for Protestants. But in Britain, Catholics were a small minority, and at the mercy of the Protestant state church and government.

are you to go on?"

[Morell]: "Why, we are to suppose an engagement, and that the Israelites have conquered, and so begin with a chorus as Fallen is the Foe or, something like it."

[Handel]: "No, I will have this," and began working it, as it is, upon the Harpsichord. "Well, go on."

[Morell]: "I will bring you more tomorrow."

[Handel]: "No, something now,"

[Morell:] "So fall thy Foes, O Lord"

[Handel]: "that will do," and immediately carried on the composition as we have it in that most admirable chorus.

Chapter 16
Guns to Good Effect

The success of the 1747 season was surely a tremendous relief to Handel. As things unfolded, he would maintain successful Lenten oratorio seasons until his death. Quite naturally, some oratorios were better received than others, but in general Handel would now make a very comfortable living from the oratorios to the end of his life. His stature as a composer (and benefactor) only grew as he aged.

With this season Handel began to sell individual tickets for each concert rather than season subscription tickets. Perhaps the fiasco of the extra-long season that he had been forced to shorten loomed large in his decision to abandon subscriptions – intertwined as subscriptions must have been in his mind with his renewed problems with the opera faction, the recurrence of his distressing and probably embarrassing mental illness, and the mortification of having to publicly offer to refund money for un-performed concerts. This new arrangement may also reflect an increasingly middle-class audience.[1]

A case in point is Catherine Talbot, whom we met previously as she delighted in arias from *Sampson*, concluding that the oratorios were a "language adapted to devotion" with the power to affect listeners morally and spiritually. Of middle-class background, she was somewhat unusual in that she was an educated woman with literary talent and interests (her uncle, Thomas Secker, was at that point Bishop of Oxford and later spent a decade as the Archbishop of Canterbury).[*] Writing to her friend Elizabeth Carter, she talked about how she was spending her time – partly with Handel's oratorios:

> ...*This play [Garrick's farce Miss in Her Teens], and one oratorio, are the sum of the public places I have been at, unless you will add two very moderate drums, and one concert. Those oratorios of Handel's are*

---

[*] Miss Talbot and her friend Mrs. Carter, both serious Christians, were of the generation thirty to thirty-five years younger than Handel. The two were among the "bluestockings," an unusual group of educated women with literary interests. Miss Talbot was a capable writer but had few works published in her lifetime. She (with her mother) lived in the household of Bishop and Mrs. Secker. Elizabeth Carter wrote published poems, essays, translations, and "notes on the Bible, and answers to objections concerning the Christian religion" (she knew both Hebrew and Greek). She was the daughter of "perpetual curate" Nicholas Carter, who gave her a fine education along with her brothers. (Her father was a friend of the editor of *The Gentleman's Magazine*, previously referred to.) Despite the "Mrs.," Elizabeth Carter was unmarried. There still exists a series of letters exchanged by the friends between 1741 and 1770, four-volumes-worth, first published in 1809.

certainly ... the most solemnly striking music one can hear. I am sure
you must be fond of them, even I am who have no ear for music, and
no skill in it. In this last oratorio he has literally introduced guns, and
they have a good effect.

The "guns" were not guns but kettle drums. But they certainly have "a good effect."

In addition to the Lenten oratorios, that spring there were benefit concerts in London featuring Handel's music for both the Sons of the Clergy and the Decay'd Musicians Fund, and continued benefit concerts in Dublin too. Perhaps because it had been nearly a year since Handel completed *Judas Maccabaeus* – and he hadn't produced a major composition since then – that summer he started not one but two oratorios and quickly completed them both. On June 1 he began work on Morell's second libretto, *Alexander Balus*, finishing it July 4; he began *Joshua* on July 19 and finished it on August 19 – the work schedule of a much younger man.

Alexander Balus continues the story that *Judas Maccabaeus* began. Like *Judas Maccabaeus*, this story comes from the Apocryphal books of the Maccabees. At first glance its plot reads somewhat more like an opera than an oratorio. The action takes place during the Diadochen wars of the third century B.C. Alexander Balus is the king of Syria with whom the Israelites, led by Jonathan, a brother of Judas Maccabaeus, are allied. Ptolomee, king of Egypt, gives his daughter Cleopatra (not to be confused with the famous Cleopatra) to Alexander to marry, but all along Ptolomee is hatching a plot against Alexander so that he can take over Syria; he takes his daughter back by kidnaping her, and tries to convince her that Alexander did exactly what he, Ptolomee, is doing: used her to plot the downfall of an enemy he pretends is a friend. But Cleopatra won't believe Alexander could be treacherous. A messenger brings word that during a battle between Alexander's and Jonathan's combined forces against Ptolomee's, her father had had Alexander beheaded. A second messenger brings word that her father had also died. In despair, and wanting to "escape this hateful light" into "endless night," she kills herself. Jonathan responds in this recitative:

Mysterious are thy ways, O Providence!
But always true and just. By Thee kings reign,
By Thee they fall. — Where is now Egypt's boast?
Where thine, O Syria, laid low in dust,
While chosen Judah triumphs in success,
And feels the presence of Jehovah's arm.

Mindful of this, let Israel ever fear,
With filial reverence, his tremendous name,
And with obsequious hearts exalt his praise.

Jonathan and all the Israelites then sing, ending the oratorio:

Ye servants of th'eternal King,
His pow'r and glory sing,
And speak of all his righteous ways
With wonder and with praise.
Amen. Hallelujah. Amen.

Alexander Balus is one of the fine oratorios that most people today have never heard of. Handel's audiences responded well to it, but many twentieth century scholars did not, considering it static, lacking "drama," and offensive in its insistence that the sad end of Ptolomee and Alexander (and Cleopatra), worshipers of false gods, was part of the "mysterious ways" and providence of the one true God.[*]

~

Amazing as it seems, that fall of 1747 there was yet another opera season of sorts by Lord Middlesex and friends. They occupied the King's Theater while Handel used Covent Garden. The first performance by Middlesex's group was a pasticcio (*Lucio Vero*) cobbled together entirely with arias from six operas – by Handel! An odd situation, he was in a sense being forced to compete with himself. He had nothing to do with this opera, though they may have asked his permission to use his music, to which he held the copyright. If so, Handel's affirmative answer reveals the essential good nature and graciousness of the great composer whom the opera faction had so often sought to bring down. It also reveals the shamelessness of Middlesex and his opera friends, and in fact they may not have bothered to ask. Yet their use of music by Handel to try to muster a season was a sort of backhanded

---

[*]Morell doesn't hint in his libretto why Jonathan and Israel ally themselves with the still idol-worshiping Alexander and Syria in direct disobedience to God's numerous commands to Israel throughout the Old Testament to remain apart and, in fact, to destroy the pagan nations because they refused to acknowledge God as God. In the scene in which word is brought to Alexander that his father-in-law has treacherously taken back Cleopatra, as Alexander and Jonathan prepare to take up arms against Ptolomee Jonathan sings: "May he return with laurel'd victory/ On his glad brow./ But oh, I fear the gods,/The creature gods he trusteth cannot help!/They are no gods, but mere delusion all." In the aria that immediately follows, Jonathan confesses that "To Him, almighty, greatest, best,/Jehovah, Lord of Hosts confest,/All victory belongs." A chorus of Israelites then joins Jonathan in singing praise to God, also acknowledging that they will praise only him.

compliment, and that may be how Handel saw it, and shrugged it off. Despite all, he knew the quality and staying power of his own music.

Handel's second oratorio written in 1747 – *Joshua* – is a compelling work. Oddly, the libretto's author is not named, but was perhaps Newburgh Hamilton.[2] *Joshua* contains exceptional choruses, outstanding arias (including the now famous soprano aria "O Had I Jubal's Lyre") and extraordinary instances of word painting. For example: Handel sets up static "walls" of sound at the parting of the Jordan River on the text, "In wat'ry heaps affrighted Jordan stood"; and at the sun and moon standing still during the battle with the Amorites (Joshua 10) an astonishing and eery thirty-two beats on a sustained A pitch make that standing still aurally obvious – a bit of word painting for which Handel took jibes from some critics who decried it as too obvious.

Joshua's best known chorus is "See the Conquering Hero Comes" – which Handel also quickly inserted into *Judas Macabaeus* (with the same text). It is in that latter context that the chorus's tune became famous; and it was transformed into a hymn when it was published in *Harmonia Sacra* in 1760, a year after Handel's death, wedded with Charles Wesley's text "Christ the Lord Is Risen Today." The frequency of the tune's usage with Wesley's Easter text declined in the nineteenth century, but late in that century it was united with the text "Thine Is the Glory," which is how it is still widely known as a hymn.[*]

Despite all that, it is another of Handel's oratorios that has not been much appreciated in modern times by scholars. It is Anthony Hicks's opinion that a "decorous love affair between the young warrior Othniel and Joshua's daughter Achsah and a sympathetic portrait of Othniel's old father Caleb" tempers the "bloodthirsty aspects of the Israelites' conquest of Canaan under the leadership of Joshua."[3] Implying that *Joshua* is included in the lot, Donald Burrows says that in December 1745 when Handel was considering what oratorios he would write next,

---

[*]The text of "Thine Is the Glory" was originally the French hymn "A toi la gloire," written in 1884 by Swiss pastor Edmond Louis Budry (1854-1939). First published in *Chants Évangéliques*, 1885, it was translated into English by Richard Birch Hoyle (1875-1839) for the first edition of *Cantate Domino*, 1924. (Hoyle was an English pastor who had ties to the English YMCA and who later went to the U.S. to teach at Western Theological Seminary in Pittsburgh.) The hymn came to be widely known in English-speaking churches worldwide. Thus, many Christians recognize this Handel tune even if they've never heard *Judas Maccabaeus* or *Joshua*. In 1974 the tune was also combined with a marriage text, "Praised Be the Father," by Calvin Seerveld (*Psalter Hymnal*, no. 582, Grand Rapids, Mich.: CRC Publications, 1987).

"he probably began to look over some oratorio librettos on bellicose Old Testament themes." If one does not accept that the Old Testament is the Word of God then, indeed, God's instructions to Israel to destroy the surrounding pagan nations (and his punishment of Israel when they repeatedly stray) is merely bloodthirsty and bellicose. Even to those who believe God is revealed in the Old Testament, and as the loving and compassionate God he claims to be, such loss of human life is deeply distressing. It can only be understood at all in the context of the almighty God's holiness and his consequent intolerance for sin. Though Britons in Handel's day had their own misconceptions and prejudices, they understood this far better than do we in our age of ala carte religion and democracy of gods made in our own image.

Burrows does suggest two points that would seem truisms to Christian scholars and listeners. First, the oratorios "might have been seen as suitably serious biblical presentations for the Lenten season"; surely Handel himself saw them that way and did not choose Lent as the time for performances only purely on pragmatic grounds: orthodox believers took Lent seriously as a time to contemplate Christ's suffering and to re-examine their own lives, as orthodox believers still do. Second, "that as such [the oratorios] may have attracted a section of London society that had been affected by the religious revival apparent in the first wave of John Wesley's influence (and in the Church of England's response to it)."Perhaps not incidentally, it was about this time (slightly earlier) that Handel wrote music for three of Charles Wesley's hymn texts. They are the only hymns Handel ever wrote.*

This is an appropriate point to take note of the relationship between Handel, the Wesleys and other Methodists. The founders of Methodism, John and Charles Wesley, grew up in the Church of England (as most people did), and, in fact, their father was a vicar. The Methodist movement began inadvertently with university Bible studies by Charles and his friends, and with preaching to the lower classes by John, after both brothers independently had conversion experiences. By the late 1730s, the movement had taken hold. But Charles, especially, did not want

---

*From the nineteenth century until rather recently, Handel was said to have written the music for "Joy to the World." The tune, named ANTIOCH, first appeared in *The Modern Psalmist*, 1839, with the designation "From George Frederick Handel." Despite a Baroque-like style, it is now clear that this carol contains no specific elements taken from *Messiah* (as was long assumed), nor from any other work by Handel. ANTIOCH was, rather, written by American music educator and hymnist Lowell Mason (1792-1872), compiler of *The Modern Psalmist*. The tune name commemorates Antioch in Syria where believers were first called Christians (Acts 11:26).

to leave the Church of England; he felt it needed reformation from within. Charles Wesley – far more agreeable and mild-mannered than his imperious though apparently charismatic brother John – was primarily a poet, so it is not surprising that he was also a music lover. He wrote more than six-thousand poems as hymn texts, dozens of which have taken their place among the great hymns of the church.

Charles Wesley and Handel may have met at home of theater manager John Rich and his Methodist wife, Priscilla. It is more likely that they never did meet face-to-face, though Wesley most likely attended some of Handel's oratorio performances, including after Handel's death. Charles's daughter Sarah ["Sally"] wrote somewhat ambiguously in an article in the *Wesleyan-Methodist Magazine*, Dec. 1826, "My Father and Mother used to hear his fine performances."[4] Charles Wesley's journal takes note of dining with the Riches, and of meeting two other notable musicians, J.F. Lampe and J.C. Pepusch, transplanted Germans like Handel. But if Wesley had met Handel he surely would have described the meeting, and an account of the occasion would have been passed down in the family, since Charles was a great admirer of Handel, and so were his sons Charles and Samuel; both sons were talented musicians who were weaned on Handel's music.

But there is no such account or story (some Internet sources to the contrary). Charles Wesley was not even aware that Handel had set three of his hymn texts to music in 1747 (Handel was then sixty-two; Wesley was forty). It was 1826 before this fact was happily discovered by Charles's son Samuel. Handel apparently took the texts for the three hymns from the then just-published *Hymns on the Great Festivals and Other Occasions*. He used the two-part titles as they appeared in that hymnal, not as Wesley entitled his poems: "The Invitation: Sinners Obey the Gospel Word"; "Desiring to Love: O Love Divine, How Sweet Thou Art"; and "On the Resurrection: Rejoice, the Lord is King." Handel's very fine, appropriately regal setting of "Rejoice, the Lord is King!" (whose tune is known as GOPSALL, home of Charles Jennens) is still commonly used in the Anglican Communion, but this text is sung to a different eighteenth century tune by most North American Protestants (DARWALL'S 148th, written two decades after Handel's death).

Handel wrote his hymn settings as a vocal line with continuo part (figured bass line) and several measures of "postlude." His early grounding in German chorales certainly gave him a knowledge of the requirements for congregational song, but these hymns were almost certainly intended for home use in family devotions. The vocal line in both "O Love Divine" and "Rejoice, the Lord is King," for example, hits high F, and "O Love Divine," particularly, is somewhat more artful than tunes intended for congregational singing were. "Sinners Obey" is in G minor and sounds ballad-like.

There are a couple of intriguing but veiled (to us) connections between Handel and prominent Methodists besides Charles Wesley. Handel expressed his Christian faith as a Lutheran who worshiped as an Anglican, as we've seen. That theological/practical dichotomy in his own life, his handful of Nonjuring friends (among them *Messiah* librettist Charles Jennens) who had their own displacement to contend with, and his own life-long generosity to the poor make it quite possible that he empathized with the Methodists' ecclesiastical displacement, with their serious biblical devotion and with their systematic work on behalf of the poor. As we shall see later, Handel did have an important meeting on his deathbed with the wealthy noblewoman who was a major benefactor for Methodists, Lady Huntington.

It was natural for Methodists and other Dissenters to be among those who attended the oratorios. Such "evangelicals" would be particularly open to the biblical messages in the oratorios, joining their Anglican neighbors in Handel's audiences. The Wesley brothers themselves are examples. Besides evidence that Charles Wesley was an avid admirer of Handel, there is an autobiographical account of John Wesley being much moved by *Messiah*.

Though there are political overtones in some of the oratorios, it is not discernable to us what percentage of Handel's audiences would have heard them, and there is no logical reason to think that the Old Testament-based oratorios were not listened to first of all at face value – that is, as straightforward "sacred dramas" which, besides being both moving and entertaining stories, present elements of the gospel. In any drama, the story is what people naturally hear and relate to first, and only then do they consider additional layers of meaning.

The modern tendency to interpret an Old Testament/ New Testament divide in which God is virtually two different Gods – vengeful, retributive and merciless in the Old Testament versus compassionate, loving and forgiving in the New – was not countenanced in Handel's day, and is still resisted by orthodox Bible scholars as a distorting misreading of Scripture. Likewise, the modern attitude which holds that the Old Testament oratorios are not "Christian" because they are Old Testament stories – that is, stories from Judaism, not Christianity – would have been strongly challenged.

The orthodox view, from the apostles to the present (maintained by Handel and his librettists and by most of their contemporaries, and put forth in the oratorios) believes the New Testament writers' presentation of Christ as the fulfillment of the Old Testament promises of the Messiah (as Christ himself claims), and from the beginning Christians understood that the Old Testament is crucial to the history of redemption. The combined Old Testament and New Testament canon, guided by the Holy Spirit, is God's unified revelation of himself and his unfolding plan for the redemption of the world; therefore all of the Bible is gospel ("good news"), and Handel and his Christian contemporaries believed it to be so. The Apocrypha (used for *Judas Maccabaeus*, *Alexander Balus*, and *Susanna*), though not part of the inspired biblical canon in the view of Protestants, is "profitable for instruction," and was particularly valued for that purpose in the centuries subsequent to the Reformation by Anglicans and Lutherans (and initially Calvinists).

Without this understanding of Christianity's confession of the fundamental unity of Scripture, a good part of the meaning of Handel's oratorios is lost. While God's saving acts – part of the gospel – are thus evident in all the oratorios, *Messiah* is unique among them in its comprehensive biblical summation of salvation in Christ, including his future glorious reign. Jennens implied that presenting the gospel was his specific motivation in compiling *Messiah's* libretto. In light of that, Ruth Smith suggests that Jennens saw its comprehensive biblical libretto as an orthodox Christian apologia against Deism.[5]

There is a passage in Eliza Haywood's *Epistles for the Ladies*, published the next year (1749), that speaks even more directly to how oratorio texts and music combined to be received by listeners. After hearing *Joshua*, Mrs. Haywood reflected on the spiritual effect of the oratorios:

> It is a vulgar Aphorism, that those who are untouched with Music, have no Soul.... I was led into these reflections by being last Night at Mr. Handel's *fine Oratorio of* Joshua, *where, though the Words were not quite so elegant, nor so well as I could have wished adapted to the Music, I was transported into the most divine Exstasy.— I closed my Eyes, and imagined myself amidst the angelic Choir in the bright Regions of everlasting Day, chanting the Praises of my great Creator, and his ineffable* Messiah.*—I seemed, methought, to have nothing of this gross Earth about me, but was all Soul!—all Spirit! ....I should be glad there were Oratorios established in every City and great Town*

throughout the Kingdom...to be given gratis.[*]

This kind of reaction to the oratorios would become commonplace. In 1756, Miss Catherine Talbot would write:

> *The only public place I have been to this winter, was last Friday to hear the Messiah, nor can there be a nobler entertainment. I think it is impossible for the most trifling [people] not to be the better for it. I was wishing all the Jews, Heathens, and Infidels in the world (a pretty full house you'll say) to be present. The Morocco Ambassador was there, and if his interpreter could do justice to the divine words (the music any one that has a heart must feel) how must he be affected, when in the grand choruses the whole audience solemnly rose up in joint acknowledgement that He who for our sakes had been despised and rejected of men, was their Creator, Redeemer, King of kings, Lord of lord! To be sure the playhouse is an unfit place for such a solemn performance, but I fear I shall be in Oxfordshire before it is heard at the Foundling Hospital [chapel], where the benevolent design and the attendance of the little boys and girls adds a peculiar beauty even unto this noblest composition....*

Handel now continued to write new oratorios and present them each Lent. The new works for 1749-50 were *Solomon* and *Susanna*. Like *Joshua*, their librettos are by unknown writers. Stylistic clues indicate they were written by the same person; a competent writer he was. He may in fact have been Newburgh Hamilton (who, recall, wrote *Samson*, part of the *Occasional Oratorio*, and possibly *Joshua*).

---

[*]Eliza Haywood (c. 1693-1756) was the most prolific female writer of the eighteenth century. Trying to earn her own living, she wrote novels, plays (including one for which Aaron Hill wrote a gracious epilogue), criticism, advice to other women regarding conduct, newspaper articles, memoir-like volumes and literary parody amounting to some seventy-five volumes. She married a clergyman, apparently had two children, and left her husband in 1721, reason unknown. Her early novels (mid-1720s) were considered scandalous, not least because, in some, the characters corresponded to real people. However, as was the expectation for art, their purported purpose, besides entertainment, was "a good Moral Use"; and Haywood's novels were also a "warning to the youth of both sexes" (Preface to *Lasselia*, 1723). She was described by Alexander Pope in his *Dunciad* (book ii 11. 157 et seq) as one of the "shameless scribblers who ... reveal the faults and misfortunes of both sexes to the ruin of public fame, or disturbance of private happiness." Haywood later had a change of heart (and/or conversion) and her late work is careful and decorous, serving as a kind of apologetic for faith and morality. Interestingly, George Washington's library contained a copy of *Epistles for the Ladies*, presumably for his wife Martha's edification, or at her request (Letterpress Edition, Colonial Series, 7:345).

The Solomon of Handel's oratorio is an altogether exemplary monarch: wholeheartedly God-fearing, constant in husbandly love and wise in his public judgments. News of the splendor of his kingdom reaches foreign lands and draws a visit by the Queen of Sheba, as in the biblical account. But the biblical Solomon's seven-hundred wives and three-hundred concubines are nowhere to be found. Nor is God's displeasure at Solomon's allowing himself to be influenced by his wives' pagan religion, and Solomon's actually building alters for their gods.

If Handel's contemporary British audiences drew parallels from the oratorio to their own king and national situation, as is generally assumed, it is difficult to imagine that they overlooked George II's faults to the extent of seeing in him a "type" of Solomon. Realistically, they may have wished and prayed that their own monarch lived up to Solomon's example – even the example of the flawed biblical Solomon, never mind the idealized oratorio Solomon. On the other hand, "warts and all" portrayals to which we're accustomed today would have shocked audiences (even when they knew that they could find such portrayals in their Bibles). The oratorio librettos based on biblical characters either leave out or smooth over at least some of the unsavory details the Bible includes. *Solomon*, however, particularly idealizes its title character. That may be a clue to the fact that the oratorio's King Solomon was intended to present a model for England's monarch; that is, England's monarch should model himself after Solomon. What is also significant is that Israel is not warring with her pagan enemies in this oratorio. It is significant that in the period when the librettist and Handel conceived this oratorio, the Treaty of Aix-la-Chapelle, which would finally end the War of the Austrian Succession, was being negotiated and was signed in October 1748.

Susanna, too, is set wholly apart from Israel's conflict with the surrounding pagan nations. Instead, its conflict is "interior": it occurs within Israel. The title character is a virtuous Israelite woman framed and wrongly accused of adultery by two Israelite judges (called "elders" in the libretto). The story comes from an apocryphal addition to the Septuagint and Theodotion, Greek translations of the book of Daniel. (This addition is considered part of the biblical canon by Roman and Orthodox Catholics).

The setting, as throughout the canonical book of Daniel, is Babylon during Israel's exile there. Susanna is a beautiful and intelligent woman who fears the Lord. She is happily married to a wealthy, honorable man named Joakim (spelled "Joacim" in the oratorio). The Apocrypha tells us (but the oratorio libretto does not) that court is held at Joacim's house. The two elders who lust after Susanna are judges who have had plenty of opportunity to observe her. When her husband Joacim is away, they conspire together to get Susanna alone so they can satisfy their lust with her. When she refuses their advances, they accuse her of adultery with a non-existent young lover. They assume that their word as respected leaders will be believed, and they're right: Susanna is condemned to die. The prophet Daniel – but a "youth" at the time – doubts the rightness of the outcome, prompted by God (in the libretto his motivation and authority aren't entirely clear). He questions the elders separately and discovers a conflict in their stories ("Let not the one the other's questions hear,/For truth will ne'er in diff'rent garbs appear.")

The story graphically illustrates, as so many biblical and apocryphal passages do, that God protects and defends the righteous who call on him. The Apocryphal incident concludes with Susanna's family praising God (this includes her children; she has no children in the oratorio). It is noted that this case first establishes Daniel's reputation among the Hebrews. The oratorio ends with praise of the virtuous wife in the manner of Proverbs 31.

As is the case with almost all of Handel's oratorios today, *Susanna* is now generally given a secular spin. Donald Burrows, in fact, calls it "what is effectively a secular story."[6] By that implied definition most of Scripture would have to be considered secular. It fails to take account of faith's informing of every-day life and action. *Susanna* is now also considered to be a pastoral comedy, that is, written in the tradition of musical-dramatic pieces with rustic mythological/pastoral stories populated by such creatures as nymphs, shepherds and gods in love, such as Handel's *Acis and Galatea*. Perhaps seeing *Susanna* as a secular story, along with the fact that its first scene celebrates the love between Susanna and Joacim, allows for that classification. It is hard to see that classification being accurate, either textually and musically.

The biblical-apocryphal story is serious and dramatically tense, and the oratorio libretto's retelling this story well-known to eighteenth century audiences maintains the Apocrypha's intent. *Susanna* opens by immediately reminding listeners of Israel's bondage in exile with a chorus of sorrowful yearning as only Handel could have written it: "How long, O Lord, shall Israel groan,/ In slavery and pain?/Jehovah, hear thy people's moan,/And break th' oppressor's chain!" Handel then continues with sixteen numbers – eight pairs of recitatives/arias – which celebrate the joys of chaste, married love (as an extended scene in *Solomon* also does, both oratorios hinting at the Song of Songs).The music is engaging and delightful – somewhat reminiscent of some of Handel's pastoral love duets, but not comedic. (It is "comedic" only in the sense that some plays have been defined that way if their characters eventually triumph over adversity – but such stories generally have elements of humor or satire along the way, which Susanna doesn't.)

Next we learn of the elders' uncontrollable lustful urges. While there's an element of the ridiculous in the panting indignity of the two purportedly dignified and supposedly righteous elders – and Handel deftly hints at that ridiculousness – they are in deadly earnest: they will secretly rush upon Susanna and rape her if she doesn't willingly cooperate ("force her to bliss," as the libretto has one of the elders euphemistically put it).

The tension mounts, but the chorus lets listeners know the elders won't get away with it. God will judge them in his own time: "Righteous Heav'n beholds their guile,/And forbears His wrath awhile./Yet His bolt shall quickly fly,/Darted through the flaming sky./Tremble guilt, for thou shalt find,/Wrath divine outstrips the wind."Pretty serious stuff. Because Burrows sees *Susanna* as secular, he has no choice but to characterize its fine choruses as "somewhat sententious." In Act 2, the temporarily separated Susanna and Joacim yearn for each other. When, eventually, through Daniel's courage and righteous judgement they are happily reunited, that, too, is not the stuff of comedy – even by a definition which sees comedy as virtually anything not "tragic."

The story of Susanna had been well known for centuries before Handel. It was sometimes interpreted allegorically. For example, initially this passage in apocryphal Daniel may have been directed against the Sadducees; later, Susanna sometimes stood for Christ's Bride, the Church. The subject captivated numerous painters, including Rembrandt – who represented the story more than once. Handel, an art lover and collector, had an affinity for Rembrandt and owned several of that great artist's works. It's quite possible that Handel saw Rembrandt's "Susanna and the Elders" (c. 1634) or "Susanna Surprised by the Elders" (1647) during one of his trips through the Netherlands, and if he did, that it helped draw him to the story as a subject for his own musical art. He may also have seen some of the many Italian renderings of the subject.

Handel looked forward to the 1749 oratorio season (which would open with four performances of *Susanna*), and Shaftesbury told his cousin James, "The old

Buck is excessively healthy and full of spirits."[7*] The season continued with two performances of *Hercules* (the first revival of this work from 1744), four of *Samson* (the first revival of another 1744 work), and three of *Solomon*. Handel closed the season with a Holy Week performance of *Messiah* (March 23) without prior advertising, the first time he brought back *Messiah* since the discontent it was still causing in 1745. After its rocky reception in London during Lent 1743, Handel omitted *Messiah* in 1744, and in 1745 he presented it just twice, without name, referring to it only as "The Sacred Oratorio"or "A Sacred Oratorio."

Of the two new works, *Solomon* was the more successful (despite three performances to *Susanna's* four) and grew in popularity. While *Susanna* was still in rehearsal, Shaftesbury noted, "I hear Susanna much commended by some who heard Galli and Frazi's parts" (two of the original soloists). And Lady Shaftsbury observed after attending the first performance, "I think I never saw a fuller house." However, she had reservations about *Susanna*: she referred to it as being "in the light operatical style," and for that reason she believed it would "not insinuate itself so much into [her] approbation as most of Handel's performances do."[**] She admitted, however, that her Harris cousins, who were also at the performance, were "much better judges than myself." After hearing *Susanna*, George Harris wrote in his diary: "Prodigious full house—but doesn't please the town."

Handel's oratorio audiences were fickle by our standards. A further diary comment by George Harris (February 12) gives a clue as to why *Susanna* was greeted indifferently: "The K[ing] told Lady Carlisle, that the new oratorio hadn't so many chorus's, & in general wasn't so well liked, as oratorios used to be." No one wrote oratorio choruses (or anthems) like Handel did. By now, audiences loved

---

*"The old Buck," "old Bucks," or "the Buck" were affectionate nicknames for Handel used among the Shaftesbury-Harris-Guernsey cousins/friends. Shaftesbury, the Harris brothers, Lord Guernsey, and Jennens were a generation younger than Handel: in 1749, Shaftesbury was thirty-eight years old, James Harris was forty, George Harris, thirty-five; Jennens was forty-nine. But Handel was sixty-four.

**What Lady Shaftesbury calls "the light operatical style" doesn't necessitate it being a pastoral comedy. She may have been referring to the low number of choruses (only seven, and they're generally short). In that, *Susanna* was more like opera than Handel's previous oratorios. *Susanna* is also dramatic in a different way than previous oratorios in that it focuses entirely on the workings-out of one incident, beginning as a kind of interior drama and ending with public-justice implications. Though some of the other oratorios contain love stories, this one contains extensive "love talk."

them, and wanted a good number of them to the balance the recitatives and arias with their different kind of appeal. Sir John Hawkins observed that Handel's oratorio choruses were set apart in kind and quality from his opera choruses (which were also far fewer in number). The oratorio choruses, Hawkins says, "answer to the sublime in poetry; they are of his own invention, and are the very basis of his reputation." Very few people would have disagreed. And once again there is an irony: Handel's early oratorio *Israel in Egypt* was apparently shunned by his audiences because it is full of choruses. Now *Susanna* was shunned because it isn't.

~

Despite opposition to the peace treaty in some camps, the end of the war, at long last, naturally called for celebration. Who but Handel could provide suitably regal music? There would be grand outdoor festivities in Green Park and they would include fireworks. But like the preparations and negotiations for the treaty itself, preparing for the celebration was an ordeal: the pavilion conceived for the purpose was begun in November after the Peace was signed, but it was not completed until the following spring. On April 25, 1749, two days before the fireworks celebration, the official service of Thanksgiving took place at the Royal Chapel in St. James's Palace. Handel provided the lovely "peace anthem" *How Beautiful Are the Feet* [of them that preach the gospel of peace]," part of which he adapted from his *Messiah* aria on that text.

The *Water Music*, though written long before, had given Handel some experience with providing outdoor music. This time around, his no-holds-barred scheme for noble music to accompany the fireworks caused consternation among those at Court responsible for the event, and for George II himself, if the Duke of Montagu, Master General of the Ordnance, is to be believed. Handel, oboe lover since childhood, planned the *Royal Fireworks Music* for copious numbers of wind instruments (traditional military instruments), among them twenty-four oboes – and nine trumpets, nine horns, twelve bassoons, a contrabassoon, a serpent (a now obsolete member of the Renaissance cornett family, then still common in military and church bands), and three sets of timpani (kettle drums).

Somewhere along the line Handel decided that the effect would be more impressive if he added strings, having them double the wind parts (the violins and oboes play the same musical line, and cellos and bassoons share their line, creating the sonority of combined winds and strings). According to the Duke of Montagu, the King was not happy about this, as he felt the addition of "fidles" would make the music less martial. Nor was Montagu happy – and by his word, nor, again, was George II – about Handel's initial refusal to hold the rehearsal at Vauxhall Gardens. (Handel probably felt it necessary to rehearse in the same venue his players would perform in.) It's possible that the King didn't really care: he allowed Handel to have his way regarding the strings as part of the band, but Handel had to compromise on the issue of the rehearsal at Vauxhall Gardens. It may have been Handel's ability to sway the King that annoyed Montagu more than anything else. Montagu threatened to ask someone else to compose the music, telling Charles Frederick, the Comptroller of His Majesty's Fireworks:

> If [Handel] continues to express his zeal for his Majesty's service by doing what is so contrary to it, in not letting the rehersal be there, I shall intirely give over any further thoughts of his overture and shall take care to have an other.[8]

This cannot have been a real threat, especially at that late date; it is doubtful that Montagu had such authority. He wrote out of annoyance, and possibly to impress Charles Frederick.

Exactly when Handel was asked to compose, or when he did compose, his *Royal Fireworks Music* is not known, but word of his intentions and other gossip about the event spread, especially among the upper classes. In a letter by a Hanover Square neighbor of Handel's, Mrs. Susan Archer, to her friend Lydia Catherine, the Duke of Chandos's wife, Mrs. Archer says she is anticipating hearing Handel's music, but adds, "His Majesty I hear is excessively out of Humour about the Fire Works.... I believe a good many people will lose their hearing...; there will be 26 Cannons & 3 Barrils of Gunpowder go [off] at once & ... Handell proposes his Musick shall be heard at the same time." Wisely, in the actual event, the music was heard before the fireworks went off.

The rehearsal at Vauxhall Gardens (without fireworks) involving Handel's "band" of one-hundred performers was itself an auspicious event. Originally scheduled for April 17, the rehearsal was finally held at noon on April 21 so that the Duke of Cumberland could be there (the *General Advertiser* had been keeping the public informed of the shifting dates). Astonishingly, 12,000 people paid half a crown each to hear the music rehearsed and to get a feel for the spectacle. This snarled traffic on London Bridge for three hours, perhaps the first traffic jam in history. The next day, the *General Advertiser* remarked on "the brightest and most numerous Assembly ever known at the Spring Garden, Vauxhall." The paper then tantalized its readers with this curious tidbit: "Several Footmen who attended their Masters, &c. Thither, behaved very saucily, and were justly corrected by the Gentlemen for their Insolence."

There were equally huge numbers of people at the April 27 celebration. For us modern people used to massive crowds, the words of a Mr. Byrom in a letter to his wife on fireworks night puts this in mid-eighteenth century perspective: "I have before my eyes such a concourse of people as to be sure I never have or shall see again...." The pavilion, envisioned and realized by a theater stage designer, had steps leading to "a grand Area before the Middle Arch," the whole structure being "extremely neat and pretty and grand to look at." Handel's one-hundred players performed from the area in front of the middle arch. The more privileged onlookers sat on scaffolding in order to get a good view of the proceedings and the fireworks.

Handel's music evidently went off without a hitch. However, the music having been played in the open air, the presence of the huge crowd and all the other goings-on allowed only those up close to hear it well, despite the hundred-member band. As part of a description of the King walking informally in the area, George Harris recorded in his diary: "...He walk'd up to the frame, & soon after[,] the music began playing from the centre, which was in a manner lost.—He heard some of it, & then walked back to the Library."

If the audibility of the music was a problem, there were far more serious problems with the fireworks. "One or two" of the "rockets ... took a wrong direction, & turned off horizontal & fell among the spectators & did some mischief," wrote Harris. Part of the great wooden structure caught fire, putting "all things into confusion." It took about an hour to extinguish the blaze – "with the help of engines." Fortunately, no one died in the fire, but one woman in the Duke of Montagu's box was badly burned after her hat and clothes caught fire. However, at least two other people died in accidents at the event: one man drowned in a nearby pond; another missed his footing at the top of the fireworks "machine" and pitched to the ground. Unfortunately we have no record of Handel's own reaction to the event, including the unusual rehearsal. He did, however, find other occasions to use the *Royal Fireworks Music*. Along with the *Water Music*, it has survived to our day as his most popular orchestral music and is, appropriately enough, increasingly being used in connection with fireworks displays.

Chapter 17
Feeding Foundlings in *Messiah's* Name

At this point in his career, Handel took time off in normal years during late spring and early summer; later in the summer he would get down to preparing music for the following year's Lenten oratorio season. But 1749 presented intervening circumstances for him that would have an impact on the last decade of his life and that would set *Messiah* on its peculiar and astonishing course through music history and the history of Christianity. An excerpt from the May 7, 1749, Minutes of the General Committee of London's Foundling Hospital reads:

> *Mr. Handel being present and having generously and charitably offered a performance of vocal and instrumental musick to be held at this Hospital, and that the money arising therefrom should be applied to the finishing the chapel of the Hospital.* Resolved—*That the thanks of this Committee be returned to Mr. Handel for this his generous and charitable offer.* Ordered—*That the said performance be in the said Chapel on Wednesday, the 24th inst., at eleven in the forenoon.* Resolved—*That George Frederick Handel Esq. In regard to this his generous proposal be recommended to the next General Court to be then elected a Governor of this Hospital.*[1]

Though *Messiah* would soon be irrevocably linked with the Foundling Hospital, it did not figure in this first concert that Handel proposed for the recently built but not yet finished hospital chapel. Instead, the concert consisted of the *Royal Fireworks Music* (an auspicious attention-getter for the first event held in a chapel), the "Peace Anthem" *How Beautiful are the Feet*, and selections from *Solomon* related to the dedication of the temple.* Handel also composed, for the occasion, *Blessed are they that considereth the Poor and Needy*, which came to be known as the "Foundling Hospital Anthem." It consisted of new arias and reworked excerpts from the *Funeral Anthem's* "She Delivered the Poor." That piece refers to Queen

---

*The inclusion of the selections from Solomon about the dedication of the temple hints that Handel initially saw the concert as a dedication of the not-quite finished chapel, even though it officially wasn't. After numerous delays, the official opening and dedicastion, in which Handel would also participate, would finally be held almost four years later, on April 16, 1753.

Caroline's good works with the poor. * A notice in the *General Advertiser* described "several Pieces composed for the Occasion, the Words taken from Scripture, and applicable to this Charity and its Benefactors." The chapel would be "sash'd [i.e., decked with bunting] and made commodious for the purpose," and tickets would cost half a guinea each. Booklets containing the texts of the anthems cost an additional one shilling; the proceeds of both, as the hospital minutes say, went to finishing the chapel. As had happened before with the performance of Handel's music, a particular august personage wanted the date changed. And so it was. The *General Advertiser* kept the public informed: the event was delayed from the 25th to the 27th at the "request" of Frederick, Prince of Wales, because he (and the Princess) found the 27th convenient to attend. The concert was a great success.

The Foundling Hospital received its charter in 1739 after an initially difficult search for support by its founder, Captain Thomas Coram (1668-1751). When Coram retired to London from his trade as a shipwright, conducted mostly in North America, he was shocked into hospitable action by the sight of starving and abandoned babies and children in the streets. He was a trustee of the Georgia colony and had previously sponsored a community in Nova Scotia for unemployed artisans. His being away from home and enduring the hardships of sea life from a very young age probably informed his generosity and played a role in his compassion for children. Coram and his wife were childless.

The Foundling Hospital described itself as existing "for the Maintenance and Education of Exposed and Deserted Young Children." In line with the times, it provided a home for babies born out of wedlock and/or abandoned. Admission standards allowed for admitting only the first infant – under one year old – of an unmarried mother whose father had deserted both the child and its mother. Prior to bearing the child the mother had to have had a good reputation. Babies accepted by the hospital were found foster homes, usually in the country, until they were four or five years old. The children were then returned to the Foundling Hospital to be educated. At adolescence they were given job training. Boys most often went into the

---

*Besides earlier work, In the last few years of her life, when Thomas Coram's long fight to get support and a charter for what would become the Foundling Hospital came to her attention, Queen Caroline backed it and may have influenced the obtaining of the charter. The anthem's finale was *Messiah's* "Hallelujah Chorus." (In Handel's lifetime that chorus was referred to as "For the Lord God Ompnipotent Reigneth," since there are other "Hallelujah" choruses by Handel.)

army; girls became ladies' maids. As is obvious from that description, the word "hospital" in eighteenth century usage was not restricted to medical facilities; it was regularly applied to charitable institutions which housed and cared for orphans and the otherwise needy. The first children under the Foundling Hospital's care were taken into a temporary home in 1741; by 1745 the large hospital itself opened, though the buildings were still incomplete. The hospital eventually became London's largest charity.*

Handel's purposeful charitable association with the Foundling Hospital for the next ten years, to the end of his life in 1759, benefited that institution in unique ways. The benefits accrued to him as the giver too, as the effects of such open-handedness often unexpectedly do; and they still echo long after he is gone. From 1749, he established the tradition of performing *Messiah* each year at the hospital, which not only greatly helped the hospital but was the beginning of *Messiah* becoming fixed in the hearts of audiences, a position it hasn't relinquished in more than 260 years.

Though Handel wasn't the first and would not be the last well-known figure associated with the hospital, his reputation and the very public nature of the association seemed to spur other prominent people to support it as well. (A hundred years later Charles Dickens would live nearby and frequently attend the chapel.**) Handel's music publisher, John Walsh, was elected a hospital governor the previous year; perhaps Walsh and Handel talked about the hospital and Walsh urged

---

*The Foundling Hospital survived into the twentieth century as the Thomas Coram Foundation for Children, and is today known as the Coram Family. A Foundling Museum, which contains Handel-related items in its collection, opened in 1998 at 40 Brunswick Square, London.

**An excerpt from Charles Dickens's observations about the hospital's admission rules, ca. 1800: "...The child must have been the first-born, and preference is given to cases in which some promise of marriage has been made to the mother, or some other deception practiced upon her. She must never have lived with the father. The object of these restrictions (careful personal inquiry being made into all such points) is as much to effect the restoration of the mother to society as to provide for her child" ("Household Words," March 19, 1853). Of Handel, the chapel and organ, and its chaplain in Dickens's day: "In the Chapel ... there is a noble organ, the gift of Handel; from whose great oratorio the "Messiah"– also his munificent contribution for their benefit – their Hospital has received ten thousand pounds. There, too, the Church service is every Sunday performed at its best, with all the assistance of devotional music, yet free from the stage-playing of any 'ism', not forgetting schism."

Handel's involvement. Well-known artist William Hogarth, a friend of Coram's and a member of the hospital's original board, contributed paintings to the hospital. (William and Jane Hogarth were, like the Corams, childless; and of course Handel had no children either.) Other prominent artists, among them Thomas Gainsborough, Francis Hayman, Allan Ramsay, Joshua Reynolds, Andrea Casali and John Rysbrack, donated paintings to the hospital. The idea was to get the public to come to view the paintings and then, it was hoped, to agree to financially support the hospital.

However Handel came to support the Foundling Hospital, once he made the decision he was committed. But he was initially reluctant to become a board member. Though he was a good businessman, he no doubt felt that his best and most effective contribution to the hospital was through his music. He thought that he "should Serve the Charity with more Pleasure in his Way [i.e., with his music] than [by] being a Member of the Corporation."

This shouldn't be seen as half-hearted support, as his subsequent involvement shows. He changed his mind and was elected a member of the governing board on May 9 the next year. Or perhaps, as such things still often go, he allowed himself to be talked into serving in that way, finding that he had no serious reason to say no. As he was already very publicly involved by providing benefit concerts, there is no reason to think that his change of heart involved ulterior motives regarding his image. In any case, he was never much concerned with how he was personally perceived ("Certain foibles in his behavior that serve only to shew that he was subject to human passions" – his "great appetite" and "when provoked ... break[ing] out into profane expressions"– "he was not studious to conceal," Hawkins said), except as people's perceptions related to his integrity (for example, when he was disturbed by the rumor of his arrogant response to those listening to him play the organ). In the remaining years of his life, besides providing annual benefit concerts of *Messiah*, Handel donated an organ to the hospital's chapel and left "a fair copy of the Score and all Parts of my Oratorio called The Messiah to the Foundling Hospital."

Handel didn't need an association with the Foundling Hospital to be seen as an established part of the culture. Besides the places where we might expect to find him mentioned, that year (1749) novelist Henry Fielding inserted Handel into his famous *History of Tom Jones*. Fielding depicts a country gentleman from Somerset and his more sophisticated daughter disagreeing over Handel's music. The father, Squire Western, is a bluff man who loves music but "he always excepted against the finest Compositions of Mr. Handel." On the other hand, though the Squire's daughter Sophia obliges her father by playing the old-time popular tunes he liked, she "would never willingly have played any but Handel's music."[2]

After that unusually busy spring, Handel allowed himself a month's break, going to Bath for a holiday. On June 28 he set to composing *Theodora*, the first of what he no doubt naturally assumed would be several new oratorios for the 1750 season. In his usual speedy manner he completed it in a month (on July 31). But he composed no other oratorio in 1749, and began no other composition at all until two days after Christmas. That work was incidental music for Tobias Smollett's play *Alceste*, which he finished on January 8, 1750. But the play was never performed and has been lost. So Handel's music for it was not heard then, though, unlike the play, it has survived; modern listeners can hear this delightful music of Handel's which his contemporaries never heard.[*]

On September 6, 1749, John Jacob Heidegger died at the advanced age of eighty-five. Though Heidegger and Handel probably never became personal friends, the death of his elderly former long-time colleague was surely noted by Handel, and possibly in terms of his own mortality. He was no longer so young himself.

At the end of September, Handel wrote to a different kind of former colleague, his friend and librettist Charles Jennens. Jennens's father had died two years earlier. The family estate at Gopsall was now his, and Jennens was conducting major and magnificent renovations to it. He collected music scores, especially Handel's, but as a further means of indulging his great interest in music he wanted to install an organ. He naturally wanted Handel's advice about what kind of instrument to get. Handel proposed a small, basic organ of seven stops, two of the seven being "mutations." (A mutation stop does not sound fundamental pitches, but a specified interval above them, based on upper partials or overtones of those pitches; mutations don't play on their own, but are combined with other stops to act as spice in the musical cake.) Jennens's organ would have no pedals, as was still the custom for English organs. And it would be without reed stops (oboe or trumpet), because, wrote Handel wisely, "They are continually wanting to be tuned, which in the

---

[*]*Alceste* has been recorded by Christopher Hogwood and his Academy of Ancient Music (Decca 458 07202). This very enjoyable two-CD set also includes the *Utrecht Te Deum and Jubilate*, the "Anthem for the Foundling Hospital," and the "Ode for the Birthday of Queen Anne."

Country is very inconvenient, and should it remain useless on that Account, it would still be very expensive" ("...althou' that may not be Your Consideration," he added).[3] He then recommended a certain well-known builder and offered to come and give his opinion of the organ when it was finished.*

Though it was the fall of 1749, Handel and Jennens may not have been in contact since sometime in 1745 after *Belshazzar* debuted. After their collaboration on *Belshazzar*, in late 1745 and early 1746 Jennens had again vacillated between admiration and speaking unkindly of Handel (and of *Occasional Oratorio* librettist Newburgh Hamilton) in letters to Edward Holdsworth. Holdsworth died later in 1746, which must have devastated Jennens, who by then had no immediate family. Holdsworth's death does not seem to have pushed him to renew his friendship with Handel, however. (Recall that Holdsworth himself had reminded the irascible Jennens that Handel was his particular friend.) Still, after all that time Jennens wasn't afraid to ask for Handel's help, and Handel must have been glad to hear from him – he replied to Jennens's request only a day after he received it. He ended his letter saying, "I am glad of the Opportunity to show you my attention, wishing you all Health and Happiness, I remain with great Sincerity and Respect ...," and then the usual formal closing.

The next year was an even better year. On February 23, 1750, Handel turned sixty-five years old, well on his way to the biblical "threescore years and ten." His admired cousin Christian Rotth wrote him an ode for the occasion, "by way of congratulation and from a sense of truest friendship."[4] A few weeks earlier Shaftesbury reported to James Harris that he had seen Handel several times since he (Shaftesbury) came to London from his country home. There was no sign of stress now. The previous year had gone well, he was confident about his upcoming oratorio season, and he was allowing himself time (and money) to indulge in his favorite extra-musical interest: viewing and collecting art. Wrote Shaftesbury:

> *[I] think I never saw him so cool and well. He is quite easy in his behaviour, and has been pleasing himself in the purchase of several fine pictures, particularly a large Rembrandt, which is indeed excellent. We*

---

*For organists: besides the mutations (twelfth and tierce), Handel recommended to Jennens an open diapason (made of "open" or "unstopped" metal pipes), a stopped diapason (treble notes metal, bass notes wood, with the pipes "stopped" or plugged), a principal, a flute, and a fifteenth (a diapason sounding two octaves about the fundamental notes).

have scarce talked at all about musical subjects, though enough to find his performances will go off incomparably.

Theodora is a departure in subject matter from the other oratorios. Its story is not biblical (neither canonical nor apocryphal), but concerns a Christian martyr (d. 304) in Antioch during the reign of Dioclesian. She is known in the Orthodox Christian lexicon of saints as Theodora the Virgin (or Virgin Martyr), not to be confused with the fifth century Theodora of Alexandria, or the sixth century St. Theodora the Empress (wife of the Emperor Justinian), or several other Theodoras. Dioclesian was the Roman emperor whose grisly claim to fame was as one of the worst of the persecutors of Christians, even though he did so for "only" three years (302 to 305) of his twenty-one-year reign (284-305). Among hundreds of others, Dioclesian killed the Christian Roman tribune from Cappadocia who became known as St. George the Dragon Slayer, and who became the patron saint of England in the fourteenth century.

To control his chaotic empire, Dioclesian formally divided it into East and West and set up three other rulers besides himself (Maximium as "augustus," and Constantius I and Galerius as "caesars"). Under Dioclesian's autocracy the Roman senate became a token assembly and all vestiges of the republic vanished. He abdicated his position in 305 (Maximian quit at the same time) and retired to a bucolic country life with his concubines. In 312, the divided power structure entirely collapsed and Constantine (caesar of the West) seized power. Constantine had his vision of the cross later that year, which changed the course of history and the church – for better or worse, or both.

Thomas Morell wrote the *Theodora* libretto, basing it on Robert Boyle's *The Martyrdom of Theodora & Didymus* (1687), an early novel-like romance that is itself based on the early church father Ambrose's lives of admirable virgins.[*] Boyle

---

[*] In the late 1990s an early draft of *The Martyrdom* was discovered. Boyle's 1687 published version expanded this, and aimed to be a "provider of virtue" rather than merely a romance. Boyle's writings have fascinating titles (and content): *The Skeptical Chemist* (which moved chemistry away from the world of alchemy), *The Mechanical Origin of Qualities, Notion of Nature, Final Causes; How the Christian Religion conforms to Reason, The Weakness of the Human Understanding Revealed in its Native Light, On the Diversity of Religions*; and there are tracts on divine love, ethics, the evil of swearing, the excellence of theology, and the style of Scripture. But Boyle is known in our time for "Boyle's Law": the pressure of a gas is inversely proportional to the volume it occupies. In February 1750, as Handel was occupied with *Theodora*, an unnamed Norwich letter writer to the *Gentleman's Magazine* quoted Boyle when referring to the London earthquake earlier that month. Boyle theorized that "fire passeth through some little subterranean clefts from one great cavity

(1627-1691) was a scientist and Christian apologist who strongly supported missions to Ireland, the Orient and the American colonies. His writings on science, theology and practical Christianity take up fourteen volumes (they are still available) and are wonderfully diverse, including romances on various moral and faith-related topics, of which *The Martyrdom of Theodora and Didymus* was in Handel's day a popular example. (A "romance" in Boyle's day was a fictional, prose narrative whose scenes and incidents were generally remote from everyday life.) All of Boyle's writings reveal what Boyle scholar Edward B. Davis calls "a profound sense of divine sovereignty," which is equally true of his *Martyrdom of Theodora and Didymus.*[5] Both Morell's adaptation of it and Handel's music capture that sensibility. But a deep awareness of divine sovereignty permeates Handel's other oratorios as well.

Theodora is a righteous virgin who has devoted herself wholly to God. She is arrested and sentenced to a life of prostitution in a brothel – a fate far worse than death – for refusing to sacrifice to the Roman gods on Dioclesian's birthday. Didymus, a Roman officer but a fellow Christian who chastely loves Theodora (and she him), tries to get her sentence reversed, then helps her escape by exchanging clothes with her; they are discovered and Didymus is arrested and sentenced to death. Theodora comes out of hiding and attempts to save Didymus by offering her life for his; instead, the prefect has them both killed. (The decorous libretto doesn't say how they die, but "racks, gibbets, sword and fire" are earlier threatened as the fate of Theodora, and anyone else who fails to bow the knee to the Roman gods). Steadfast in their faith, Theodora and Didymus go calmly to their deaths. In Didymus's words:

> Yet deem us not unhappy, gentle friend,
> Nor rash; for life we neither hate, nor scorn,
> But think it a cheap purchase for the prize
> Reserv'd in Heav'n for purity and faith.

The chorus ends the oratorio by praying, on behalf of all Christians, for equally steadfast and passionate faith. *Theodora* is introspective in a way that most of the oratorios are not. Handel's music profoundly captures the important faith struggle

---

to another," causing "vehement tremulous motion ... a very great way beyond where the explosions are made" (*Philosophical Transactions*).

of the libretto and exudes the depth and breadth of numerous emotions and states of mind: steadfast faith, tenderness, devotion, longing, rage, disdain.

This oratorio is one of the few about which we have Handel's personal opinion: it was his favorite and, he believed, his best oratorio, which "he valued more than any Performance of the kind." When Morell himself asked Handel "whether he did not look upon the Grand Chorus in the Messiah ['Hallelujah'] as his Master Piece," Handel replied, "No ... I think the Chorus at the end of the 2d part in Theodora far beyond it." That chorus is "He saw the lovely youth." Theodora's anxious friends, personified in the character of Irene, have just expressed their grief at her impending death, but they have hope in the Resurrection. They take refuge in prayer "to Him who rais'd, and still can raise, the dead to life and joy." The chorus – a resurrection chorus – then follows; the "He" of its title is Christ. In five succinct lines of text the chorus calls to mind Jesus's raising from the dead the son of the widow of Nain (Luke 7:11-17): "He saw the lovely youth, death's early prey,/Alas, too early snatch'd away!/He heard his mother's fun'ral cries:/'Rise, youth,' he said. The youth begins to rise./Lowly the matron bow'd, and bore away the prize."[*]

Handel apparently alternated between being vexed and philosophical about the fact that Theodora did not become popular. On the vexed side, Burney says:

> Theodora *was so very unfortunately abandoned, that he was glad if any professors, who did not perform, would accept of tickets or orders for admission. Two gentlemen of that description, now living, having applied to* HANDEL, *after the disgrace of* Theodora, *for an order to hear the* MESSIAH, *he cried out, 'Oh your sarvant, Mien-herren! you are tamnaple tainty! You would no co to* TEODORA – *der was room enough to tance dere, when dat was perform.*[**]

---

[*]Ruth Smith says "Morell's habit of reporting others' favourable opinion of his work must color our reading" of the letter in which he mentions Handel's comments on Theodora (and this chorus)."It seems plausible that Morell meant that Handel thought Morell's text for Theodora the best oratorio libretto he had ever seen." However, Morell's question to Handel was specifically about his favorite *music* among all his music, not about his favorite librettos/stories. And Handel answered the question as asked.

[**]"Oh, your servant, gentlemen, you are damnably dainty [by which Handel likely meant fickle in your tastes]. You would not go to Theodora – there was room enough to dance there when that was performed."

On the other hand:

> *'I have heard him, as pleasantly as philosophically, console his friends, when, previous to the curtain being drawn up, they have lamented that the house was so empty, by saying, "Nevre moind; de moosic vil sound de petter."*

Again philosophically, Handel quipped about *Theodora*, showing that his sense of humor was in tact: "The Jews will not come to it (as to *Judas* [Maccabaeus]) because it is a Christian story; and the Ladies will not come, because it [is] a virtuous one." Jews and Christians in the audiences at the Old Testament and Apocryphal oratorios would, of course, have interpreted those oratorios quite differently – Handel and his fellow Christians always seeing the Old Testament in the light of Christ as the promised Messiah, the God of Israel having become their God through Christ. Jews would not have wanted to encounter *Theodora* at all, it being set in the early centuries of the persecuted church and depicting those who endured with Christ to the end as the true people of God.

Plainly, there is something about the subject matter of *Theodora* that Handel found compelling, beyond his satisfaction with how he had set it. Its central depiction of a faith that remains steadfast amidst persecution and death is a subject that all devoted Christ-followers – from Simon Peter to the present – think on from time to time in reference to themselves: would *I* maintain my faith in such circumstances, or would I deny my Lord to escape ridicule, torture or death? And, apart from persecution, which may or may not come, there is the self-examination required by daily Christian life: Does my life testify to my faith or do I "sacrifice" to other gods?

As such questions have never been foreign to Christians, they could not have been foreign to Handel. But their special resonance for him may also have arisen in a specific way from his Lutheranism, and indeed numerous Lutheran chorales raise such questions. Every Lutheran grew up learning Luther's own hymns too, Luther's catechism, reading Luther's German translation of the Bible, hearing stories from Luther's life and revering the Reformer for his principled stand against the Pope and other church leaders who he believed were leading themselves and the church to doom – "Here I stand, I cannot do otherwise."* That stand, were it not for Elector

---

*Luther wrote, "Unless I am convinced by Scripture and plain reason I do not accept the authority of the popes and councils, for they have contradicted each other. My conscience is captive to the Word of God. I cannot and I will not recant anything for to go against conscience is neither right nor safe. God help me. Amen."

Friedrich the Wise of Saxony, would almost certainly have led to his death (as such stands did for Reformers John Hus and William Tyndale), and which did lead to his excommunication and the eventual development and spread Lutheranism.

Thus, refusing to recant one's beliefs even in the face of death was a subject woven into the warp and woof of Handel's formative faith. Luther's struggle, of course, occurred in the context of the Roman church being his persecutor (as it did Handel's own great-grandparents and grandparents on both sides, who, as we've seen, moved out of Catholic regions "for the love of the pure evangelical truth"). Given Handel's early association with Catholic cardinals in Italy, and in later working with Catholics in London's theaters, it is not at all likely that he would have thought of the conflict in *Theodora* in terms of the pagan Roman persecutors being equated with the Catholic Church (though this oratorio is currently being interpreted as being anti-Catholic). Times had changed since the sixteenth and early seventeenth century. Luther's fight was still of grave importance to devout Lutherans, but the crucial element in contemplating Luther's struggle is the stand he took in faith and integrity – his refusal to recant his beliefs (as Theodora and Didymus refuse), not first of all who his enemy was.

Faithfulness to God amidst adversity was also relevant to Handel in terms of his own personal experiences with his opera adversaries – "enemies" is not too strong a word – and their attempt to destroy him. Clearly, he knew what it was like to feel besieged, and bouts of serious illness were related to his enemies' relentless attacks. Though the resulting stress wreaked havoc on him, he remained strong and free of bitterness. Handel "frequently declared" to Hawkins "... how much the contemplating the many sublime passage in the Psalms had contributed to his edification." "Edification" implies spiritual growth, and often includes comfort. It is not hard to see why he frequently drew comfort – as many millions of Christians did before him and have since – from contemplating the Psalms, full as they are of heartfelt cries to God to save the psalmist from his enemies (who trifle with God).

Theodora is one of Handel's oratorios that has been neglected in modern times primarily because of its story and presumed "values." It is no longer so neglected, but has been reworked to fit modern secular sensibilities. For example, in an acclaimed staged (and filmed) performance at Britain's Glyndebourne Festival in 1999, theater director Peter Sellars depicted *Theodora's* conflict as being between an intolerant right-winged government (the Roman soldiers became security forces with stars and stripes on their helmets) and the "heretical," free-thinking citizens who oppose that government. Sellars had Theodora and Didymus executed on stage by lethal injection, completing the allusion to the American government. Most modern critics seem unaware that the face-value subject matter of *Theodora* was then, and still is, a "live issue." Enduring torture and even death for refusing to deny one's Christian faith is presumed to be a (mostly disreputable) thing of the foggily distant past when people routinely killed each other in the name of "religion." There is no awareness that more Christians were executed in the twentieth century for refusing to deny their faith than were put to death for that reason in all previous centuries since the age of the Apostles.* In fact, the "religious intolerance" in the oratorio (perpetrated by the Romans) is often transposed in our time to Christians themselves, though that turns on its head the oratorio's main point.

Handel himself had associations and friendships with Catholics and Methodists, so in our time some interpreters assume that the oratorio's Roman persecutors were meant to be seen as England's anti-Catholics. But Anglicans and virtually *all* Protestant Christians – essentially Handel's whole audience – saw Catholics as heretics in some form. Handel's own open-mindedness was real (and based on genuine tolerance, not on a fudging or shrugging off of doctrine and genuine theological differences), but it is unlikely that he (or librettist Morell) was indicting his own audiences in that way.

The oratorios became Handel's means of making a living. At times they were lucrative for him, but that doesn't mean they were *only* a living to him. It doesn't negate the strong likelihood that he came to feel that he was testifying to his faith in the composing of oratorios, and that he had to continue to do so. He signed his oratorio manuscripts "S.D.G.G.F.H".: "*soli Deo gloria* George Frederic Handel." It should be noted that the concept of *soli Deo gloria* – to the glory of God alone – though something all Christians are taught to strive for, has a peculiar resonance for Lutheran Christians (Bach signed his manuscripts with the same designation). Luther strongly emphasized – and thus, Lutherans learned in no uncertain terms – that *all* one's work must be a thankful returning to God what he

---

*Reviewer John Yohalem shows his incomprehension of *Theodora*, and ignorance of modern-day persecution, torture and martyrdom of Christians in many parts of the world, when he distills the intended deadly serious and eternally significant conflict in *Theodora* down to "the tale of a princess in Roman Antioch who refuses to offer incense to the Roman gods in the Emperor's honor – which is something like refusing to salute the flag or sing the national anthem nowadays." (<culturevulture.net/opera>)

has given: "Nothing more than the finding and collecting of God's gifts," in Luther's words. "Man must and ought to work" because God commanded it, says Luther, "not to his own labor but solely to the goodness and blessings of God... God wants the glory as the one who alone gives the growth."*

Given both the context of Handel's faith and his recent personal experience before *Theodora*, then, it doesn't take a great leap of imagination to think that the faith-under-siege aspect of the *Theodora* libretto strongly resonated with Handel. A third attraction for him is no doubt embodied in the strength of faith and character of the heroine – qualities he had found compelling before then, and which he knew especially well in his mother and sisters. Morell's remarks on his working relationship with Handel don't indicate if the subject of *Theodora* was his idea or Handel's, or if they came to it jointly. He simply says, after commenting on *Alexander Balus*, "The next I wrote was Theodora...." That may imply that he chose the subject and Handel quickly warmed to it.

A well-attended but not "so accurate as usual" performance of *Saul* opened the 1750 Lenten, but George Harris was looking forward to *Theodora*:

Handel I believe has never had a better set of voices for his oratorio; & when he brings on his new piece, where no doubt he'll contrive to have 'em all appear to advantage, I dare say he'll meet with success.[6]

But as the new oratorio of the season, *Theodora* wasn't talked about much; it did not "please the generality of people." Thomas Harris, however, thought far more highly of it. He told James:

I differ widely in my opinion, for I think it has many excellent songs, composed with great art and care, and such as I am sure you will highly approve. Dr. Fawcett & Mr. Granville [Mary Delaney and Ann Dewes' brother] whom I met there, are entirely in the same sentiments as I am. Last night was the thinest house he has had at all; but they have hitherto been so good that I am certain he must be a considerable

---

*Nor did Luther (or Calvin) divide work into "sacred" and "secular" pursuits: "Govern, and let Him give his blessing. Fight and let him give the victory. Preach, and let him win hearts. Take a husband or a wife, and let him produce children. Eat and drink, and let him nourish and strengthen you. And so on.. In all our doing he is to work through us, and he alone shall have the glory from it.... Don't be lazy or idle, but don't rely solely on your own work and doing. Get busy and work, and yet expect everything from God alone" (*Luthers Werke*, 31¹, 436f: Althaus, p. 109).

gainer at all events.

Shaftesbury, too, was deeply moved by *Theodora*, writing his opinion to James Harris on March 22:

> *I can't conclude a letter and forget Theodora. I have heard it three times, and will venture to pronounce it, as finished, beautifull and labour'd a composition, as ever Handel made. To my knowledge this took him up a great while in composing. The town don't like it at all; but Mr. Kelloway and several excellent musicians think as I do.*[*]

The following season, Ann Dewes hoped that Handel would repeat *Theodora*. "Surely [it] will have justice at last," she told her brother Bernard Granville, "if it was to be again performed, but the generality of the world have ears and *hear not*."

~

There was an unusual distraction that season: earthquakes in London. Two small earthquakes (estimated magnitude three by the modern-day British Geological Survey) struck directly beneath central London, on February 8 and March 8. The second one caused slight damage to Westminster Abbey. There were no deaths or serious injuries, but the quakes elicited great alarm: fear of physical danger, but more so fear of impending judgment, earthquakes having had long connotations of God's wrath against sin, and associations with the dissolution of the world. Consequently, there was moral and spiritual examination, spurred by exhortations from many pulpits. Since the previous quakes had occurred on the 8th of February and 8th March, there was apprehension about what might happen on April 8 – a Sunday: would the Lord's Day turn into the Day of the Lord? Many people apparently thought so. They literally headed for the hills (of Highgate, Hampstead and Islington). Few people knew that forty-six years earlier, the renowned Sir Isaac Newton had predicted that severe storms and earthquakes would occur in February 1750 because the moon and Jupiter would be at their closest points to earth, and because of the appearance of the *Aurora Borealis*. Newton was right, but astro-meteorology, the study the influence of the heavenly bodies on earth's weather, was by 1750 considered unscientific. Besides Boyle's theory, a common theory of the

---

[*]In calling *Theodora* "labour'd" Shaftesbury means carefully, painstakingly wrought. Handel composed *Theodora* from June 28 to July 31, 1749, a normal span for him.

origin of earthquakes involved electrical shocks – which did not rule out their also being seen as spiritual omens.

Bishop Thomas Sherlock, who had succeeded Edmund Gibson as Bishop of London just two years earlier, immediately wrote and published *A Form of Prayers for the Use of Private Families, on occasion of the late Earthquakes.* Sherlock also produced *A Letter to the Clergy and People of London and Westminster on occasion of the late Earthquakes.*[7] This latter work, which vigorously condemned the vices of Londoners and urged them to repent, sold an astonishing 100,000 copies in less than a month, said the printer-bookseller John Nichols. Charles Wesley observed in his diary, "Such distress, perhaps, is not recorded to have happened before in this careless city." Soon after, he published *Hymns Occasion'd by the Earthquake.*[*]

It was the March 8 quake that George Harris described as occurring between five and six in the morning, whose shock was "felt very sensibly, attended with a very odd noise."[16] Elizabeth Montagu, in a letter to her sister, wrote, "I was not under any apprehension about the earthquake, but went that night to the oratorio, then quietly to bed." Though Elizabeth Montagu reacted calmly, many people were "under apprehension" about the earthquake, and unlike Montagu, stayed home. Montagu continued, "The Wednesday night oratorio was very empty, though it was the most favorite performance of Handel's." Some Londoners were thus drawn to Handel's biblical oratorios; but others kept away out of fear of being away from home and in a public place should another quake hit.

Thomas Harris, a lawyer, insightfully critiqued Bishop Sherlock's public letter. Harris wrote to his brother James on March 17 when people were still talking only of the earthquakes. Thomas was critical of the Bishop's selective list of vices. The Bishop

> *describes us as a parcel of vile people; but I dare say it will please, for every body loves to have the world abused in general* [loves to hear others raked over the coals]. *He is severe upon infidelity, lewdness, blasphemy, plays, routs, public gardens &c but omits wicked ambition, prostitution of principles in high life, griping avarice; with other such,*

---

[*]An example of a stanza from Wesley's collection: "Tremendous Lord of Earth and Skies,/Most holy, high, and just,/We fall before Thy glorious eyes,/And hide us in the Dust:/Thine Anger's long suspended Stroke/With deepest Awe we feel,/And tremble on, so lately shook/Over the Mouth of Hell."

which I am afraid abound, and call for a judgment as much as those he has enumerated: one thing in particular, that when his topic naturally led him to masquerades [there was one the night following the first shock] he is so complaisant as not to say a single word about them.

Harris implies that the Bishop had self-serving motives in not including the masquerades and the sins of attitude and principle which Harris mentions. The sins Harris alludes to involving attitudes and principles were those emanating especially from the upper classes, and they were precisely the sins the Bishop "forgot" to mention.

The furor over the quakes finally subsided. In the latter part of this 1750 season a French woman, poet Madame Anne-Marie Fiquet du Bocage, described her experience of the oratorios while visiting London, and in doing so left us a fine picture of Handel as composer-conductor. She was perfectly happy with what she heard:

The Oratorio, or pious concert, pleases us highly. English words are sung by Italian performers, and accompanied by a variety of instruments. HANDEL is the soul of it: when he makes his appearance, two wax lights are carried before him, which are laid upon his organ. Amidst a loud clapping of hands he seats himself, and the whole band of music strikes up exactly at the same moment. At the interludes he plays concertos of his own composition, either alone or accompanied by the orchestra. These are equally admirable for the harmony and the execution. The Italian opera, in three acts, gives us much less pleasure....[8]

Chapter 18
Considering the Uncertainty of Human Life

Though Handel was in good health and for all he knew might well live, "by reason of strength," to fourscore, it was time that he considered what would happen to his worldly goods when he was gone. On June 1 he wrote a will. (Bach died that summer, on July 17, July 28 by the modern calendar.) Handel's relative longevity, however, would later cause him to attach four codicils to the will — in 1756, twice in 1757, and once more in 1759 just before his death — as he outlived people to whom he had bequeathed money or goods, and needed to redistribute and account for his remaining resources.

The will begins: "In the name of God, Amen." This common, though no longer universal, introduction to wills in Britain and the American colonies was an acknowledgment that what will follow is an oath witnessed by God. Though Handel did not include specific reference to his faith in his will (a practice already waning in his day), this six-word oath is a tacit acknowledgment that God is the bequeather of worldly goods and is responsible for the signatory's very life and the number of his days. Thinking of one's own death, as writing a will made one do, focused the mind away from the very material goods a will is concerned with toward things of the spirit and the writer's eternal destiny. Almost no one denied an afterlife and the certainty that at death we meet our Maker. It had an appropriately sobering effect.

In that context Handel decided it would be prudent to make a will: "I George Frideric Handel considering the Uncertainty of human Life doe make this my Will in manner following...." He left most of his estate to his closest relative, his niece and goddaughter Johanna Friderica Flöerken, whom he named "My sole Exec[trix] of this my last Will." He bequeathed money to other more distant relatives; gave his clothing and £300 to his primary male servant and a year's Wages to his other servants; allotted £500 to a friend, a Mr. James Hunter; and gave his "large Harpsicord, my little House Organ, my Musick Books, and five hundred Pounds sterl" to "M[r].Christopher Smith."[1]

J.C. Smith the elder was one of Handel's oldest friends, the music copyist who had emigrated from Germany to London at Handel's urging. Because they knew each other so well, and there is a mystery surrounding Handel's bequeathals to John Christopher Smith which brings to the fore a longstanding disagreement between the two men, we will consider both their friendship and that mystery.

In the official copy of the will the designation "Senior" was added to

Christopher Smith and then crossed out. Since J.C. Smith's son had the same name, there has been some question about whether Handel intended the father or the son to inherit his considerable musical treasures.

The younger J.C. Smith would be a great help to Handel after the onset of his blindness (one year in the future), and would be his "successor" in the production of the oratorios. But for some time (years, apparently) Handel and the elder Smith had not been on good personal terms, though Smith continued to work for Handel and to hold him in high regard musically. From Smith's point of view the rift came at Handel's instigation and made Smith feel ill-used, but the reason for it is elusive. As long as seven years earlier Smith had told James Harris:

> My manner of writing of Mr Handels great merit in musick shall allways be the same, though I cannot say so much of his behaviour towards me, and according to his repeated promises I expected a better reward for 24 years slavery & services I have done him; time will shew what counsel he has and whether he will be the better for it[;] hithertho [sic] I cant say much of it, and think he is very ill adviced as to fly in the Prince of Wale's and the Quality's face as he has done; I am sorry to see it & wish him heardily well, and don't doubt but all his friends do the same. I beg you will excuse this liberty.[2]

Smith's speaking to his social superior about a man who was a mutual friend and also an employer of Smith's could easily have been seen by Harris as taking liberties, and Smith knows it – thus his begging to be excused for it. The fact that Smith mentioned Handel's flying in the face of his aristocratic opera opposition in the same breath, as it were, with what he saw as Handel's bad behavior towards *him* makes the two issues seem connected. He plainly says that Handel should have succumbed to the Prince of Wale's and the "Quality's" wishes. Did the two men argue about the issue? The implication is that they did. Perhaps Smith thought Handel was simply being stubborn, arrogant and acting "above his station," which foolish action would have severe consequences for Handel and, not incidentally, also for Smith if Handel's fortunes waned because of the composer's obstinance. Especially because Smith was Handel's primary copyist and was therefore intimately involved in what Handel decided to do each season, the issue must have come up, probably on more than one occasion. Since the two men had been long-time friends, and had a working relationship and their ethnic, social and religious heritage in common, it is probably that they talked with each other in a particular way, with a degree of frankness that Handel could not do or was shy about with his English friends. But there is a limit to the degree of unvarnished forthrightness even close friends can tolerate from each other. This interpretation is reinforced by Smith's telling Shaftesbury in a summer letter, before he wrote to Harris in October, "It seems [Handel] has taken an aversion to see me, for having been to[o] much his Friend."

Perhaps from Handel's point of view Smith had crossed that line, not only wounding Handel's pride but making him feel that Smith had misunderstood his motives in opposing the "Quality," and also preventing him from further confiding his personal thoughts to Smith, at a particularly stressful time when it would have been helpful to be able to do so. When Smith says "time will shew what counsel he has and whether he will be the better for it" he is implying that Handel had begun to get advice from other quarters (from where, Smith didn't know). Though Smith seems to try to be fair – at least in addressing James Harris, who revered Handel – he was leery of the quality or rightness of that counsel.

At the same time, Smith felt that Handel's reaction to *him* was unfair. His melodramatic pout about unfulfilled promises from Handel ("reward for 24 years slavery & services I have done him") may indicate that Handel had told him he would remember him in his will. (It is doubtful Smith had any inkling of just what, and how much, Handel intended to bequeath to him.) The fact that Handel meant to leave Smith not only his large Ruckers harpsichord, his organ, his music manuscripts and £500 besides, indicates the degree of friendship between them and probably also the debt Handel felt he owed Smith for his long and excellent work.

But Smith wrote about that particular disagreement in 1743, and Handel was writing his will in 1750. Handel had been able to put the offense behind him. Or had he? It has been surmised that the adding of "Senior" to the name Christopher Smith in Handel's will meant to clarify that the elder Smith was the inheritor, and the crossing out of the word at some point meant that Handel decided to favor Smith the younger instead. Alternatively, Handel's original designation "Christopher Smith" referred to the younger Smith, and he later changed his mind and clarified the change by adding "Senior" – and then changed it again and indicated it by crossing out "Senior."

However, Handel initially, and probably always, intended the elder Smith to be his inheritor. It is true that their personal estrangement seems to have lasted some years, and it is not unthinkable that in his worst moments Handel wanted to disinherit his friend. But for Handel to have overlooked the elder Smith, who had been so faithful to him, in favor of Smith's son, would have humiliated the older man. (Smith the Younger would also render great service to Handel, though almost entirely in the years after Handel wrote his will and after Smith Senior had died.) For the estrangement to have gone on so long, Handel had to have felt deeply wounded by his friend, which then may have turned to anger (which Smith also felt). But by all accounts Handel was not a malicious or spiteful man.[*] And in an eighteenth century context, leaving such treasures to the son of a man who had been a friend and had served him so well professionally instead of to the man himself *would* be malicious and spiteful. In any case, the son would no doubt eventually inherit these treasures from his father anyway, which, in fact, happened. In the end, the elder Smith was the inheritor, and at Smith's death four years after Handel's, Smith Jr. inherited Handel's instruments, music and not £500 but £2000: in the first codicil to the will (August 6, 1756), Handel added £1500 to the monetary legacy to Smith already indicated in the will itself.

William Coxe, J.C. Smith Jr.'s son-in-law, unfortunately does not clear up the matter when he writes in the Anecdotes:

> Smith Sr. and Handel had a falling out in over something trivial in Tunbridge in 1755. Handel wanted to put Smith Jr. in his will in place of his father. Smith Jr. refused, and said he'd not assist with the oratorios any longer. Handel conceded.

Smith had written to James Harris about Handel long before 1755. Coxe could have gotten both the reason for the conflict and its date wrong (as sources contemporaneous with Handel do relatively frequently). Or there could also have been more than one occasion during which Handel and Smith were estranged and then reconciled. It is believable that if Handel mentioned wanting Smith Jr. in his will instead of his father the younger Smith would object. Coxe may have gotten that part right, but virtually all the details surrounding the story wrong.

From Coxe, via Smith, there also comes a moving story about Handel and the elder Smith being reconciled not long before Handel's death. Again there are

---

[*]William T. Whitley in *Artists and Their Friends in England 1700-1799* (London, 1928) suggests that Handel intended to leave Joseph Goupy a legacy, and changed his mind after Goupy's venomous cartoon of Handel as a glutton If that is so, Handel's withdrawal of his friendship from Goupy (which was permanent) was also caused by a deep-felt emotional wound.

incorrect details regarding Smith's legacy from Handel. But the gist of this story makes complete sense given the purpose and effects of the Christian sacrament of Communion/the Eucharist – and it is something that only Smith Jr. could have told Coxe:

> *About three weeks before Handel's death, he desired Smith junior to receive the sacrament with him. Smith asked him how he could communicate, when he was not at peace with all the world, and especially when he was at enmity with his former friend; who, though he might have offended him once, had been faithful and affectionate to him for thirty years. Handel was so much affected by this representation, that he was immediately reconciled.*

Communion in the Church of England then resembled its Calvinist counterpart in many respects, and the Anglican practice had grown from its Calvinist heritage. Most English churches celebrated Communion only about four times a year, making it an all the more weighty event. As a remembrance of Christ's sacrifice and one of the two sacraments in Protestant churches, it was no trifling matter. The "spiritual food and sustenance in that holy Sacrament ... [is] received in remembrance of [Christ's] meritorious Cross and Passion; whereby alone we obtain remission of our sins, and are make partakers of the Kingdom of heaven," said the *Book of Common Prayer* then in use. It is "so divine and comfortable a thing to them who receive it worthily"; but it is "so dangerous to them that will presume to receive it unworthily."[3] At least a week before the sacrament was administered the congregation (or individual, if a person was ill, as in Handel's case) was exhorted by the minister "to search and examine [their] consciences, (and that nor lightly, and after the manner of dissemblers with God; but so) that ye may come holy and clean to such a heavenly Feast..." There was much emphasis on reconciliation between those who had caused or been the recipient of offenses, and willful refusal to do so could have dire spiritual consequences:

> *By the rule of God's commandments; and whereinsoever ye shall perceive yourselves to have offended, either by will, word, or deed, there to bewail your own sinfulness, and to confess yourselves to Almighty God, with full purpose of amendment of life. And if ye shall perceive your offences to be such as are not only against God, but also against your neighbours; then ye shall reconcile yourselves unto them; being ready to make restitution and satisfaction, according to the uttermost of*

your powers, for all injuries and wrongs done by you to any other; and being likewise ready to forgive others that have offended you, as ye would have forgiveness of your offences at God's hand: for otherwise the receiving of the holy Communion cloth nothing else but increase your damnation....

So when Smith refused to join Handel in Communion and questioned Handel's own taking of it Handel would instantly have "gotten the message." Handel (and Smith) had heard this exhortation for years, and a form of it in their Lutheran experience as well, and understood it perfectly. Handel knew what he had to do. And before Handel died he would go further. He would make sure that there was no impediment between him and any of his friends which would stand in the way of his facing "his sweet Lord" with a clear conscience. In this context, there is nothing far-fetched about intractable human spirits yielding to reconciliation.

From June 28 to July 5 that summer of 1750, Handel composed one more work *(The Choice of Hercules)* before setting out for a visit to his homeland – a return to Germany perhaps spurred by ways of The Netherlands. On August 29 (continental date) the Dutch newspaper *Oprechte Haarlemse Courant* reported Handel in Haarlem visiting Henricus Radeker, organist at the Groote Kerk, whom Handel first met during his 1740 visit.[4] On August 27 Handel had heard Radeker play the huge Christian Müller organ. Radeker was not only organist of the world's largest and most famous organ, but he grew up in a Dutch organ culture that was similar to what Handel had known in Germany, and Radeker's own father (Johannes) was a well-known builder. Handel surely enjoyed talking with Radeker and relished the setting – the more so because he would soon also see his fond friend and former music student, Princess Anne (Princess of Orange since 1734). Though a traveler to Germany from Britain would naturally pass through the Netherlands, it's no wonder Handel spent quite some time there.

There is another reason Handel possibly stayed in Haarlem a little longer than he intended, why there's no report of him playing the Groote Kerk organ himself at that time, and why he may not have wanted to continue traveling just then. He was very likely still feeling the effects of a coach accident that occurred on his way to Haarlem sometime during the last week of August. On August 21 (Sept. 1, continental) the *General Advertiser* reported to Londoners:

Mr. Handel, who went to Germany to visit his Friends some Time since, and between the Hague and Harlaem [sic] had the Misfortune to be overturned, by which he was terribly hurt, is now out of Danger.

Handel traveled north from The Hague to Haarlem. Both these cities lie near the North Sea (The Netherlands' west coast), about thirty-five miles apart. Handel would have sailed from Britain across the North Sea, landed at Rotterdam, then traveled by coach, passing through The Hague on the way to Haarlem. Depending on the terrain and weather, a coach might be expected to travel thirty-five to forty-five miles a day without a change of horses. The news report makes the accident sound serious, and indeed a coach overturning was no minor matter. There is no tale of broken bones or internal injuries, but the sixty-five-year-old Handel must have felt the ache of his inevitable bruises and abrasions for some days.

By September 12, two Dutch newspapers reported Handel in Deventer, eighty miles inland (east) from Haarlem. On the 10th he gave an impromptu organ recital at Deventer's Groote Kerk. His presence and reputation caused the church to fill. Princess Anne and her husband, the Prince of Orange, were present, as were "various nobles of the court ... among a great mass of people, both the first and least of this town." The listeners, high and low, were "extremely satisfied." The Royal Palace was at Het Loo, nearby, and Handel likely stayed to visit a while. From there he probably continued east into Germany, and to Halle, remaining in Germany for the some or all of the rest of the fall, until sometime in November, when he made his way back through The Netherlands. This would be Handel's last trip to his homeland, and at his age he surely had a premonition of that.

There is word of Handel being back in The Hague on December 2, when once again "Heer Handel ... allowed his extraordinary gifts on the organ to be heard in the Nieuwe Kerk. The entire court, most of the foreign ambassadors and other distinguished persons of both sexes were present, and he was greatly praised by all." Later in the week (December 7), and still in The Hague, there was a. report of him playing "for the last time" for the Prince and Princess of Orange and their family, and then departing the next day for England, via Rotterdam.

Meanwhile, his friends and admirers in Britain were thinking of him. On December 3 Ann (Granville) Dewes' warm thoughts of Handel were kindled by strains of *Messiah* running through her head. She confided her thoughts to her brother, giving another clear contemporary picture of the spiritual impact of *Messiah*, and of the oratorios in general. Notably, she confessed to Bernard that there were few people to whom she could say such things for fear of being branded an "enthusiast":

I hope you find Mr. Handel well. I beg my compliments to him: he has not a more real admirer of his great work than myself; his wonderful Messiah will never be out of my head; and I may say my heart was raised almost to heaven by it. It is only those people who have not felt the leisure of devotion that can make any objection to that performance, which is calculated to raise our devotion, and make us truly sensible of the power of the divine words he has chose behond any human work that ever yet appeared, and I am sure I may venture to say ever will. If anything can give us an idea of the Last Days it must be that part— "The trumpet shall sound, the dead shall be raised." It is [to] few people I can say so much as this, for they would call me an enthusiast; but when I wish to raise my thoughts above this world and all its trifling concerns, I look over what oratorios I have, and even my poor way of fumbling gives me pleasing recollections, but I have nothing of the Messiah, but He was despised, &c.[5]

Coincidentally, the other member of the Granville sibling trio, Mary Delaney, was also thinking of Handel and *Messiah*. From Dublin, she told Ann that on November 29 she heard a benefit performance of Handel's Te Deum and Jubilate "and two anthems," and she would be attending *Messiah* on Dec. 11 "for the benefit of debtors."

~

Handel returned to view on December 14 (Christmas Day by the continental calendar) in a lengthy, fascinating letter to Telemann. Clearly, the affection between the two composer-friends had not diminished over the years. The letter is an answer to one he had just received from Telemann. Handel expresses himself warmly and openly in French – somewhat reminiscent of his letters to his brother-in-law. Typical of his generosity, and further demonstrating his fondness for Telemann, he also sent an unusual gift that related to an extra-musical passion of Telemann's:

I was on the point of leaving the Hague for London when your most agreeable letter was delivered to me by [violinist] Mr. [Giuseppe] Passerini. I had just enough time to be able to hear his wife sing. Your patronage and approval were enough not only to excite my curiosity but also to serve her as sufficient recommendation; however I was soon convinced myself of her rare quality. They are leaving for Scotland to fulfil concert engagements there for a season of six months. There she will be able to perfect herself in the English language; after that (as they intend to remain some time in London) I shall not fail to be of service to them in all ways that may depend on me.

[Christina Passerini did sing in the oratorios from 1754 to Handel's death.] Moreover I was deeply touched by your most friendly expressions of goodwill; your kindness and your renown made too much impression on my heart and mind for me not to reciprocate them as you deserve. Pray be assured that you will always find in me a like sincerity and true regard.

I thank you for the splendid work on the system of intervals which you were good enough to send me; it is worthy of your time and trouble and of your learning.

I congratulate you on the perfect health that you are enjoying at your somewhat advanced age, and I wish you from my heart every prosperity for many years to come. If your passion for exotic plants etc. could prolong your days and sustain the zest for life that is natural to you, I offer with very real pleasure to contribute to it in some sort. Consequently I am sending you as a present (to the address enclosed) a crate of flowers, which experts assure me are very choice and of admirable rarity. If they are not telling the truth, you will [at least] have the best plants in all England, and the season of the year is still right for their bearing flowers. You will be the best judge of this; I await your decision on the matter. But do not let me have to wait for your agreeable reply about this for too long, since I am, with perfect friendship and devotion,*

Sir,

Your humble and most obedient servant,

George Frideric Handel.[6]

The "system of intervals" for which Handel thanks Telemann is a reference

---

*Telemann would be 70 in March 1751, Handel would be 66 in February. Handel's actual words were not "many years to come" but "several years" ("plusieurs Ans"). Even in his kind wishes for Telemann, he was realistic the possible length of his friend's future. As it happened, Telemann had a very long life: he died eight years after Handel, in 1767, at age 86.

to the latter's *Das neue musikalische System* (*The New Musical System*), which would be published in 1752 in Leipzig, in the periodical *Neu-eröffneter musikalischer Bibliothek* (*Newly Published Musical Library*). The periodical had been founded in 1736 by Lorence Christoph Mizler von Kolof, a student of Bach's. In 1738 Mizler had inaugurated a professional society for "musical scientists."[7] The society, called the Correspondirenden Societät der Musicalischen Wissenschaften (Corresponding Society of Musical Sciences), is of interest because Bach, Handel and Telemann were all members. Also in the group were fourteen good but lesser composers, and Mizler himself (Leopold Mozart, Amadeus's father, was being recommended as the twentieth member). Bach joined only in 1747, as the fourteenth member; Handel had joined earlier, as the eleventh member, and Telemann had joined in 1739 as the sixth member. Unfortunately, Mizler's journal contains no contributions from Handel, and little is known of Handel's membership.

There were strict membership requirements. For two thalers annually, subscribers could maintain correspondence with other members. At least once a year each member had to contribute a "scientific communication." That could take the form of a "scientific" composition, but it must follow the principles of Christian Wolff (1679-1754), and written analysis had to be in the literary style of J.C. Gottsched. (Members aged sixty-five or older were exempt from this submission requirement.) Each member was also to present his portrait to the society (Bach's, by E.G. Haussmann, 1746, is the only one which survives.) A member was also supposed to remember the society in his will. On its side, the society would provide a cantata or ode when a member died, along with publishing his obituary and portrait in *Neu-eröffneter musikalischer Bibliothek*. Both the periodical and the society survived to 1754.

Handel was first mentioned in the journal the year after its founding (1737): "Does not the admirable *Händel* delight the ears of the discerning English above all other composers living in England? And who is he? A German.... Where can other nations evince such keyboard masters as *Händel*, and our Bach here?"

Mizler, perhaps surprisingly, figures in the puzzle about Handel's doctorate. He was the man to whom Handel commented about the doctorate on May 25, 1744, causing Mizler to write in the *Neu Musickalische Bibliothek* of 1747:

> The author [Bellermann] ... praises the custom, introduced in England, of making Bachelors, Masters and Doctors of Music, an honour which has befallen Pepusch and the prince of composition, the excellent *Händel*. As

far as Herr Händel is concerned, I must contradict Herr Bellermann, because I know more of the facts. This admirable musician, from whom indeed six Doctors of Music could be fashioned, wrote the following words to me in a letter of 25ᵗʰ May 1744: "I neither could nor would accept the Doctor's degree, because I was overwhelmingly busy."

The day after Handel wrote to Telemann, Mary Delaney once again wrote from Dublin about Handel. She tells her sister, "This week I have had a feast of music": both a rehearsal and benefit performance of *Messiah*. "The pleasure of the music," Mary says, "was greatly heightened by considering how many poor prisoners would be released by it."[8] This was the *Messiah* performance she was anticipating in her earlier letter. It was conducted by the Italian violinist Giovanni Battista Marella ("Morella") in a manner better than she had expected, "considering he was *not before acquainted* with such sublime music."

A few days later Mary elaborated on that *Messiah* performance to her brother. She had earlier criticized Marella's "French taste" for excessively florid and fussy ornamentation. ("I shall not be able to endure his introducing froth and nonsense in that sublime and awful piece of music," she had said.) She had feared what Marella would do to awe-inspiring *Messiah*, as she had heard him take Corelli's eighth concerto (the "Christmas Concerto") and "fill it up with frippery and graces which quite destroyed the effect of the sweet notes, and solemn pauses that conclude it." That being the case, Marella's restrained interpretation of *Messiah* was a pleasant surprise to Mary. And she adjures Bernard, as Ann had, "Pray make my compliments to Handel."

Chapter 19
How Dark, O Lord, Are Thy Decrees

Handel's long sojourn with family and friends in Germany and the Netherlands had a wondrously rejuvenating effect. On February 16, four days before the start of the 1751 oratorio season, Shaftesbury told James Harris, after having either seen Handel himself, or by word from J.C. Smith the elder:

> *Belshazar is now advertis'd, and Smith tells me the parts will go off excellently. Handel himself, is actually better in health, and in a higher flow of genius than he has been for several years past. His late journey has helped his constitution vastly.* [1]

What was not apparent in Handel's renewed spirits and good health was a looming problem with his eyesight and general health, which would sadly and abruptly change the course of his remaining eight years. On January 21 he began a new oratorio, *Jephtha*. Under normal circumstances he would have completed it easily by the time the Lenten season was to begin; but on February 13 his circumstances became abruptly abnormal.

Unknown to Shaftesbury (and to all of Handel's friends), on that day, while composing the last chorus of *Jephtha's* Act 2, he was forced to stop composing. Where he stopped, and why, he poignantly noted, in German, in the margin: "Got as far as this on Wednesday, February 13, 1751, unable to go on due to [the] 'relaxation' of the sight of my left eye." After writing that sentence in German, Handel evidently crossed out the word "relaxation" – the one English word in the midst of this sudden reversion to his mother tongue – and added it at the end in more Germanic form: "so relaxt."* As we've already noted, Handel tended to revert to writing in German in times of grief or experiences which deeply affected him. Now he did the same. Assuming he had recently been in Germany for up to several months, the German may have come more readily this time – though he apparently couldn't think of a word in German to express the nature of his sudden eye abnormality. Only his left eye was affected on that day; but within not much more than a year, his blindness would be total.

There is an aching poignance in the fact that the text Handel was setting to

---

*Handel wrote: "Biss hierher komen den 13 Febr. [Wed.] 1751 verhindert worden wegen relaxation des gesichts meines linken auges." (He denoted "Wednesday" with the sign for that day used in both astrology and astronomy, a common shorthand of his.)

music when he so abruptly had to stop says:

> *How dark, O Lord, are thy decrees,*
> *All hid from mortal sight*
> *All our joys to sorrow turning,*
> *And our triumphs into mourning,*
> *As the night succeeds the day.*
> *No certain bliss,*
> *No solid peace,*
> *We mortals know*
> *On earth below,*
> *Yet on this maxim still obey:*
> *"Whatever is, is right."* (Chorus ending Act II)

What caused Handel's sudden unilateral blindness? The diagnosis at the time and a reasonable diagnosis now are two quite different things. Eye diseases were not well understood. Both Mainwaring and Hawkins call Handel's condition "gutta serena," following the lead of surgeon Samuel Sharp. Hawkins explained:

> *In the beginning of the year 1751 [Handel] was alarmed by a disorder*
> *of his eyes, which, upon consulting with Mr. Samuel Sharp, Surgeon*
> *of Guy's Hospital, he was told was an incipient Gutta serena.*[2]

What was meant by *gutta serena* becomes apparent when we take a brief look at the ancient Greek theory of the humors which still underlay medicine in the eighteenth century. The elements water, fire, earth and air were believed to give matter the characteristics of moisture, warmth, dryness and coldness; and those, in turn, related to human physiology as the four humors: blood, mucus, yellow bile and black bile. If the body maintained a proper balance of these humors, health was the result; an imbalance caused illness. If left to itself, the body responded in three stages: crudity (the appearance of disease/humor imbalance), coction (the body preparing to rid itself of the disordered humors), and crisis (the actual process of doing so, the body trying to restore its balance of humors).

Besides the four basic humors there were seven dangerous ("morbid") humors that passed from the brain into the tissues, two of which affected the eyes. One of these produced eye disorders ("opthalmias"), causing inflammation and discharge; the other affected vision without producing a discharge. Thus, eye abnormalities were slotted into one of two categories: *gutta opaque* or *gutta serena*. In the first category, the eye was clouded by one of the two morbid humors of the eye; in *gutta serena* the morbid humor did not cloud the eye, so the eye appeared essentially normal (without the kind of twenty-first century equipment, of course, which allows for the magnification and minute examination of the interior of the eye).

There were refinements on these concepts over the centuries; the anatomy of the eye was the subject of considerable study in the sixteenth and seventeenth centuries, and there was pathological and clinical progress on that study in the eighteenth century – surgical attempts at treating cataracts, for example. But the fundamental basis of the humors had not yet been rejected.

Handel's condition described as *gutta serena* meant, then, that there was no obvious swelling or discharge (cataracts do, however, cause an affected eye to look cloudy). The normal treatment was "couching" for cataracts. Because cataracts were common in Handel's day and little was known about other causes of blindness or how to treat them, an assumption of cataracts is not surprising.* The Greeks thought a cataract to be a morbid humor in front of the lens of the eye. It wasn't until 1705 that Frenchman Pierre Brisseau (1631-1717) described cataracts as affecting the lens itself; and it wasn't until decades later (1753) that another Frenchman, Jacques Daviel, attempted surgical extraction of a cataract rather than the normal "couching" procedure that put pressure on the cataract. And it took more decades still for Daviel's method to be accepted in England.

In that pre-anesthetic age, "couching" was not submitted to by the faint of heart; but at no time in his life was Handel faint-hearted. Robert James's *Medicinal Dictionary* (1743-45) tells the surgeon that he should "strike the needle thro' the *tunica conjunctiva*, something less than one tenth of an inch from the cornea, even with the middle of the pupil, into the posterior chamber, and gently endeavor to depress the cataract with the flat surface of it." In modern terms, this was an attempt – without benefit of anesthetic – to dislocate the cataract by shoving it into the eye's vitreous cavity.

---

*Another commonly cited cause of blindness was glaucoma (it, like cataracts, does not cause sudden blindness). "Glaucoma" as a term goes back to Hippocrates' time, but for centuries was not applied to the specific condition we know as glaucoma. In 1622 British oculist Richard Banister recognized that condition and rightly noted that "if one feele the Eye by rubbing upon the Eie-lids, that the Eye be growne more solid and hard than naturally it should be." However, his observations "failed to attract any attention" and glaucoma remained to be rediscovered in the early nineteenth century (C.N. Chua, "A Historic Tour of Ophthalmology, <www.mrcophth.com>).

In June 1751, Handel traveled to Cheltenham Wells to take the waters for two or three weeks. Since hot springs had been beneficial to him in the past, he no doubt hoped that they would help revive his sight as well as improve any other ailments he may have been feeling. Of course, "the waters" did nothing to improve his sight, though they may well have helped alleviate his stress and lift his spirits. On his return he "consulted" Samuel Sharp. Neither Hawkins nor Mainwaring say that Handel's consultation included being couched by Sharp and there was no such report in the newspapers. However, by November 4, 1752, the *General Advertiser* informed Londoners:

> *Yesterday George-Frederick Handel, Esq; was couch'd by Willaim Bromfield, Esq; Surgeon to her Royal Highness the Princess of Wales, when it was thought there was all imaginable Hopes of Success by the Operation, which must give the greatest Pleasure to all Lovers of Musick.*

Handel's nineteenth century French biographer Victor Schoelcher quotes "a journal" dated January 27, 1753, which mentioned one couching incident and Handel's total blindness, set in an ambiguous time span:

> *Mr. Handel, at length, unhappily, quite lost his sight. Upon his being couch'd some time since, he saw so well, that his friends flattered themselves his sight was restored for a continuance; but a few days have entirely put an end to their hope.*

Whether Handel was couched in one or both eyes, and on exactly how many occasions, is unknown, but the implication that his sight was actually restored, even if for a few days, is highly unlikely. The source of this quotation seems to have vanished. Deutsch points out that "the notice is not to be found in the collection called *Theatrical Register*, nor in the *London Daily Advertiser, Public Advertiser, London Evening Post*, etc."

Years after his complete blindness, Handel was apparently couched again. That time it was at Tunbridge Wells by "Chevalier" Taylor, John Taylor the elder (1703-1772), a well-known traveling oculist (or, as he called himself, an "ophthalmiater"). From a modern standpoint he was a quack, aided by the ability to appear to be reasonably knowledgeable. He had a thriving practice, as such practitioners often do; his son, also named John, was in the same lucrative and apparently ego-massaging profession. Konrad Pesudovs and David Elliott in the *Ophthalmology Times* describe such itinerant oculists:

In the eighteenth century traveling quacks were common. They attracted patients through vigorous self-promotion and operated on cataracts, and other common maladies, in town centres and marketplaces [and, as in Chevalier Taylor's case, in higher class venues such as the Tunbridge Wells]. *The outcome from the patient's point of view lagged well behind the claims of the cataract lancer.*[3]

C.N. Chua further describes the state of eye treatment at the time, specifically mentioning Taylor the elder and another dubious oculist, Woolhouse:

The conflict between orthodoxy and quackery was to last for the rest of the [eighteenth] century, largely because of the indifference of the profession to ophthalmic matters. Benedict Duddell had to complain in 1729 that surgeons undertook treatment of eye conditions without the necessary knowledge: 'to the question how a certain surgeon did to know the different natures of the distempers of the eye: His answer was that he undertook all. If his operation succeeded, so much the better; if not the patients could but be blind, or in danger of being so, as they were before.' In such an atmosphere charlatanism could not but prosper, especially as the charlatan was often well grounded in the subject; Woolhouse and the Chevalier Taylor were certainly the equals in knowledge to most of the more orthodox oculists.

"Chevalier" Taylor falsely claimed that, as a result of his treatment, Handel regained his sight. From the diary of barrister John Baker, we do know that Handel was at Tunbridge Wells in August 1758, and that Morell was with him:

Left horse and took post chaise ... to River Head 12 miles – thence fresh chaise 14 [miles] to Tunbridge Wells.... At Wells then and after Handel and his Dr. Murrell [Morell], Taylor the occulist....

On August 24, 1758, the *London Chronicle* saw fit to print a nine-stanza ode "On the Recovery of the Sight of the Celebrated Mr. Handel, by the Chevalier Taylor."* Set in Greek mythology populated by Apollo and the Muses, the ode is both wretched poetry and brimming with Taylor's conceit.

An example:

---

*The placement of the phrase "by the Chevalier Taylor" can be taken one of two ways, or both: either naming Taylor as the author or meaning to say that Taylor was the one who was responsible for the "recovery."

[Euterpe speaking to Apollo]:
"Great Father of Music and every Science,
In all our distresses, on thee our reliance;
Know then in yon villa, from pleasures confin'd
Lies our favourite, Handel, afflicted and blind.

"For him who hath travers'd the cycle of sound,
And spread thy harmonious strains the world round,
Thy son Aesculapius' art we implore,
The blessing of sight with a touch to restore. "

Strait Apollo replied: "He already is there;
By mortal's call'd, Taylor, and dubb'd Chevalier:
Who to Handel (and thousands beside him) shall give
All the blessings that sight in old age can receive.

~

The fact that Handel was couched several times for one or more cataracts does not mean that he actually had cataracts. Even if he was beginning to develop them, it is certain that his sudden loss of vision in one eye in February 1751 and his subsequent loss of vision in the other eye cannot have been caused by them: cataracts do not result in sudden blindness (strangely, a fact still often overlooked by Handel scholars). There is nothing to indicate that Handel had been suffering from deteriorating eyesight before the onset of his sudden left-eye blindness. The way he worded his note in the score of *Jephtha* does not imply that this was a worsening of a vision problem, but rather, something new, unexpected and disconcerting that he didn't quite know how to describe in either English or German.

The most likely explanation for the loss of Handel's sight is that he had a form of ischemic optic neuropathy (which we will refer to as ION). According to Dr. Sohan Singh Hayreh, for four decades a pioneer in research of the disease, ischemic optic neuropathy can be explained in a layperson's terms as "a stroke in the back of the eye," a "blocked blood vessel" or "a broken blood vessel at the back of the eye."[4] This occurs most often in the elderly, in one eye, painlessly and usually without warning. The vision loss frequently progresses to the other eye, sometimes almost immediately, sometimes over a somewhat longer period, as it did in Handel's case. The loss of vision may show itself as anything from a narrowing of the visual

268

field and decreased acuity (ability to focus), to "blind spots," to complete blindness, and color vision may be affected. It occurs because of reduced or interrupted blood flow to the optic nerve. (Sudden vision loss can also occur because of stopped circulation to the retina, which is a different, less common condition.)

While vision may sometimes actually improve temporarily – which possibly happened to Handel, but which was attributed to the couching he underwent – the condition is irreversible because the optic nerve begins to die for lack of blood supply. ("Ischemia" is an interruption of blood supply to any body tissue, resulting in decreasing oxygen levels and nutrition – rather like putting a rubber band around a finger and leaving it there. "Neuropathy" is any inflammation of the nerves, in this case causing the ischemia.)

"Ischemic optic neuropathy" is most often preceded with the word "anterior," because interruption of the blood supply to the anterior (front) part of the optic nerve where it is attached to the eyeball is by far the most common form (abbreviated here as AION). A further descriptor applied is either "arteritic" or "non-arteritic." "Arteritic" comes from *arteritis* – inflammation that effects arteries supplying blood to the head and eyes. Inflammation causes arteries to swell and become tender (an inflamation that would not have been visible to practitioners in Handel's day). The result is restricted or stopped blood flow, clotting and subsequent loss of vision. Because arteritic AION is a vascular disease (affecting blood vessels and the circulatory system) it is generally accompanied by one or more of a host of symptoms: mental status changes, *including "acute confusional states"* (my emphasis), headache, achy joints, general fatigue, neck pain, scalp tenderness, jaw or tongue pain when chewing, temple pain, facial swelling, cardiovascular and/or neurological symptoms.[*] To complicate matters, there is a variant arteritic form of AION that is not accompanied by any of these symptoms, and in which the patient appears to be in good health, as Handel initially appeared to be. Though arteritic

---

[*]The non-arteritic form of AION, while somewhat more common, seems to fit less well our admittedly sketchy knowledge of Handel's symptoms. It shows a less severe vision loss, with some recovery of vision possible over time. Involvement of the second eye is also much less frequent than in the arteritic form. Because Handel was a life-long indulger in rich foods and was somewhat overweight, he may well have had high blood pressure, and may have been developing arteriosclerosis for years without experiencing any specific symptoms. General hardening of the arteries can contribute to ischemia in the eye. However, the non-arteritic condition itself has no effect on long-term health in the way that arteritic AION does, and Handel's health did deteriorate after the onset of his blindness.

AION is more common in women than men, it occurs most frequently among people of European ancestry, and particularly those of Scandinavian and German descent. Handel, then, was a member of an ethnic group that can be presumed to have had a high frequency of arteritic AION, as that group does today.

He may have had the form of arteritic AION that doesn't readily manifest systemic symptoms. Shaftesbury's remark about how much good Handel's European trip had done him demonstrates that Handel wasn't showing any obvious symptoms of ill health just before his sudden encounter with blindness. He had always been a man of strong constitution; but he was to live only eight more years. Periodic remarks by friends about his health and how ill he looked after his blindness indicate that his health deteriorated from that point. This suggests that his blindness *was* accompanied by or caused by "significant systemic disease," as arteritic AION is, without that systemic disease initially manifesting itself.

Arteritic AION can result in paralysis of cranial motor nerves (nerves in the head which control eye and facial movements) because of the choked blood supply. Most commonly affected is the nerve which controls eye and eyelid movement and pupil dilation. Paralysis of this (third cranial) nerve can result in a permanently dilated pupil, drooping eyelid and/or the inability to focus on an object due to lack of eye-movement control. It may have seen such nerve paralysis as a result of arteritic AION that Handel initially experienced as the "relaxation" of his left eye. (Treatment today involves taking corticosteroids, which can help arrest the progression of the disease but not restore vision loss.) There may have been a connection – though not one necessarily well understood even now – between Handel's three bouts of right-arm paralysis and mental confusion and this later manifestation of presumed ischemic optic neuropathy. These vascular and neurological conditions also fit with the later sudden "Paralytick Disorder" which resulted in blindness in Handel's other eye.* In August 1752 the *General Advertiser* reported:

---

*When I devised this theory of the cause for Handel's blindness and its relation to prior vascular problems causing his bouts of right-arm paralysis and mental confusion when under severe stress, I had not seen any research suggesting this cause. Then I discovered ophthalmologist Donald L. Blanchard's article "George Handel and His Blindness" in *Documenta Ophthalmologica* 99: 247-258, 1999. Blanchard, too, suggests anterior ischemic optic neuropathy as the cause of Handel's blindness, though of the nonarteritic variety. I am gratified by Blanchard's concurrence with "my" theory, as he is a physician and I am not. While all diagnoses are speculative, anterior ischemic optic neuropathy as the cause of Handel's blindness (whether arteritic or nonarteritic) merits wider dissemination and discussion. It is clear, as I pointed out and as Blanchard also points out, that the traditional cause of cataracts cited by most music historians does not fit Handel's symptoms.

*We hear that George-Frederick Handel, Esq; the celebrated Composer
of Musick was seized a few Days ago with a Paralytick Disorder in the
Head, which has deprived him of Sight.*

This seems to be a description of Handel's loss of sight in his other, right eye. While
Chevalier Taylor's word has to be taken with the proverbial grain of salt, he, too,
mentions a "paralytic disorder" in connection with Handel in a work he wrote about
himself and his travels two years after Handel's death. However, his "clinical" talk
about Handel is obscure. Taylor at first thought he would succeed in restoring
Handel's sight, but that changed. He later acknowledged that he could do nothing
(his earlier pretentious ode claiming restoration of Handel's sight notwithstanding).
He could admit his ophthalmological impotence in 1761 because Handel was dead
by then. In mentioning Handel, Taylor first claims to have restored the sight of an
eighty-eight-year-old "celebrated master of music" from "Leipsick" with whom

> *the famous Handel was first educated, and with whom I thought to have
> the same success, having all circumstances in his favour, motions of the
> pupils, light, &c. But upon drawing the curtain, we found the bottom
> defective, from a paralytic disorder.* [*]

~

Morell wrote the libretto for *Jephtha*. At the point in the oratorio where
Handel was forced to stop composing, the "mighty warrior" Jephtha, one of Israel's
Judges, has just discovered that a rash vow he made must result in the death of his

---

[*] As we've seen, Handel was "first educated" in Halle with Zachau, who was long dead. Taylor's
statement is no doubt a convoluted reference to Bach, who lived in Leipzig from 1723-50 and who also went
blind. Bach died in 1750 at age sixty-five. At the best of times Taylor was not careful with details, and he wrote
his account a decade after the story he tells, so his memory may have been fuzzy as well. There are reports in
the *Berlinische Privilegirte Zeitung*, April 4 and 7, 1750, that Taylor was then in Leipzig giving lectures, that
he had previously operated on Bach (which took place in January 1750), and that Bach received his sight again
(*The New Bach Reader*, ed. Hans T. David and Arthur Mendel. New York: Norton, 1998, pp. 243-244).
That Bach was cured is untrue (as in Handel's case, and doubtless many others). In fact, Taylor so botched
Bach's operation that "not only could he no longer use his eyes, but his whole system, which was otherwise
thoroughly healthy, was completely overthrown by the operation and by the addition of harmful medicaments
and other things, so that, thereafter, he was almost continuously ill for full half a year" – and he died shortly
thereafter (Bach's obituary by C.P.E. Bach and Johann Friedrich Agricola, 1750, published 1754; in *The
New Bach Reader*, p. 303).

only daughter and only child. He had bargained with God: "If you give the Ammonites into my hands, whatever comes out of the door of my house to meet me when I return in triumph from the Ammonites will be the LORD'S, and I will sacrifice it as a burnt offering" (Judges 11:31; see Judges 10-12 for the whole story and its context). Jephtha's daughter (called Iphis in the oratorio, unnamed in the Bible) is the first person who joyously comes to greet him upon Israel's victory, and Jephtha can't renege on his vow.

In Judges, this vow is a tragically careless act on Jephtha's part (and in its almost certain requirement of human sacrifice, a reflexive reversion to the pagan worship of Molech, of which the Israelites had recently repented). Though there has been debate throughout the centuries as to the exact nature of Jephtha's vow, Morell changed the details and implications of the vow. He absolves Jephtha by having an angel appear to tell him that it was actually the Holy Spirit who had "dictated the vow," and that what would be required to fulfill the vow was Iphis's life-long setting apart as a virgin dedicated to God's service.* This makes for a far happier ending to the oratorio, of course, than if Iphis had had to die by her own father's "slaught'rous hand." And putting the onus of the vow on God instead of on Jephtha also allows Morell to bring up the issue of the providence and "decrees" of God, and the nature of God's care and control of his world.

Morell had at least one "free-thinking" friend, but he himself was no Deist. Deism still had a slim audience in England at this point, as we've said, but it was beginning to make in-roads. This, because of its audacious unorthodoxy was causing dismay among biblical Christians. So Deism's denial that God is a loving, providential God who is concerned for his world and continues to act within it for our good, amidst the presence of evil, was a particularly current, much discussed issue as Morell and Handel wrote *Jephtha*. Morell's libretto reinforces a traditional Christian interpretation of God as revealed in Scripture: God's decrees can be "dark" – veiled and incomprehensible to mortals as they often are – but despite "no certain bliss, no solid peace" on *this* earth, we can know that events, good and bad,

---

Jephtha, Recitative, Act III: "Rise, Jephtha, and ye rev'rend priests, withhold/The slaught'rous hand. No vow can disannul/The law of God, nor such was its intent/When rightly scann'd; yet still shall be fulfill'd./Thy daughter, Jephtha, thou must dedicate/To God, in pure and virgin state fore'er,/As not an object meet for sacrifice,/Else had she fall'n an holocaust to God./The Holy Sp'rit, that dictated thy vow,/Bade thus explain it, and approves thy faith."

are unfolding rightly, as God intends, according to his commands — commands that his people must obey. God is not seen as the *author* of evil, but as allowing and controlling evil, ultimately working out his good purposes through it.

In the Act II chorus that Handel was setting when he first lost his sight, Morell's final line was originally, "What God ordains is right." Handel himself indicated the change to "Whatever is, is right,"which is a line from Alexander Pope's *Essay on Man* (1733). For Handel, Morell's text would likely have called to mind the Lutheran chorale "Was Gott tut, das ist wohlgetan" ("What God does, that is rightly done"; or, in the translation better known, "What'ere My God Ordains is Right"). This chorale text was written by the Pietist Samuel Rodigast ten years before Handel was born. The chorale as sung in Lutheran worship was the collective believers' communal yet personal confession of trust in God and the rightness of his acts, and reliance on his will.*

In our time, Handel's change of this line has occasioned discussion about his motive for making the change. Why would he alter Morell's phrase, replacing it with a phrase by Pope which, ostensibly, is less overtly Christian? Did he do it for philosophical or theological reasons, or for aesthetic or other reasons that had nothing to do with a possible sudden change of heart about Providence — as sudden as the onset of his blindness?

Winton Dean concludes that Handel was "devoutly religious" and did not mean to "attack Christianity" even while simultaneously producing a "damning indictment of the providence that inflicts capricious suffering on the guiltless." Dean adds: "There are indeed signs that he wished to distinguish the Christian God from Jehovah, for he carefully expunged the name of God from several movements." So when Dean notes the wording change, he interprets it as the composer's "grim acceptance of Pope's maxim from the *Essay on Man*" and "his own submission to

---

*Rodigast never wrote any other chorale texts, as far as is known. He lived in Berlin as headmaster of the principal Gymnasium there and was a friend of Pietist founder-leader Philipp Jakob Spener. He wrote "Was Gott tut" in 1675 for another friend who was seriously ill. Its first stanza says: "What God does, that is rightly done *(Was Gott tut, das ist wohlgetan),*/His will is just for ever *(Es bleibt gerecht sein Wille);*/Whatever course he sets [for] my life, *(Wie er fängt meine Sachen an),*/ I will trust him with calmness *(Will ich ihm halten stille)./* He is my God *(Er ist mein Gott),/* Who in [my] distress *(Der in der Not)/* Knows well how to support me (*Mich wohl weiß zu erhalten);/*So I yield him all power *(Drum laß ich ihn nur walten)"*. Bach used the chorale as the basis for cantatas BWV 98-100 and used stanzas 2 and 6 in BWV 75.

destiny"which "submission" the composer simultaneously turns into an "impassioned protest" by "point[ing] an accusing finger at the dark impenetrability of the government of the universe."[5] This is a misinterpretation of both Pope and Handel.

Dean prefers to see Handel as a "great humanist" rather than a great Christian. Humanism and Christianity are compatible in the sense that Christians should be fully engaged with all humanity by daily "loving their neighbor as themselves," as Jesus said ("neighbor" being interpreted as anyone and everyone one comes in contact with). In the philosophical sense, however, the humanist worldview has deep points of incompatibility with a biblically Christian view, the primary one being that it sees humanity, not God, as "the measure of all things." Dean also seems unaware that a "devoutly religious" Christian was (or is) hardly likely to overthrow a life-time of reliance on God and trust in his providential care after just two weeks of anguish, however bitter. Also ignored is Hawkins's first-hand report (cited earlier) of an increase in Handel's obvious piety and devotion to God rather than a wavering of faith after his blindness and as his health continued to deteriorate

Dean infuses Handel with his own views, which do not relate to Handel's views and context Christianity. This is substantiated by the way Dean writes of the God revealed in Handel's oratorios; he fully accepts the Old Testament/New Testament God approach, which Handel clearly did not: "The God of the greater oratorios is not the jealous Jehovah of the Old Testament, still less the Christian God of the Atonement, but rather the remote and impartial controller of man's destiny, a being akin to the Aeschylean conception of Zeus. It is only in the weaker examples – Deborah, Judas Maccabaeus, Joshua – that the librettist has forced on Handel the notion of a tribal deity, and so conspired to smother his inspiration. If Handel's God has a chosen people, it is the entire human race."

Dean assumes that Pope's intent in the line "whatever is is right" was humanist, and certainly not a Christian apologia for God's providential control of the world. But that is not the case. Pope's entire poetic stanza containing the line Handel used says:

> All Nature is but art unknown to thee;
> All chance direction, which thou canst not see;
> All discord, harmony not understood;
> All partial evil, universal good;
> And spite of pride, in erring reason's spite,
> One truth is clear, Whatever is is right.[6]

"Whatever is is right" is a rephrasing of Dryden's line "Whatever is, is in its causes just." (Pope was a great admirer of John Dryden, the author of the poems on which Handel's *Alexander's Feast* and *Ode for St. Cecilia's Day* are based). Pope's reworking of Dryden's phrase has sometimes been read to be a repudiation by Pope of his own faith (he was a Catholic) and/or of the traditional Christian view of God and his providence, and of good and evil. But the context of "whatever is is right" makes clear that Pope is neither disclaiming his own faith, minimizing evil (or good), nor positing a disinterested God at whose capricious whims we can only shrug fatalistically in hopeless acceptance.

Pope's introduction to his essay, called "The Design," lays out the ten arguments he will make – and Providence is an important subject amidst these "arguments." Pope's fourth argument addresses "the impiety of [man] putting himself in the place of God, and judging of the fitness or unfitness, perfection or imperfection, justice or injustice, of his dispensations." The sixth argues "the unreasonableness of [human] complaints against Providence." The tenth, the "consequence of all,"summarizes by arguing "the absolute submission due to Providence, both as to our present and future state" – an "absolute submission" due to God because he is God, which has nothing in it of grim forced surrender.

It is true that aspects of the *Essay on Man* did raise questions at the time. This was inadvertently due largely to Samuel Johnson's English translation and publication of Swiss Calvinist Jean Pierre de Crousaz's negative critique.[*] Johnson, acknowledging that Pope was a far better poet than philosopher, said bluntly, "The poet was not sufficiently master of his subject." According to Johnson, this was compounded by Pope having been deliberately misled by Bolingbroke, whose Deist ideas Pope did not recognize as such because Bolingbroke had hidden them from Pope, and then denied that he did so.

That being the case, William Warburton (1698-1779), later Bishop of Gloucester, and a well-known defender of Christianity against Deism, undertook to

---

[*]When, thanks to Johnson, the *Essay on Man* became known on the Continent, Jean Pierre de Crousaz (1663-ca.1648) dissected it. He was a pastor, theologian and mathematician who Johnson called "no mean antagonist"; "his mind was one of those in which philosophy and piety are happily united" (Johnson, *The Life of Pope*, par. 182).

vindicate Pope, succeeded and became his friend and literary executor.* In response, Pope told Warburton, "You have made my system as clear as I ought to have done, and could not."

During Handel's lifetime Warburton became a well-known figure in the defense against Deism. Because Handel also knew Pope personally, he may well have known Pope's mind on these matters. (Pope was in the group that gathered frequently as guests of James Brydges, later Duke of Chandos, when Handel was providing anthems for Brydges).

Handel's own thoroughly trusting view of God's care, and of his prerogative as sovereign God to "give and take away," was now tested. He had to grapple with this issue in an acutely personal way, likely more than any previous grief or stress had ever forced him to do.

Ten days passed during which he could do no composing. We can imagine they must have been agonizing days – days and nights when he may have thought, and thought again, about the nature of God's care, particularly for himself. On the tenth day, his sixty-sixth birthday, he returned to *Jephtha*. He then wrote in the margin: "den 23. dieses etwas besser worden, wird angegangen" ("On the 23rd it is a little better, I will resume.") And then he promptly changed "whatever God ordains is right" to "whatever is is right."

So what about that rewording? There were likely two things that informed the change: Handel's own newly acquired burden, and his discomfort or even disagreement with Morell's setting of the text and it's implications for Jephtha, and by extension for listeners to the oratorio. Hawkins's observation, which he relates to the onset of Handel's blindness, of a mellowing of Handel's character and a deepened and deepening faith in the last years of his life indicates that Handel's new handicap increased rather than decreased his reliance on God.

"Whatever God ordains is right" makes a theological point, an objective stating of a belief about Providence, to which one may assent – or not. "Whatever is is right" doesn't remove God and his often unfathomable acts from the picture –

---

*In a two-volume work, *The Divine Legation of Moses* (1737-41), Warburton used the Deists' principles against them to argue for the divine inspiration of the biblical books of Moses. His work, in which he often employed satiric wit, sometimes caused controversy. In *The Alliance Between Church and State* (1736) he advocated tolerance by the Church of England of those who were Dissenters; but two decades later (1762) he took the Methodists to task in *The Doctrine of Grace*, which did not win him friends in all quarters.

as Pope made clear in his "arguments" – so much as it brings things down to the nitty-gritty of life as it's lived, an assent that whatever happens, and happens to *me*, is right. There's a difference between a theological "reality" one assents to and a lived reality one accepts; a difference between an intellectual acknowledgment of God's grace and the lived experience of it. Handel no doubt agonized over his blindness, but in his agony he also experienced God's compassionate grace. Then he apparently related his own hard experience and the acceptance of it through God's grace to what was going on in the oratorio he was setting.

He would have heard the story of Jephtha since boyhood, and his Lutheran interpretation of Scripture would not have allowed him to easily blame God for Jephtha's rash and foolish vow and its tragic consequences. Morell's phrase "whatever God ordains is right," occurring as it did at the end of a chorus of Israelites after Jephtha spiritually writhes over his own recklessness, essentially blames God for Jephtha's stupidity – something even Jephtha himself didn't dare to do, and something which Handel would have been loathe to do. So in changing the words to "whatever is is right," he was actually acknowledging that human agency exists, and that when we make tragic choices, we must not blame them on God.

Given Handel's saturation in both the Lutheran and Anglican worldview, and his extensive, lifelong knowledge of the Scriptures, he was also very likely uneasy about Morell bringing on an angel who tells Jephtha not to worry because his vow was actually urged by the Holy Spirit. Handel accepts it because the oratorio, by convention, needed a positive ending.* And in the end, in using Pope's phrase from the *Essay on Man*, which was then well known, two decades after Pope adapted it from Dryden, Handel understood that he could instantly call to the minds of his audience the larger context of that phrase: a vindication of God and his providence.

Theodora, Handel's previous oratorio, had ended with the execution (martyrdom) of Theodora and her male counterpart Didymus. It was Handel's only oratorio to end in such a manner and was not accepted by audiences. Morell, and very possibly Handel himself, was apparently unwilling to end *Jephtha*, too, with the martyrdom of an innocent young woman, and this time at the hands of her own father.

Chapter 20
His Muses Have Not Left Him

Handel was quite naturally despondent for some time. The blindness was a grievous and unexpected burden. It took away the means through which he felt and expressed his deepest joy on earth – and the means through which he had surely staved off loneliness throughout his life. The loss of sight was then still partial, but he was realistic enough to realize that it would number his days as a composer, conductor and even performer. Yet if in his worst hours in this newly infirm state he experienced God as either far too remote or rather too close for comfort, he determined quickly that he had to accept his condition and go on. He didn't brood, as was shown by his determination to go about completing *Jephtha* ten days later.

This let's-go-on-amidst-adversity was typical of Handel; but his soldiering on was not a matter of stoic acceptance. Hawkins noted later that Handel changed after his blindness: "The loss of his sight, and the prospect of his approaching dissolution, wrought a great change in his temper and general behavior."[1] It was a positive change. The extremes of his strong and sometimes fiery temperament softened. Hawkins' statement does not imply that Handel suddenly turned pious and interested in matters of faith when he hadn't been before. Nor does Hawkins minimize the devastating and lingering emotional effect of Handel's blindness. Immediately after saying Handel changed, Hawkins indicates that "throughout his life he manifested a deep sense of religion." But it became deeper still.

This is the context of Hawkins' well-known statements recalling that Handel "would frequently declare the pleasure he felt in setting the Scriptures to music; and how much the contemplating the many sublime passages in the Psalms had contributed to his edification." That habit of meditating on Scripture strengthened Handel's faith. Christians across the centuries who lived with or through adversity have understood that. Though Handel could no longer read the Psalms, or read them easily, he surely had learned many by heart through his early education and training, his own earlier Bible reading and the weekly liturgy. Hawkins concludes in language typical of the time: "These sentiments were improved into solid and rational piety, attended with a calm and even temper of mind." There was one other obvious consequence:

> For the last two or three years of his life he was used to attend divine
> service in his own parish church of St. George, Hanover-square, where,
> during the prayers, the eyes that at this instant are employed in a fain

portrait of his excellencies, have seen him on his knees, expressing by his looks and gesticulations the utmost fervour of devotion. [*]

Burney describes Handel as attending not only daily services, but twice-daily – morning and evening, winter and summer, both in London and Tunbridge.

When Handel resumed work on *Jephtha*, he managed to complete in four days the second act he had been working on. His condition soon became known to the public when he had the fortitude to go on with his Lenten oratorio season as planned. The season opened with two performances of *Belshazzar* on February 22 and 27, and Handel maintained his tradition of providing an organ concerto (previously composed) at intermission. *Belshazzar* was followed by four performances of two shorter pieces paired, *Alexander's Feast* and *The Choice of Hercules*, along with another organ concerto (this a new one that he had finished before his blindness struck). Given his prodigious memory and improvising ability, he was able to play organ concertos with or without sight in his left eye, as he indeed continued to do for some time after he was wholly blind. By the time his season started (February 22) he had begun to feel a little better, if temporarily.

The organ concertos seemed to come off as superbly as they always had. On March 14, Sir Edward Turner wrote: "Noble Handel hath lost an eye, but I have the Rapture to say that St. Cecilia makes no complaint of any Defect of his Fingers." On March 15 the oratorio season continued with the first revival of *Esther* in eleven years; and then with *Judas Maccabaeus* on March 20. But that performance would unexpectedly end the season: that very evening Frederick, Prince of Wales died at age forty-four. Theaters closed beginning March 22 for a period of mourning that extended through the rest of Lent. So Handel would not need a new oratorio after all in 1751.

Handel's still partial blindness did not prevent him from playing the organ and conducting at a *Messiah* benefit performance at the Foundling Hospital in April; this raised the considerable sum of £600. In fact, "at the Request of several Persons of Distinction," Handel "very charitably agreed to" a repeat performance on May 16 (Ascension Day), the *General Advertiser* told its readers on May 9.

---

[*] It can be inferred that in his previous, active life Handel often attended church outside his own parish. Hawkins is not implying that Handel was not a churchgoer before the last two or three years of his life. Church attendance was expected (and technically, required in each parish), so even those who were only nominal Christians (which Handel wasn't) went to church.

After that unexpectedly arduous season, Handel traveled to Bath for a rest, and from there went on to Cheltenham Wells. On his return he worked on Act III of *Jephtha* for a month (June 18 to about July 15) and finally finished the oratorio. But his normal composing days were gone. Handel now knew he would need help if he was going to try to continue any kind of public career. Mainwaring says, "Finding it no longer possible for him to manage alone, he sent to Mr. Smith [the younger] to desire that he would play for him, and assist him in conducting the Oratorios."[2] (Handel "sent to" Smith because Smith was in France; he returned to England at Handel's request.) Hawkins confirms this, and poignantly adds about Handel:

> *From the moment [Sharp's] opinion of his case was communicated to him, his spirits forsook him; and that fortitude which had supported him under afflictions of another kind [the opposition of the opera faction], deserted him upon being told that a freedom from pain in the visual organs was all that he had to hope, for the remainder of his days. In this forlorn state, reflecting on his inability to conduct his entertainments, he called to his aid Mr. Smith, a son of him who had for many years been his copyist and faithful friend; and with this assistance oratorios continued to be performed even to that Lent season in which he died, and this with no other abatement in his own performance than the accompaniment by the harpsichord; the rich vein of his fancy ever supplying him with subjects for extempore voluntaries on the organ, and his hand retaining the power of executing whatever his invention suggested.*

For the rest of 1751, apart from four bank transactions, there is no record of Handel's activities. No doubt he was still adjusting to the profound changes in lifestyle his handicap was forcing on him – including the difficulty of reading with just one eye. Still, he was considering what kind of Lenten oratorio season he would present in the spring of 1752. And despite his new affliction he nearly outdid himself.

Probably with help of J.C. Smith the younger, he mounted a full and prosperous Lenten concert season featuring his most popular oratorios and the debut of *Jephtha*. In January, Thomas Harris had told his brother James:

> *I hope you have thoughts of coming to town this spring. Handel, you know, has composed Jephtha: and I am sorry to say that I believe this*

Lent will be the last that he will ever be able to preside at an oratorio; for he breaks very much [i.e., takes breaks often], & is I think quite blind on one eye.[3]

Thomas repeated his fears to James a few weeks later, and told his brother that Lord Brooke (Francis Greville, First Lord Brooke of Warwick Castle) was of the same opinion. Thomas was no doubt still hoping that James would make the trip from Salisbury to London for this last chance to revel in their friend Handel's genius while it could still be communicated through the composer in the flesh. But Thomas Harris and Lord Brooke hadn't reckoned with Handel's emotional and spiritual depth and iron will, which would take him through that season and subsequent ones to the end of his life – seven years later.

The 1752 season began on February 14 and 19 with a revival of *Joshua*. Two days later it was *Hercules* (performed just once).[*] *Jephtha* debuted on February 26 (repeated on the 28th and March 4). Three performances of *Samson* followed (March 6, 11 and 13), then *Judas Maccabaeus* (March 18 and 20). The season ended with *Messiah* (March 25 and 26). On April 9 the annual *Messiah* at the Foundling Hospital took place, once again with Handel playing the organ.

However, things were not to continue in that manner. Sometime in August 1752 Handel suffered the "Paralytick disorder in his Head" that blinded his other eye, and the couching by Bromfield occurred that November. To add to his misery, at the end of that year (December 5) his cousin and good friend Christian August Rotth died. If Handel's total blindness "did not totally incapacitate him from study, or the power of entertaining the public," as Hawkins put it, it exacted an ever greater toll.[3] His general health noticably deteriorated, as contemporary comments reveal, which can be interpreted as the systemic problems associated with arteritic AION beginning to show themselves.

Besides an unreliable report in the *Cambridge Chronicle* in January 1753 that Handel had regained his sight, there are mentions of him in his friends' letters in 1753: he went on with his oratorio season, despite his waning health. Comments

---

[*]When Handel first presented *Hercules* on Jan. 5, 1745, he had called it a "musical drama," and on Feb. 24, 1749, an "oratorio"; in this 1752 season he uses no descriptor at all. Calling *Hercules* an oratorio betrays a looser definition of the word, which had always previously been applied only to biblically based works. Handel seems to have preferred the traditional definition, since he now does not call *Hercules* an oratorio, and in no other case does he refer to a "secular" work as an oratorio.

by John Upton on February 12 are upbeat, but Upton hadn't yet seen Handel at the oratorios. Upton was on his way from London to Rochester, but hoped first "to steal to town to hear our blind bard, whose muses have not left him though they have amerc'd him of his eyes." (The previous February, a year after Handel's initial blindness, Upton had told James Harris, "I am constant attendant on Mr. Handle; just as the brutes were on Orpheus; to hear, admire, & stare.")

In March 1753, Lady Shaftesbury described Handel at a Lenten performance of *Alexander's Feast* as "the great[,] th'unhappy Handel dejected, wan and dark." While several of those adjectives of course refer to Handel's state of mind and spirit, "wan" indicates that he looked pale and ill, and in fact, Lady Shaftesbury originally wrote "pale," instead of "dark." (That need not be a contradiction. She probably realized that "wan" implied "pale," so she changed "pale" to "dark" to indicate Handel's general spirit as well as an allusion to the darkness caused by his blindness.) At the same time, Lady Shaftesbury chided those of her society who were too arch and superficial to support Handel in his need:

> [He was] sitting by, not playing on the harpsichord, and to think how his light has been spent by being over-ply'd in musicks cause; I was sorry too to find the audience so insipid and tasteless (I may add unkind) not to give the poor man the comfort of applause, but affectation and conceit cannot discern or attend to merit.

Another rumor about Handel, reported in three London papers, was highly disconcerting to his fellow members of the Foundling Hospital board. A most unusual resolution in the April 11 general committee (board of directors) minutes is concerned with the unnerving "news" that Handel was at work on his own funeral anthem for posthumous performance at the hospital:

> The Committee taking Notice of an extraordinary Paragraph, in three of the Daily Papers on Tuesday the 3rd instant, relating to a Funeral Anthem preparing by Geo. Frederick Handel Esqr to be performed in the Chapel of this Hospital after his Death, and expressing their surprize thereat.
>
> RESOLVED[:] That the Secretary do acquaint Mr. Handel, That the said Paragraph has given this Committee great Concern; they being highly sensible, that all Well-wishers to this Charity must be desirous for the Continuance of his Life, who has been and is so great and generous a Benefactor thereto.[4]

We can only imagine how Handel might have reacted to a letter or visit from the board secretary conveying this information! This rumor-disguised-as-news traveled fast. A little later that spring a paper in Handel's hometown, the *Hallische Zeitung*, took it up, surely causing Handel's remaining relatives even greater consternation that it had the Foundling Hospital board. This Halle report gives a clue as to what the London papers had said. Likened to two of history's previous blind masters Homer and Milton in not allowing "his muse to remain idle," Handel was said to be working on "perhaps his last opus" which "is to become his echo, and after his death is to be sung in the Foundling Hospital, and the profits which are earned by it he this made over to this House."

That year's Foundling Hospital *Messiah* was presented on May 1. Presumably, Handel's presence there, along with his (unrecorded) earlier verbal reassurances, put the hospital representatives and some portion of the public at ease regarding his supposedly imminent death.

Not a week after *Messiah* another of Handel's oratorios (*Judas Maccabaeus*) was heard, with his blessing, and for the benefit of another charitable institution, the Lock Hospital. Lock Hospital – despite its medieval-era name, which connoted unwilling incarceration of patients – was London's first voluntary hospital for the treatment of venereal diseases in both women and men. Handel would soon become a governor of the hospital, while he continued to maintain his close association with the Foundling Hospital. But we don't know whether he was in attendance at this concert. William Bromfield, who was surgeon to the Princess of Wales and who had couched Handel, was a founder of the hospital (1746). Perhaps through his medical association with Handel, Bromfield convinced him of the necessity and worthiness of this somewhat controversial charity. The necessity of treating those who were spreading venereal diseases, both for the patients' sake and society's, had become quite clear. Handel was not the kind of person to shy away from helping such an institution just because some would frown on offering such help to presumed willful sinners.*

---

*Near the end of the century the hospital would propose an "Asylum for the Reception of Penitent Female Patients," which would open in 1792, five years after the proposal. It would be a refuge for "fallen" women who had been treated at the hospital and who wanted to leave lives of promiscuity, but who had no home or steady life to which to return. They were taught skills which it was hoped would help them get jobs in accordance with their social "station."

There was at the time, of course, a stigma on venereal diseases: in most cases such poxes could be presumed to be self-inflicted by immoral behavior (albeit immoral behavior that cut across all class lines). As a consequence, some people thought that treatment would encourage such behavior, and so they did not support Lock Hospital. This is no doubt why the advertisement which announced the benefit performance of *Judas Maccabaeus* on May 7 at the King's Theater does not mention Lock Hospital by name. It says merely that money raised would go "towards the Increase of a Fund for Extending the BUILDING of a PUBLIC CHARITY."[5] (The hospital chaplain from 1758 to 1780 would be Martin Madan, whose life we will see intersecting with Handel's in the year leading up to the composer's death.)

At the end of 1753, Handel's charitable spirit further showed itself. He subscribed to the four volumes of *The Works of late Aaron Hill*. Hill had died in 1750, and this posthumous collection was published to benefit his widow and children. Hill wasn't an exceptional writer, but Handel no doubt had fond memories of the man who wrote the libretto for the first, wildly successful opera by the confident young Saxon newly arrived in London – and Handel could now smile at the wisdom of Hill's early attempts to get him to turn his prodigious talent to dramatic works with English texts.

Amidst several reports of Handel playing organ concertos at the oratorio concerts as well as he ever did, there is also a heart-rending description of him during that same oratorio season. It shows the extent to which his health was deteriorating (but at the same time, his strong will to continue with his work), written in May 1753 by Miss C. Gilbert to Elizabeth Harris:

> You ask'd me about poor Handel. I paid my _devoir_ to him at the oratorio, and cou'd have cry'd at the sight of him[.] He is fallen away, pale, feeble, old, blind, in short every thing that cou'd most affect one, & his playing is the monument of a great genius, not at all a living one. There is not in the man soul or spirit enough left to make it so. I was told, at the Total Eclipse in Samson, he cry'd like an infant. Thank God I did not see it.[6]

The reference to "Total Eclipse" is the aria Samson sings after having had his eyes gouged out by the Philistines. This aria and its surrounding scene, which speaks of the effect of blindness on body and soul, and offers a prayer to the Author of Light, must have pierced Handel's dispirited heart, inevitably causing him to put himself in Samson's place:

20. His Muses Have Not Left Him

Total eclipse! No sun, no moon!
All dark amidst the blaze of noon!
Oh, glorious light! No cheering ray
To glad my eyes with welcome day!
Why thus depriv'd Thy prime decree?
Sun, moon, and stars are dark to me!

Earlier, in Dublin, Mary Delaney had drawn her own connection from Handel's blindness to how hearing his "Total eclipse" might affect him. Out of her deep empathy for her old friend, she wrote to her sister Ann on Nov. 25, 1752: "Poor Handel! How feelingly must he recollect the *'total eclipse.'*" On December 16 in another letter to Ann, Mary described having been at a *Messiah* rehearsal in Dublin. (The letter provides further proof of the talkativeness of eighteenth century audiences – a characteristic which, particularly because of the nature of the work, Mary couldn't abide.) Because *Messiah* always affected her so deeply, spiritually and emotionally (and perhaps brought tears), she admitted:

I was a little afraid of it ... but am glad I went, as I felt great comfort from it, and I had the good fortune to have Mrs. Bernard sit by me, the Primate's sister, a most worthy sensible woman, of an exalted mind; it adds greatly to the satisfaction of such an entertainment to be seated by those who have the same relish for it we have ourselves. The babblers of my acquaintance were at a distance, indeed I took care to place myself as far from them as I could. Do you remember our snug enjoyment of Theodora? I could not help thinking with great concern of poor Handel, and lamenting his dark and melancholy circumstances; but his mind I hope will still be enlightened for the benefit of all true lovers of harmony.

Also at the end of 1752, Benjamin Victor, a slightly more distant Handel admirer (he did not personally know Handel) wrote of the profound reaction *Messiah* elicited in him. He recalls a mesmerizing London performance that Handel conducted. His vivid personal testimony to a clergyman friend, written while still in the after-glow of a performance, succinctly describes what many people to this day have experienced in *Messiah*:

You must be a lover of music—If Handel's Messiah should be performed in London, as it undoubtedly will in the lent season, I beg it as a favour to me, that you will go early, and take your wife with you,

285

your time and money cannot be so well employed; take care to get a book of the oratorio some days before, that you may well digest the subject, there you will hear glad tidings and truly divine rejoicings at the birth of Christ, and feel real sorrows for his sufferings—but, oh! When those sufferings are over, what a transporting full chorus! where all the instruments, and three sets of voices are employed to express ... "Lift up your head, O ye gates! ... As much as I detest fatigue and inconvenience, I would ride forty miles in the wind and rain to be present at a performance of the Messiah in London, under the conduct of Handel–I remember it there–He had an hundred instruments, and fifty voices! O how magnificent the full choruses.[7]

~

Burney's account of Handel's blindness (written in 1785) puts the composer in the august company of Homer and Milton, as the 1753 newspaper story of his work on his own funeral anthem had. Burney accentuates the positive, writing at length about how Handel was able to keep working. His description of Handel at concerts in his last years may give an inadvertent clue to at least part of the reason why some in the audiences reacted callously, as Lady Shaftesbury described. Though loss of sight was not uncommon if one had managed to live into old age, blindness seems to have been a condition that elicited either pity or revulsion (as is also evident in the tenor of a remark by Mainwaring about Handel's elderly blind mother).[*]

This is confirmed by Burney when he says that Handel was embarrassed by his blindness; this embarrassment was no doubt caused in the supremely independent Handel by his perceived "weakness," which required a childlike dependence on others. Despite the fact that his mental vigor and playing ability had not abated, audiences reacted as if his person and manhood had been diminished by

---

[*]*Mainwaring's account of Handel's visit to his elderly mother near the end of her life exhibits pity, and perhaps something more: the visit "promised [Handel] but a melancholy interview" due to her "extreme old age and total blindness"; and her condition "rendered this influence of [Handel's] duty and regard the more necessity" (Mainwaring, p. 73). Frau Händel had suffered a reduction in vision the year before a paralytic stroke in 1729 (the year of Handel's last visit) which affected her right side, tongue and functional vision. She died of *"marasmum senile"* (Charles de St. Yves, A New Treatise of the Diseases of the Eyes, translated by J. Stockton, London, 1741, in Donald L. Blanchard, "George Handel and His Blindness," *Documenta Ophtalmologica* 99: 247-258, 1999).

his blindness. Seeing him blind and dependent on others made them so uncomfortable that their pleasure in the music was diminished. They couldn't cope with the sight of a man of such powerful genius, energy and spirit now having to be led to the organ as a child might be:

> However it might dispirit and embarrass him[,] at other times, had no effect on his nerves or intellects, in public: as he continued to play concertos and voluntaries between the parts of his Oratorios to the last, with the same vigour of thought and touch, for which he was ever so justly renowned. To see him, however, led to the organ, after this calamity, at upward of seventy years of age, and then conducted towards the audience to make his accustomed obeisance, was a sight so truly afflicting and deplorable to persons of sensibility, as greatly diminished their pleasure, in hearing him perform.[8]

Not everyone reacted in that manner, however. A letter to Elizabeth Harris in Salisbury from a neighbor staying in London indicates that many people in Handel's audiences were able to become reconciled to his blindness, and his friends fully supported him:

> The oratorios were never more constantly full than this spring and I am told that many people make such a point of serving Handle under his present calamity that if they are prevented from being there in person they send their half guineas.

Handel's "inventive powers" did not quickly abandon him, and his oratorios were drawing good crowds. Burney describes how Handel dealt with playing his organ concertos:

> During the Oratorio season, I have been told, that he practiced almost incessantly; and, indeed, that must have been the case, or his memory uncommonly retentive; for, after his blindness, he played several of his old organ-concertos, which must have been previously impressed on his memory by practice. At last, however, he rather chose to trust to his inventive powers, than those of reminiscence: for, giving the band only the skeleton, or ritornels of each movement, he played all the solo parts extempore, while the other instruments left him, ad libitum; waiting for the signal of a shake, before they played such fragments of symphony as they found in their books.

Thomas Harris was enthusiastic about Handel's organ playing at the March

28, 1753, performance of *Judas Maccabaeus* to "a very full house of good company." Handel played a voluntary, "full as well in point of invention, execution & all other respects as ever was heard, and I think I never heard so good a one from him but once before, which was I think the last time of last season."* After remarking on Handel's excellent playing, Thomas couldn't resist speculating on his friend's monetary take for the season (as others had before him): "I suppose he won't get less than fifteen hundred or two thousand pound."

Despite his ebbing health, Handel's seasons went very well in 1752 and 1753. His music – oratorios, operas or opera excerpts, *te deums*, anthems, songs and various orchestral works – was ubiquitous (in spite of signs that musical tastes were changing, ushering in of a new musical age). Handel, Handel everywhere was no doubt resented by those who disliked both him and his music. All these years, a variety of Handel's works was still being regularly performed, often for charity: in other venues in London, in various English cities outside London (including an ongoing concert series in Salisbury run by James Harris), in Dublin, and on the Continent. During February and March 1754, Handel's works appeared in the ads of three different London theaters.

In January 1754, a misunderstanding between the Foundling Hospital and Handel erupted. In a most uncharitable gesture the hospital attempted to take for itself the exclusive right to perform *Messiah*, based on their association with Handel and the oratorio's annual performances at the hospital. In Hawkins' words, they wished to "prohibit, under penalties, the performance of the Messiah by any others than Mr. Handel and themselves." In order to do this, the hospital board had to approach Parliament so that such an act could be passed, which they prepared to do. Their drafted petition for Parliament reads:

> ...*That in order to raise a further sum for the benefit of the said charity, George Frederick Handel, esq;, hath been charitably pleased to give to this Corporation a composition of musick, called 'The Oratorio of the*

---

*Thomas Harris says Handel played a voluntary, not a concerto (he surely knew the difference). A voluntary for solo organ rather than a concerto accompanied by orchestra would be the easiest and most satisfying way for Handel to play in public now, as it would allow him to invent and play whatever he pleased, without reference to the orchestra. However, at the April 4 performance of *Samson* Handel played a concerto (Thomas Harris to Elizabeth Harris, April 5, 1753). Its seems logical that Handel might sometimes still play concertos and at other times voluntaries, depending on how he was feeling.

Messiah' composed by him the said George Frederick Handel, reserving to himself the liberty only of performing the same for his own benefit during his life: and whereas the said benefaction cannot be secured to the sole use of your petitioners except by the authority of Parliament your petitioners, therefore, humbly pray, that leave may be given to bring in a Bill for the purpose aforesaid.[9]

Whoever among the hospital governors proposed this attempt to acquire exclusive rights to *Messiah* greatly misunderstood Handel and his charitable spirit. He was not amused. In fact, he was furious. Even some time later, the thought of it greatly perturbed him:

To facilitate the passing of a law for the purpose, Mr. Handel's concurrence was asked, but he was so little sensible of the propriety of it, that upon the bare mention of it he broke out in to a furious passion, which he vented in the following terms: 'For vat sal de Foundlings put mein oratorio in de Parliament? Te Teuffel! Mein musik sal not go to de Parlement.'[*]

We can imagine what Handel told the board members who must have visited him to explain the idea and read the petition to him. The subsequent board minutes, in supremely veiled understatement, noted, "The same did not seem agreeable to Mr. Handel for the present." But, as in other instances when his temper flared and cooled, Handel put the incident behind him. It is very unlikely that in the heat of this incident he ever considered cutting off his association with the hospital. Not only did the Foundling Hospital *Messiah* performances continue, but later, in the third codicil to his will drawn up on August 4, 1757, he stipulated: "I give a fair copy of the Score and all Parts of my Oratorio called The Messiah to the Foundling Hospital."[**]

---

[*]"For what [Why] shall the Foundlings put my oratorio in Parliament? The devil! My music shall not go to Parliament!"

[**]Hawkins's account of the Parliamentary petition incident sets the hospital's presumptions about *Messiah* against the background of Handel's benefit performances and having given the hospital a copy of the score, which together "gave them such a title to it as seemed to import an exclusive right to the performance of it" (Hawkins, p. 891). It is possible that Handel had already in 1753-54 mentioned his intention to bequeath a "fair copy" of the score to the hospital. Or Hawkins assumed that the hospital's great presumption in trying to claim exclusive rights must have been based on their ownership of this score as well as on Handel's personal

Another kind of agitation of Handel's spirits occurred a few months later (in 1754) with the re-publicizing of the mean-spirited pig-snouted caricature of him as a glutton by his former friend from the theater world, Joseph Goupy. An engraving of Goupy's cartoon, "The Charming Brute," reappeared on March 21, 1754, along with two stanzas of verse concluding that Handel's sole devotion was to eat. Only Handel's worst enemies would have thought that that had ever applied to him; but now, in his elderly, blind and declining state, it is hard to imagine that even they could truly believe it. If this was a calculated move by Goupy or others (why else would the caricature have been resuscitated from a forgotten past?), the cartoon's reappearance at this point bordered on the sadistic.*

Times were changing. A company producing a new generation of Italian operas had some time since been reincarnated at the Haymarket Theater. In fact, its operas were "flourish[ing] beyond any that have been in England for many years," according to Elizabeth Harris's friend Miss Gilbert.[10] Yet, almost unbelievably, during the 1755 season several of the opera's aristocratic backers were yet again trying to undermine the elderly Handel and his oratorios by deliberately planning other entertainments on Wednesdays and Fridays, the two nights when oratorios were performed. Again, the news came from Thomas Harris, to his brother James:

I am sorry to give so bad account as I am obliged to do about oratorios. Handel has performed Alexander's Feast twice, and yesterday Allegro & Pens[eroso] & the new ode [for St. Cecilia's Day]: his houses have been very thin, especially last night when he hardly paid his expenses. I am told that Lady Coventry has routs at her house on Wednesdays and Lady Carlisle on Fridays where the world assemble to the no small detriment of our great genius[,] now almost worn out with age and loss of sight.

At the beginning of February, Thomas Harris wondered to James whether

---

association with them. On the other hand, compression of events into time periods that don't actually fit the details of the facts is fairly common in the contemporary biographical accounts of Handel – of which we've seen other examples.

*A surprisingly tenacious story, first stated by William T. Whitley in 1928, has survived to our day: that Goupy forfeited a legacy from Handel because of the caricature. But there is no reliable primary source that says Handel ever intended to remember Goupy in his will.

a satirical soliloquy that the famous actor David Garrick had used to introduce the February 3 debut of an English opera *The Fairies* by Handel's amenuensis J.C. Smith Jr. would "stirr up a party ... from among the friends of the Italian opera ... to oppose" Smith's opera, and by extension, Handel's oratorios. Garrick's prologue satirized Italian opera but had ended with praise of Handel's ability to "the coldest breasts inspire." That being so, Garrick questioned why the Master's pupil would be so rash as to attempt an opera; the actor concluded that "if through the clouds appear some glimm'ring rays,/They're sparks he caught from his great master's blaze!" Garrick's appreciation of Handel was apparently genuine (but his questioning of Smith's audacity was at least partly tongue-in-cheek, since he himself had written the libretto). Still, Harris surmised that Garrick's praise of Handel might irritate the opera faction and make them more determined to undermine Handel (and Smith). Smith, who not only worked for Handel but would be seen as his "successor," was conducting his opera on Monday and Thursday and Handel's oratorios on Wednesday and Friday during the week of February 17.

On the other hand, like the renewed opera faction, composer Thomas Arne had no scruples about directly competing with Handel. That Lent (1755) he scheduled several of his own oratorios on two Wednesdays and two Fridays, which, Thomas Harris noted disgustedly, "from the perverse spirit of the generation may probably be crowded." (As much as two years earlier, when some in the theater world tried to get around the general prohibition against performances during Holy Week itself, the Lord Chamberlain came down on them, "strictly charg[ing] and command[ing]" that there be no such performances "for the future on any Pretence whatsoever.") Mary Delany was in London for the 1755 season and told her sister:

The oratorio was miserably thin; the Italian opera is in high vogue, and always full, though one song of the least worthy of Mr. Handel's music is worth all their frothy compositions.

On March 30, 1755, William Shenstone told Lady Luxborough, "I was shewn a Letter yesterday from Sr Harry Gough to Mr. Pixell [a minister and amateur composer] which said Sir H. laments that the town at Present is much fonder of Arne than Handel." Yet even though London's tastes were now moving toward a new style – a sign of the Enlightenment beginning to take hold there –

Handel's oratorios were being heard outside London more than ever.*

The reappearance of Goupy's caricature during the 1754 oratorio season must have been meant to strike at Handel and stir up controversy, and to divert the aristocratic, fashionable segment of his audiences. In contrast, at the end of Handel's season, "at the particular Desire of several Persons of Quality," performances of *L'Allegro ed il Penseroso* and the *Ode for St. Cecilia's Day* were performed at the Covent Garden Theater (where John Rich was still the manager), likely as a specific show of support for Handel by the aristocrats who were in his camp.

However, that was again followed the next season by the concerted efforts of Lady Coventry and Lady Carlisle to siphon off Handel's audiences. With all this going on, it is no wonder that early the next spring, Miss Gilbert expressed concern to Elizabeth Harris for Handel's weakening state, and the fact that many who claimed to appreciate him were not "protecting" him and were being swayed by fashion (the new opera faction). Miss Gilbert showed great sympathy for Handel as a person even while admitting, "[His music] never gave me pleasure." She recognized its merit, however, and considered herself "never worthy of him." She then asserted:

> *Poor Handel has been most ungratefully neglected this year, and whoever were admirers of him when in perfection ought I think to protect him in his decline. Fashion in every thing will have most followers, and consequently he is quite forsaken.*

---

*In 1755 and early 1756, besides Handel's own oratorio season, his music was heard throughout England: an unnamed oratorio, a benefit for "Miss Turner" (March 11, Great Room, Dean Street, Soho); *Judas Maccabaeus* and *Messiah* (March 17, 31, Music Room, Holywell, Oxford); miscellaneous pieces at a benefit for the Decay'd Musicians Fund (March 17, King's Theater, Haymarket, London); *Athalia* (May 5, July 10, Music Room, Oxford); *Acis and Galatea, Alexander's Feast, Judas Maccabaeus, L'Allegro ed il Penseroso* (June 23 and 30, July 2, Aug. 4, Oxford); *Judas Maccabaeus* and *Sampson* (April 30 and May 3, Theater in Orchard-Street, Bath); *Alexander's Feast* and *Messiah* (May 14 and 17, Mr. Wiltshire's Room, Bath); a benefit: *Samson* and miscellaneous pieces (Sept. 10-11, "Three Choirs" festival, Cathedral Church, Worcester); the *Ode for St. Cecilia's Day* and *Utrecht Te Deum* (Nov. 24, Oxford); *Messiah*, inauguration of the new Music Room (Jan. 14, 1756, Bristol).

Jackson's Oxford Journal reported, Jan. 24, 1756, that a Feb. 2 performance of *Esther* had been postponed from a week earlier "with the Hopes of making the Boys tolerably perfect in their Parts; being all very young and inexperienced, and upon that Account hope favourable Allowances will be made." *Acis and Galatea* was performed on Feb. 26 at Trinity College Hall, Cambridge, "before a numerous Audience" And in the distant American Colonies two "songs" (arias) by Handel graced the March 18 dedication of a new organ at the City Hall of New York. (See Deutsch, pp. 758-767, 769-770.)

For those Londoners not inclined toward music, there were plays, masquerades, and other entertainments to beguile them, and tastes in all the arts and across society were changing. While Handel's music, and especially *Messiah*, would peculiarly endure through the subsequent generations, for now he and his oratorios were showing signs of belonging to the previous age. A new age was emerging and, in fact, had just dawned. By mid-century, the Baroque period – the last manifestation of the spirit of the Reformation era – gave way to the Age of Enlightenment. In music, the "gallant" style was the rage. It is frothy and superficial by Baroque standards, and particularly by the standards of the Baroque's greatest representatives, Handel and Bach.

Chapter 21
The Third & Last & Degenerate Age of Music

The changing social and cultural context elicited increasingly frequent discussions among music lovers about the future of the art. James Harris's prognosis, written on New Year's Eve 1753 in a long letter to Sir John Hawkins, was glum:

> *I fear we now live at the conclusion of ["the age of perfection"], & that the days are hastening on, when harmony will be forgot, & melody alone be cultivated. This I call the third & last & degenerate age of music, when it will hardly deserve the name of an art, being wholly bereft of all principles of science. Most of the Italian pieces of music (for compositions I can not call them) which have been lately printed in England, fully answer this last character.* [1]

Handel's music, however, was still giving Harris reason to rejoice:

> *You could not do better than begin your musical studies, as you tell me, with Corelli, Geminiani, & Handel.... Handel for rapidity of invention, & for the universality of his ideas, the sublime, the terrible, the pathetic & every other, has exceeded all that ever I have yet heard of, or ever expect to hear of. Nor is he more to be admired for his invention, than his art, in which he has given samples, that none have transcended, & but few been able to equal.*

An example of a public discussion of the issue came in an exchange between the minor composer, organist and critic Charles Avison (1709-1770) and an Oxford music professor, William Hayes, in 1752-53. Avison, a native of the northern city of Newcastle, had briefly gone to London early in his career (ca. 1734-35) to study with violinist-composer Francesco Geminiani. Burney called Avison the first English music critic, and generally approved of him, though there were others who felt that Avison's critical skills were not well-honed. In 1752, in an *Essay on Musical Expression*, Avison defends Geminiani and a small handful of other composers (especially Rameau, Scarlatti and Benedetto Marcello) while saying very little about Handel, the greatest of them all. (That he doesn't mention Bach is another reminder that Bach's music was almost unknown outside Germany; and even within Germany, Bach was now dead and gone and his music part of the previous age.)

Avison's "ridiculous Fondness and Partiality to some Masters," Hayes asserted, caused him to deliberately – but quite unsuccessfully – "draw a Veil over and eclipse [Handel's] great and glorious character." Avison describes at length the excellencies of Rameau's opera choruses, but in response Hayes called Avison's opinions "industriously placed directly under the *little* he says of Mr. Handel, or as it were in his very Face." Avison ignored Handel's acknowledged reputation as the master of chorus writing. But, Hayes declared:

> Were a thousand of these puny Performances [of Rameau's opera choruses] opposed to one Oratorio Chorus of Mr. Handel, it would swallow them up, even as the Rod of AARON converted into a Serpent, devoured those of the Magicians. *

Hayes also called Avison to task for ignoring the native-born English composers; and for neglecting to discuss, in an essay on musical expression, Handel's superb talent in creating such "*pictoresque* Arrangement[s] of musical Sounds" that "his Pictures *speak*." As examples, Hayes cited *L'Allegro ed il Penseroso* and *Israel in Egypt*. In the latter "truly sublime Composition," Handel "exerted every Power human Nature is capable of" to create musical sounds that so aptly describe "inarticulate Nature." (Hayes reference is to the musical "word painting" and evocative power of Handel's depiction of Israel's oppression, the Ten Plagues, the frenzy of the pursuing Egyptians and Israel's rejoicing at deliverance.)

Hayes had several more criticisms of Avison's critique. He figured Avison defended Geminiani out of duty or gratitude to his old teacher, and that he set Geminiani up against Handel out of envy of Handel's supremacy in both instrumental and vocal/choral music, and of the acclaim he had long received. Hayes ends with a summary of Handel, as composer and man, with which most music lovers would have concurred. That he mentions Handel's person along with his works is not surprising: it was self-evident that one's good works, musical and otherwise, revealed one's excellent character; conversely, it was considered a truism that a person of questionable or immoral character was not capable of producing *sublime* works:

> The Man ... hath maintained his Ground against all Oppos-
> ers:—Who at the Age of Seventy, with a broken Constitution, produced
> such a Composition [Jephtha] which no Man mentioned in the Essay

---

*A carefully chosen illustration, as Hayes's readers would recognize his allusion to Moses and Aaron before Pharaoh, thus to Handel's *Israel in Egypt*, which he afterwards mentions by name.

beside, either is, or ever was (so far as it hath appeared to us) equal to, in his highest Vigour;—And, to the Astonishment of all Mankind, at the same Period of Life, performed Wonders on the Organ, both set Pieces and extempore:—*I say, perhaps you may expect me to enter into Particulars, to defend and characterize this Man;—but the first would be an endless Undertaking;—his Works being almost out of Number.—The second, a needless one, the Works themselves being his best Defence:—And the third, I must acknowledge is above my Capacity; and therefore once more refer you to his Works, where only his true character is to be found; except in the Hearts of Thousands [of] his Admirers. Thus far as a Musician only[.] As a moral, good, and charitable Man, let Infants, not only those who feel the Effects of his Bounty, but even such who are yet unborn, chaunt forth his Praise,* whose annual Benefaction to an Hospital for the Maintenance of the Forsaken, the Fatherless, and those who have none to help them, *will render HIM and his MESSIAH, truly Immortal and crowned with Glory, by the KING OF KINGS and LORD OF LORDS.*

Avison, naturally, wrote a response to Hayes. He set it down in the form of a letter to a friend in London and later published it as an appendix to the second edition of the *Essay on Musical Expression*. Avison pulled no punches, as he must have felt Hayes had not. Hayes's accusation that Avison had denigrated their own English composers drew this retort:

Everyone will easily perceive his Reason for quoting and perverting [my Essay, namely,] to take off the Odium from such meagre Composers as himself, and to throw it all upon the Character of Mr. HANDEL.

Avison chided Hayes for inappropriate over-familiarity towards Handel (having called him "brother"), and defends his own neglecting to discuss Handel with the English composers because, after all, Handel was not an Englishman; the fact that he had long since become a naturalized citizen did not make him an Englishman in people's perceptions, though they were happy to acknowledge his choosing to settle among them). Further, Handel was "first educated in the Italian School" and composed and directed Italian operas for many years. (Not surprisingly, Avison seemed unaware of the extent to which Handel's grounding in the German Lutheran tradition affected his style.)

Avison concluded by likening Handel to the great poet Dryden: what

Dryden is to poetry Handel is to music. This turns out to be a somewhat backhanded compliment, however. Both Dryden and Handel are "nervous" ("vigorous" and "powerful" in eighteenth century meaning) and "exalted and harmonious" – but "voluminous" as well, "and consequently, not always correct." Thus, though their abilities are equal to those of anyone, "their Execution [is] frequently inferior." By *voluminous* Avison means full of turnings, windings or convolutions. He was referring to Handel's frequent use of the fugue and other counterpoint, which was already at that point striking modern listeners attuned to the new style as far too complicated and thickly textured. It is also notable that this assessment doesn't admit that Handel's abilities were superior to those of the other composers Avison discusses, as virtually any music lover of the previous decades would readily have acknowledged (and which superiority we, even more readily, can see). In fact, in saying that Handel's (and Dryden's) execution didn't live up to his abilities Avison went further:

> Born with Genius capable of soaring the boldest Flights they have
> sometimes, to suit the vitiated Taste of the Age they lived in, descended
> to the lowest.

Feeling perhaps that he had gone too far, or possibly to shield himself a little from too-harsh criticism, Avison quickly adds: "Yet ... their Excellencies are infinitely more numerous than their Deficiencies." Though Handel and Dryden are not "Models of Perfection," they are "glorious examples of those amazing Powers that actuate the human Soul," said Avison.

~

The last years of Handel's life were by no means unremitting drudgery and sorrow. Though his health generally declined and he could no longer compose on a grand scale, or conduct, he could of course still hear his music. He could still do some revising of old music and even a little composing of new, with J.C. Smith's help. He could instruct Smith on how he wanted the oratorios performed. He could still play the harpsichord and organ. He could accept visits from friends, and occasionally make visits to them. And he was not financially destitute – nor anything close to it. He could also dictate letters. We have one of these, from September 20, 1754. (Only the signature is in Handel's handwriting. And there is now just one date on it: in 1752, Britain had finally adopted the Gregorian calendar, causing it to "lose" eleven days, but bringing it in line with continental Europe.) From this letter we learn a startling fact related to Telemann. The "admirably rare" plants that

Handel had sent to Telemann in 1750 were never delivered, and for an unusual reason:

> *Some time ago I had a selection of exotic plants made ready to be sent to you, when Captain John Carsten (to whom I spoke about delivering them to you) informed me that he had learnt of your death. You will not doubt that this report caused me extreme sorrow. You will therefore judge of my joy on hearing that you are in perfect health. The same Captain John Carsten, who has just arrived here from your part of the world, sent me this good news by a friend, and also [told me] that you had entrusted to him a list of exotic plants to be procured for you. I profited by this occasion with the greatest pleasure, and I have been at pains to have these plants found, and you shall have nearly all of them. As Captain Carsten is not due to leave till next December, he has been good enough to see to their despatch by the first vessel leaving here; you will find the name of the captain and the vessel on the enclosed paper. I trust that this little present which I take the liberty of offering you, will be acceptable. I pray you to send me news of your health, which I trust is excellent. I wish you all prosperity....[2]*

By modern standards it is astonishing that this scenario could take four years to play out. But merchant ships were often away for months, carrying goods to various ports and picking up others in return, and always biding time for the right conditions of tide, wind and weather – and then sailing at sedate speeds. When Captain Carsten's ship returned to its English port the first time, he may have written Handel with the news that the would-be recipient of the plants had died. But it was a more common practice to bring such news face-to-face when possible, and it is likely that Carsten traveled up to London personally to carry the sad news to Handel (indeed, the captain may have lived in London). The second time, when Carsten had *good* news, he sent a friend to convey it to Handel.

Given the probable duration of the first trip, Handel's receipt of the distressing news about Telemann may have come when he was particularly distraught about his blindness and still learning to cope with it. We can imagine his joy when Carsten's ship returned months later from a second voyage with the news that Telemann was very much alive. In fact, seventy-three-year-old Telemann was still avidly pursuing horticulture as a hobby and was still looking for specific exotic plants – a perfect opportunity for Handel to supply them once more, an opportunity Handel relished.

Given the length and warmth of their friendship, it might seem surprising that Handel told Telemann nothing of having been struck by blindness. But Handel's embarrassment may have come into play, perhaps along with his knowledge that Telemann was still apparently vigorous despite being older than Handel himself. It is quite unlikely that Handel ever talked of his struggles with blindness to any of his friends (until on his deathbed, perhaps), much less that he would dictate his very personal thoughts to J.C. Smith Jr. to be written down in stark black and white, even to a life-long friend like Telemann.

~

In 1756, Handel and Smith opened the oratorio season with *Athalia* on March 5, which was repeated on March 10 and 12. Though *Athalia* had been heard the previous year in Oxford – recall that Handel wrote it for Oxford University in 1733 – he himself had not repeated since 1735. Handel went back to several other early oratorios as well: *Israel in Egypt, Deborah, Jephtha* and the old favorite *Judas Maccabaeus*; again, the season ended with two performances of *Messiah*.

Though Handel was now forced to be idle to a degree which was completely foreign to his previous life, he tried to maintain some normalcy in contact with his friends, as his health allowed. Bernard Granville was looking for an organ suitable for his house, and he naturally got advice from Handel. Granville was still Handel's neighbor as well as friend, and would inherit from Handel a Rhine landscape painting presumed to by Rembrandt, and another presumed Rembrandt landscape which Granville had given to Handel in the first place.

Mary Delany's friend Anne Donellan, whom we met earlier, got to know Handel through Mary. She, too, had recently bought an instrument: a harpsichord, constructed by the well-known German builder Jacob Kirkman. In December (1755) she invited Handel to come and try it out.

Unusually, the following March Mary Delany attended a social gathering at the home of her friend Anne Donellan instead of going to hear *Israel in Egypt*. But she chided herself for it, as the company of the other women present left something to be desired. "How provoking!" she complained. "[Mrs. Donellan] had Mrs. Montagu, Mrs. Gosling, and two or three fiddle faddles, so that I might as well have been at the oratorio."[3] Given her earlier expressions of the spiritual worth and impact of Handel's oratorios it would be odd if she were tired of them. And her next words show that indeed she was not: "I was last night at 'Judas Maccabaeus,' it was

charming and full. 'Israel in Egypt' did not take, it is too solemn for common ears."
Mary also attended *Jephtha*, astutely telling her sister, "I never heard it before: I
think it a very fine one, but very different from any of his others." Though she didn't
elaborate on how *Jephtha* was different, she was no doubt struck by its peculiar
introspection and emotional immediacy, and her reaction was informed by her
knowledge of not only decades of Handel's music but of her friendship with the man
himself.

Mary's attendance at Mrs. Donellen's "conversation party" is notable in that
the other women present who were so unimpressive to her were part of the prominent
women's group called the Bluestockings. These were women of the new Age of
Enlightenment; they were perplexing to many because they had unconventional ideas
about how women should act and be treated. (They are often now anachronistically
described as feminists.) Their male friends included such political, philosophical and
literary luminaries as Horace Walpole, Edmund Burke and Samuel Johnson. The
universe Handel now lived in was becoming a brave new world.

That season (1756), Thomas Harris noted that the oratorios were
performed to less than full houses – "his houses have been but indifferent especially
in the pitt" – but the performances went very well, and "his own on the organ as
good as ever."[4] The pit was not what we would call the orchestra pit but the main
floor (now called the orchestra seats) where the aristocrats sat. The aristocrats'
attention was taken up once again with Italian opera, plays and other diversions.
Thomas Harris was at the season-ending April 9 *Messiah*, too. That performance
he described to James with the line, "Handel had another crowded house...." And
George Harris, also present, noted to himself in his diary that Handel played a
concerto (not a voluntary). By "another crowded house" Thomas meant that the first
performance of *Messiah* on April 7 was full, even if the previous oratorios were not.
Meanwhile, Miss Catherine Talbot reported:

> *Handel[,] who could suit such music to such words[,] deserves to be*
> *maintained, and these two nights [April 7 and 9], I am told, have*
> *made amends for the solitude of [sparse attendance at] his other*
> *oratorios. How long even this may be fashionable I know not, for next*
> *winter there will be (if the French come) two operas [opera companies];*
> *and the opera and oratorio taste are, I believe, totally incompatible.*
> *Well they may!*

Miss Talbot's surmise that "the French" might come the next season to present *opera comique* offers an opportunity to look outward to the broader world in 1756. In fact, that year marked the beginning of what would be known as the Seven Years' War, a complicated struggle in which France and Britain were enemies.

The war involved fighting across Europe (though not on English soil), in India (one of the arenas in which the British and French were rivals) and North America (the French and Indian War). It ignited, on the one hand, because of the smoldering animosity of France's and Britain's competing interests as colonial powers, and on the other hand was a struggle in Germany between the Austrians and Prussians, with Britain's and France's interests intertwined. George II was, of course, concerned for his interests in Hanover. Eventually, France, Austria, Saxony, Sweden and Russia lined up on one side, with Britain, Hanover and Prussia on the other. By the end of the war, after the Treaty of Paris of 1763, France lost most of its colonial possessions (including those in North America) and Britain emerged as *the* great colonial power – paving the way to its becoming an empire in the nineteenth century.[5] George II would die in 1760 before the war ended, so it was his grandson George III who would sign the Treaty of Paris. Nor would Handel see the end of the war, nor the reign of a new monarch.

About this time there is another account of Handel socializing; the event occurred after his 1756 season. George Harris's diary tells us:

> *Dined at Mr. Jenning's, Ormond Street.... Handel quite blind, but pretty chearfull, & after dinner play'd finely on Mr. J's piano forte. / Handel said, that Corelli was at the head of the orchestra at Rome when he [Handel] first went thither; that twas a rule with Corelli's band of music that when any one made a grace [ornamented his musical line], he should forfeit a crown; & one poor fidler lost his whole salary before he could be cured of gracing. // Handel was 2 years at Rome in Cardinal Ottoboni's family.—Handel by birth a Saxon. When first he came over to England, he played on the fiddle; but this not succeeding, he then took to the harpsichord.*[6]

Jennens, as host of this intimate dinner party, had obviously invited Handel, indicating that there was no ongoing animosity between the two men. Handel entertained the group by reminiscing about his past, telling stories from his early career. His story about Corelli surely amused his friends, and he undoubtedly told it well. He had not lost his early knack for telling a story and making humorous quips.* These last years demonstrate that, consonant with Handel's stalwart character and faith, he had accepted his blindness, adjusted adeptly and seemed determined to live well whatever remaining days God would give him.

However, the details of the mention of Handel's early career are not quite accurate: Handel's short-lived career as a violinist occurred in Hamburg; and his sojourn in Rome was apparently as much with the Marquis Ruspoli's household as with Cardinal Ottoboni's. Are these "mistakes" of Thomas Harris's in remembering the details of Handel's stories, or did the fault lie with Handel, due to a failing memory? Accounts of Handel's memory and mental state in his last few years seem contradictory. According to Mainwaring,

> *His faculties remained in their full vigour almost to the hour of his dissolution, as appeared from Songs and Chorusses, and other Compositions, which from the date of them, may almost be considered as his parting words, his last accents! This must appear the more surprising, when it is remembered to how great a degree his mind was disordered, at times, towards the latter part of his life.*

But remarks by Shaftesbury near the beginning of the next year indicate that Handel's memory (if not his inventiveness) *had* been failing, but then was suddenly "strengthened of late to an astonishing degree." Both this episodic memory loss and mental confusion could have been manifestations of systemic ailments that accompanied Handel's blindness.

Even if his memory of his early life was to some degree faulty, the evening at Jennens's home was another demonstration that neither his expert keyboard playing nor his improvising had been affected – nor would they be. His innate talent, combined with those skills ingrained in him since childhood, assured that he would never lose this ability. As Burney wrote, Handel "manifested his power of invention in extemporaneous flights of fancy to be as rich and rapid, a week before his decease, as they had been for many years."

---

*Handel's delightful Corelli story demonstrates a problem which can still plague Baroque music: performers who get carried away with improvised ornamentation. Most ornaments (trills, ad libbing melodic lines, etc.) were applied on the repeat of a section of music, as, for example, in a **da capo aria** such as *Messiah*'s "The Trumpet Shall Sound." But if players and/or singers get caught up in the "more is better" spirit, the ornamentation feels fussy and obtrusive; or as Mary Delany aptly put it, it would "introduce froth and nonsense" (Dec. 10, 1750).

That summer of 1756 Handel decided he had better update his will. It had been six years since the will was written and some of its intended benefactors had since died. His gradually declining state of health contrasted with his now very comfortable state of wealth. He added £200 to his servant Peter le Blond's bequest and made various other additions to legacies for relatives, and for two of his oratorio librettists, Thomas Morell (£200) and Newburgh Hamilton (£100). In case anyone had forgotten, Handel described Hamilton as he "who has assisted me in adjusting words for some of my Compositions."[7]

As co-executor of his estate along with his niece, Handel named George Amyand, a businessman and fellow native German who had moved to England. Handel no doubt concluded that it would be prudent to have at least one executor who actually lived in London. The £200 awarded Amyand would be a token of thanks "for the Care and Trouble he shall take in my Affairs." Thomas Harris and John Hetherington, witnesses to this first codicil, were both lawyers whom Handel had seen at Jennens's home a few months before; perhaps that gave him the idea to ask that favor. Thomas Harris was, of course, a staunch supporter and friend of Handel's – and personally the closest to Handel of the three Harris brothers.[*] In a third codicil drawn up the next year, Charles Jennens, who was vastly wealthy, would be remembered with paintings of an old man and an old woman by Denner. Clearly, that gift, too, was one of friendship, not based on need like most of the bequests Handel made.

Sometime that same year Handel subscribed to a "Collection of Songs With Symphonies and a Thorough Bass, With Six Lessons for the Harpsichord."[8] The composer was a woman, Elizabeth Turner, who was active in London during the 1750s, and perhaps as late as the 1780s. Her collection exhibits the emerging Classical style. Though the details of Turner's life are mysterious, her main interest seems to have been vocal and biblically based choral works, and she herself wrote choral music; she, therefore, appears to have had a keen interest in Handel's

---

[*]James Harris is almost always cited as the Harris who was "Handel's friend." As the eldest brother James was the head of the family and was thoroughly committed to disseminating Handel's music via his own concert series in Salisbury. But if the letters between the Harris brothers and their cousin Shaftesbury are an indication, James had considerably less personal contact with Handel, and heard far fewer performances of the oratorios than did Thomas, and than did Shaftesbury and perhaps George Harris as well. James's affairs in Salisbury often kept him from coming to London.

oratorios. It is possible, even probable, that she and Handel met in the context of his oratorio performances and/or rehearsals and got to know each other to some degree. She may have showed him some of her works, and he encouraged her. That she was generally known among those involved in Handel's oratorios can be surmised from the fact that Handel's tenor John Beard also subscribed to Miss Turner's collection.

Though Handel's subscription to this collection is but a blip in his affairs from our point of view, it once again demonstrates his generosity: realistically, since he was blind, elderly and aware that his life was near its end, he had no use for such a collection. But besides the music sale, which helped Miss Turner make a living, how encouraging it must have been to her to have *Handel* subscribe to her music. (The collection, incidentally, was "printed for the author and sold in the College of Physicians, Warwick Lane." Deutsch thinks that may indicate that Miss Turner had a male relative or friend who was a physician, and who undertook helping her sell the collection.) This act is also an indication of Handel's interest in and willingness to support women whose interests and unmarried state branded them as slightly – or more than slightly – unorthodox. Elizabeth Turner was not afraid to call herself *Miss* Turner on the title page of her collection. But being a "spinster" was so socially uncomfortable (as it would be well into the twentieth century despite great advances for women) that many unmarried women called themselves *Mrs.* to avoid automatic stigma, as Ann Donellan did. Being also unmarried, Handel was surely aware that were it not for his sex, he too would have suffered the peculiar problems that unmarried women faced.

He would soon also show appreciation and support to several other unmarried women by leaving them small bequests in the fourth and final codicil to his will, drawn up three days before his death: to Ann Donellan (50 guineas) and the widows Mayne (50 guineas) and Palmer (£100). Handel also helped widows in his own family, as he had long previously aided Zachau's widow. It is safe to assume that his life-long empathy for widows developed in large part from his knowledge of what widowhood was like for his mother.

Chapter 22
Before the Bard is Silenced

The new year, 1757, turned out to be exceptional. Shaftesbury told James Harris in early February:

Mr. Handel is better than he has been for some years: and finds he can compose chorus's as well as other music, to his own (and consequently to the hearers) satisfaction. His memory is strengthened of late to an astonishing degree. This intelligence must give you pleasure.[1]

Handel took advantage of his temporary physical and mental reprieve, and it naturally heartened him and gladdened his friends. He showed an interest in composing again, and began to add arias to various works (the actual writing done by J.C. Smith the younger). Most modern scholars see these insertions as primarily composed by Smith, based on ideas Handel gave him. If so, the best of the new insertions is an exception: the duet and chorus "Sion now her head shall raise," which Handel originally used in *Esther* and then in *Judas Maccabaeus* "were dictated to Mr. Smith, by HANDEL, after the total privation of sight," says Burney – long after Handel went blind, in fact.

Handel also created a new oratorio (libretto by Thomas Morell). Most of it wasn't newly composed; nevertheless, it was new to London audiences and can be considered his last work: *The Triumph of Time and Truth*, an English version of the 1737 version of *Il trionfo del Tempo e della Verità*. It is called an oratorio though not biblically based or "sacred"in the way the other oratorios are. But it has a distinct moral, as such works always did. So once again Handel presented a varied oratorio season, reviving a different batch of works and rejuvenating them with new additions.

The 1757 season opened with *Esther* two days after Handel's seventy-second birthday. *Esther* was repeated March 2, then *Israel in Egypt* returned (it had been heard the previous year) for one performance on March 4. Despite the cool reception *Israel in Egypt* had received in 1739 as a new work, and despite Mary Delany's feeling that it is "not for common ears," there must have been enough "uncommon ears" to experience it as a "truly sublime composition," as Oxford's William Hayes did. Handel resurrected it frequently in the two decades between its creation and his death. As the extraordinary power of Handel's choruses became more and more apparent to his audiences, this chorus-heavy oratorio came to be much appreciated. (Handel himself may have particularly liked it as well.) On

March 9 *Joseph and His Brethren* appeared, followed by the debut of *The Triumph of Time and Truth* on March 11, repeated on the 16th, 18th, and 23rd. Handel's publisher John Walsh quickly made the score available, promoting it in the *Public Advertiser* on April 18.

The new oratorio was advertised on the day of performance as "altered from the Italian, with several new Additions." It is an allegorical work whose five soloists personify Time, Truth /"Counsel," Beauty, Pleasure and Deceit. *The Triumph of Time and Truth* is thoroughly typical of the mid- and late eighteenth century, both in its type of moral instruction and in the language and allegorical method it uses to get its message across.

In Act I, Beauty realizes she is "horrid Time's devoted prey." Pleasure tries to cheer her. Deceit, too, encourages her to "despise Old Time" and focus on Pleasure. But Time urges her to face him, and his counterpart Truth. Counsel, the son of Truth, then sings of the brevity of Beauty; but Pleasure vies with him for Beauty's heart. It's not difficult to guess whose side Beauty chooses. Deceit enters again and urges Beauty to "beguile" Time and "live free from all care and all strife." Counsel then returns and urges Beauty to think on human frailty, but Pleasure tells her not to think about how fast Time flies. Counsel, however, begs her to heed his own instructive lesson before it's too late.

Act II begins with a chorus reminiscent of Ecclesiastes' "For everything there is a time...." But once again Pleasure returns and entices Beauty with music and dancing and all his splendid court. Deceit urges Beauty to submit to Pleasure's uncontrolled reign so that she will sail toward, and reach, the port of bliss. Beauty now believes Time is sleeping, but Counsel warns against such a self-deceiving thought. Time tells Beauty that if she wishes to quit dreading his "hated power" she must prepare "for a nobler flight,/Amidst the realms of light" – Time assures her that once she attains immortality she is out of his reach. Counsel joins in, telling Beauty that Pleasure's lies and flattery have deluded her. Truth is recognizable because she is not all decked out (as Pleasure is), but because she is "fairest in simplicity"and wears "white robes of innocence." Predictably, Pleasure and Deceit try to get Beauty to close her eyes to what Truth and Counsel are showing her. So yet again, Time must warn Beauty that she will not see the bliss Pleasure insists will be hers forever. Counsel, in turn, tells her that the delights of both youth and old age are vain without "the sanction and applause of Truth": eventually she will regard with contempt and disbelief the choices she made at the prompting of Pleasure and

Deceit. Time exhorts Beauty to be wise, and Counsel prods, "Hear the call of Truth and Duty,/And to Folly bid adieu./Ere to dust is chang'd thy beauty,/Change thy heart, and good pursue." A chorus ends Act II reiterating that Beauty must change her heart before it is her beauty which changes – to dust.

In Act III, Deceit argues one more time that Beauty must have regard for her own happiness. But Beauty is now leaning in the direction she knows is right, and she begs Deceit to quit tempting her; Deceit's words no longer give her relief. But Deceit isn't about to give up yet, and presses Beauty to enjoy the rose, not its thorns. Counsel now comforts Beauty, telling her to disregard Deceit: though sorrow's tears may be unvalued here on earth, each one will prove as a precious pearl in heaven.

Beauty now finally shuns Pleasure and sets herself toward Virtue. She now has in her possession Truth's "immortal mirror," and she dashes Pleasure's "deluding glass" to earth. She addresses Truth – "O mighty Truth! Thy power I see,/All that was fair seems now deformity" – and sees that she was a "slave to vanity." Because that's true, she feels as if she should live out her days in "some sequester'd penitential cell." As Beauty's long struggle with Pleasure and Deceit shows, this was no easy transformation. Though repentant, Beauty has been in Pleasure's courts so long that she is still uneasy in the presence of Truth and finds no contentment there. Therefore, her final prayer is that that will change, and that she will be granted help from heaven to stay on her new path: "Guardian angels, oh, protect me,/And in Virtue's path direct me,/While resign'd to Heav'n above./Let no more this world deceive me,/Nor let idle passions grieve me,/Strong in faith, in hope, in love." We can assume, of course, that her prayer will be answered, and the last word (from the chorus) is one of rejoicing in heaven and on earth: "Hallelujah."

Unfortunately, there are no surviving contemporary comments from Handel's friends or from anyone else about their reactions to the new oratorio. It was well enough received, though, to merit four performances, and two more to open the season the following year.

On Handel's last free day between the third and fourth performances he drew up the second codicil to his will. We learn from it that his long-time servant Peter Le Blond had recently died. (Handel had intended to leave Le Blond his "Clothes and Linnen" besides several hundred pounds.) In the 1750 receipts related to the Foundling Hospital *Messiah*, Le Blond was mentioned (he had received a guinea for his services to Handel in connection with that performance);

but he may have worked for Handel a good deal longer than that. He was someone Handel relied on, and chief among the servants, so Handel would certainly miss Le Blond and no doubt grieve for him, servant or not. Handel's ambivalence toward, and more distant relationship to, the male servant who remained, and who moved up into Le Blond's position, is also reflected in the codicil: "I give to my Servant Thomas Bramwell the Sum of Thirty Pounds in case He shall be living with me at the time of my Death and not otherways."[2]

The last performance of *The Triumph of Time and Truth* the next day no doubt helped to get Handel's mind off his domestic affairs. Two days after that, *Judas Maccabaeus* was presented. The season ended with *Messiah* on March 30 and April 1, followed by the Foundling Hospital *Messiah* on May 5 (once again, patrons were requested to leave swords and hoops at home). From a modern viewpoint this performance was notable in that the replacement for Giulia Frasi, the principle soprano soloist the previous three years, was a boy: "Mr. Savage's celebrated boy." Young Savage was probably a relative, possibly the son, of the organist William Savage, then Master of the Chorister at St. Paul's Cathedral, who himself had debuted for Handel as a boy in 1735 in *Athalia* and *Alcina*, and who continued as an adult soloist in Handel's operas and oratorios. The boy Savage must have been celebrated indeed if he could handle the most difficult of *Messiah's* soprano arias. Afterwards, the *London Chronicle* didn't mention his performance, but it did sing an old and happy refrain:

> *Yesterday was perform'd at the Foundling Hospital, under the Direction of George Frederick Handel, Esq.; the sacred Oratorio called the Messiah, to a numerous and polite Audience, who expressed the greatest Satisfaction on that Occasion.*[3]

"Under the direction" of Handel almost certainly meant under his general musical and administrative directorship because of his blindness, not that he himself conducted the performance. Still, because he was blind, and elderly, and of gradually failing health, even that kind of oversight of his oratorio concerts would have been something of a feat.

Handel was surely pleased with Master Savage. The boy did so well that he was invited to sing in a performance of *Messiah* in Oxford that July to commemorate the University's benefactors. Among the "considerable Number of Voices and Instruments, from London and other Places" who would participate in this performance, in the notice of the event he was the only one noted by name –

more or less. Again he was "Mr. Savage's celebrated Boy," who "supplied the place of Signora Frasi in the last Performance of Messiah at the Foundling Hospital." Perhaps partly as a result of his presence, the Oxford *Messiah* was populated by "a very numerous Audience" (as was *Esther* the next night).

Handel continued in good health and spirits for the rest of 1757 and into the next year. In July, Thomas Harris told James, "I see Handel frequently[,] who is in good health."[4] On August 4, 1757, Handel had a third codicil to his will drawn up. Its most important stipulations from a musical point of view: he bequeathed his "Great Organ," which was still at the Covent Garden theater, to John Rich, who was still the theater manager; and he officially allotted "a fair copy" of *Messiah* to the Foundling Hospital.

In spite of J.C. Smith's now prominent position in Handel's affairs, Handel himself was still very much in control of who performed in his oratorios, and he was especially interested in the soloists. It is understandable if he jealously guarded that control. Though he had learned to accept his limitations and to be cheerful in the face of his handicap, he was not the type to meekly acquiesce to being sidelined. Rehearsals – at least for the singers – were still being held at Handel's house, allowing him to influence tempos and other variables of interpretation, and to hear how well his soloists were doing. (John Baker noted in his diary that he and a friend attended the rehearsal of *Judas Maccabaeus* at Handel's house the day before its performance in March.)

The Triumph of Time and Truth opened the 1758 oratorio season on February 10 and 15. On the 18th, Walsh advertised the fourth volume of Handel's songs available in score. A month later there was a benefit performance of *Sampson* at the King's Theater (Handel's own season was at Covent Garden) on behalf of Guilia Frasi at the King's Theater, the singer whose place had been taken the previous year by Mr. Savage's boy. Besides *Sampson* being Handel's music, there was an interesting parallel to Handel himself at this concert: the blind composer and organist John Stanley (1712-1786) provided an organ concerto at intermission. (Stanley, blind since age two, was known for having a prodigious memory.) Despite Stanley having been taught by Maurice Greene, whom Handel didn't particularly value, his composing style shows Handel's influence. After Handel's death, in fact, Stanley would direct the Foundling Hospital *Messiah* from 1769 to 1777 (after J.C. Smith directed it from 1760-68).

Though Handel and Stanley were on good terms, once Handel had become blind himself he had doubts about Stanley's ability to help him. Coxe recounts a witty quip of Handel's regarding himself and Stanley. Handel made the remark during his consultation with the surgeon Sharp:

> *His surgeon, Mr. Sharp, having asked him if he was able to continue playing the organ in public, for the performance of the Oratorios Handel replied in the negative. Sharp recommended Stanley, as a person whose memory never failed; upon which Handel burst into a loud laugh, and said, 'Mr. Sharp, have you never read the Scriptures? do you not remember, if the blind lead the blind, they will both fall into the ditch?'*[5]

Hawkins puts the start of Handel's final decline "towards the beginning of the year 1758."[6] Generally, Handel had been steadily declining. But he was so determined to keep going that he tried to ignore it, and mostly succeeded until then. John Upton told James Harris that he had heard only one oratorio up to March 4, 1758, because, as he quaintly put it, "[I am] nursing myself up against the Messiah" Upton suffered frequent ill health but was pampering himself in hopes of being able to hear *Messiah* in a week or so. At the oratorio he did hear, he thought Handel looked quite well, but was keenly aware that wouldn't last:

> *Your old friend Handel looks plump, & large, & fat: I applauded his broad shoulders & spatious wig.—Are you not well enough recovered & reinstated in your health to come up before the Bard is silenced?*[*]

The Foundling Hospital *Messiah* of 1758 occurred on April 27. A foundling born at the hospital on the 15th of April, a girl, started a trend that would span the next century: she was named after Handel. As the baby had no family connections she was given Handel's surname in his honor: Maria Augusta Handel. No one thought that the least bit odd, nor any reflection on the child's possible paternity. There are several later instances of the name "George Frederick Handel" being applied to a newborn boy along with the child's own surname.

---

[*]Handel was sitting somewhere at the front with his back to the audience, therefore when Upton and the rest of the audience showed their appreciation of the oratorio they "applauded his broad shoulders & spatious wig." Handel no doubt did turn to acknowledge the audience's applause, but Upton shows a peculiar personal style for stating ordinary things in slightly unusual ways and he no doubt liked this phrase he had come up with. Upton and Handel knew each other, and not just through their mutual friend James Harris. In 1737, when Handel was taking the waters at Tunbridge Wells, Upton happened to be there too. The composer and the clergyman-classical scholar spent a week dining together every day (Upton to James Harris, Sept. 1, 1737, Harris Family Papers, p. 36).

The next personal reference to Handel comes from banking records on May 19. Those Bank of England records show that on May 19, 1758, he withdrew his cash balance of £2169 18s and bought £2500 in annuities.[7] Financially he had done extremely well with the oratorios these last years, even though he didn't always have full houses. He needed little money to live on, and it was not nearly as expensive to produce a Lenten oratorio season as it had been to present an opera season, since there were no sets, no costumes, and no superstar foreign soloists who expected to be paid commensurate with their stardom.

As previously noted, speculating on exactly how well Handel did with his performances was a minor form of entertainment among his contemporaries. A friend of Burney's was one of those intrigued by Handel's income, and Burney provided this colorful picture:

> The last season of HANDEL'S personal attendance and of his life was remarkably successful. One of my friends, who was generally at the performance of each Oratorio that year, and who used to visit him after it was over, in the treasurer of the theater's office, says, that the money he used to take to his carriage of a night, though in gold and silver, was as likely to weigh him down and throw him into a fever, as the copper-money of the painter Coreggio, if he had had as far to carry it.

Conjecture about Handel's financial affairs also took root in his native land. Jakob Adlung's *Anleitung zu der Musikalischen Gelahrtheit* (*Primer of Musical Erudition*) published in Erfurt in 1758 took time out from erudition to speculate:

> Hendel or Händel, (Georg Fr.) of Halle of Magdeburg, at present in his 71st year [sic], is said to have no definite appointment or service at the Court in London; but yet earns a great deal through operas, concerts and occasional music. Ist May 1753 he performed in the Chapel of the [Foundling] Hospital an oratorio, The Messiah, of two hours' duration. They counted more than 800 coaches; the tickets brought in 995 guineas, which amount to nearly 9,000 Fl.

If Handel persevered, so his music had staying power, despite the dawning of the new, Classical age. On May 11 there was another *Messiah* performance, this one by the Academy of Ancient Music. It was one of dozens of Handel performances that continued throughout the country and in Ireland in the next months, some of them in festivals, many as benefits for hospitals, and sometimes for individuals. On May 10, a variety of Handel's music was heard at the anniversary service and sermon for the Middlesex Hospital for the Sick and Lame and for Lying-in Married Women (i.e., women about to give birth). This, again, involved some of Handel's oratorio singers. On August 17, John Wesley noted in his journal: "I went to [Bristol] cathedral to hear Mr. Handel's Messiah. I doubt if that congregation was ever so serious at a sermon as they were during this performance. In many parts, especially several of the choruses, it exceeded my expectation."[8] (Wesley's wording indicates this was the first time he had heard *Messiah*.)

A new Charitable Foundation of Church-Langton was proposed by Rev. William Hanbury that summer, with the stipulation that at the charity's annual meeting each September not only should a sermon be preached, but that "Handel's or Purcel's *Te Deum* be performed" so that "God in all things may be glorified" and for the congregation it would "excite an holy emulation in all Christian duties." William Hayes, the Oxford professor who had championed Handel's music, conducted the first performances on September 26 and 27 the next year.

On April 19, 1758, the *Public Advertiser* carried this notice:

To *the* Lovers of Music, *particularly those who admire the Compositions of* GEO. FREDERICK HANDEL, *Esq[.]* F. BULL, *at the White House on Ludgate Hill, London, having at a great Expence procured a fine Model of a Busto of Mr. Handel, proposes to sell by Subscription, thirty Casts in Plaister of Paris. The Subscription Money, which is to be paid at the Time of subscribing, and for which A Receipt will be given, is one Guinea; and the Cast, in the Order in which they are finished will be deliver'd in the Order in which the Subscriptions are made. The Busto, which will make a rich and elegant Piece of Furniture, is to be twentty-three Inches and a half high, and eighteen Inches broad. The Model may be viewed till Monday next, at the Place abovementioned....*[9]

Though Mr. Bull certainly hoped to recoup his expenses, if not make a profit, this is yet another clear-cut example of the esteem in which Handel was held. About this time, Rev. William Hughes of Worchester, calling himself "A Lover of Harmony," wrote a summation of Handel in his "Remarks upon Musick, To Which are Added Several Observations Upon Some of Mr. Handel's Oratorios, and Other Parts of His Works." He parodied lines from Shakespeare's *Julius Caesar*:

Why Man! He does bestride the Musick World
Like a Colossus; and We poor, petty Composers,

Walk under his huge Legs, and pick up a
*Crotchet [quarter note] to deck our humble Thoughts.**

That summer of 1758 was when Handel went to Tunbridge with Morell, met the "Chevalier" Taylor there and was couched by him. Even at that late date, Handel simply wasn't letting go of the remote possibility that he might see again. Nor did Taylor's lack of success seem to dishearten him much. The next report of him shows that he had been exceedingly mentally active, thinking over and planning his 1759 season. On November 21, Thomas Harris reported to James:

Handel was with me yesterday: he says he has worked hard, and has made a considerable part of a new oratorio. He ... seems in good spirits to go on with his design. Taylor did something to his eye at Tunbridge, but has not been of any real service to him.[10]

Throughout December and January we hear nothing further of Handel himself. Then we learn from Thomas Harris that Handel had once again paid him a visit: on Saturday, February 24, the day after his seventy-fourth birthday. Lent of 1759 began early, on February 28, and the oratorios would commence two days after that. Handel was still cheerfully looking forward to this new, busy season, yet his friends apparently saw in him disturbing signs of decline. Amidst the matter-of-fact information about Handel's new season, there is a slight prodding in the tone of Thomas's February 27 letter to James in which he tried to get his brother to come to London for at least some of the oratorios, and to see Handel, before it was too late. Thomas Harris also mentioned Charles Jennens, and Jennens too warned of their last opportunity to hear an oratorios performed by Handel:

I am very glad to find for certain that you have some thoughts of coming to London. Handel was here last Saturday: he begins with Solomon, of which I find there is a great deal which is entirely new, the first act being omitted: this may probably be performed twice: then Susannah: then possibly Theodora, but I rather think Time & Truth; then Samson: then Judas: then the Messiah. The first performance is on Friday next.

---

*The lines from *Julius Caesar* are from Act I, Scene 3. In 1749 Hughes had preached a sermon entitled "The Efficacy and Importance of Musick" at Worcester Cathedral at the annual meeting of the Three Choirs [Festival].

By this you will judge about your coming to town: I should think the first performances would be most agreable to you. I dined today with Charles Jennens, who desired his compliments & that he thought these would be the last oratorios you would ever hear performed by Handel; which I am afraid is too likely to be the case.

A few days earlier, John Upton had urged James Harris to come to London, his concern concealed in his emphasis on James's seeing Handel rather than in talking about the oratorios: "I take it for granted you will pay a visit to the old blind prophet." James Harris took their advice.

The 1759 season went much as Handel had laid it out for Thomas Harris. The "new oratorio" he worked so hard on was *Solomon*, with its "new Additions and Alterations." It opened the season on March 2 and 7. *Susanna*, with its own "new Additions and Alterations" (but less changed than *Solomon*) followed on March 9. The ever popular *Samson* was heard three times (March 14, 16 and 21) and *Judas Maccabaeus* twice (the 23rd and 28th). *Messiah* ended that fine season, on March 30, April 4, and one final time, April 6. The Foundling Hospital *Messiah* was scheduled for the 3rd of May.

Then, Handel's days of reprieve were over. His health was now rapidly deteriorating but he continued to be present at the oratorios, and he still played the organ or harpsichord for at least some of them – even, it seems, at the season-ending performance of *Messiah*. After February 27, Thomas's next mention of Handel came on April 3, when he told James, "Handel had a full house at the Messiah last Friday, and performs the same tomorrow and Friday next, when he concludes."[11] According to Coxe's account – from J.C. Smith, who would know – Handel was still able to attend the season's last *Messiah* performance on April 6. That completed the 1759 season. Handel had endured to the end. He knew his life's work was complete. He then seemed to let go, knowing he could. His strength gave out and he was forced to his bed, fatigued, ill and without appetite:

Nature at last became exhausted, he exhibited evident symptoms of decay; his appetite failed him, and he saw without dismay his dissolution approaching. But his extraordinary faculties continued to the end of his life: his last public performance took place only a week before he died.[12]

Chapter 23
His Pen to the Service of God

At some point that spring of 1759, as the probability of Handel's death had loomed ever greater, he and Selina Countess of Huntington visited together "at his particular request." Lady Huntington was immensely wealthy and a generous benefactress to the Methodist movement and to numerous dissenting Methodist clergy who at that time were not allowed to be educated at Oxford or Cambridge or ordained in the Church of England (and thus could not administer the sacraments). According to Lady Hungtington's *Life*, she had gotten to know Handel some years earlier. But she had had no personal contact with him for some time before his request that she visit him near what he knew was the end of his life.

Handel probably had been hearing news of Lady Huntington periodically, especially from Rev. Martin Madan through Madan's and Handel's mutual association with the Lock Hospital. Madan was also a Methodist and a close friend of Lady Huntington. Since the previous year (1758) Madan had been the chaplain at Lock Hospital. He was also a music lover and a hymn writer who introduced hymn singing to the services held at the hospital. He would publish *A Collection of Psalms and Hymns, Extracted from Various Authors* the next year, and eventually would be responsible for the building of an 800-seat chapel there.[*]

An entry in Lady Huntington's diary records her visit with Handel:
I have had a most pleasing interview with Handel – an interview which I shall not soon forget. He is now old, and at the close of his long career; yet he is not dismayed at the prospect before him. Blessed be God for the comforts and consolations which the Gospel affords in every situation, and in every time of our need! Mr. Madan has been with him often, and he seems much attached to him.

The reason Lady Huntington would "not soon forget" her visit with Handel lay, she implies, in their sharing together their experiences of faith in the midst of adversity, and Handel's clear testimony to the "comforts and consolations" he

---

[*] Published in 1760, Madan's hymnal would be enlarged in 1763 and 1769; a second edition, 1792 would be prepared by hospital organist Charles Lockhart after Madan's forced departure in 1780 over his *Thelyphthora or Female Ruin*. Guided by compassion and a looking back to the Old Testament to what God had allowed (but not ordained), Madan argued that polygamy could be the solution to prostitution. That well-meaning but misguided view did not go over well with the hospital board or patrons.

received from the gospel, which she also experienced. That made facing his impending death a prospect that did not dismay. He was unafraid. Madan's frequent visits were undoubtedly pastoral as well as personal, and surely (as a chaplain as well as friend) included praying with Handel and reading to him from Scripture, which his blindness prevented him doing himself. By then, the men were good friends.[*]

The only business Handel attended to after that last *Messiah* performance was to make some further changes to his will, from his sickbed on Wednesday, April 11. The most unusual and often remarked upon aspect of this last addition to Handel's will is this:

> *I hope to have the permission of the Dean and Chapter of Westminster to be buried in Westminster Abbey in a private manner at the discretion of my Executor, Mr Amyand and I desire that my said Executor may have leave to erect a monument for me there and that any sum not Exceeding Six Hundred Pounds be expended for that purpose at the discretion of my said Executor.*[1]

This plainspoken request is extraordinary. No one previously buried in Westminster Abbey and celebrated with a monument there had requested that favor, much less in writing and in quite this manner. But Handel was an extraordinary man who had an extraordinary place in British music history; and he knew it. There was no hubris involved. Handel had, all his life, valued his familial, musical and theological roots in Germany. But his real significance as a composer developed in England, and his lasting fame and the assigning of *sublimity* to his music arose through his biblical oratorios set to the English language. Nor had everyone forgotten his many operas – nor his anthems or many dozens of other works. It was wholly appropriate that he be buried in Westminster Abbey, as so many of England's greatest native sons are. Handel's straightforward request on his own behalf, not the notion itself, was what was unconventional. A rumor printed in a London paper three days after his death said he was to be buried at the Foundling Hospital's cemetery, near the hospital founder, Capt. Coram. That is a plausible story: it made

---

[*]In Lady Huntington's sentence "Mr. Madan has been with him often, and he seems much attached to him," grammatically "he" refers to "Mr. Madan." But the sense of the sentence is that Lady Huntington meant "he" to be Handel, referring back to "him," who is definitely Handel. Regarding pastoral visitors, it is interesting to note that despite Handel's constant worship in Hanover Square in his last years, there are no records of visits to him in his last days by clergy from St. George's.

sense. The public could not yet have known the actual state of affairs.

Handel had expressed a desire to die on Good Friday, to meet his Savior on that worst and best day of the year for Christians. Burney writes:

Having been always impressed with a profound reverence for the doctrines and duties of the Christian religion, that he had most seriously and devoutly wished, for several days before his death, that he might breathe his last on Good-Friday, 'in hopes, he said, of meeting his 'Good God, his sweet Lord and Saviour, on the day of his resurrection,' meaning the third day, or the Easter Sunday.[2]

But even after a week of quick deterioration, including being unable to eat, Handel's strength was such that he lived through Good Friday night and died on Saturday morning at 8 o'clock, April 14, 1759.* The *Whitehall Evening Post* reported that evening:

This Morning, a little before Eight o'Clock, died (between 70 and 80 Years of Age) the deservedly celebrated George Frederick Handell, Esp; When he went home from the Messiah Yesterday Se'nnight [April 6], he took to his Bed, and has never rose from it since; and it was with great Difficulty he attended his Oratorios at all, having been in a very bad State of Health for some Time before they began.[3]

Eulogies for the great man quickly appeared. On April 17, three papers printed a version of this poem written the day before, signed H—y:

...To melt the soul, to captivate the ear,
(Angels his melody might deign to hear)
T'anticipate on Earth the joys of Heaven,
Was Handel's task; to him the pow'r was given!
Ah! When he late attun'd Messiah's praise,
With sounds celestial, with melodious lays;
A last farewel his languid looks exprest,
And thus methinks th' enraptur'd crowd addrest:

---

*The *Whitehall Evening Post* reported, April 12, "Mr. Handel ... was in Hopes to have set out for Bath last Saturday" (the 7th) for the waters but was too ill" (quoted by Deutsch, p. 816). When the fact got out that Handel was actually very near death, his death was then reported prematurely. That same day, April 12, five London papers (the *Gazetteer*, *Daily Advertiser*, *Public Advertiser*, *Evening Post* and *Universal Chronicle*) reported that he had died that day; but he was not yet dead (Deutsch, p. 816).

"Adieu, my dearest friends! and also you,
"Joint sons of sacred harmony, adieu!
"Apollo, whisp'ring, prompts me to retire,
"And bids me join the bright seraphic choir!
"O for Elijah's car," great Handel cry'd;
Messiah heard his voice—and Handel dy'd.

The same day, this appeared in the *Public Advertiser*:

He's gone, the Soul of Harmony is fled!
And warbling Angels hover round him dead.
Never, no, never since the Tide of Time,
Did Music know a Genius so sublime!
Each mighty Harmonist that's gone before,
Lessen'd to Mites when we his Works explore.

A few days later this "Attempt towards an EPITAPH" appeared:

Beneath this Place
Are reposited the Remains of
GEORGE FREDERICK HANDEL.
The most excellent Musician
Any Age ever produced:
Whose Compositions were a
Sentimental Language
Rather than mere Sounds;
And surpassed the Power of Words
In expressing the various Passions
Of the Human Heart.[*]

There are more such verses.

It seems peculiar that the prolific letter writer Thomas Harris and the steady diarist George Harris set down nothing about the death of their good friend, whose music and company they so admired and enjoyed. The brothers, probably along with their cousin Shaftesbury, must have been together when they talked of Handel,

---

[*]"Sentimental language" is that characterized by refined and elevated feeling – not by excessive or superficial emotion, as in the modern definition of "sentimental." This epitaph was not used on Handel's monument.

his life and his death, and his significance for the age, eliminating the need for letters between them. Thomas Harris and Shaftesbury, especially, "seem to have lost interest in attending the London theaters after Handel's death." It was left to their brother James to leave us a brief comment on Handel's death, written two weeks after it occurred, to a friend of his in Venice:

> Our great genius Handel is dead, the Homer of music, of whose work it may be said, as Quintilian I think says of Cicero[']s eloquence, that then a man may be said to have proficiency in the art when he has taste and skill enough to relish their superior merit.

Harris then continues with news about Handel's estate – worth the substantial sum of £20,000 – a tidbit he had likely heard from his brother Thomas.

If we have no other written words from the Harrises about Handel's death, two other close friends of Handel's – James Smyth (the "perfumer of Bond Street" mentioned in Handel's will) and his neighbor Bernard Granville – exchanged this touching and highly informative letter three days after Handel was gone, written by Smyth:

> According to your request to me when you left London, that I would let you know when our good friend departed this life, on Saturday last at 8 o'clock in the morn died the great and good Mr. Handel. He was sensible to the last moment; made a codicil to his will on Tuesday, ordered to be buried privately in Westminster Abbey, and a monument not to exceed £600 for him. I had the pleasure to reconcile him to his old friends; he saw them and forgave them, and let all their legacies stand! In the codicil he left many legacies to his friends, and among the rest he left me £500, and has left to you the two pictures you formerly gave him. He took leave of all his friends on Friday morning, and desired to see nobody but the Doctor and Apothecary and myself. At 7 o'clock in the evening he took leave of me, and told me we "should meet again"; as soon as I was gone he told his servant "not to let me come to him any more, for that he had now done with the world." He died as he lived—a good Christian, with a true sense of his duty to God and man, and in perfect charity with all the world. If there is anything that I can be of further service to you please let me know. I was to have set out for Bath tomorrow, but must attend the funeral, and shall then go

*next week.**

This clear picture of Handel's preparation to die is a final reinforcement of all the other portraits we have of Handel as a man of faith, whose generous spirit and irreproachable morals bore witness to that faith.

As we would expect, Handel's friend Mary Delany, too, wrote her thoughts of him. She, like Thomas Harris and Lord Shaftesbury, suddenly felt a keen lack of interest in music. She confided to her sister:

> *I was very much pleased with Court's lines on Mr. Handel; they are very pretty and very just. D.D. [Dr. Delany] likes them extremely. I could not help feeling a damp on my spirits, when I heard that great master of music was no more, and I shall now be less able to bear any other music than I used to be. I hear he has shewed his gratitude and his regard to my [i.e., our] brother by leaving him some of his pictures; he had very good ones.... I am sure you were pleased with the honours done him by the Chapter at Westminister.*

Handel had requested a private burial. Even in his realistic assessment of his worthiness to be buried in Westminster Abbey, he did not entirely realize the esteem in which he and his music were held. A private funeral was impossible. Instead, a very public funeral was held in the evening on Friday, April 20. "The Gentlemen of his Majesty's Chapels Royal, as well as the Choirs of St. Paul's and St. Peter's, will attend the Solemnity, and sing Dr. Croft's Funeral Anthem," reported the *Public Advertiser.* They sang to a full house:

> *On Friday Night the Remains of the late Mr. Handel were deposited at the Foot of the Duke of Argyle's Monument in Westminster-Abbey; the Bishop, Prebendaries, and the whole Choir attended, to pay the Honours due to his Memory; and it is computed there were not fewer than 3000 Persons present on this Occasion.*

---

*Smyth's account of Handel being reconciled to friends he with whom he was at odds reinforces Coxe's account of Handel and J.C. Smith the elder's reconciliation at the end of Handel's life. Handel had apparently been at odds with a few other people he had named in his will, and with death at his door let go of whatever grievances he felt, and did so by reconciling in person. James Smyth added after his signature, "He has left the [manuscript of] Messiah to the Foundling Hospital, and 1,000 pounds to the decayed musicians and their children, and the residue of his fortune to his niece and relations in Germany. He has died worth £20,000, and left legacies with his charities to nearly £6000. He has got by his Oratorios this year £1952 12s 8d."

As another paper put it, the Bishop and his entourage, the other clergy, choirs and "a vast concourse of people of all ranks" attended "from the respect due to so celebrated a man." And few doubted that the monument that would be erected for him "his works will even outlive."[4] William Coxe (son-in-law of J.C. Smith the Younger) understood as well as any of Handel's contemporaries the spirit that animated Handel and his works:

> *Few men composed more; no man better. Handel was in music all things to all persons; the audience feel it, and in the language of that poetry, which he himself so happily made the strong example of his art, 'The list'ning crowd admire the lofty sound.' Such is the force and effect of his productions;–but he has the highest claim for moral and religious excellence. His pen was never debased to the disgraceful practice of an effeminate or seductive style of composition: it is entitled to the first attribute of praise.–It is sublime, affecting, animated, and devoted, without the gloom of superstition, to the service of God.*

Epilogue
Handel's Impact

Two and a half centuries after Handel's death, Roubiliac's monument still marks the composer's grave in Westminster Abbey's "Poet's Corner." And since 1869, Charles Dickens has lain buried at his feet.* If Handel's monument still stands, so do his musical works, and they are the real monuments to the extraordinary gift with which God endowed him. Not only do Handel's works still exist: the whole range of them is better known than at any period since his lifetime – and perhaps better than even then.

In the Westminister monument, "his figure is represented standing before the organ, and listening to the harp of an Angel," wrote William Coxe.[1] "On the scroll are recorded his own divine notes, set to those emphatical words, comprising the sum of Christian hope, 'I know that my Redeemer liveth.'"** Those words from the book of Job, long cherished in Handel's family, were set by him in *Messiah* with such profound effect that millions of people since then cannot read them without inwardly hearing Handel's music. And so, too, many other portions of Scripture.

The first retrospective of Handel's work occurred just twenty-five years after his death in the form of a three-day celebration of the centennial of his birth in 1784 (the actual centennial was 1785). Not only was Handel's general impact spoken to, so were specific genres among his works, particularly the oratorios. It was believed then – as many people still find – that Handel's choruses are his best works, and that in them "he is without a rival," as Mainwaring put it. "And it may be said without extravagance," he added, "that the sublime strokes they abound with, look more like the effects of illumination, than of mere natural genius."[2]

---

*There is this matter-of-fact assessment of gravesites by "Mr. Gordin, U.T." (undertaker) in the Abbey's Funeral Book, April 20, 1759 – perhaps slightly macabre to anyone but an undertaker : "No. 14.... George Frederick Handel Esq' ... was buried by the Dean ... in the South Cross; 8 feet from the Duke of Argyle's Iron Railes; 7 feet from his Coffin; which is Lead: N.B. There may be made very good graves on his Right and Left by Diging up a Foundation of an old Staircase; Room at the feet" – where Dickens would be buried (Deutsch, p. 820).

**Coxe said of Handel's death, "That great event happened, as he had often expressed his earnest wish, on Good Friday." Handel died on Holy Saturday, but Coxe is right in calling death "that great event." The context shows he is not merely referring to the death of a well-known and highly regarded man, but to "that great event" that brings Christians face to face with their living Redeemer – "the sum of Christian hope."

Mainwaring concluded his biography by writing of Handel's contribution, through music, to the "interests of religion and humanity." Such interests refine and elevate our ideas of pleasure, he wrote; and pleasure, when properly understood, is the very purpose of our existence (cf. the *Westminster Confession's* statement of humankind's chief aim: "to glorify God and fully *enjoy* him forever"– my emphasis). Religion is given great assistance by music when the music is such as Handel's, Mainwaring asserted. It improves our ideas of taste, heightens the effect of whatever is beautiful and excellent, civilizes, polishes and ultimately softens the cares of life. Mainwaring hoped that Handel's music would open the curious to new sources of beauty and sublimity in music, and spur future musicians to study it, "and so check the progress of those corruptions in taste which in every period have threatened destruction to the Art, and in none perhaps more than in the present." He concluded:

> *Little indeed are the hopes of ever equalling, much less of excelling so vast a Proficient [as Handel] in his own way: however, as there are so many avenues to excellence still open, so many paths to glory still untrod, it is hoped that the example of this illustrious Foreigner will rather prove an incentive, than a discouragement to the industry and genius of our own countrymen.*

In 1785, Burney wrote a lengthy assessment of Handel in *An Account of the Musical Performances in Westminster-Abbey, and the Pantheon in Commemoration of Handel.* He published his *General History of Music* in 1789. Burney saw a peculiar suitability in music, and particularly in Handel's music, for aiding the human heart to "expand in charity and beneficence." Handel's music "supported life in thousands by its performances for charitable purposes," Burney, said, and charities throughout the kingdom were particularly indebted to it for their support.

Hawkins concluded that no one was really aware that there a "sublime" quality about music in the way it was seen to exist in poetry until Handel came along:

> *The character of an author is but the necessary result of his works, and as the compositions of Handel are many and various, it is but justice to point out such of them as seem the most likely to be the foundation of his future fame. Many of the excellencies, which as a musician recommended him to the favour and patronage of the public during a*

323

residence of fifty years in this country, he might perhaps possess in common with a few of the most eminent of his contemporaries; but, till they were taught the contrary by Handel, none were aware of that dignity and grandeur of sentiment which music is capable of conveying, or that there is a sublime in music as there is in poetry. This is a discovery which we owe to the genius and inventive faculty of this great man; and there is little reason to doubt that the many examples of this kind with which his works abound, will continue to engage the admiration of judicious hearers as long as the love of harmony shall exist.

Though musical tastes and styles regularly change as the decades and centuries roll by, it is notable that musically literate people who were alive at the time of Handel's death assumed that his music would be still be known, and still have the power to move the human heart, long after they, too, were gone. They could not have known the degree to which that would be true in a future age of communication marvels that now include not only live concerts but the availability of recordings of virtually all of the hundreds of Handel's works, ready access to videos and DVDs of operas and oratorios, and the instant, nearly universal access to his music through radio and the Internet.

But in between Handel's own listeners and us would lie the Classical Enlightenment of Haydn and Mozart, the wide-ranging emotional Romanticism of the nineteenth century, and the avant garde world of early- to mid-twentieth century experimentation with, rejection of, and eventual reinstatement of, the **tonal system.** During that span, Handel's music – especially the oratorios – would move not only millions of listeners, but the greatest composers as well.

Franz Joseph Haydn was, with Mozart, the greatest exemplar of the late eighteenth century Classicism that supplanted the intricate-textured, contrapuntal style of the Baroque. Nevertheless, as a result of having been introduced to Handel's oratorios (most notably *Messiah* and *Israel in Egypt*) during well-publicized stays in London, 1791-92 and 1794-95, Haydn wrote two of his own oratorios, *Die Schöpfung* (*The Creation*) and *Die Jahreszeiten* (*The Seasons*). Upon hearing *Messiah's* "Hallelujah" Chorus at Westminster Abbey, Haydn was said to have risen to his feet with the crowd and exclaimed, with tears in his eyes, "He is the master of us all." While another account places this anecdote at a 1784 performance of *Israel in Egypt*, it is not disputed that Haydn (himself a devout man) had such high praise for Handel, and was deeply moved, musically and spiritually, by the Handel oratorios he heard. Mozart also took Handel and *Messiah* to heart. He arranged the entire oratorio to suit the Classical tastes of 1788.[*]

In the second decade of the turbulent nineteenth century, Beethoven was asked by Cipriani Potter (1792-1871), pianist, composer and director of London's Royal Academy of Music, which of the previous generations' composers he considered the greatest. He answered that "he had always considered Mozart as such, but since he had been made acquainted with Handel he had put him at the head." Six years later in 1823, Edward Schulz left London to visit the fifty-three-year-old Beethoven in Vienna. Schulz reported:

> In the whole course of our table-talk there was nothing so interesting as what he said about Handel. I sat close by and heard him assert very distinctly in German, "Handel is the greatest composer that ever lived." I cannot describe to you with what pathos, and I am inclined to say, with what sublimity of language, he spoke of the Messiah of this immortal genius. Every one of us was moved when he said, "I would uncover my head, and kneel down at his tomb!" H. and I tried repeatedly to turn the conversation to Mozart, but without effect. I only heard him say, "In a monarchy we know who is the first" – which might, or might not apply to the subject.

Felix Mendelssohn (1809-1847), well known for permanently altering the musical landscape by revealing Bach's music to the broader world, also esteemed Handel. Mendelssohn was keenly influenced by Handel's oratorios when he created his own oratorios, *St. Paul* and *Elijah*. That developed during visits to Scotland in 1829 and London in both 1832 and 1833.

And so during his tenure as a conductor in Düsseldorf, 1833-35, Mendelssohn concentrated on Handel's oratorios. If Men-delssohn was influenced by Bach's unsurpassed genius for fugues and by Bach's *Passions* in general, he was also powerfully affected by Handel's varied and masterful choruses, and specifically by Handel's harmonic progressions and rhythms.

---

[*]Mozart's arrangement is a re-orchestration using the larger Classical orchestra, which, besides more strings, included more woodwinds and brass than Handel used, including clarinets and trombones. The clarinet did not come into its own until Mozart's time (largely because of him), and Handel had used trombones on only a couple of occasions (notably in *Saul*). "Mozart *Messiah*" recordings are readily available.

While some of Handel's music did travel during his lifetime, it is a lovely irony that a German composer of the nineteenth century should visit London, the eighteenth century German Handel's adopted home, and introduce Handel's English oratorios to a new generation in Handel's (and Mendelssohn's) own native land. Mendelssohn felt kinship with Bach and Handel on another level: he shared with them a committed Christian faith. His family had converted from Judaism, thus the story of Paul's conversion which Mendelssohn depicts in *St. Paul* had deep and peculiar meaning for him.

In the mid-nineteenth century, Johannes Brahms, whose music blended Romantic characteristics with earlier elements, wrote piano *Variations and a Fugue on a Theme by Handel* (1861). While a conductor in Vienna, Brahms, too, introduced audiences to works by Handel and Bach. The long-dead (and consequently unfashionable) Handel also captured the imagination of Camille Saint-Saëns (1835-1921). Saint-Saëns, too, visited London, and he, too, wrote choral works which show the influence of Handel.

In our own time, Briton John Tavener, whose music consciously reflects his Orthodox Christianity, has said that until he heard a recording of *Solomon* in the late 1990s, he hadn't made any great effort to listen to Handel. But *Solomon* changed that. "I think it's Handel's spontaneity more than anything that I like," says Tavener, "and also the fact that he never does what you expect him to. Unlike Bach, when he starts a fugue he doesn't go through all the motions; he'll go off at a tangent and stop the fugue and do something amazing. I'm also knocked out by his amazingly beautiful vocal lines, especially the vocal lines he wrote for women. The music he wrote for the Queen of Sheba or Solomon's wife is some of the most exquisite female music every written."

~

After the first centennial commemoration in 1784 other such gatherings that employed as many as 500 musicians were held during George III's reign. Oratorios festivals sprang up in the following century. By the 1820s these were being held in London, Birmingham and Leeds. *Messiah* came to the U.S. in 1818, performed in Boston by amateur music lovers. By 1834, 644 performers took part in the Royal Music Festival in Westminster Abbey.

But that was a chamber group compared to the Crystal Palace Handel Festivals that began in 1857. Generally held every three years until 1926, these festivals incorporated 3000 performers and were witnessed by many thousands more

326

audience members.

"Humongous Handel" remained in vogue well into the twentieth century, as is obvious from the recordings of *Messiah* even into the 1950s and most of the 1960s. Large symphony orchestras and massive choirs inevitably meant Handel was heard at slow tempos. But gradually, Baroque music was "rediscovered." Musicologists, conductors, performers and listeners became interested in how Handel and his contemporaries might have performed his music, and how Baroque music in general was heard in its own time. The apparent answer: faster, lighter, more finely, cleanly textured, and embodying the simultaneous warmth and edginess of gut strings. "Historically informed performance" (HIP) was born. It thrives, and has drastically changed the way we hear and perceive Baroque music.

~

From Handel's own time to our modern era his music has been publicly celebrated and privately relished. Handel's operas once again have enthusiastic audiences. So do his Italian cantatas, orchestral works and chamber pieces. But for many listeners the oratorios and other choral works remain the music they particularly love, among which *Messiah* will always hold a unique and cherished place.

Back in 1733 for a benefit performance of the *Utrecht Te Deum* for the Sons of the Clergy, Aaron Hill wrote an ode to Handel, addressing it directly to the composer and summing up his impact. "The Thoughts of Men, in Godlike Sound he sung," wrote Hill of the biblical David, shepherd, king, lyre-player and psalmist *extraordinaire*. But, Hill wondered, "Where has thy Soul, O Musik! slept, since then? ... Say, sacred Origin of Song! Where hast thou hid thyself so long?" Hill suggested that perhaps Handel's then yet unembodied soul was entertaining (and out-singing) angels, as it were: "What wond'ring angels hast thou breath'd among,/By none, of all th'immortal Choirs out-sung?" But once Handel was flesh and blood he took what he had learned in heaven, creating music mightier than David's, "as if in ev'ry Orb,/From every *Note*, of *God's*, which thou were shown,/Thy Spirit did th' Harmonious Pow'r absorb,/And made the moving Airs of Heav'n thy *own*!"

Hill knew Handel's music in general had "charms to sooth the savage breast," as Congreve put it. But Handel's music did – and does – that and more. It could – and can – embody the profoundest prayer and praise, and even (as a result) elicit contentment and peace. Hill finished his ode this way:

327

Ah! Give thy Passport to the Nation's Prayer,
Ne'er did Religion's languid Fire
Burn fainter—never more require
The Aid of such a fam'd Enliv'ner's Care:
Thy Pow'r can force the stubborn Heart to feel,
And rouze the Lucke-warm Doubter into Zeal.
  Teach us to pray, as David pray'd before;
Lift our Thanksgiving to th'Almighty's Throne,
  In Numbers like his own:
    Teach us yet more,
Teach us, undying Charmer, to compose
Our inbred Storms, and 'scape impending Woes:
Lull our wanton hearts to ease,
Teach happiness to please;
And, since they Notes, can ne'er, in vain implore!
Inspire Content, and Peace, in each proud Breast,
  Bid th' unwilling Land be blest.
If Aught we wish for seems too long to stay,
Bid us believe, that Heav'n best knows its Day:
Bid us, securely, reap the Good we may,
Not, Tools to other's haughty Hopes, throw our own Peace away.[3]

By secular twenty-first century standards Hill's ode is flowery, formal and fantastical (and, some may think, even a bit farcical). But this man who knew Handel and his music and was so concerned that Handel set that uncommon music to listeners' common language, caught the importance and power of that music. It was not merely art; it was a gift of God. Millions still believe it so.

Notes

Chapter 1: A Thriving Shoot from a German Lutheran Root

[1]On Francke and Lutheran education: Lutheran Journal, v. 51, no. 2 1984.

[2]On the social, economic, political and cultural influences on the practice of medicine see Mary Lindemann's *Health and Healing in 18th Century Germany* (Baltimore: Johns Hopkins University. The Johns Hopkins Studies in Historical and Political Science, 2001) and *Medicine and Society in Early Modern Europe* (Cambridge: Cambridge University Press, 1999). These works also provide contextual information for considering Handel's paralytic and mental ailments in 1737, 1740, 1743 and 1745, and how such ailments were then seen and treated.

[3]Georg Händel's tombstone: Otto Erich Deutsch. Handel: A Documentary Biography (New York: W.W. Norton & Company, 1954), p. 5. The tombstone no longer exists.

[4]Sermon for Dorothea Händel, by Johann Georg Francke, Dec. 16/27, 1730 (Deutsch, p. 263-265). And subsequent quotations about Frau Händel.

[5]Georg Händel: Donald Burrows. *Handel* (New York: Schirmer Books, 1994), p. 3.

[6]On Handel's Gymnasium education see John Butt, "Germany – education and apprenticeship," in *The Cambridge Companion to Handel*, ed. Donald Burrows (Cambridge: Cambridge University Press, 1997), p. 12.

[7]Boy Handel's funeral poem for his father. English and German, Deutsch, pp. 6-8.

[8]Luther on God's Providence: *D. Martin Luthers Werke* (Weimar: Kritische Gesamtausgabe, 1883, 21, 521) in Paul Althaus, The Theology of Luther, 2nd ed., trans. by Robert C. Schultz (Philadelphia: Fortress Press, 1966), p. 105; and on the proper attitude towards death.

[9]Georg Händel's charity: Butt, ibid, p. 13.

[10]Character of Handel's father: Romain Rolland, *Händel* (AMS Press, 1916; French edition, 1910).

[11]Funeral sermon for Georg Händel, Feb. 18, 1697: Johann Christian Olearius, "Die Gnädige Zulage Zu dem Lebens Ziel der Frommen Welche Als der Leichmann Tit. Herrn Georg Händels (*Handel Handbuch*, v. 4: "Dokumente zu Leben and Schaffen." Leipzig: HHA, Deutscher Verlag Für Musik, 1985), p. 14.

[12]Charles Burney on charity and Messiah: "An Account of the Musical Performances in Westminister-Abbey, and the Pantheon in Commemoration of Handel," *A Sketch of the Life of Handel*, p. 27. (London: Printed for the Benefit of the Musical Fund; and Sold By T. Payne and Son, at the Meuse-Gate; and G. Robinson, Pater-noster Row, 1785.)

Chapter 2: First Immersion in Music

[1]Young Handel's influence on Telemann: Burney, *Sketch of the Life of Handel*, p. 5.

[2]Georg Händel's supposed opposition to music: John Mainwaring [unnamed author], *Memoirs of the Life of the Late George Frederic [sic] Handel: To Which is Added, a Catalogue of His Works and Observations Upon Them* (London: Dodsley, 1760), pp. 4-5.

[3]Further re: Georg Händel:Paul Henry Lang, *Handel* (New York: W.W. Norton, 1966), p. 10; and Charles Cudworth, *Handel* (London: Linnet Books & Clive Bingley, 1972), p. 8. A correction: Christopher Hogwood, *Handel* (Thames & Hudson: Pitman Press, 1984) p. 12; and Burrows, Handel (ibid), p. 6.

[4]The clavichord in the garret, William Coxe. *Anecdotes of George Frederick Handel and John Christopher Smith*. London, 1799, p. 4.

[5]On Handel's father and opera in Halle: Butt, ibid., p. 15.

[6]Boy Handel: at court, Coxe, p. 5.

[7] Taught by Zachau: Mainwaring, pp. 14-15.

[8] His composing: Coxe, p.6.

[9] In Berlin, meeting Bononcini: Mainwaring, p. 23.

[10]Dislike of servanthood: Mainwaring, p. 19; and the next quotation.

[11]Organist duties: Handel's job contract, March 13, 1702; and further, Deutsch, p. 9.

[12]Teenaged Handel aware of his own abilities: Mainwaring, p. 26; sends money home: ibid, p. 29, his later support of Zachau's widow, ibid, p. 29-30.

[13]In Hamburg: on Kaiser in the theater: Burrows, *Handel*, p. 17.

[14]Handel meets Mattheson: trip to Lübeck, Coxe, p. 9; Mattheson likes Handel's wit: Burney, p. [*4]; their duel: ibid, p. [*4], and [*5].

[15]Handel's dislike of teaching: Jacob Wilhelm Lustig, *Inleiding tot de Muziekkunde* (*Introduction to the Art of Music*. 2nd ed. Groningen, 1771, p. 172). Deutsch, p. 360.

Chapter 3: A Brave New World in Italy

[1]Handel on Italian music: Mainwaring quoting Mattheson, pp. 40-41, and subsequent quote; his melodic style in need of remedial help: Mattheson, in Burrows, p. 21; political "fragments" remind him of home: Carlo Vitali on eighteenth century Italy: "Italy – Political, Religious and Musical Contexts," *Cambridge Companion to Handel*. Donald Burrows, ed. (Cambridge: Cambridge University Press. Cambridge University Press, 1997), p. 29; and subsequent quotations of Vitali, pp. 64-65; musical "duel," with Scarlatti, Mainwaring, pp. 59-60; pressed to convert to Roman Catholicism: Mainwaring, pp. 50-51, and his later thankfulness for religious freedom in England, Sir John Hawkins. *A General History of the Science and Practice of Music*. (London, 1776), p. 911.

[2]On a secular Handel, cf. Winton Dean, Paul Henry Lang, Jonathan Keane, Christopher Hogwood; and William Frosch, M.D., in his essay on Handel's illnesses.

[3]On Italian oratorio: see Anthony Hicks."Handel and the Idea of an Oratorio," *The Cambridge Companion to Handel*, ibid.

Chapter 4: Rumors of Love, Matters of Character

[1]Home again in Germany: *Kapellmeister* for Elector Georg Ludwig: Mainwaring, p. 61; help from Steffani, Hawkins, p. 857.

[2]Rumors link "handsome" Handel with Vittoria: HHB, p. 45 Quoted by Burrows, *Handel*, p. 30; and Mainwaring, pp. 50-51; Handel and women: William A. Frosch. "The 'Case' of George Frideric Handel." (*New England Journal of Medicine*, v. 321, no. 11: Sept. 14, 1989), pp. 765-9.

[3]Handel's morality: Burney, p. 31; and Hawkins, p. 910.

[4]Early consideration of marriage: Coxe. *Anecdotes*, pp. 28-29.

[5]Homosexual Handel?: Gary C. Thomas."'Was George Frideric Handel Gay?': On Closet Questions and Cultural Politics."(*Queering the Pitch: The New Gay and Lesbian Musicology*,

ed. Philip Brett, Elizabeth Wood, and Gary C. Thomas. New York: Routledge, 1994), pp. 155-204; and Ellen T. Harris. *Handel as Orpheus: Voice and Desire in the Chamber Cantatas.* (Cambridge, Mass.: Harvard U. Press, 2001), p. 14; and Burrows' *Handel*, pp. 9, 374, n51.

[6]Handel's character: Coxe, p. 26-28, and subsequently; treatment of his singers: Burney, p.36, and subsequently p. 37; as epicurean: Burney, pp. 31-32; his manner, wit: Burney, ibid.

Chapter 5: Early Imprints on England

[1]London's taste for things Italian: Mainwaring, p. 77.

[2]London's theaters: see Burrows, pp. 64ff.

[3]Handel's quick writing: Rossi quoted by Coxe, *Anecdotes*, p. 14.

[4]The Queen pleased: Abel Boyer, *The History of the Reign of Queen Anne digested into Annals*, 11 v., 1702-12 (Burrows, *Handel*, p. 66); and Mainwaring, p. 89.

[5]Godparents/Lutheran baptism: *Luthers Werke*, 2, 728; 30[1], 220 (Althaus, p. 354).

[6]London's liberty: *Encylopaedia Britannica*. 3rd ed. London, 1788-97.

[7]Fired by the Elector: quoted by Burrows, translated from the French, in both *Handel*, p. 72-73 and *Handel and Hanover*, pp. 43-45; then Mainwaring, p. 89.

[8]Reconciliation with the Elector, who had become King: Burrows, *Handel*, p. 76-77; court intrigue: ibid, pp. 72-73, and the subsequent quotation. Burrows quotes the entire letter.

Chapter 6. A Passion for Opera, a Passion for Home

[1]Bad opera attendance, 1714-15: Hogwood, *Handel*, p. 70.

[2]Brockes's reputation: Anthony Hicks. Performance notes for *Brockes Passion*, HWV 48, March 11-15, 2002, Royal College of Music, London, p. 13.

[3]Objections to Passion oratorios: Christian Gerber, translated by Stiller, p. 265. Quoted by John Butt, *Oxford Composer Companions: J.S. Bach*, p. 426. Malcolm Boyd, ed. (Oxford: Oxford University Press, 1999); and subsequent quotes: Anthony Hicks, ibid, p. 13; and a letter, March 19, 1743, signed "Philalethes," to the *Universal Spectator* (ed. Henry Baker, London).

[4]Interest in the Brockes Passion: Hicks, ibid., p 14.

[5] Duke of Chandos: "Chandos, Marlborough and Kneller: Painting and 'Protest' in the Age of Queen Anne," *National Gallery of Canada Bulletin* 17; on his artistic taste: Deutsch, p. 79.

[6]Character of Handel's sister: Johann Michael Heineck. Funeral sermon for Dorothea Sophie (Händel) Michaëlsen, ibidJuly 31 (Aug. 11), 1718, excerpt in Deutsch, p. 81. The sermon was printed, as usual, in a booklet with poems about the deceased. Dorothea Sophie's was 30 pages and contained seven elegies. See Chrysander, I. p. 490 ff. A short sermon excerpt (translated) is in Deutsch, p. 81.

[7]Projected profitability of the new Royal Academy: Quoted by Anthony Hicks. *New Grove Dictionary of Music and Musicians*, 2nd ed. online, 2001. "Handel" entry; and Handel's place in the Academy: quoted by Christopher Hogwood, *Handel*, p. 76; the Academy usurps his time: Handel to his brother-in-law, Feb. 29, 1719. Deutsch, pp. 84-86, in French and in English.

[8]Eighteenth century comparison of Bach and Handel: Friedrich Wilhelm Marpurg, *Beyträge zur Geschichte der Musik*, p. 450, in "A Comparison of Bach and Handel," (possibly by C.P.E. Bach), *The New Bach Reader* (ed. Hans T. David and Arthur Mendel; revised and

enlarged by Christoph Wolf. New York: W.W. Norton & Co., 1998), p. 407; and the next quote.
[9]Looking for singers in Dresden: Burrows, *Handel*, p. 105.
[10]South Sea Bubble: David MacNeil, Dalhousie University Collaborative and Interdisciplinary Research Initiative on the South Sea Bubble. Web version, p. 1; and MacNeil, pp. 1-2; then librettist Rolli to Riva, Deutsch, from the Italian, p. 113; and the subsequent quote of Rolli, p. 115.

Chapter 7. Glory and Grim Reality in the Land of Angels

[1]On the Royal Academy years: Mainwaring, p. 106-107; then Hogwood, *Handel*, p. 83.
[2]GFH's Bible knowledge and the *Coronation Anthems*: Burney, *Sketch of the Life*, p. 34.
[3]Star singers and their egos: Hawkins, p.874.
[4]*The Beggars Opera*: Mary Pendarves, January 29, 1728 (actual date uncertain). Deutsch, p. 220; and Hawkins, pp. 874-875, and the subsequent quote.
[5]Problems at the Royal Academy: Diary of Royal Academy member Viscount Percival, January 18, 1729, Deutsch, p. 234; and the subsequent quote, Deutsch, p. 235. 6-238.
[6]Last visit to his mother: Christian August Rotth to Handel, 1730 (no month/day) Deutsch, p. 858, translated in précis from the German; and the subsequent quotation, p. 858-859.
[7]More on opera "dying": Mary Pendarves, in Deutsch, p. 254; and Rolli, ibid, p.254-255.
[8]Handel on his mother's death: Deutsch, p. 269; and Rotth, ibid.
[9]On clergy poverty: "Introduction: the Church and Anglicanism in the 'long' eighteenth century," John Walsh and Stephen Taylor. In The Church of England c. 1689 - c. 1833: From Toleration to Tractarianism,(ed. John Walsh, Colin Haydon, Stephen Taylor. Cambridge: Cambridge U. Press, 1993), p. 6; and subsequently, on Handel's help alleviating it: *The Daily Courant*, Feb. 24, 1731 (Deutsch, p. 270) and *The Craftsman*, Feb. 24, 1731 (Deutsch, p. 271).
[10]Handel's music suitable to charitable use: Burney, Preface to *Sketch of the Life*, vi-vii.

Chapter 8. A Novel Species of Entertainment

[1]On *Esther*: Bernard Gates's promotion: Burrows, *Handel*, p. 166; impressions on first hearing: Diary of Viscount Percival, February 23, 1732 (Deutsch, p. 286); and re: an anonymous production: London *Daily Journal*, April 19, 1732 (Deutsch, p. 288).
[2]On opposition to staging biblical drama, and to masquerades: Anthony Hicks, *New Grove Dictionary of Music and Musicians* (2nd ed., online, 2001), "Handel" entry; Terry Castle, *Masquerade and Civilization: The Carnivalesque in Eighteenth-Century English Culture and Fiction* (Stanford, Calif.: Stanford University Press, 1986), p. 59; also the subsequent quotation by Bishop Gibson, p. 7; and Burrows, *Handel*, p. 167.
[3]Attempt to get GFH to use English texts: Aaron Hill, Dec. 5, 1732 (Deutsch, p. 299).
[4]*Esther* as a "religious farce" (Deutsch, p. 300-301).

Chapter 9. A Matter of Degrees

[1]On *Deborah*: magnificent performance: Viscount Percival diary, March 27, 1733 (Deutsch, p. 309); backlash against Handel doubles as criticism of Walpole (Deutsch, p. 313); and the subsequent quotations *from The Craftsman* (ibid, p. 312).
[2]Growing opposition from the elite: Hicks, New Grove Dictionary, ibid; support from

Princess Anne, opposition from Frederick, Prince of Wales: Lord Hervey (Deutsch, p. 380); opposition to Senesino's firing: *The Bee*, June 1733 (Deutsch, pp. 315-316).

[3]On *Athalia*: its success: *Weekly Journal*, July 14, 1733 (Deutsch, p. 326) and The *Bee*, July 14, 1733, about July 10 performance (Deutsch, pp. 326-27); Oxford don's negative opinion: Thomas Hearnes diary, July 5, 1773. And entries July 8, 11, 12, 13, 19 and Aug. 8 (Deutsch, pp. 319-20, 323-325, 328-329); and a public pamphlet: Deutsch, pp.366-368. Schoelcher, Chrysander, Mee, Eland all print the pamphlet's contents.

[4]Handel on the Oxford doctorate: in Hogwood, *Handel*, p.117. Hogwood notes that "this fragment only of the letter is quoted by L.C. Mizler in *Neu eröffnete Musikalische Bibliothek*, Leipzig, 1736-54"; and Burrows, *Handel*, p. 174.

[5]Handel's contemporaries on the doctorate: Mainwaring, p. 117; Hawkins, p.889; Burney, "Sketch of the Life," p. 23; and another modern conclusion: Hogwood, *Handel*, p. 117.

[6]Versified praise of Handel at Oxford: Henry Baynbrigg Buckeridge of St. John's College, *Musica Sacra, Sive Oratorium*. The entire "carmine lyrico" appears in Deutsch, pp. 320-322, in Latin and in English, translated by Henry Gifford.

[7]Use of pasticcios, 1733-34: Burrows's theory, *Handel*, p. 178.

[8]On listeners ignoring spiritual importance of oratorio texts: Mary Pendarves to Ann Granville, March 28, 1734 (Hogwood, *Handel*, p. 122. Truncated in Deutsch, pp. 361-362.)

[9]Handel entertaining his friends: Mary Pendarves to Ann Granville, April 12, 1734; and from a letter, April 30 (Deutsch, pp. 363-364).

[10] Handel's opera not drawing: Mary Pendarves to Jonathan Swift, May 16, 1735 (Deutsch, p. 390).

[11]Dr. Johnson on Arbuthnot: *The Lives of the Most Eminent English Poets. Pope*, I, 425.

[12]Handel at the organ: playing his concertos: Hawkins, p. 912; up against Bach: "A Comparison of Bach and Handel," first published anonymously in the literary magazine *Allgemeine Deutsche Bibliothek*, ed. Friedrich Nicolai, 1788. *The New Bach Reader* (ed. Hans T. David and Arthur Mendel; revised and expanded by Christoph Wolff. New York: W.W. Norton & Company, 1998), pp. 400-409.

Chapter 10. So Great a Shock: Palsy, Lunacy and Recovery

[1]Rumor of ruin: Prevost's *Le Lour et Contre*, v. 4, no. 54, p. 17. Paris, 1734, probably July (Deutsch, pp. 368-69); *General Evening Post*, March 29, 1735, and *Old Whig*, May 22, 1735 (ibid, p. 390).

[2]*Handel in high spirits: Music and Theatre in Handel's World: The Family Papers of James Harris, 1732-1780*, ed. Donald Burrows and Rosemary Dunhill (Oxford: Oxford University Press, 2002), p. 12. In subsequent quotations this work will be referred to as the Harris Papers.

[3]*Alexander's Feast*: lines 5-10 of Newburgh Hamilton's dedication in the wordbook of this work, Feb. 17, 1739 (Deutsch, p. 476).

[4]Lord Hervey on Handel and opera: to Mrs. Charlotte Digby, a sister of Hervey's friends Stephan and Henry Fox, Nov. 25, 1735 (Deutsch, p. 396); and the following lengthy quotation.

[5]On Frederick, Prince of Wales, shunning Handel's *Atalanta*, Anthony Hicks, *New Grove Dictionary*, "Handel" entry; but offering financial support: Hogwood, Handel, p. 120.

[6]Opera will destroy Handel: Benjamin Victor to Matthew Dubourg, ca. May 15, 1736 (Deutsch, pp. 408-09).

[7]Handel on his niece's engagement: Deutsch, p. 414-415.

[8]Mary Pendarves on opera singers: to Ann Granville, Nov. 27, 1736 (Deutsch, p. 418).

[9]Mary Pendarves on GFH's future and the oratorios' impact : to Ann Granville, April 2, 1734; then, to her mother, Mary Granville, March 15, 1735 (Deutsch, pp. 362, 383).

[10]On Handel's first paralysis, 1737: the Fourth Earl of Shaftesbury to James Harris, Harris Papers, p. 26; and the subsequent quotations.

[11]On Handel's "temper and conduct": Hawkins, p. 911; and initial reactions to Handel's illness: ibid, p. 879; the subsequent statement by Burney, p. 34.

[12]The "media" on the illness: *London Daily Post*, April 30, 1737; the *London Evening Post*, May 14, 1737 (Deutsch, pp. 432-433, 434).

[13]Handel's contemporaries and friends on his illness: Mainwaring, pp. 121-122; Coxe, *Anecedotes*, p. 21; Hawkins, p. 879; Shaftesbury, Memoirs of Handel, responding to Mainwaring's biography (Deutsch, p. 846); and James Harris to Shaftesbury, from Salisbury, May 5, 1737.

[14]Modern views of Handel's illness: Milo Keynes. "Handel's Illnesses," *Lancet* Dec. 20 & 27, 1980, pp.1354-5, and Frosch's gout theory spelled out in "The 'Case' of George Frideric Handel," *New England Journal of Medicine*, v.. 321, no. 11. Sept. 14, 1989, pp. 765-9).

[15]Handel's win shopping list: Deutsch, p. 397.

[16]On his astonishing cure: Marinwaring, p. 123.

Chapter 11. Another Direction to His Studies

[1]On the *Funeral Anthem for Queen Caroline*: Duke of Chandos to Theophilus Leigh, Dec. 18, 1737; and Francis Hare, Bishop of Chichester, to his son Francis Naylor, Dec. 18, 1737 (Deutsch, p. 443).

[2]Handel's use of Lutheran chorales: Burrow, *Handel*, pp. 252-253.

[3]Handel affected by his own compositions: Hawkins, p. 913.

[4]Krummacher. "Handels Verhältnis zur Tradition der lutherischen Kirchenmusik." *Göttinger Händel'Beiträge*, 5 (1993), pp. 65-94. Translated/quoted in Roberts' "German Chorales in Handel's English Works," Händel-Jahrbuch 42-43 (1997): 77-100.

[5]Hawkins on Handel's religious principles , p. 911.

[6]Handel suited to "sacred subjects": Hawkins, p. 889.

[7]A benefit concert for Handel: Burney, *A General History of Music*, p. 426; its success: Diary of the Earl of Egmont, March 28, 1738 (Deutsch, p. 455).

[8]On Vauxhall Gardens and its monument to Handel: Hawkins, p. 888, and the subsequent quote; ibid, p. 912; and the next two quotations by Hawkins.

Chapter 12. Maggots and a *Faux Pas*

[1]Jennens, George Steevens and Shakespeare: Ruth Smith in "The Achievements of Charles Jennens," *Music & Letters*, v. 70, no. 2, May 1989, p. 171 (and see pp. 161-190); and Brian Vickers, *Shakespeare: The Critical Heritage*, v: *1765-1774*. London, 1979, p. 35, quoted by Smith, ibid; and Gordon Crosse, "Charles Jennens as Editor of Shakespeare," *The Library*, 4th

series, xvi, 1935-6, pp. 236-240, quoted by Smith, ibid, n66.

[2]This and subsequent reference to a letter from Charles Jennens to Lord Guernsey, Sept. 19, 1738 (Deutsch, pp. 465-466, and Burrows, with slight corrections, pp. 202-203).

[3]Saul: Winton Dean, Handel's Dramatic Oratorios and Masques, p. 305.

[4]Handel and Jennens: Burrows, Handel, p. 245; Jennens's second "Scripture Collection": letter, July 10, 1741 (HHB, p. 334); Burrow, ibid; re: collaborating on Saul: Burrows, p. 202-203.

[5]Church and state in Handel's day: W.M. Jacob. Lay People and Religion in the Early Eighteenth Century (Cambridge: Cambridge University Press, 1996), p. 11, p. 14, and the following quotations on the relation of faith and community, sacred and secular.

[6]Rumor of Handel being churlish: Shaftesbury to James Harris, Nov. 15, 1739 (Harris Papers, p. 78).

[7]Socializing: Shaftesbury, Nov. 24, 1739 letter (ibid, p. 80).

[8]The weather Handel's enemy: London Daily Post, Nov. 17, 1739 (Deutsch, p. 490); and Daily Post quotations: Feb. 11, 1739 (ibid, p. 495) and Feb. 14, 1739 (ibid).

[9]Princess Mary: Burrows, Handel, pp. 210-211.

[10]R ecurrence of Handel's paralysis: Thomas Harris to James Harris, May 17, 1740 (Harris Papers, p. 98), and the subsequent quotation; his recovery: Oct. 6, 1740, Shaftesbury to James Harris, quoting his "Uncle Ewer" (Harris Papers, p. 105).

[11]Mattheson's pique at Handel: Deutsch, pp. 501-506, translated from the German.

[12]On Monza: Mary Pendarves to Ann Granville Dewes, Dec. 21, 1740 (ibid, p. 508).

[13]On Handel's infamous faux pas: "J.B.'s" letter to the London Daily Post, April 4, 1741 (ibid, pp. 515-517); and the subsequent quotes of J.B.

[14]Handel's public response: London Daily Post, April 8, 1741 (Deutsch, pp. 517-518); the quotation of Anne Donellan to Elizabeth Robinson, April 11, 1741 (ibid, p. 518); concern for Handel from his friends: Earl of Radnor to James Harris, Aug. 8, 1741 (Harris Papers, p. 119).

Chapter 13. The Subject is *Messiah*

[1]On Handel setting Scripture to music: Cox, pp. 27-28, and the subsequent quote by Hawkins, p. 889; and Charles Jennens to Edward Holdsworth, July 10, 1747 (HHB, p. 334; Burrows, Handel, p. 259).

[2]Handel merry at bad opera: to Jennens, Dec. 29, 1741 (Deutsch, pp. 530-531).

[3]Taking Messiah to Ireland: Burney, Sketch of the Life, p.26, and the subsequent lengthy anecdote, p. 27; in Dublin: Shaftesbury to James Harris, Dec. 10, 1741 (Harris Papers, pp. 130-131); Handel to Charles Jennens, Dec. 29, 1741, ibid. And subsequent references to this letter; and Shaftesbury to James Harris, Jan. 9, 1742 (Harris Family Papers, p. 133).

[4]Newspapers announce Messiah: Faulkner's Dublin Journal, March 20, 1742 (Deutsch, p. 542); accommodating the crowds:April 10, 1742 (ibid, p. 545); two quotations, Dublin Journal, April 14, 1742 and May 29, 1742 Dublin Journal (ibid, p. 545 and 550).

[5]Handel's accolades to the Irish: to Charles Jennens, letter Sept. 9, 1742 (Deutsch, p. 554); and subsequent quots from that letter.

[6]Handel's plans: to Charles Jennens, ibid; and Earl of Radnor to James Harris, Sept. 28, 1742 (Harris Papers, p. 142), and the next two quotations, Oct. 9, 1742 and Oct. 21, 1742.

[7]London controversy over *Messiah* and presenting biblical texts in the theater: "Philalethes," *Universal Spectator*, March 19, 1743 (Deutsch, p. 563); and the following lengthy quotes, pp. 563-564, and p. 565.

[8]Handel himself wasn't faulted: on the congruence of his faith and life: Burney, *Sketch of the Life of Handel*, p. 31; then William Coxe, *Anecdotes*, p. 29; and Hawkins, p. 911, p. 910.

[9]*Messiah* in the theater an ongoing issue: letter from George Harris to James Harris, May 1, 1750 (Harris Papers, p. 270); Handel is cautious as a result: *Daily Advertiser*, March 19, 1743 (Deutsch, p. 562).

[10]Gentleman defense Messiah: *Daily Advertiser*, March 31, 1743 (ibid, pp. 565-566).

[11]The Nobility's opposition to *Messiah*: Hawkins, p. 890; then Burney, *Sketch of the Life*, p. 24; and Horace Walpole, letter to Horace Mann, Feb. 24, 1743 (Deutsch, p. 560); and the next quote by Walpole; then from a March 3, 1743 letter to Mann (ibid, p. 561).

[12]Handel and Middlesex: July 28, 1743 (HHB, pp. 363-364); and J. C. Smith the elder to James Harris, Oct. 4, 1743 (Harris Papers, p. 167).

[13]On depression: National Institute of Mental Health, NIMH Publication No. 00-3561, printed 2000; and Ruth Smith, "The Achievement of Charles Jennens," p. 164.

[14]Jennens's complaint about Handel: Jennens to Edward Holdsworth, March 24, 1743 (HHB, pp. 360-361; also in Burrows *Handel*, p. 271, with incorrect year); and Sept. 15, 1743, letter (HHB, p. 365); and the reply from Holdsworth to Jennens, Oct. 23, 1743 (Christie's auction catalogue, p. 25).

Chapter 14. Grand Chorusses – Ineffectual Labours

[1]GFH's growing esteem: private letter, author unknown, London, March 8, 1743, to an addressee in Dublin. In Faulkner's *Dublin Journal*, March 15, 1743 (Deutsch, p. 562).

[2]Oratorio effects: Catherine Talbot to Elizabeth Carter, Dec. 27, 1743 (ibid, p. 577).

3Return of GFH's confusion: Thomas Harris to James Harris, June 18, 1743 (Harris Family Papers, p. 163); its subsiding: Shaftesbury to James Harris, Nov. 22, 1743 (ibid, p. 178).

[4]On the *Dettingen Te Deum*: Mary Delany, letter to her sister Ann Dewes, Nov. 10, 1743 (Deutsch, p. 573); and the quote from the *Daily Advertiser*, Nov. 28, 1743 (Deutsch, p. 575).

[5]Amazement at Handel's talent and resiliency: Shaftesbury to James Harris, Dec. 17, 1743 (Harris Papers, p. 180).

[6]On *Semele*: Mary Delany to Ann Dewes, Feb. 21, 1744; and Charles Jennens to James Harris, Nov. 30, 1744 (Harris Papers, p. 208).

[7]Handel's friends must support him: Shaftesbury to James Harris, Jan. 12, 1744; and the two subsequent quotations (ibid, p. 183).

[8]On *Joseph and His Brethren*: Duncan Chisholm, "New Sources for the Libretto of Handel's *Joseph*. (*Handel Tercentenary Collection*), edited by Stanley Sadie And Anthony Hicks. Ann Arbor, Mich. and London: UMI Rsearch Press, 1987), p. 191.

[9]Oratorios' success: despite Handel's enemies: Mary Delany to Ann Dewes, March 10, 1744 (Deutsch, p. 587); and: Mary Smith to James Harris, April 3, 1744 (Harris Papers, p.191).

[10]Charles Jennens to Edward Holdsworth, May 7, 1744 (Burrows, Handel, p. 277).

[11]Handel "at play": Mary Delany to Ann Dewes, April 3, 1744 (Deutsch, p. 589).

[12] Opera substitute: Burrow, Handel, p. 278.

[13] Handel-Jennens correspondence re: Belshazzar: Handel to Charles Jennens, June 9, 1744 (Deutsch, p. 591-92), and the subsequent quotations in this series of letters: letters of July 19, 1744 (ibid, p. 592); Aug. 21, 1744 (p. 594); Sept. 13, 1744 (p. 595).

[14] Trouble with the double season: Daily Advertiser, Nov. 5, 1744 (Deutsch, p. 598).

[15] Handel's music and reputation outside London: General Advertiser, June 11, 1744. (Deutsch, p. 591); then Daily Advertiser, Aug. 25, 1744 (Deutsch, p. 594); and Johann Adolf Scheibe, Critischer Musikus, 2nd ed., Leipzig, 1745 (short excerpt, Deutsch, pp. 620-621).

[16] Mrs. Brown's boycott, and aftermath: Mainwaring, pp. 134-35; and on the same subject, John Walsh to James Harris, Nov. 27, 1744 (Harris Papers, p. 207); Jennens to Edward Holdsworth, Feb. 21, 1745: (HHB, p. 386, Burrows, Handel, p. 282); Shaftesbury to James Harris, Jan. 8, 1745 (Harris Family Papers, p. 210). From Handel himself, to the public, via the Daily Advertiser, Jan. 17, 1745 (Deutsch, p. 603); Lines 23 and 37 from an anonymous writer's verse "To Mr. Handel," Daily Advertiser, Jan. 21, 1745 (Deutsch, p. 604), the next reference, the writer's quoting of Virgil, Aeneid, Book 6, Line 95. From Handel again, first in the Daily Advertiser, Jan. 25, 1745 (Deutsch, p. 606), then to His Grace the Lord Chamberlain, as recalled by Shaftesbury to James Harris, Feb. 12, 1745 (Harris Papers, p. 214).

[17] Praise from a writer in the Daily Gazetteer, March 13, 1745 (Deutsch, pp. 608-09); and the stanza from his poem.

Chapter 15. A 'Blast of Hell': Civil War, Personal Pain

[1] Supporters' reactions to the oratorios: Excerpts from "An Ode, to Mr. Handel" by an anonymous writer. "Printed for R. Dodsley at Tully's Head in Pall-Mall" (Deutsch, pp. 614-618); then Mrs. Elizabeth Carter to Miss Catherine Talbot, [April] 2, 1745 (Deutsch, pp. 610-611); letter to either Elizabeth or James Harris, Feb. Or March 1747, (Harris Papers, pp. 233-34); and Countess Shaftesbury to Elizabeth or James Harris, Feb. or March 1747, (ibid, pp. 233-234).

[2] Handel: Horace Walpole to George Montague, May 25, 1745 (Deutsch, p. 619).

[3] Handel with his friends: James Noel to Shaftesbury, June 23, 1745 (HHB, p. 393; Burrows, Handel, p. 285); then William Harris, presumably to his sister-in-law, wife of his brother Thomas, Aug. 29, 1745.

[4] Ill again (1745): Charles Jennens to Edward Holdsworth, Oct. 16, 1745 (HHB, p. 395; Burrows, Handel, p. 286); and Shaftesbury to James Harris, Oct. 24, 1745 (Deutsch, p. 624); and in the Harris Papers, p. 220, and the subsequent quotation by Shaftesbury.

[5] On the Occasional Oratorio and the Rebellion: General Advertiser, Jan. 31, 1746 (Deutsch, p. 629); Charles Jennens to Edward Holdsworth, Feb. 3, 1746 (HHB, p. 400); Burrows, Handel, p. 289); then Rev. William Harris to Mrs. Thomas Harris, Feb. 8, 1746 (Deutsch, pp. 629-630); Jennens again, ibid.; and Burrows, Ibid, p. 291.

[6] Handel recovers, resumes his music: Shaftesbury to James Harris, Jan. 20, 1747 (HHB, p. 405); Burrows, Handel, p. 292, Harris Papers, p. 233, and the next quote by Shaftesbury, ibid.

[7] Simon Fraser's trial: Shaftesbury to James Harris, March 17, 1747 (Deutsch, p. 637).

[8] On Judas Maccabaeus: Shaftesbury, Memoirs of Handel, from the London Chronicle, responding to earlier excerpts in the Chronicle from Mainwaring's biography of Handel, Autumn

1760 (Deutsch, p. 848); and the letter excerpt by Thomas Morell to John Nichols, ca. 1779-80; see footnote 403 (Deutsch, pp. 851-852). The letter details working with Handel on *Judas Maccabaeus, Alexander Balus, Theodora* and *Jephtha*.

Chapter 16. Guns to Good Effect

[1]An increasingly middle-class audience: Burrows, *Handel*, p. 292; an example: Miss Catherine Talbot to Mrs. Elizabeth Carter, April 18, 1747 (Deutsch, p. 640).

[2]On *Joshua*: Libretto authorship: according to Merlin Channon, cited by Ruth Smith, *Handel's Oratorios and Eighteenth Century* (Cambridge: Cambridge University, 1995), p. 401, n1.

[3]On the oratorios' "bellicose" Old Testament themes: Hicks, *New Grove Dictionary* (2nd ed., online), "Handel" entry, sect. 10; and subsequently, Burrows, *Handel*, p. 287, and p. 294.

[4]Handel and the Wesleys: See Donald Burrows's introduction to his compilation of *The Complete Hymn and Chorales, including complete source materials for the Handel-Weley hymns* (London: Novello, 1988).

[5]The oratorios' meaning for audiences: See Smith's "The Achievements of Charles Jennens," p. 182; then Eliza Haywood. *Epistles for the Ladies.* "*From* Eusebia *to the* Bishop of * *, *on the Power of Divine Music*," London, 1749; and Catherine Talbot to Elizabeth Carter, April 13, 1756 (Deutsch, p. 773).

[6]On Susanna: Burrows, *Handel*, p. 295; and ibid., p. 325.

[7]Re: the 1749 season: Shaftesbury to James Harris, Jan. 3, 1749 (Harris papers, p. 253); and the comments about *Susanna's* reception: Shaftesbury to James Harris, Jan. 3, 1749 (Ibid, p. 253); Lady Shaftesbury, to Elizabeth Harris, Feb. 11, 1749 (Harris Papers, p. 255); her comments about *Susanna* itself: Ibid, (p. 254); and George Harris on *Susanna*: Harris's Diary, Feb. 10, 1749 (Harris Family Papers, p. 254).

[8]On the *Royal Fireworks Music*: Montagu to Charles Frederick, Comptroller of His Majesty's Fireworks, April 9, 1749 (Deutsch, p. 663); then an April 15, 1749, letter from the correspondence of the first Duchess of Chandos, now in the Buckinghamshire Records and Local Studies Service: Dinton Hall Estate, ref. D 63/8/7/1. The rehearsal: *General Advertiser*, April 22, 1749 (Deutsch, p. 666). The celebration: the crowd: A Mr. Byrom to his wife, written "before [in front of] Squib Castle" in Green Park, 7 p.m., and completed at 11 p.m., April 27, 1749 (Deutsch, p. 667); the pavilion: the first quotation is from an unofficial program for the event, "A View of the Public Fire-Works, etc.," which includes the information about the number of musicians (Deutsch, p. 666). The second quotation is from the letter by Byrom to his wife. The king: Diary of George Harris, April 21-27, 1749 (Harris Papers, p. 258); the pavilion catching fire: ibid.

Chapter 17. Feeding Foundlings in *Messiah's* Name

[1]Handel and the Foundling Hospital: from May 7, 1749 Foundling Hospital Minutes, reproduced by Deutsch, p. 669; *General Advertiser*, May 19, 1749, from "ad" copy clearly provided by the Foundling Hospital (Deutsch, pp. 670-71); board membership: in Burrows, *Handel*, p. 299; Hawkins, p. 911; bequeathals to the hospital: Third Codicil to Handel's will, dated, signed by Handel and witnessed by Thomas Harris and John Maxwell, Aug. 4, 1757 (Deutsch, p. 789).

[2]Mention in a Fielding novel: Henry Fielding. *History of Tom Jones*. Dublin, 1749

(Deutsch, p. 677). The Handel-loving Sophie is based on Fielding's first wife, Charlotte Cradock.

[3]Handel helps Jennens choose an organ: Handel to Jennens, Sept. 30, 1749 (Deutsch, pp. 675-676), and the following quotations.

[4]Handel at sixty-five: Christian Rotth. Title page, an editorial note by Johann Friedrich Grunert, who printed the ode (Deutsch, p. 680). The poem itself is lost; and Shaftesbury to James Harris, Feb. 13, 1750 (Deutsch, p. 680; Harris Papers, p. 264).

[5]On *Theodora*: Robert Boyle as libretto source: Edward B. Davis, in a talk "Robert Boyle, the Christian Virtuoso," given at the Massachusetts Institute of Technology, Jan. 9, 1998, in the series, *The Faith of Great Scientists*, organized by Dr. Ian Hutchinson. Quote used with Davis's permission. Handel's view: Thomas Morell to John Nichols, ca. 1776-84, (Deutsch, p. 852), and the subsequent quotations from this letter; and Ruth Smith, "Thomas Morell and His Letter About Handel," *Journal of the Royal Music Association*, v. 127, 2002, p. 221. Audience reaction: Burney, *Sketch of the Life*, p. 29, the subsequent quote. Handel and *Theodora*'s message: Hawkins, p. 910; *Luthers Werke*, 15, 366f.

[6]More on *Theodora*: George Harris to Elizabeth Harris, March 8, 1750 (Harris Papers, p. 266); and the comments by Thomas Harris to James Harris, March 22, 1750 (ibid, p. 269) and Shaftesbury to James Harris, March 22, 1750 (ibid, pp. 269-270); and Ann Dewes to Bernard Granville, Dec. 3, 1750 (Deutsch, p. 695).

[7]London earthquakes: Bishop Thomas Sherlock's post-earthquake "letter" is in *The Cambridge History of English and American Literature, Encyclopaedia in 18 Volumes*, v. X: *The Age of Johnson*. Pt. XV. *Divines. Thomas Sherlock* (Cambridge: University Press; NY: G.P. Putnam's Sons, 1907–21); then George Harris to Elizabeth Harris, ibid; and Mrs. Elizabeth Montagu to her sister, Miss Sarah Robinson, March 20, 1750? (Deutsch, pp. 683-684). Deutsch points out there is confusion about the date of this letter, and so also about which oratorio Mrs. Montagu is referring to. On Bishop Secker's public letter after the earthquake: Thomas Harris to James Harris, March 17, 1750 (Harris Papers, p. 268).

[8]Frenchwoman's view of Handel: Madame Anne-Marie Fiquet du Bocage to her sister, Mme du Perron, April 15, 1750 (Deutsch, p. 686).

Chapter 18: Considering the Uncertainty of Human Life

[1]Handel's will, June 1, 1750, and subsequent references to it. Deutsch, p. 691.

[2]On the Handel-J.C. Smith falling-out: John Christopher Smith the elder to James Harris, Oct. 11, 1743 (Harris Papers, p. 171); and Smith to Shaftesbury, July 28, 1743 (HHB, p. 364), also in Burrows, *Handel*, p. 273; and Coxe, *Anecdotes*, p. 48, and the next quote, p. 49.

[3]About Communion: this, and the subsequent two longer quotations from the *Book of Common Prayer*, "Holy Communion" (1662).

[4]Handel in the Netherlands. In Haarlem: see Richard G. King, "Handel's Travels in the Netherlands in 1750," *Music & Letters*, v. 72, 1991, p. 372. Coach travel: from charts in *The Chronology of British History* by Palmer, Century Ltd, 1992 0-7126-5616-2. Figures are for ca. 1730. In Deventer: *Oprechte Haerlemse Courant*, Sept. 12, 1750; the *Amsterdamse Courant*, same date, "with minor variants" (Richard G. King, ibid, p. 374), and *'s Gravenhaegse Courant*, Dec. 3, 1750, and the subsequent report from the same paper, Dec. 8, 1750.

[5]Thinking of Handel: Ann Dewes to Bernard Granville, Dec. 3, 1750 (Deutsch, p. 695); Mary Delaney to Ann Dewes, Nov. 30, 1750 and Dec. 10, 1750 (Deutsch, pp. 694-695).

[6]Handel to Telemann, Dec. 25/14, 1750, in French and Eng. (Deutsch,, pp. 696-698).

[7]The Corresponding Society of Musical Sciences: "Mizler" entry, *Oxford Composer Companion: J.S. Bach*, ed. Malcom Boyd, Oxford: 1999, pp. 300-301; and the subsequent quote from the society's journal.

[8]"Compliments" to Handel: Mary Delaney to Ann Dewes, Dec. 15, 1750 (Deutsch, p. 698), and quotations from letters written to Ann Dewes on Dec. 10 and Nov. 30, and to Bernard Granville on Dec. 18.

Chapter 19. How Dark, O Lord, Are Thy Decrees

[1]Post-Netherlands trip: Shaftesbury to James Harris, Feb. 15, 1751, Harris Papers, p. 274.

[2]On Handel's blindness: Mainwaring, p. 138; Hawkins, p. 910; treatment: Robert James. *A Medicinal Dictionary, Including Physic, Surgery, Anatomy, Chymistry, and Botany.* 3 v. London: 1743-45. A modern view: William A. Frosch in "The 'Case' of George Frideric Handel." *New England Journal of Medicine*, vol. 321, no. 11 (Sept. 14, 1989), pp. 765-9; and Konrad Pesudovs and David B. Elliott. "The Evolution of Cataract Surgery," *Ophthalmology Times*, Oct. 19, 2001, p. 30. A contemporaneous press account: Victor Schoelcher. *The Life of Handel*. London: Robert Cocks & Co., 1857. New York: Da Capo Press (Music Reprint Series), 1979, p. 322; Deutsch's comment on this account, p. 727.

[3]On quacks like "Chevalier" Taylor: Konrad Pesudovs and David B. Elliott, ibid.; and following: C.N. Chua. Oxford Eye Hospital. *A Historic Tour of Ophthalmology*, "Ophthalmalogy in the British Isles" (<www.mrcophth.com>); at Tunbridge Wells: John Baker diary, Aug. 26, 1758 (Deutsch, p. 806); Taylor: "On the Recovery of the Sight of the Celebrated Mr. Handel, by the Chevalier Taylor," stanzas 2-4, dated Tunbridge Wells, Aug.15 [1758] (ibid, pp. 804-805).

[4]Re: my theory on the cause of Handel's blindness see Sohan Singh Hayreh. Explanation of ischemic optic neuropathy. U. of Iowa Dept. of Ophthalmology and Visual Sciences website; Handel's symptoms: the *General Advertiser*, Aug. 17, 1752 (Deutsch, p. 726); Chev. Taylor, "History of the Travels and Adventures of the Chevalier John Taylor, Ophthalmiater," 1761 (Deutsch, p. 849).

[5]On *Jephtha*: Winton Dean, *Handel's Dramatic Oratorios and Masques* (London, New York, Toronto: Oxford University Press, 1959), pp. 18-19,22; and subsequently, ibid p. 39.

[6]"Whatever is is right": Alexander Pope. *Essay on Man* (Epistle I, lines 284-289), and following, Pope's rephrasing of Dryden: John Dryden, *Oedipus* (1679), Act iii. Sc.1. "In [Pope's] perusal of the English poets he soon distinguished the versification of Dryden, which he considered as the model to be studied...." Samuel Johnson. *The Life of Pope*, 1780 (ed. Hill), par. 13; Johnson on Pope's *Essay on Man: The Life of Pope. From The Lives of the Poets*, originally 10 short volumes, 1779-81. Ed. G. B. Hill, 3 v. (Oxford: Clarendon Press, 1905), par. 184-185; and the subsequent comment about Bolingbroke lying to Pope, p. 192. Available electronically, ed. Jack Lynch, at <http://andromeda.rutgers.edu/~jlynch/Texts/pope.html>; and Pope to Bishop William Warburton, March 24, 1743, quoted by Johnson (*The Life of Pope*, ibid, par. 190).

Chapter 20: His Muses Have Not Left Him

[1]Blindness changes Handel: Hawkins, p. 910, and the quotes by Hawkins; and Burney, *Sketch of the Life*, p. 34; his playing unaffected: Sir Edward Turner to Sanderson Miller, March 14, 1751 (Deutsch, p. 703).

[2]On hiring J.C. Smith Jr. to help him: Mainwaring, p. 138; and Hawkins, p. 910.

[3]His friends fear for his future: Thomas Harris to James Harris, Jan. 7, 1752 (Harris Papers, p. 281); and the subsequent quote, Jan. 23, 1752, ibid, p. 282; the toll on his health: Hawkins, p. 891; John Upton to James Harris, Feb.12, 1753 (Harris Papers, p. 285); and Feb. 25, 1752, ibid, p. 282; Fourth Countess of Shaftesbury to Elizabeth Harris, March 13, 1753 (ibid, p. 287); Burrows and Dunhill's commentary on Lady Shaftesbury's letter, ibid.; and subsequently, Lady Shaftesbury on audience reaction to blind Handel, also to Elizabeth Harris (Deutsch dates this letter "1751?"; Burrows and Dunhill say 1751 is correct, based the specific play performances she mentions elsewhere in the letter).

[4]Rumor of Handel writing for his own funeral: Minutes of the General Committee of the Foundling Hospital, April 11, 1753 (Deutsch, p. 740); and *Hallische Zeitung*, May ?,1753, translated (Deutsch, p. 742).

[5]Handel and the Lock Hospital: *Public Advertiser*, May 7, 1753 (Deutsch, p. 743).

[6]On "Total Eclipse"from *Samson*, and blind Handel's response to it: Miss C. Gilbert to Elizabeth Harris, May 21, 1753 (Harris Papers, p. 291); text of quoted aria, *Samson*, Act 1, Scene 1, No. 12; and the comment by Mary Delany to Ann Dewes, Nov. 25, 1752 (Deutsch, p. 727); and Mary Delany's comment on Handel and his blindness, to Ann Dewes, Dec. 15 or 16, 1752 (ibid, pp. 728-729).

[7]Reaction to *Messiah* a decade after its debut: Benjamin Victor to Rev. William Rothery, Dec. 27, 1752 (Deutsch, p. 729).

[8]Audience reaction to Handel's blindness, *Sketch of the Life*, pp. 29-30; and the next quote, by Frances Griesdale to Elizabeth Harris, April 12, 1753 (Harris Papers), p. 289; organ playing when blind: Burney, *Sketch of the Life*, pp. 29-30; Thomas Harris to James Harris, March 31, 1753 (Harris Family Papers, p. 288).

[9]Draft of petition to Parliament by the governors of the Foundling Hospital (Deutsch, pp. 756-757); Handel's reaction, quoted by Hawkins, p. 891; and the hospital's reaction to him: Foundling Hospital General Committee Minutes, Jan. 23, 1754 (Burrows, *Handel*, p. 360).

[10]On new competition for Handel: Miss C. Gilbert to Elizabeth Harris, March 11, 1755 (Harris Papers, p. 303); and the subsequent quotes by Thomas Harris to James Harris, Feb. 22, 1755 (ibid, p. 302), and Feb. 6, 1755 (ibid, p. 301); on J.C. Smith's avoidance of date conflicts with Handel: Burrows and Dunhill commentary (ibid, pp. 301-302); Thomas Arne's competing with Handel, and more on waning audiences: Thomas Harris to James Harris, Feb. 22, 1755 (ibid); and subsequently, Mary Delany to Ann Dewes, March 3, 1755 (Deutsch, p. 761); William Shenstone to Lady Luxborough, March 30, 1755 (Deutsch, p. 762). Decree by the Lord Chamberlain, Charles, Duke of Grafton, April 11, 1753 (Deutsch, p. 740); and Miss C. Gilbert to Elizabeth Harris, March 11, 1755 (Harris Papers, p. 304), and the subsequent quotation of Miss Catharine Talbot to Elizabeth Carter, April 13, 1756 (Deutsch, p. 773).

Chapter 21: The Third & Last & Degenerate Age of Music

[1]Gloomy future for music: James Harris to Sir John Hawkins, Dec. 31, 1753 (Harris Papers, p. 296); the place of Handel's music: William Hayes, "Remarks on Mr. Avison's Essay on Musical Expression," 1753 (Deutsch, p. 732). Hayes' remarks were first published anonymously; and the next quotations; then Charles Avison, "Reply to the Author of Remarks on the Essay on Musical Expression," Feb. 22, 1753 (Deutsch, p. 736). And the quotes of Hayes and Avison.

[2]GFH to Telemann, Sept. 20, 1754 (Deutsch, in French and in translation, pp. 754-755).

[3]On the Bluestockings and the oratorios: Mary Delany to Ann Dewes, March 27, 1756 (Deutsch, p. 772), and the subsequent quote; then from an April [3] letter (ibid).

[4]Handel perseveres with the oratorios: Thomas Harris to James Harris, March 27, 1756 (Harris Papers, p. 310); and the subsequent quote from a letter dated April 10, 1756, along with a comment from the George Harris diary, April 9, 1756 (ibid., p. 312, 311); and Catharine Talbot to Elizabeth Carter, April 13, 1756 (Deutsch, p. 773).

[5]For a general understanding of this "first world war," see The Encyclopedia of World History (gen. ed., Peter N. Stearns. Houghton Mifflin, 2001), <http://www.bartleby.com/ 67/ 662.html>. For a compelling study from a North American perspective see Fred Anderson's Crucible of War: The Seven Years' War and the Fate of Empire in British North America, 1754-1766 (New York: Knopf, 2000). For those interested in the American Revolution, this work provides the often missing, broader European context of the American move toward independence. See also Karl W. Schweizer's England, Prussia, and the Seven Years War: Studies in Alliance, Policies, and Diplomacy. Lewiston, NY: Edwin Mellon, 1989.

[6]Elderly Handel musing: on Corelli: Thomas Harris diary, May 29, 1756 (Harris Family Papers, p. 314); his memory in his late years: Mainwaring, p. 139; then Shaftesbury to James Harris, Feb. 8, 1757, Harris Family Papers, p. 321; and Burney, Sketch of the Life, p. 31.

[7]First Codicil to Handel's will, Aug. 6, 1756 (Deutsch, p. 776).

[8]Elizabeth Turner's "Songs": 19 musical settings of poems by both male and female poets, including Ben Jonson, Matthew Prior and Sir Charles Sedley. The sonata-like "lessons" are available in score (The Six Lessons for Harpsichord or Piano by Elizabeth Turner, ed. by Barbara Harbach. Pullman, Wash.: Vivace Press, 1993; VIV 1804; and a facsimile edition, produced by JPH Publications (Jack, Pipes and Hammers), Alston, Cumbria, available by writing <j.edmonds@ jphbaroque.co.uk>, or from Old Manuscripts & Incunabula, New York, tel: 212-758-1946). There is also a recording of the "lessons"on "Eighteenth Century Harpsichord Music by Women Composers, vol. II," Barbara Harbach, harpsichord (Gasparo CD 281).

Chapter 22. Before the Bard is Silenced

[1]Handel at seventy-two: Shaftesbury to James Harris, Feb. 8, 1757 (Harris Papers, p. 321); and Burney, Sketch of the Life of Handel, p. 30.

[2]Second codicil to Handel's will, March 22, 1757 (Deutsch, p. 784).

[3]Satisfaction with the oratorios: London Chronicle: or Universal Evening Post, May 5-7, 1757 (Deutsch, p. 786); and with "Mr. Savage's celebrated Boy": Jackson's Oxford Journal, July 2, 1757 (Deutsch, p. 787).

[4]Continued health: Thomas Harris to James Harris, July 21, 1757 (Harris Papers, p.

326); rehearsals still at Handel's home: John Baker's Diary, March 2, 1758 (Deutsch, p. 795).

[5]Humorous comment re: himself and John Stanley: Coxe, p. 44.

[6]He begins to decline: Hawkins, p. 910; and John Upton's comment to James Harris, March 4, 1758 (Harris Papers, p. 331).

[7]On Handel's finances: Deutsch, pp. 802, 841; then Burney, quoting a friend, *Sketch of the Life*, p. 28; and Jakob Adlung, *Anleitung zu der Musicalischen Gelahrtheit*, Part 1, chap. 1, par. 26 (translated from the German, Deutsch, p. 810).

[8]More on spiritual effects: John Wesley on *Messiah*: Journal, v. 4, p. 282 (Deutsch, p. 804); a charity would use Handel's music so that "God would be glorified": William Hanbury's Proposal's for the Charitable Foundation of Church-Langdon, 1758 (Deutsch, p. 802).

[9]Handel's impact: Mr. Bull sells busts of Handel: the *Public Advertiser*, April 19, 1758 (ibid, p. 798); and seen by Rev. William Hughes, Worchester, 1758 (ibid, p. 809).

[10]G FH's state of affairs and health: Thomas Harris to James Harris, Nov. 21, 1758 (Harris Papers, p. 335), and subsequently, Feb. 27, 1759 (ibid, p. 338); and John Upton to James Harris, Feb. 24, 1759 (ibid, p. 338); his "new oratorio" (*Solomon* revised): *Public Advertiser*, March 2, 1759 (Deutsch, p. 812).

[11]On his last *Messiah* performance: Thomas Harris to James Harris, April 3, 1759 (Harris Papers, p. 339); and Coxe, p. 26.

[12]His last days: Coxe, p. 26; and Diary of Selina, Countess of Huntington, not specifically dated (Huntington, *Life*, v. 1, p. 229; Deutsch, p. 813).

Chapter 23. His Pen to the Service of God

[1]Handel's request to be buried in Westminster Abbey: Fourth Codicil to his will, April 11, 1759 (Deutsch, p. 814).

[2]Wishing to die on Good Friday: Burney, *Sketch of the Life of Handel*, p. 31.

[3]On his death. The announcement: *Whitehall Evening Post*, April 14, 1759 (Deutsch, p. 816). Eulogies: "On GEORGE FREDERICK HANDEL, Esq.," *Gazetteer* (and two other papers), April 17, 1759 (Deutsch, p. 817); "He's gone, the Soul of Harmony is fled!", the *Public Advertiser*, April 17, 1759 (Deutsch, p. 818); "Attempt toward an EPITAPH, *Universal Chronicle*, April 21, 1759 (Deutsch, p. 820). Effect on, comments by his friends: Shaftesbury and Thomas Harris lose interest in music: Burrows and Dunhill, Harris Papers, p. 341; James Harris to Louis de Visme in Venice, April 28, 1759 (Harris Papers, p. 339); James Smyth to Bernard Granville, April 17, 1759 (Deutsch, p. 819); Mary Delany to Ann Dewes, May 5, 1759.

[4]The funeral: choirs participating: *Public Advertiser*, April 20, 17959 (Deutsch, pp. 819-820); 3,000 attending: *London Evening-Post*, April 24, 1759 (Deutsch, p. 821).

Epilogue

[1]The Westminster Abbey monument: *Universal Chronicle*, April 28, 1759 (Deutsch, pp. 821-822); Coxe, p. 26, and the following quote.

[2]His legacy: his oratorio choruses: Mainwaring, pp. 187, 190; his contribution to religion and humanity: ibid, pp. 204-206. Support of charities: Burney, *An Account of the Musical Performances in Westminster-Abbey, and the Pantheon in Commemoration of Handel* (London:

Printed for the Benefit of the Musical Fund; and Sold By T. Payne and Son, at the Meuse-Gate; and G. Ronbinson, Pater-noster-Row, 1785), vi-vii; his music defines the *Sublime*: Hawkins, p. 914; highest claim for moral and religious excellence: Coxe, p. 33-34; Beethoven on Handel: Alexander Wheelock Thayer. *Life of Beethoven* (2 v., ed. Elliot Forbes, Princeton, N.J.: Princeton University Press, 1992, originally published 1879), p. 683; and the subsequent quotation by Edward Schulz, *The Harmonicon*, January 1824 (monthly musical journal published in London, 1823-1833); John Tavener on "discovering" Handel: in an interview with Michael Stewart, after the "Ikons of Light" festival, 2000. See the whole interview at < http://www.imageandmusic.co.uk > .

[3]"An Ode, On Occasion of Mr. Handel's Great Te Deum, a the Feast of the Sons of the Clergy." The (unnamed) author is Aaron Hill; the poem is in Hill's collected works, published 1753, III. 167-169 (Deutsch, pp. 306-307).

Glossary of Musical Terms

air/aria. A "song" in an opera, oratorio, passion or cantata, written for a soloist, or as a duet or sometimes a trio, with orchestral accompaniment. Almost always sung by a specific character in the drama, it reveals the character's thoughts, faith, regrets, actions or intended actions, and in that way moves the drama forward. (In *Messiah*, whose libretto has no character roles, the arias reveal God's action or future action, comment on the human state of affairs, describe Christ or confess faith, and are integral to the oratorio's message.) Along with recitatives and choruses (and chorales in passions and church cantatas), arias are integral to the structure of the large Baroque choral works.

Baroque period. The historical period during which Handel lived and flourished. The dates of the period are generally cited as 1600-1750. Baroque music (and art, architecture, literature) has certain discernable characteristics, regardless of composer. Its primary texture is polyphonic (harmony is created by combining two or more independent melodic lines combine to create canons, fugues, etc.) as opposed to homophonic (emphasizing a melody with subordinate harmony).

basso continuo. See continuo.

cantata. Literally "sung." The term has somewhat different meanings in different historical periods. In the Baroque age, it is a multi-movement vocal or choral work made up primarily of recitatives and arias, either biblically based, as Bach's 300-odd church cantatas which musically illuminate the Scripture readings for a given Sunday, or based on a secular story (often a love story between mythological characters), as in Handel's Italian cantatas.

cantus firmus. Literally a "fixed song": a pre-existing melody (originally Gregorian chant, but in the hands of the German Lutheran composers, usually a chorale) in a polyphonic composition, occurring (usually) in one voice, around which are woven other fragmentary melodies. E.g., the complete chorale melody might occur in the tenor voice ("voice" meaning the musical line, which can be sung *or* played) while the singers or instruments in soprano, alto and bass range independently dance around it, ornamenting or elaborating on it. All the independent voices together form a piece with polyphonic texture (polyphony = "many sounds").

castrato. Plural **castrati**. A male singer castrated during boyhood so that his voice would remain unchanged, making him a life-long soprano or alto. Castrati were employed in Italy throughout the seventeenth and eighteenth centuries, primarily in opera, and in the Vatican chapel. (There were still a few at the Vatican chapel in the very early twentieth century.) The mature castrato voice had a unique character which set it apart from the mature female soprano or alto voice. It was peculiarly bright and sensuous, and the best castrati were capable of phenomenal feats of flexibility and breath control. In Handel's day Italian castrati were popular all over Europe; he regularly used "star" castrati in his operas in London. But only Italy was willing to sacrifice some of its pre-pubescent boys for this purpose. There was no guarantee for parents who submitted their sons to the knife, or for the singer himself, that an exceptional boy soprano or boy alto would make an equally exceptional castrato soprano or alto. And there were psychological effects. But for those who had the gift it paid off handsomely.

chorale. The basis of Lutheran church music: a Lutheran hymn for singing by the congregation. Though Handel left his German Lutheran homeland early in life, he incorporated chorales into some of his English choral works.

chorale prelude. An organ work based on a chorale, originally intended to act as an introduction to a chorale to be sung in worship.

concerto. A multi-movement work featuring one or more solo instruments, with orchestra.

concerto grosso. A typically Baroque genre, a (usually) three-movement work in which a small group of instruments acts as the solo group, alternating with the entire orchestra. Italian plural: *concerti grossi.*

continuo. The foundational instrumental group in Baroque music which plays the music's bass line and the chords implied by it. It consists of cello and harpsichord, and/or organ, sometimes with the addition of a string bass or bassoon and/or a plucked stringed instrument, such as the theorbo, lute or archlute.

counterpoint/contrapuntal. The term comes from the Latin phrase *punctus contra punctum*: point against point, or note against note, thus counterpoint is the combining two or more independent parts, as in a fugue. This forms a contrapuntal or polyphonic texture.

countertenor. The voice range of an adult, uncastrated male, equivalent to alto.

da capo aria. An aria constructed in ABA form, i.e., with a first section, a contrasting section, and the first section repeated. On the repetition, the Baroque custom was for the soloist to ornament his or her melody so that the repeat of A was never exactly like A when first heard. *Da capo* (literally "from the head" or beginning) comes from the abbreviation D.C. seen in the musical score at the end of the B section, telling the performer to return to the beginning and sing until the word *Fine* or a fermata sign (at the end of the A section).

figured bass. Music of the Baroque period (ca. 1600-1750) is constructed from the bottom up, built on a bass line to which the composer added "figures": for each bass note, a number or numbers written vertically below the note indicates which chord is to be built upon that note, and whether the chord occurs in its root position (e.g., C,E,G), or in an inversion of that position (e.g., E,G,C).

fugue/fugal. The fugue is the form *par excellence* of the Baroque period in music (ca.

1600-1750). It is a sophisticated sort of round or canon in which independent melodies enter successively and imitate each other. Each melody is called a "voice," whether played or sung. The opening melody or theme is the "subject." If there is another theme it is the "counter-subject." Sections of the fugue in which the subject is not restated are called "episodes."

Kapellmeister. *See* **Maestro di cappella.**

libretto. The text of an opera, oratorio, passion or cantata. A libretto may be entirely prose, a mixture of prose and poetry, or entirely poetry. Many opera and English drama librettos took off from Greek or Roman myth or other ancient stories (e.g., Handel's *Semele*). Handel's oratorio librettos are elaborations of characters and stories from the Bible (including the Old Testament Apocrypha), and in the case of *Theodora*, the story of an early Christian martyr. The Italian plural is *libretti*, but the Anglicized plural *librettos* is now more common.

librettist. A person who writes librettos – seldom the composer. Some librettists were professional writers or poets, but many were men of letters who had an interest in the subject(s) they wrote of, and/or a friendship or professional relationship with the composer(s) who would set their librettos.

Maestro di cappella. "Master of the chapel," in Italy, music director of a church or an aristocrat's chapel. Generally synonymous with *Kapellmeister* in Germany.

movement. A "stand alone" piece which is part of a larger work; e.g., a concerto grosso usually has three or four movements. Handel's oratorio *Messiah* has fifty-three, and *Saul* has more than eighty.

ode. A choral work of ceremonial significance and/or celebrating a particular personage or occasion, as in Handel's *Ode for St. Cecilia's Day* (which he himself originally merely called a "song").

opera. Sung drama, in Handel's case in the Italian *opera seria* ("serious opera") style, consisting of recitatives, arias, and ensemble pieces (and occasionally full-fledged choruses); most are based on mythological or other ancient stories.

oratorio. Large choral work with biblical or biblically based text and story, consisting of recitatives, arias and choruses, but giving special prominence to the choruses. Handel devised his own particularly successful blend of these elements, set to English-language texts.

overture. The orchestral movement that generally begins an oratorio or opera.

Passion. In the Lutheran tradition, a major choral work based on one of the gospel accounts of Christ's Passion, consisting of arias, recitatives, chorales and choruses.

pasticcio. Musical recycling. An eclectic combination of music gathered from various sources (some may be newly composed), pulled together into a new work. Handel presented both pasticcio operas and a pasticcio oratorio on various occasions.

recitative. In operas, oratorios, passions or cantatas, a section or movement of declamatory, speech-like singing which serves as dialogue or narrative to move the plot or story forward. *Secco recitatives*, ("dry" i.e., unaccompanied) are the most common. They are actually lightly accompanied by continuo (cello, harpsichord, etc.), as opposed to the full orchestral accompaniment of *accompanato recitatives*. The latter are less declamatory and more song-like.

sublime. In music, a quality that imparts to the listener a sense of combined intellectual, emotional and spiritual power and overwhelming grandeur because of the music's beauty, pathos, majesty or splendor, which inspires awe or deep reverence. Handel's oratorios, particularly, were frequently cited as *sublime*. The designation implies and assumes a loftiness of ideas, nobility of character, and refined sense of morality.

tonal system. The system of major and minor keys (scales) which has been the melodic-harmonic foundation of music in the Western world since the early Baroque period. The scale of each key is formed by a specific pattern of intervals (whole- and half-steps or tones: do, re, mi, etc.). The first note of a key or scale, the "tonic," has a strong pull as the key's home-base, causing a feeling of resolution when a piece (or section) is finished. Bach was the first composer to systematically write pieces in every major and minor key (his *Well-Tempered Clavier*). In the early twentieth century some composers overthrew the system, replacing it for a while with a system without "resolution," in which all tones were given equal importance. There have been other innovations and constant stretching of the system. However, the tonal system is still the basis for virtually all of the music we hear every day.

wordbook. A booklet containing the libretto of an oratorio which Handel's audiences used to follow the text/story during a performance. Wordbooks could be bought ahead of time. Several of Handel's contemporaries urged their fellow oratorio-goers to read and study the wordbook before they attended a performance, allowing them to become familiar with the text so that they could experience its full spiritual impact when they heard the oratorio.

Bibliography

Books.

Andrew, Donna T.. *Philanthropy and Police: London Charity in the Eighteenth Century*. Princeton, N.J.: Princeton University, 1989.

Bach, Handel, Scarlatti Tercentenary Essays. Ed. Peter Williams. Cambridge: Cambridge University Press, 1985.

    Handel's 'Chandos' and Associated Anthems: An Introductory Survey -- Gerald Hendrie

    Handel's Early London Copyists -- Winton Dean

    Beeks, Garydon. Handel and Music for the Earl of Carnarvon.

    Handel in Hanover -- Donald Burrows

Bell, A. Craig. *Handel before England*. Darley ?: Grian-Aig Press, 1975.

Book of Common Prayer, 1662.

Bullard, Roger, A. *Messiah - The Gospel according to Handel's Oratorio*. Grand Rapids, Mich.: William B. Eerdmans, 1993.

Burney, Charles. *An Account of the Musical Performances in Westminster-Abbey, and the Pantheon in Commemoration of Handel*. "A Sketch of the Life of Handel." London: Printed for the Benefit of the Musical Fund; and Sold By T. Payne and Son, at the Meuse-Gate; and G. Robinson, Pater-noster Row, 1785.

_____. *A General History of Music From the Earliest Ages to the Present Period*, v. IV, 1789.

Burrows, Donald. *Handel*. New York: Schirmer Books, 1994.

_____. *Handel: Messiah*. Cambridge: Cambridge University Press, 1991.

The Cambridge Companion to Handel. Ed. Donald Burrows. Cambridge: Cambridge University Press, 1997.

    - Beeks, Graydon. "Handel's sacred music."

    - Burrows, Donald. "Handel's oratorio performances."

    - Butt, John. "Germany: education and apprenticeship."

    - Hicks, Anthony. "Handel and the idea of an oratorio."

    - Hurley, David Ross. "Handel's compositional process."

    - LaRue, C. Steven. "Handel and the aria."

    - Vitali, Carlo. "Italy: political and musical contexts."

    - Milhous, Judith, and Robert D. Hume. "Handel's London: the theaters."

    - Smith, Ruth, "Handel's English librettists."

    - Weber, William. "Handel's London: political, social and intellectual contexts."

Coxe, William. *The Anecdotes of George Frederick Handel and John Christopher Smith.* London: 1799.

Cudworth, Charles. *Handel.* London: Linnet Books & Clive Bingley, 1972.

Deutsch, Otto Erich. *Handel: A Documentary Biography.* New York: W.W. Norton & Company, 1954.

Dreyhaupt, Johann Cristoph von. *Die diplomatisch-historische Beschreibung des Saalkreises und der Stadt Halle.* 1749-50.

Händel-Handbuch, v. 4: Dokumente zu Leben und Schaffen. Leipzig: HHA, Deutscher Verlag für Musik, 1985.

Handel Tercentenary Collection. Ed. Stanley Sadie and Anthony Hicks. New York: MacMillan Press, 1987.
- Scholarship and the Handel Revival, 1935-85 -- Winton Dean
- Sources, Resources and Handel Studies -- Donald Burrows
- Handel and his Central German Background -- Bernd Baselt
- The Case for Handel's Borrowings: the Judgement of Three Centuries -- George J. Buelow
- Why did Handel Borrow? -- John Roberts
- The Royal Academy of Music (1719-28) and its Directors -- Elizabeth Gibson
- Handel's Disengageent from the Italian Opera -- Carole Taylor
- New Sources for the Libretto of Handel's 'Joseph' -- Duncan Chisholm
- 'A Club of Composers': Handel, Pepusch and Arbuthnot at Cannons -- Graydon Beeks

Harris, Ellen T. *Handel as Orpheus: Voice and Desire in the Chamber Cantatas.* Cambridge, Mass.: Harvard University Press, 2001.

Hawkins, Sir John. *A General History of the Science and Practice of Music.* London, 1776.

Henry, Matthew. *Matthew Henry's Commentary on the Whole Bible.* 5 vol. (to Acts). London, 1708-1710. Finished by other clergy from Henry's notes, ed. G. Burder and John Hughes, 1811.Available online.

_____. *Matthew Henry's Concise Commentary on the Whole Bible.* Nashville: Thomas Nelson Publishers, 1997.

Hicks, Anthony. Handel entry. *The New Grove Dictionary of Music and Musicians.* 2nd ed., online, 2001.

Hogwood, Christopher. *Handel.* Thames & Hudson: The Pitman Press, 1984.

Hurley, David Ross. *Handel's Muse: Patterns of Creation in his Oratorios and Musical Dramas, 1743-1751.* Oxford Monographs on Music. Oxford: Oxford

University Press, 2001.

Jacob, W.M. *Lay People and Religion in Eighteenth Century England*. Cambridge: Cambridge University Press, 1996.

J.S. Bach. Oxford Composer Companions, ed. Malcolm Boyd. Oxford: Oxford University Press, 1999.

Kavanaugh, Patrick. *The Spiritual Lives of Great Composers*. Nashville: Sparrow Press, 1992.

Keates, Jonathan. *Handel: The Man & His Music*. London: Victor Gollancz Ltd., 1985; New York: St. Martin's Press, 1985.

Lang, Paul Henry. *Handel*. New York: W.W. Norton, 1966.

Lewis, C.S. *Mere Christianity*. New York: Collier Books/Macmillan, 1943, 1960.

Lindemann, Mary. *Health and Healing in 18th Century Germany*. Baltimore: Johns Hopkins University. The Johns Hopkins Studies in Historical and Political Science, 2001.

_____. *Medicine and Society in Early Modern Europe* (Cambridge: Cambridge University Press, 1999).

[Mainwaring, John]. *Memoirs of the Life of the Late George Frederic Handel. To which is added, A Catalogue of his Works, and Observations upon them*. Facsimile edition. London: R. And J. Dodsley, 1760.

Mays, James O'Donald. *The Splendid Shilling: A Social History of an Engaging Coin*. Burley: Pardy & Son, 1982.

Music and Theatre: Essays in honour of Winton Dean. Ed. Nigel Fortune. Cambridge: Cambridge University Press, 1987.
* Handel and Charles Jennens's Italian opera manuscripts -- John H. Roberts
* Handel, Jennens and Saul : aspects of collaboration -- Anthony

Music and Theatre in Handel's World: The Family Papers of James Harris, 1732-1780, ed. Donald Burrows and Rosemary Dunhill. Oxford: Oxford University Press, 2002.

Music in Eighteenth-Century England: Essays in Memory of Charles Cudworth. Ed. Christopher Hogwood and Richard Luckett. Cambridge: Cambridge University Press, 1983.
- Intellectual contexts of Handel's English oratorios - Ruth Smith
- Handel's successor: notes on John Christopher Smith the younger - Alfred Mann
- The late editions to Handel's oratorios and the role of the younger Smith - Anthony Hicks.

The Nelson Study Bible, gen. ed. Earl D. Radmacher. Based on the New King James

Version of the Bible. Nashville: Thomas Nelson Publishers, 1997.

The New Bach Reader, ed. Hans T. David and Arthur Mendel. New York: Norton, 1998.

The NIV Study Bible. Kenneth Barker, gen. ed. Grand Rapids, Mich.: Zondervan, 1985.

The NIV Bible Library, consisting of *The NIV Bible Commentary; The NIV Bible Dictionary; The NIV Bible Study Notes; Encyclopedia of Bible Difficulties; an Exhaustive Concordance; Expository Dictionary of Bible Words;* the Bible in three translations: NIV, KJV, NASB.. Grand Rapids, Mich.: Zondervan, 1997. Software.

Nichols, R.H. and F.A. Wray. *The History of the Foundling Hospital*. London: 1935.

Oxford Composer Companion to J.S. Bach, ed. Malcom Boyd. Oxford: 1999.

Parker-Hale, Mary Ann. *G. F. Handel: a Guide to Research*. Ed. Guy A. Marco. ??: Garland Publishing, Inc. 1995 (Garland Composer Resource Manuals, v.19); ??: Taylor & Francis, Inc. 1998 (ISBN: cloth 0824084527)

Psalter Hymnal. Grand Rapids, Mich.: CRC Publications, 1987.

Psalter Hymnal Handbook, ed. Emily Brink and Bert Polman. Grand Rapids, Mich.: CRC Publications, 1998.

Rolland, Romain. *Händel*. [city]: AMS Press, 1916 (French ed. 1910).

Schoelcher, Victor. *The Life of Handel*. London: Robert Cocks & Co.,1857. New York: Da Capo Press (Music Reprint Series), 1979.

Smith, Ruth. *Handel's Oratorios and Eighteenth-Century Thought*. Cambridge: Cambridge University Press, 1995.

Stapert, Calvin. *My Only Comfort: Death, Deliverance, and Discipleship in the Music of J.S. Bach*. Grand Rapids, Mich.: Wm. B. Eerdmans, 2000.

Strohm, Reinhard. *Dramma Per Musica: Italian Opera Seria of the Eighteenth Century*. New Haven, Conn.: Yale University Press, 1997.

Wheelock, Alexander Thayer. *Life of Beethoven*. 2 v., ed. Elliot Forbes, Princeton, N.J.: Princeton University Press, 1992, 1879.

Shorter works and journal articles

Blanchard, Donald L. "George Handel and His Blindness," *Documenta Ophthalmologica*, v. 99: pp. 247-258, 1999.

Channon, Merlin. "Handel's Early Performances of 'Judas Maccabaeus': Some New Evidence and Interpretations, *Music & Letters*, 77, no. 4: Nov. 1996, pp.

499-526.

Chua, C.N. *A Historic Tour of Ophthalmology*, "Ophthalmalogy in the British Isles" (www.mrcophth.com).

Corp, Edward. "Handel, Scarlatti and the Stuarts: a response to David Hunter," *Music & Letters*, v. 82, no. 4: Nov. 2001, pp. 556-8.

Dean, Winton. "Handel's Farewell to Oratorio," *Jephtha* recording, cond. John Eliot Gardiner (Philips 422 351-2), 1988, pp. 16-22.

Frosch, William A.
   "The 'Case' of George Frideric Handel." *New England Journal of Medicine*, v. 321, no. 11: Sept. 14, 1989, pp. 765-9
   "Moods, Madness, and Music. Was Handel Insane? *The Musical Quarterly*, v. 74: Spring 1990, pp. 3-56.

Hunter, David. "Handel among the Jacobites," *Music & Letters*, v. 82, no. 4: Nov. 2001, pp. 543-56.
   "Patronizing Handel, Inventing Audiences. The Intersections of Class, Money, Music and History," *Early Music*, v. 28, no.1,. Feb. 2000, pp. 32-49.

King, Richard G. "Handel's Travels in the Netherlands in 1750," *Music & Letters*, v. 72, 1991.

Lutheran Journal, v. 51, nol 2, 1984.

McCann, Bill. "Earthquakes in London," web article on < www.storyoflondon.com >, a site outlining London's history.

Mirelle Langier Benchimol. "Ocular Manifestations of Some Systemic Diseases: Giant Cell (temporal) Arteritis." < http://www.medstudents.com.br/oftal/ oftal3.htm >

Neurologic Clinics, Nov 1997; 15(4), pp. 893-902."Giant cell (temporal) arteritis."

Pesudovs, Konrad, and David B. Elliott. "The Evolution of Cataract Surgery," *Ophthalmology Times*, Oct. 19, 2001.

Pope, Alexander. *Essay on Man*, "The Design"; "Epistle I: Of the Nature and State of Man, With Respect to the Universe," 1733. Published electronically at < http://classiclit.about.com/library/bl-etexts/apope/bl-apope-essay-1.htm >

Royal College of Surgeons of England. London Lock Hospital records, GB 0114 Add Mss 112.1.

Smith, Ruth. "The Achievements of Charles Jennens (1700 - 1773)," *Music & Letters*, v. 70, no. 2: May 1989, pp. 161-90.
   _____. "The Meaning of Morell's Libretto of *Judas Maccabaeus*," *Music & Letters*, v. 79, no. 1: Feb. 1998, pp. 50-71.

Sohan Singh Hayreh. Explanation of *ischemic optic neuropathy*. University of Iowa Dept. of Ophthalmology and Visual Sciences website.

Sons of the Clergy. Stated purpose, <www.bishports.clara.net/welfare/corporation.htm>.

Tavener, John. Interview with Michael Stewart. "Ikons of Light" festival, 2000. <http://www.imageandmusic.co.uk>

University of Illinois at Chicago Eye Manual, produced by the faculty and residents at the Department of Ophthalmology and Visual Sciences. <mail.ml.usoms.poznan.pl/eyemanual/Download/neuro.doc.>

Windsor, Richard, and Laura Windsor, "Understanding A Stroke of the Optic Nerve: Anterior Ischemic Optic Neuropathy," <www.visionww.org/drswindsor-opticnerve.htm>.

Index

Index

GEORGE FRIDERIC HANDEL

Handel, George Frideric
    Adaptability, 34, 36, 41, 63, 69, 158
    Bach, Johann Sebastian, relation to, 27, 30, 71, 72, 80, 81, 160, 225, 241, 277, 292, 303, 328, 363, 364
    Blindness, 55, 70, 283, 295-303, 305, 306, 309, 311-322, 325, 334, 337, 338, 340, 341, 345, 346, 351, 353
    Composition, speed of, 39, 157, 177, 188, 268
    Duel with Mattheson, 31, 135
    Education, 9-11, 19, 24, 28, 38, 312
    Excessive eating, 55, 211
    Faith, vi, vii, 4-6, 7, 8, 10, 11, 29, 30, 31, 42, 47, 62, 78, 85, 86, 87, 95, 134, 146, 137, 138, 158, 166, 244-245, 246, 247, 275, 277, 279, 280-281, 303, 316, 321, 327
    Faux pas, 139, 184
    Generosity, 2, 29, 38, 90, 112, 125, 252, 265, 290, 340
    Independence, 25, 33, 35, 52, 63, 69, 90, 91, 122, 124, 206, 321
    Lutheran chorales, use of in English choral music, 152-155, 160, 161, 177-179, 252, 305
    Lutheran upbringing, ties, 50, 51, 60, 61, 79, 90, 131, 152-156, 202, 241, 252, 274, 277, 287, 309, 332
    Mental confusion, 146, 157, 210, 212, 235, 301, 302, 338
    Monuments to, 55, 75, 163, 164, 208, 353, 356, 358, 359
    Morality, 2, 38, 46, 47, 199
    Oratorios, 1, 13, 16-17, 39-41, 57, 72-74, 89, 92, 102, 108-110, 113, 127, 130-131, 136-137, 139, 141, 143, 151, 153, 157-159, 165, 167-171, 174, 176, 187-188, 196, 198-201, 203-205, 209-211, 213, 216-217, 219, 225-226, 228-233, 241-242, 244, 246-248, 250, 253-255, 258, 260, 272, 274-277, 280, 283, 286, 289-291, 306, 313-315, 322-323, 325-326, 328, 333-336, 339-341, 344-347, 349-351, 354, 357, 360-364
    Organ playing, 23-24, 26-28, 30, 35, 81, 132, 144, 148-149, 167-168, 174-175, 181, 189, 191-192, 194, 268, 281, 312-315, 318, 321-322, 331, 333, 336, 346, 351
    Paralysis, 143-144, 157, 180, 202, 216, 235, 302
    Pianoforte, and the, 180, 337
    Roman Catholics, relation to, 2, 34, 36, 62, 275, 276
    Sexuality, 46, 50
    Singers, relation to, 17, 27, 33, 40, 48, 52, 53, 55, 64, 89, 97, 119, 131, 345, 348
    Sisters, relationship with, 8, 13, 17, 21, 26, 28, 43, 60, 61, 76-79, 95, 100, 277
    Temper, 52, 56, 144, 175, 311, 324
Händel, Johanna Christianne, 10
Händel, Karl, 8, 9, 22
Händel, Sophie Rosine, 9

Index

Index

Printed in the United States
86283LV00006B/22/A